Chandra Manning

WHAT THIS CRUEL WAR WAS OVER

Chandra Manning, a graduate of Mount Holyoke College, received an MPhil from the National University of Ireland, Galway, and took her PhD at Harvard in 2002. She has lectured in history at Harvard and taught at Pacific Lutheran University in Tacoma, Washington. Currently, she is assistant professor of history at Georgetown University and lives in Alexandria, Virginia, with her husband and son. This is her first book.

WHAT THIS
CRUEL WAR
WAS OVER

WHAT THIS CRUEL WAR WAS OVER

Soldiers, Slavery, and the Civil War

CHANDRA MANNING

VINTAGE CIVIL WAR LIBRARY

VINTAGE BOOKS

A DIVISION OF RANDOM HOUSE, INC.

NEW YORK

FIRST VINTAGE CIVIL WAR LIBRARY EDITION, MARCH 2008

Copyright © 2007 by Chandra Manning

The Library of Congress has cataloged the Knopf edition as follows:
Manning, Chandra.
What this cruel war was over : soldiers, slavery, and the Civil War / Chandra Manning.
p. cm.
Includes bibliographical references and index.
1. Soldiers—United States—Attitudes—History—19th century. 2. Soldiers—Confederate States of America—Attitudes—History. 3. United States—History—Civil War, 1861–1865—Causes. 4. Slavery—United States—Public opinion—History—19th century. 5. Slavery—Confederate States of America—Public opinion—History—19th century. 6. United States—Race relations—History—19th century. 7. United States—History—Civil War, 1861–1865—Social aspects. 8. United States. Army—History—Civil War, 1861–1865. 9. Confederate States of America. Army—History. 10. Public opinion—United States—History—19th century. I. Title.
E607.M32 2007
973.7'4—dc22 2006048733

Vintage ISBN: 978-0-307-27732-9

Author photograph © Claudio Vazquez
Book design by Virginia Tan

www.vintagebooks.com

Printed in the United States of America
10 9 8 7 6 5 4

Dedicated to the memory of my grandmother and my grandfather, who did not laugh when I, at the age of three, promised to dedicate my first book to them;

and to Derek, with all my love.

"When This Cruel War Is Over"
Charles C. Sawyer, 1862

The title What This Cruel War Was Over *comes from the title of the most popular (at over one million copies of sheet music sold) song of the Civil War, at home and in camp, North and South, "When This Cruel War Is Over," (sometimes also known as "Weeping, Sad and Lonely"). The tune is so mournful that some officers forbade men from singing it in camp, out of worries that it would harm morale. The prohibitions met with only limited success; white Americans everywhere continued to sing the song. Union and Confederate lyrics to the song were nearly interchangeable, except for the last two lines of the first verse. Below is the Union version; Confederates simply changed the last two lines of the first verse to read: "Oh! How proud you stood before me, in your suit of gray/When you vow'd from me and country ne'er to go astray."*

Dearest Love, do you remember, when we last did meet,
How you told me that you loved me, kneeling at my feet?
Oh! How proud you stood before me, in your suit of blue,
When you vow'd to me and country, ever to be true.

CHORUS:
Weeping, sad and lonely, hopes and fears how vain!
When this cruel war is over, praying that we meet again.

When the summer breeze is sighing, mournfully along,
Or when autumn leaves are falling, sadly breathes the song.
Oft in dreams I see thee lying on the battle plain,
Lonely, wounded, even dying, calling but in vain.

CHORUS
If amid the din of battle, nobly you should fall,
Far away from those who love you, none to hear you call—
Who would whisper words of comfort, who would soothe your pain?
Ah! The many cruel fancies, ever in my brain.

CHORUS
But our Country called you, Darling, angels cheer your way;
While our nation's sons are fighting, we can only pray.
Nobly strike for God and Liberty, let all nations see
How we loved the starry banner, emblem of the free.

CHORUS

CONTENTS

WHAT THIS CRUEL WAR WAS OVER

Above: Union soldiers of the Seventh New York state militia at Camp Cameron, 1861. *Courtesy of the Library of Congress*

Left: A Confederate soldier: Georgia Private Thomas Kitchen. *Courtesy of the Library of Congress*

Below: Company E., Fourth United States Colored Infantry at Fort Lincoln. *Courtesy of the Library of Congress*

Introduction

"THE FACT that slavery is the sole undeniable cause of this infamous rebellion, that it is a war of, by, and for Slavery, is as plain as the noon-day sun."[1] So claimed the farmers, shopkeepers, and laborers who made up the Thirteenth Wisconsin Infantry Regiment in February 1862. The white Southerners of Morgan's Confederate Brigade might not have seen eye to eye with the Wisconsin men on much in 1862, but they agreed that "any man who pretends to believe that this is not a war for the emancipation of the blacks . . . is either a fool or a liar."[2] Two years later, black men in the Fourteenth Rhode Island Heavy Artillery reminded each other, "upon your prowess, discipline, and character; depend the destinies of four millions of people and the triumph of the principles of freedom and self government of this great republic."[3] These soldiers plainly identified slavery as the root of the Civil War. Just as plainly, by "slavery," they did not mean some abstract concept or a detached philosophical metaphor for ideas about freedom, but rather the actual enslavement of human beings in the United States based on race.

Yet to say that soldiers placed slavery at the center of the war is to open rather than solve a mystery. Neither the authors nor the intended audiences of these remarks held high office or made policy. Few owned slaves, and few of the white soldiers thought of themselves as abolitionists. They were instead very ordinary men of the type unlikely to figure in historical inquiries into the causes of the Civil War; they were men often assumed, even by historians from both the North and the South who for decades have acknowledged that without slavery there would have been no Civil War in the United States, to be little more than pawns swept up in events they probably did not understand, let alone consent to or shape. Members of the general public recognize even less of a connection between soldiers, slavery, and the Civil War. My most recent reminder of this sobering truism came at a wedding in September 2005, when a man from Buffalo, New York, who had no idea what I do for a living, spent more than an hour insisting to me that slavery had nothing to do with the conflict. And who can blame him? The Confederate ranks consisted primarily of men who owned no slaves, and historians have not convincingly explained why those men would fight a war they knew was waged to prevent the destruction of slavery. At the same time, scant numbers of the white men who filed into the Union Army had ever laid eyes on a slave, though most harbored their own prejudice against black people, so why would they fight to end slavery? And why would more than 180,000 black men fight for a government that, for its entire existence, had smiled on the enslavement of members of their race? What, in other words, did a "war about slavery" mean to the men who fought the Civil War, and why would it be important enough to fight?

This book is about what ordinary soldiers thought about the relationship between slavery and the Civil War. It is not about soldiers' motivations for enlisting, for individuals chose to do that for widely varied reasons. Seldom did a man enlist for the pay, which was low and unreliable. Few joined the military because they were forced; both Union and Confederate armies overwhelmingly consisted of volunteers. Many enlisted out of a sense of duty or personal honor. Some became soldiers in order to take part in what they assumed would be the biggest adventure of their lives. While some Northerners entered the ranks to help eradicate slavery, others enlisted to preserve the Union, with small concern for enslaved African Americans. In the South, many took up arms to safeguard their own slave property or their hopes to own slaves one day, while others shouldered rifles out of the belief that doing so protected their homes and families. Yet in spite of these and the countless other reasons that sent individual Northerners and Southerners into the ranks, broad consensus existed within each army as to why a war needed to be fought in the first place. Whatever else occupied their minds, ordinary Union and Confederate soldiers recognized slavery as the reason for the war, and the purpose of this book is to figure out why that was, and what it meant for the war and the nation.

Most Confederate soldiers owned no slaves, and more than anything else in the world, they cared about the interests and well-being of their own families. Why, then, would an ordinary, nonslaveholding white southern man readily identify slavery as the reason for the war, and why would he consider it important enough to himself and his family to imperil both in a fight to prevent its abolition? Why would men continue to fight for four desperate years, through military catastrophes like Gettysburg and

Atlanta and through political disasters like the reelection of President Abraham Lincoln, and then stop in the spring of 1865?

Why would most white Northerners, who knew no black people, and who may or may not have viewed slavery as vaguely distasteful but certainly would not have sympathized with the antebellum abolitionist movement, care enough about an abstract concept like the "Union" to fight a war that they too knew would never have happened if not for the institution of slavery? And if enlisted Union troops so vigorously opposed emancipation (as many historians and even more members of the general public, including the wedding guest from Buffalo, have long supposed), then why did the mass desertions predicted to occur in the wake of emancipation not happen? Did soldiers possess different attitudes toward slavery and its abolition than we have assumed? How did those attitudes compare to their ideas about racial equality and civil rights for black people? And how did the experiences of war and of interacting with black Americans (for the first time, in the case of many white Union soldiers) influence ordinary men's views?

Black men who joined the Union ranks harbored few delusions about the United States' long and complicated relationship to slavery or about white Northerners' attitudes toward blacks. As the soldiers of the Fourteenth Rhode Island Heavy Artillery pointed out, by 1860 slavery might have existed only in the southern states, but it still cast its "baleful shadow over the whole land from Maine to Texas." Even after the war began, "the North . . . despised the offer of her most loyal men" and barred blacks from the Army.[4] Why would African American men struggle so determinedly to join an army that at first refused them, and then once it did accept them, paid them less and prohibited them from becoming officers until the final year of the war? What did black troops expect the war and its aftermath to bring?

These questions enter into several ongoing conversations about the Civil War, including one about the relationship between military factors and social and political influences. What happened on the battlefield and what happened on the home front could not be separated in the Civil War, sometimes because the two arenas melted into one (for example, during Sherman's March), but more often because the cultures and societies from which Civil War soldiers came influenced how they and their leaders carried out the war.[5] Specifically, cultural values and attitudes molded the unique senses of Confederate and Union patriotism that in turn shaped how each side fought the war and weathered its turmoil.

Some historians have argued that a passionate, emotional connection to the abstract notion of an independent Confederacy transcended divisions among white Southerners, especially class divisions, while others have argued that internal fault lines dividing the wealthy from the nonwealthy prevented any true sense of patriotism from congealing in the white South. Those who argue for an emotional sense of patriotism run up against the hard reality of white southern behavior that directly and sometimes intentionally harmed the Confederacy and its war effort, and they must struggle to explain the apparent contradictions away.[6] Historians who argue that class conflict led to such resentment that nonslaveholders either never felt an attachment to the Confederacy and its war for independence or else abandoned that sense of attachment early in the war miss the strong and real commitment that even nonslaveholders felt to the institution of slavery, and therefore struggle to explain why an army made up primarily of nonslaveholders held on for four punishing years.[7] The soldiers in this book attest to a particular and distinctive sense of Confederate patriotism that transcended without erasing class division; self-interested behavior could and did damage the Confederate cause, but rather than negating the existence of Confederate patriotism, such behavior was actually the logical manifestation of white Confederates' unique brand of patriotism, based firmly on white men's perceptions of the best material and ideological interests of their loved ones, which they assumed to depend upon the survival of slavery. Far from splintering Confederates along class lines, slavery served as the cement that held Confederates together even under almost impossibly trying circumstances.

Historians have devoted less attention to Union patriotism, but among those who have considered it, questions center less on its relationship to self-interest than on whether emotional attachment to the American government predated or was created in the midst of the Civil War.[8] The soldiers in this study show that they did feel a strong sense of connection and duty to the United States government, which grew in part out of an antebellum millennialist understanding of the United States' unique mission in the world.[9] In the main, Union soldiers cared about the United States government not primarily because it served their families' interests, but because its survival mattered for the survival of ideals like liberty, equality, and self-government for all humanity. It was not that Union soldiers cared less about their families and interests than Confederate soldiers did, or that white Southerners were inherently more selfish than Northerners; instead, the relationship between individual and family interests and the nation worked differently for Confederates than it did for Union men. One irony of the Civil War was that the struggle placed far greater demands on Confederates than it did on white Northerners, even as it provided Confederates with a version of patriotism less well suited to sacrifice.

This book also enters into an even longer-running historical conversation about Civil War soldiers. Bell Wiley began the first serious study of common soldiers with his classics *The Life of Johnny Reb* and *The Life of Billy Yank,* works that surely must bear the credit or blame for inspiring as many budding Civil War historians as any publishing event since the South Carolina Ordinance of Secession.[10] Other than Wiley, most historians concentrated on officers or political leaders until the 1980s and 1990s, by which time social history's emphasis on history from the "bottom up" prompted increased attention to the lot of common soldiers.[11] Interest in social history also began to inspire pioneering works on black Union soldiers, although most studies then and since segregate white and black soldiers' ideas and experiences as thoroughly as Civil War military policy did.[12] Influenced partly by Wiley and even more by studies of World War II soldiers and by the national experience of the Vietnam War, historians for quite a while anachronistically projected modern notions of the nonideological soldier onto the Civil War generation.[13] The problem with such projections is that they impose modern views backward rather than trying to come to grips with nineteenth-century Americans on their own terms. Civil War–era Americans were not just like us, but dressed in funny clothes; instead, they were shaped by the culture and values of their day, which we need to try to understand in order to get a glimpse of how the war looked from their point of view. Eventually, important studies like Reid Mitchell's *Civil War Soldiers* began to call assumptions about ranks full of unthinking automatons into question. *Civil War Soldiers* awards more weight to elusive but important values like honor, duty, and manhood than it does to sharply articulated ideas, but it led the way in focusing historians' attention on the significance of soldiers' thoughts to their perceptions of the war.[14] James McPherson's *For Cause and Comrades: Why Men Fought in the Civil War* has done the most to shatter the misconception of the unthinking soldier by demonstrating the importance that Northerners and Southerners assigned to ideas about freedom, equality, the American Revolution, and the place of slavery within the American Republic.[15]

After all that, the reader could creditably be wondering what could possibly be left to say about Civil War soldiers. This book veers from the beaten path in a number of ways. First, unlike in most books about sol-

diers, which are organized thematically (a chapter on soldiers and patriotism, a chapter on soldiers' views of the enemy), Chapter One begins with
the opening shots of the war and the rest of the book proceeds chronologically through the four years of conflict, which was the way that soldiers
experienced the struggle. Moreover, the chronological organization allows
the book to convey change over time, a perspective that is essential in
understanding a long and bruising conflict that challenged every ideal and
preconceived notion that enlistees held dear. Further, few other books
compare Union and Confederate soldiers' views, either because they consider only one army or the other, or because they operate from the assumption (or at least seem to imply) that northern and southern troops harbored
nearly interchangeable ideas.[16] In contrast, this book explicitly compares
what Union and Confederate soldiers thought about slavery, including
when, how, and why soldiers' ideas changed. In addition, most books
about soldiers address either white or black soldiers, but this book includes
both white and black soldiers because the Union Army contained white
and black troops, so both must be included to represent the Union Army. At
the same time, this book resists the common practice of lumping all black
Union soldiers together, and aims instead to arrive at a fuller understanding
of black soldiers' views on slavery, the war, civil rights, and racial equality.

As the inclusion of black soldiers suggests, this book also draws on the
voices of more and slightly different soldiers than any of its predecessors.
While most books about soldiers rely disproportionately on the opinions
of officers, 1861 recruits, Easterners, and men who fought in the Virginia
theater, this book casts a net broad enough to capture members of traditionally underrepresented groups such as immigrants, African Americans,
western soldiers, late enlisters, and soldiers who served in the West, in
order to approximate cross sections of the actual Union and Confederate
ranks. It draws on letters and diaries written by men during the war itself,
rather than postwar memoirs, in which nostalgia, revisionism, and selective memory often cloud the ideas that soldiers entertained at the time they
actually served. For every soldier whose writings I read, and for whom I
could obtain sufficient biographical detail, I created a data sheet that
recorded such information as birth date, home, occupation, marital status,
regiment, rank, battle participation, and experiences such as capture,
wounding, or death. These 477 Confederate soldier data sheets and 657
Union soldier data sheets helped place soldiers' words in appropriate
social and demographic context, and also helped ensure that my cross section of soldiers resembled the actual makeup of the enlisted ranks as

closely as possible. In addition, I drew on the letters and diaries of hundreds of additional recruits for whom biographical information was too scanty to compile, and on letters written by soldiers to newspapers.

Uncensored and composed by men who, if war had not called them away from their homes, would have had no reason to express their innermost thoughts to their loved ones in writing, Civil War soldiers' letters and diaries offer unparalleled insight into the thoughts of ordinary Americans during a defining time in the nation's history.[17] It is no wonder historians and members of the general public remain fascinated with them. Countless letters and diaries reside in repositories throughout the United States, which means that source shortage presented no problems, but choosing collections wisely sometimes could. The letters and diaries used in this book come from forty-five state and local historical societies and libraries located from the Atlantic coast to Kansas, and from large archives like the Library of Congress and the United States Army Military History Institute. They were written mainly by enlisted men (though some junior officers appear) from every state that took part in the war. To preserve soldiers' own voices, their innovative spelling and grammatical habits appear exactly as written, without intrusion by *sic* or correction, except when absolutely necessary to avoid confusion. The resulting sample of soldiers, large in size and carefully reflective of the makeup of the actual armies, consists of men chosen not for their extraordinary ideas but rather for their very ordinariness; it provides a base from which to draw conclusions about the army as a whole.

In the course of this project, I unearthed more than one hundred regimental newspapers whose survival and whereabouts have escaped historians' attention, which makes this book the first study to use this unique type of source extensively and systematically.[18] These newspapers, unofficial, uncensored publications written almost entirely by enlisted men with whatever resources they could find, differ from one another in many details, but taken together, they offer valuable insights. Intended primarily for other soldiers as heartily sick of mud marches, oppressive heat, and wormy rations as the writer, camp newspaper articles had less need to keep up appearances for the benefit of worried wives or parents. Soldiers' newspapers were also written by many authors and therefore provide diverse perspectives to supplement the deep ones found in individuals' letters and diaries, although the preponderance of articles signed with initials or pseudonyms (if at all) can make the identification of individual authors difficult. Both Union and Confederate soldiers created camp newspapers, though many more Union than Confederate examples survive, especially from the later years of the war.

This book's inclusion of black Union troops presents its own challenges in terms of sources. While most black Union soldiers were slaves until the time of their enlistment, most surviving letters and diaries and the two black soldiers' camp papers I found were written mainly by northern free black soldiers, not least because the overwhelming majority of slaves were illiterate. Former slaves, then, stand out as the most seriously under-represented group in this book, though I have made every effort to find their voices in other places, such as verbal testimony given to Congress or army officers, letters dictated to literate comrades, and proceedings of meetings held in camp where the illiterate made their voices heard. African American newspapers such as the *Anglo-African* and the *Christian Recorder* regularly included letters from soldiers, as well as accounts of soldiers' camp gatherings. Letters to the *Anglo-African* and *Christian Recorder* appear often, because while public letters differ from private ones and must be read with care, they provide better insight into the war than the exclusion of black soldiers altogether, which has been the solution adopted by many studies to date.

Letters, diaries, and camp newspapers allowed Civil War soldiers to release pent-up frustrations and explore their own emotions, but just as important, they also provided places for soldiers to deliberate on slavery's role in the war. Throughout the conflict, troops continued to identify themselves as citizens first, and as soldiers only temporarily and by necessity, which meant that they retained the privilege of holding their own opinions. It is possible—even easy—to find a Civil War soldier's letter, diary, or newspaper article that says almost anything. Because dissent jangled constantly throughout the Union and Confederate ranks, it occupies considerable space in the pages that follow. Yet despite the persistence of disagreement and opposing viewpoints, soldiers' letters, diaries, and newspapers point to definite trends and patterns in soldiers' predominant understandings of the war. In other words, the wind of rank and file opinion always blew in multiple directions, but it generally blew harder in some directions than in others. Where the fundamental, underlying cause of the war was concerned, it amounted to a full-blown gale.

To determine the direction of prevailing winds, I built a series of gauges in the form of long compilations on each of the topics that soldiers themselves identified as important, including patriotism, politics, slavery, and race. Each compilation was organized chronologically. For instance, every time a soldier made a remark about politics, I made a new entry in the politics compilation. If the letter dated from May 5, 1863, I transcribed the relevant portion into the politics compilation between any remarks made by any other soldiers on May 4 and May 6, 1863. I used one font for Union soldiers and another font for Confederate troops, which permitted me to compare men from the two armies and still distinguish between them at a glance. The chronological organization of these gauges allowed me to chart change over time, while the topical nature of each compilation enabled me to measure the relative strength of each position taken on an issue. As I used quotations to write chapters, I reread each soldier's excerpt in the context of the entire letter, diary entry, or camp paper article in which it appeared, which helped adjust for any unusual stimuli or circumstances. In order to conclude that any one position dominated among Union or Confederate soldiers at a particular time, I stipulated that expressions of the prevalent view had to outnumber expressions of the dissenting view by a ratio of at least three to one. I indicate in the Notes any instances in which the proportion is lower.

More important than differences in sources or approach, this book departs from other books about Civil War soldiers because it places its primary focus on what soldiers thought about slavery. It does so because soldiers themselves did so. Rather than discussing slavery as one among many topics that soldiers addressed during the war, this book rescues slavery from the periphery of soldiers' mental worlds, where subsequent generations have tried to relegate it, and returns slavery to its rightful place at the center of soldiers' views of the struggle. In so doing, it alters our view of the Civil War in several ways. It eliminates the need to explain away a war about slavery as either a war about something else or a war imposed on unwitting nonslaveholding soldiers (despite those soldiers' own clear statements to the contrary) and instead helps unravel precisely why nonslaveholding Southerners would fight a war to protect slavery. Trying to understand why slavery mattered to the Confederate rank and file, rather than fabricating a view that we find more comforting or appealing, illuminates how and why enlisted Confederates held on as long as they did, and it also modifies our understanding of the timing of the war's end.

Seeking to understand, rather than deny or assume, the centrality of slavery also sheds light on how nineteenth-century Americans, especially Southerners, defined what it meant to be a man. While white Union soldiers did not articulate a clear relationship between slavery and manhood, white Southerners closely linked the two. A true man protected and con-

trolled dependents, which for white Southerners meant that a man compe-
tently exercised mastery over blacks (whether or not he owned any) as well
as over women and children. It also meant that a man took care of his family and sheltered his loved ones from harm, including the almost unimaginable harm that white Southerners feared emancipation would bring,
because they assumed that slaves released from bondage would terrorize,
murder, and violate vulnerable white women and children. Ironically,
black Southerners (and even northern free blacks) also took for granted a
relationship between slavery and manhood. For bondmen, the institution
of slavery made true manhood impossible because it robbed a black man
of the ability to protect his family from sale or to shelter his loved ones
from violence or sexual violation at the hands of white masters. While
slavery was necessary to white Southerners' conception of manhood, in
other words, it was antithetical to manhood among black men.

   In placing slavery at the center of soldiers' ideas about the war, we
recast much of what we know about white Union soldiers by providing a
new understanding of *when* Union soldiers began to support emancipation,
which in turn reveals a new emphasis on ordinary enlisted Union soldiers
as agents of change who shaped the progress and outcome of the war. Few
white Northerners initially joined the Union rank and file specifically to
stamp out slavery, and most shared the antiblack prejudices common to
their day, especially when the war began. Yet the shock of war itself and
soldiers' interactions with slaves, who in many cases were the first black
people northern men had ever met, changed Union troops' minds fast. At
first, white Union soldiers had little trouble separating their ideas about
slavery from their racist attitudes and saw no contradiction between
demanding an end to slavery and disputing any notion of black equality or
opposing any suggestion of increased rights for black people. Yet as the war
dragged on, even attitudes as stubborn as white Union troops' antiblack
prejudices shifted with the tide of the war, sometimes advancing and other
times regressing. By the end of the war, white northern opinions about
racial equality and civil rights, intractable though they had seemed in 1861,
were far more malleable and vulnerable to intense self-scrutiny among
Union troops than anyone could have imagined when the war began.

   Attention to Union soldiers' early shifts on slavery allows this book to
enter yet another ongoing conversation about the Civil War, the conversation about how slavery ended. Some historians chiefly credit slaves themselves, who weakened the institution of slavery by their actions during the
war, and who forced a war for Union to become a war against slavery by

using their physical presence to make it impossible for Union Army generals and political leaders like President Abraham Lincoln to ignore or shunt aside the question of slavery.[19] Other historians acknowledge individual slaves' actions as instrumental in securing their own individual freedom (a slave who ran away to the Union Army did indeed free himself), but argue that ending the institution of slavery required the exercise of governmental power; therefore, President Lincoln, who issued and stuck with the Emancipation Proclamation and championed the Thirteenth Amendment (unlike his 1864 presidential opponent, George McClellan, who would have done neither) bears primary responsibility for destroying slavery in the United States.[20] This book argues that the enlisted men in the Union Army forged the crucial link between slaves and policy makers. Slaves themselves did force emancipation onto the Union agenda even when most white Northerners would have preferred to ignore it, but one of the most important and earliest ways they did so was by converting enlisted Union soldiers, who, in 1861 and 1862, developed into emancipation advocates who expected their views to influence the prosecution of the war. Slaves convinced enlisted soldiers, who modified both their beliefs and their behavior. In turn, the men of the rank and file used letters, camp newspapers, and their own actions to influence the opinions of civilians and leaders who, lacking soldiers' direct contact with slaves, the South, and the experience of living on the front lines in a war that most people wanted over, lagged behind soldiers in their stances on emancipation.

By recognizing the centrality of slavery to Union soldiers' understanding of the war, this book also provides a key to understanding President Lincoln's immense popularity among the Union rank and file. When soldiers voted in 1864, nearly 80 percent of them cast their ballots for Lincoln, but the bond between president and soldiers was formed years earlier than that. In explaining the bond, historians have habitually emphasized Lincoln's humble demeanor, his accessibility, and his visits to the Army of the Potomac in the field.[21] Each of these characteristics helped enhance Lincoln's appeal among soldiers who saw the president, either by visiting the White House or by witnessing one of Lincoln's visits to camp, but they do not explain the love for him that even soldiers who never laid eyes on him expressed. Union troops believed that Lincoln shared their vision of the war's cause and purpose, even when nobody else at home seemed to understand. Although black Americans had advocated the destruction of slavery even before the war began, few white troops initially believed that the Union had any authority to interfere with slavery (and some would not have wanted it to regardless of authority), but their wartime experiences convinced them that slavery must be destroyed in order to win the war and redeem the American Republic from sin, and they believed that the president's views had evolved along a similar (though somewhat later) trajectory. When in the Gettysburg Address Lincoln avowed that the Union mattered for all humanity, and especially in later speeches like the Second Inaugural when he portrayed the war as punishment for the shared sin of slavery, the president validated a version of the war that soldiers had already espoused, but that their loved ones at home could not seem to grasp. A soldier's father might not see eye to eye with him about slavery and the war, and so as the war progressed, the soldier came to rely on Father Abraham instead.

White Union soldiers' commitment to emancipation was created by and during the war itself, but the issues of slavery and abolition had not appeared out of the blue in 1861. Tensions between North and South over slavery had been mounting for the entire lives of the men (most of whom had been born between the mid-1820s and mid-1840s) who enlisted in the Union and Confederate armies, even as the institution of slavery itself had been strengthening and growing.[22] The number of slaves jumped from 800,000 to 4,000,000 in just two generations, while the prosperity of southwestern cotton states like Mississippi and Alabama and the addition of Texas to the Union pushed the institution from the seaboard into the interior of the continent.[23]

The first real conflict over slavery arose in 1819, when Missouri applied to enter the Union as a slave state. Misled by Missouri's small number of slaves and the peripheral role that slavery at that time played in Missouri's economy, Representative James Tallmadge of New York miscalculated that Missouri would be an easy place to enact a gradual form of emancipation. He introduced the Tallmadge Amendment, which would not have freed existing slaves, but would have permitted no new slaves to be carried into Missouri after statehood, and would have stipulated that any children born in Missouri to slave parents would become free once they reached the age of twenty-five. To Tallmadge's surprise, southern leaders reacted with outrage, which did not die down until the so-called Missouri Compromise resolved the controversy and determined the fate of slavery in western territories for the next three decades by admitting Missouri as a slave state and drawing a boundary across the Louisiana Purchase territories at 36° 30' latitude. Territories below the line would be slave; above it would be free.[24]

In the wake of the Missouri Compromise, a proslavery ideology that abandoned the earlier habit of identifying slavery as a necessary evil in favor of forcefully arguing for it as a positive good took shape among white Southerners, even as an abolitionist movement increasingly critical of southern slavery emerged in the North.[25] Eager to avoid controversy over such an uncomfortable topic, most white Northerners and Southerners did their best to suppress troubles over slavery in the 1830s. They usually succeeded, despite exceptions like the gag rule controversy of 1836–44 (in which a southern-controlled Congress prevented the reception of antislavery petitions over howls of protest from some white Northerners who objected to the violation of the First Amendment rights of white petitioners). Occasional outbreaks of violence, such as the killing of antislavery advocate Elijah Lovejoy in 1837, sometimes broke the tenuous calm, but not very often.[26] Beneath the surface, tensions smoldered, and they sparked again in the 1840s when the rapid acquisition of Texas, New Mexico and Utah Territories, and California all reintroduced the question of slavery's expansion into western territories. When Pennsylvania Democrat David Wilmot proposed the Wilmot Proviso, which would have prevented the United States from introducing slavery into territories gained from Mexico (where slavery had been abolished), he ushered the slavery issue back into politics, and there it stayed, even after the Compromise of 1850 uneasily quelled the controversy stirred up by the proviso. Among other measures, the Compromise of 1850 threw out the Wilmot Proviso, admitted California as a free state, and enacted an unprecedentedly stringent Fugitive Slave Law.[27]

The Fugitive Slave Law prevented the slavery issue from disappearing in the 1850s. Article IV of the United States Constitution permitted masters to recapture slaves who fled to free states, but said nothing about the role of northern states or civilians in that process. The Fugitive Slave Law broke new ground because it mandated that states and individuals participate in the capture of fugitives and imposed harsh penalties for noncompliance. In response to the Fugitive Slave Law, Harriet Beecher Stowe wrote *Uncle Tom's Cabin,* a sentimental novel that sold better in the North than any previous work of fiction and that touched off angry protest in the South, where the book was banned.[28] Meanwhile, federal and state jurisdiction came into conflict throughout the North, as evidenced by fugitive slave rescue cases such as the Anthony Burns case in Massachusetts, the Joshua Glover case in Wisconsin, the Oberlin-Wellington case in Ohio, and others. Some northern states passed personal liberty laws, which overtly flouted the Fugitive Slave Law by exempting individuals, including those who worked for the state, from participating in the capture of fugitive slaves if their personal consciences so dictated; in response, white Southerners threatened violent retaliation.[29] The notoriety stirred up by fugitive rescues and the vitriolic southern response to northern states' personal liberty laws inflamed public opinion over slavery throughout the nation, dramatically limiting the effectiveness of Congressional compromise.

While the Fugitive Slave Law, *Uncle Tom's Cabin,* and personal liberty laws raised tensions, Kansas provided the ground on which those tensions led to armed battle. Kansas Territory was opened to white settlement in 1854. As a part of the Louisiana Purchase located above the 36° 30′ line, Kansas should have been free territory according to the Missouri Compromise, but a solution that worked in 1820 proved wholly inadequate to the hotter climate of the 1850s, by which time the extension of slavery seemed too important an issue to white Southerners, too vital to their very existence, to settle with the outdated Missouri Compromise. Instead, white southern leaders insisted, slavery followed the flag: it was a legitimate national institution that could not be barred from any U.S. territory. Senator Stephen Douglas of Illinois tried to douse the flames with cool reason in the form of the Kansas-Nebraska Act, which threw out the Missouri Compromise and replaced it with "popular sovereignty," which meant that white male voters in Kansas should decide at the ballot box whether Kansas would be slave or free. For his pains, Douglas was seen as a traitor to the Missouri Compromise by many Northerners and as a public danger by many white Southerners who did not believe an issue as important as slavery could be left to any mechanism as haphazard as voting. In Kansas itself, violence between proslavery and antislavery settlers erupted. Accounts by eastern correspondents such as James Redpath painted a lurid (and often exaggerated) picture in which voicing antislavery opinions or reading antislavery literature was branded a crime, aiding a fugitive slave was punishable by death, elections were fraudulent, and proslavery ruffians murdered and sacked with abandon. In 1857, it looked like all the violence might succeed in forcing slavery on Kansas. A fraudulently elected proslavery convention not recognized by most settlers in Kansas drafted the Lecompton constitution, a state constitution that would have made Kansas a slave state, and submitted it to Congress. Despite the strong opposition of most Kansas voters, President James Buchanan, thought to be under the thumb of southern Democrats, tried to force the proslavery constitution through Congress.[30] When Congress rejected the Lecompton constitution, white

Southerners like Georgia Congressman Lucius Gartrell lashed out. Gartrell called opposition to the Lecompton constitution the latest in a long series of "continual aggressions" against white Southerners, and newspapers throughout the South echoed similar protests.[31] Meanwhile, troubles mounted nationally. Even before the controversy over the Lecompton constitution arose, Chief Justice Roger B. Taney of the U.S. Supreme Court declared in the Dred Scott decision that Congress could not ban slavery from any territory. In the midst of the Lecompton controversy, a prominent Democratic newspaper, the *Washington Union,* called northern states' prohibition of slavery within their own boundaries unconstitutional.[32] Taney began to write a decision that would declare state laws against slavery unconstitutional.[33] In 1860, a slaveholder's case against the state of New York would have provided Taney with the opportunity to issue his decision effectively nationalizing slavery if secession had not intervened.[34]

A new, exclusively northern political party, the Republican Party, arose in the 1850s and added to white southern fears for the safety of slavery. Republicans made rapid gains among northern voters by portraying the dangers of a "Slave Power conspiracy" of wealthy Southerners designing against the liberties of free white men and attempting to undermine the dignity of white labor by associating it with the menial condition of slavery. The Republican Party's central focus was stopping the spread of slavery into western territories. Although the party claimed no authority to touch slavery where it existed, its emergence alongside growing (if lukewarm) antislavery feeling in the North alarmed white Southerners, who warned that the rise of the "Black Republicans" would doom the Union. The party's first presidential candidate, John C. Frémont, lost the election of 1856, but his strong showing in many northern states further worried the white South, as did Republican victories in many northern state and local contests.[35]

In 1859, warnings about the inevitable violence that growing northern antislavery sentiment would bring seemed to come true when abolitionist John Brown tried to capture the federal armory at Harpers Ferry and ignite a slave revolt throughout the South. Brown did not identify himself as a Republican (or a member of any party), but his actions struck white Southerners as the logical result of the growth of a sectional, antislavery party. The failure of Brown's mission and the horror with which most of the white North viewed it did not matter: a white man marching South to arm blacks and end slavery corresponded to white Southerners' worst nightmares.[36] The survival of slavery and the South required decisive action. In January 1860, Mississippi Senator Albert G. Brown submitted resolutions charging the Senate with the duty of passing laws protecting and promoting slavery in a territory if a territorial legislature failed to enact its own sufficiently strong proslavery laws. In February 1860, Senator Jefferson Davis followed up with a set of resolutions stating that neither Congress nor a territorial legislature could ban slavery from a territory, and that if "judiciary and executive authority" or "the territorial government shall fail or refuse to provide" protection for the "Constitutional Rights" of slaveholders to bring and keep slaves in a territory, "it will be the duty of Congress to supply such a deficiency." In short, white southern leaders were demanding an expanded role for the federal government in promoting slavery. Such demands provided a platform for southern Democrats when the Democratic Party met for its 1860 convention. Southern Democrats insisted on some version of a federal slave code while northern Democrats espoused popular sovereignty. The party split virtually assured the victory of a Republican candidate in the 1860 election.[37]

Such was the world in which Civil War soldiers had come of age. To be sure, they did not spend night and day thinking about the slavery issue, and most probably preferred to push it as far from the forefront of their minds as possible, but once the war came, they could not, and more importantly, did not, ignore it. Some historians have criticized (implicitly or explicitly) the study of Civil War soldiers as something of an escape hatch offering authors and readers a way to avoid wrestling with difficult and sometimes painful ideological questions about the war.[38] Even some veterans in their later years did their best to suppress the role of slavery, and even to deny that soldiers possessed any ideological awareness at all. Most famously, an aging Oliver Wendell Holmes, Jr., sighed three decades after the end of the war, "there is one thing I do not doubt . . . and that is that the faith is true and adorable which leads a soldier to throw away his life in obedience to a blindly accepted duty, in a cause which he little understands."[39] But that wistful sentimentalism flies in the face of the reality that soldiers confronted during the war itself. If we listen to what soldiers had to say as they fought the Civil War, the men in the ranks do not allow us to duck the uncomfortable issue of human slavery, but rather take us right to the heart of it. They force us to look at it unflinchingly, and what is more, to see it as a national, not simply southern, issue that defined a war and shaped a nation.

"Lincoln and Liberty":

Why an Antislavery President Meant War

CHARLESTONIANS crowded the city's rooftops, craning their necks to watch as ribbons of fire arced their way toward Fort Sumter. Beginning in the early morning hours of April 12, 1861, the batteries ringing Charleston Harbor bombarded the federal garrison for thirty-four hours. As daylight advanced, the barracks caught fire, the flagstaff fell, and the U.S. soldiers inside the fort ate their last rations. On April 14, Maj. Robert Anderson surrendered Fort Sumter to Confederate officer Pierre Beauregard. After decades of arguing and compromising, the northern and southern United States had gone to war.

As thousands of militiamen stared across Charleston Harbor at the scanty U.S. Army force occupying Fort Sumter, communities everywhere gathered to discuss the crisis facing the nation in early 1861. At a meeting of Louisiana students attending the University of North Carolina, nineteen-year-old Thomas Davidson recorded the proceedings. The Louisianans accused "fanatics of the North" of robbing "the South of her most cherished liberties," and pledged their lives to the protection of slavery, "that Institution at once our pride and the source of all our wealth and prosperity."[1] Nearly seven hundred miles away, Stephen Emerson, a Harvard College student who hoped to become a minister, attended a campus meeting that also passed resolutions. "We see our beloved country in imminent peril, our institutions of civil liberty threatened, [and] the genius of freedom & human progress assailed by the spirit of slavery and despotism," the Harvard students noted, before affirming their "chief allegiance" to God, the heritage of the American Revolution, and the Union.[2] Mean-

---

"Lincoln and Liberty" was an 1860 campaign song set (like many nineteenth-century campaign songs) to the tune "Rosin the Bow."

Union soldiers confront slavery in 1861: slave pen in Alexandria, Virginia. *Courtesy of Local History/Special Collections, Alexandria Public Library*

Slave woman in slave pen, Alexandria, 1861. *Courtesy of Local History/Special Collections, Alexandria Public Library*

while, black Philadelphians flocked to the Masonic Hall on South Eleventh Street. There, Alfred Green, a prominent man of color, reminded listeners that black soldiers defending Philadelphia in 1777 helped secure victory in the American Revolution. Now the time had come to realize the ideals of the Revolution by overthrowing "the tyrant system of slavery," and bringing "truth, justice, and equality to all men."[3]

Davidson, Emerson, and Green echoed many of one another's concerns, but they spent the bloodiest war in United States history on different sides. None of the black men to whom Green spoke could legally enlist in the Union Army for more than a year, and Green's own age made him an unlikely recruit, yet before the war ended, more than 180,000 African Americans had joined the Union war effort. Thomas Davidson served the Confederacy as a private in the Nineteenth Louisiana Infantry until he was killed at Atlanta. And Pvt. Stephen Emerson, First Massachusetts Infantry, fought for the Union until he died at Chancellorsville.

The words and actions of Green, Davidson, and Emerson show that to many of its participants, the Civil War was nothing less than a clash between competing ideas about how Americans should interpret and enact their founding ideals. The problem, as soldiers on both sides saw it, was that the opposing section posed a direct threat to everything that mattered. The opposing side threatened self-government. It threatened liberty and equality. It threatened the virtue necessary to sustain a republic. It threatened the proper balance between God, government, society, the family, and the individual. And no matter which side of the divide a Civil War soldier stood on, he knew that the heart of the threat, and the reason that the war came, was the other side's stance on slavery. From first to last, slavery defined the soldiers' war among both Union and Confederate troops, though how it did so would change over time. In the early months of the conflict, little budged in Confederates' initial understanding of the war as necessary resistance to the destruction of slavery. In contrast, Union soldiers' newfound acquaintance with the South, firsthand observations of slavery, and first taste of combat quickly led them to take a much firmer stand against slavery than many could have imagined before the war.

"No earthly Power can prevent Secession and revolution"

The immediate catalyst for secession and the outbreak of war was Abraham Lincoln's election to the presidency on a platform that pledged to halt the expansion of slavery. As one Virginia private put it, "the poisonous germ which must have sooner or later brought about a conflict between the two sections of the United States" was Northerners' apparent determination to bar "slaveholders from introducing slavery" into the territories.[4] A majority of northern voters had, after all, just cast ballots in the 1860 election for a candidate who ran on a platform of preventing slavery from spreading into the territories. Following the election, a slave trader complained that Lincoln's victory disturbed his business and caused slaves to act up. "No earthly Power can prevent Secession and revolution," he told his wife.[5] Even before Lincoln was inaugurated, seven slaveholding states had left the Union.

Most states seceded through the action of conventions, which voted to repeal state ratification of the U.S. Constitution. Secessionist and unionist candidates campaigned for election to these state conventions by asking voters to decide if slavery, their best interests, the well-being of their families, and the legacy of the American Revolution were safer inside or outside the Union. Just days after the presidential balloting, Thomas Cobb campaigned for the Georgia state convention by insisting that "the memory of our fathers" as well as Georgians' "property, our liberty, and our reputation" were all endangered by an antislavery president. Furthermore, he reminded voters that states like Wisconsin and Vermont had personal liberty laws, which permitted individual citizens to refuse to help capture runaway slaves within the boundaries of their own states, and that compounded the threat.[6] Georgia unionists like Alexander Stephens, Benjamin Hill, and Herschel Johnson countered that they, too, sought to protect the spirit of 1776, slavery, and white families' best interests, and that "the only real ground of difference now is: some of us think we can get redress in the Union, and others think we cannot." How, these men asked, could remaining in a Union with a Fugitive Slave Law do a worse job of protecting slavery than establishing a national boundary between the slave and free states, which would release the northern states from any obligation to return slaves to their owners? Shoring up protections for slavery within the Union served southern interests better, Georgia unionists argued.[7]

The electorate mirrored the difference of opinion voiced by secessionist and unionist candidates. Realizing this uncomfortable truth, Cobb and other secessionists hoped to hurry secession along without a vote that might reveal divisions in white southern opinion. "Wait not till the grog shops and crossroads shall send up a discordant voice from a divided people," Cobb urged, and although he failed to prevent an election, the returns showed he was right to worry about the outcome.[8] The results were so close that the count was never revealed; although Georgia Governor Joseph Brown claimed that 58 percent of the vote went to secessionist candidates, the actual total either resulted in a virtual tie or squeaked out a bare secessionist majority.[9] The state convention opted for secession, but deep differences in public opinion hinted that popular attitudes toward a new Confederate nation would be complex, with connections to a Confederacy created through secession remaining tenuous among some segments of the population.

Divisions like those present in Georgia emerged everywhere, but as the winter progressed, even initially reluctant white Southerners resolved their doubts in strikingly similar ways throughout the South. They began by weighing secession against the threat Lincoln's election posed to the expansion of slavery, white Southerners' best interests, and the Revolution as white Southerners interpreted it. John Halliburton, a young man from Memphis, Tennessee, spent the winter wooing his cousin, Juliet, through letters that discussed everything from politics to marriage. Juliet, an ardent secessionist from Arkansas, maintained that the Declaration of Independence enshrined the right of secession, which the election of an antislavery president gave southern states reason to invoke. Halliburton disagreed, insisting, "I can hate [Lincoln] and still love the Union." Further, Halliburton argued, "no state has a right to secede" because the Constitution followed and therefore superseded the Declaration, and its spirit forbade secession. Besides, the Declaration must be treated with caution. "Why if we had to do as the declaration of Independence says we should have to assert 'that *all* men were born free and equal' . . . and fight for Nigger equality." Better to abide by the Constitution, "*the* bulwark of slavery," and stay in the Union, Halliburton concluded.[10] Initially, Virginian Hodijah Meade agreed that secession was neither legal nor in the best interests of the South, but that was before he learned that some northern states "refused to repeal those Personal Liberty laws." Reasoning that Lincoln was unlikely to interfere with states' personal liberty laws, Meade asked his mother, "are you not for Secession now?"[11] Even John Halliburton eventually capitulated and enlisted in a Confederate regiment. However torn, many white Southerners accepted the logic that a Lincoln presidency threatened slavery, and threats to slavery justified—even demanded—drastic measures, including secession and war.

Threats to slavery meant secession and war for many reasons. For one thing, they made the privileged place that southern states held within the Union insecure, and without a dominant role for the South, the Union seemed less valuable. Louisianan Rufus Cater agreed with his cousin Fannie that "the United States government was once a glorious and prosperous one," under which white Southerners profited. For most of the nation's existence, the South had masterfully used the Constitution and political structure of the United States to dominate the federal government, despite the region's smaller size and slower-growing white population. The "three-fifths clause" of the U.S. Constitution, which provided for the counting of three-fifths of the slave population when determining Congressional apportionment despite slaves' obvious exclusion from the body politic, gave white Southerners disproportionate voting clout. In addition, Southerners controlled key Congressional committees and dominated powerful positions like the speakership of the U.S. House of Representatives, the chief justice's seat, and the presidency (with a small number of exceptions) throughout the first eight decades of the United States' national existence. The election of a president who did not share the South's concern for the safety of slavery, along with growing northern hostility to slavery's expansion, threatened the favoring of southern interests to which white Southerners felt entitled, and in so doing, dissolved any federal claim on southern allegiance. As Rufus Cater put it, when northern "fanatics" like Lincoln "misinterpreted and . . . perverted" the Constitution to bar slavery from the western territories, they relieved white Southerners of all obligations of loyalty, and licensed the southern states to frame a new government "suited to themselves," even if doing so precipitated war.[12]

Threats to slavery, even indirect ones like the Republican Party's opposition to slavery's westward extension, also posed a frightening public safety problem in the minds of many white Southerners. Because the institution of slavery rested on a foundation of force and violence, tensions always smoldered beneath the surface of southern society, where they kindled a contradiction that southern whites were forced to confront.[13] If slaves were truly happy in slavery, as proslavery ideologues insisted, then whites should have had nothing to fear from the approximately four million enslaved human beings who lived among them.[14] Yet the fear of slave revolt haunted white Southerners constantly, inflamed by actual uprisings such as the Denmark Vesey conspiracy of 1822, the Nat Turner rebellion of 1831, and John Brown's failed uprising in 1859. White men, slaveholders and nonslaveholders alike, shared constant responsibility for ensuring community safety by serving together in slave patrols that safeguarded neighborhoods while also testifying to the community standing, commitment to slavery, and manhood of patrol members.[15] Southern whites generally coped with the contradiction between supposedly contented slaves and the concerted need for vigilance by assuming that slaves would not rebel of their own accord; they would have to be contaminated by northern ideas released into the atmosphere like infectious spores every time Northerners agitated on any aspect of the slavery question. Consequently, Republican claims to oppose slavery's spread but not to touch it where it existed did nothing to assuage white Southerners' concerns that slavery was in imminent danger in 1860.

Because most white Northerners did not want war, they clung to the comfortable belief that there would not be one, regardless of white Southerners' warnings. Despite the concerns of some northern Democrats such as defeated presidential candidate Stephen Douglas, many northern onlookers dismissed the howl of protest from the South as theatrical posturing. Northerners had listened for decades to what they believed was southern saber rattling on the issue of slavery, but it had not led to war during the Nullification Crisis of 1828–33, the Wilmot Proviso crisis of 1846, or even the Nashville Convention in 1850. Troubles in Kansas showed that slavery *could* lead to violence, but most white Northerners preferred to believe that Southerners with their impetuous ways were simply bluffing again.[16] With the 1860 presidential race looming, some northern whites looked for signs of southern moderation. Lucius Brown, a draftsman from Columbus, Ohio, was working on a building project in Nashville, Tennessee, in November 1860. After watching a full day and night of torchlight processions on behalf of John Bell, a Constitutional unionist candidate who ran on a platform of saving the Union, Brown assured his father that "folks are very moderate here," and he saw no "probability of . . . any trouble."[17] Even after the election, the *New York Daily Tribune* claimed, "the secession strength in the South is over-rated. Vociferous, ostentatious and intolerant, it appears greater at the hustings than the polls."[18] To go to war over such folly seemed neither wise nor probable. "War is the last, the very last argument to be resorted to among children of a common parentage," warned the *Chicago Tribune*. "Let it be avoided by every sacrifice short of the legacy which our fathers left us in the *Constitution of the United States*."[19]

When southern states actually began to leave the Union, secession shifted from a melodramatic threat to a genuine danger to republican self-government. It repudiated the results of a fair and free election, the only basis on which self-government could function, and it was anarchy, according to newspapers, individuals, and President-elect Lincoln. More-over, secession showed that a self-governing nation would self-destruct and betrayed the hopes for representative government shared by millions throughout the world. As South Carolina threatened secession, the *New York Daily Tribune* reminded readers that the United States was "engaged in trying a great experiment, involving not merely the future fate and wel-fare of this Western continent, but the hopes and prospects of the whole human race." The American experiment would determine if "the demo-cratic principle of equal rights, general suffrage, and government by a majority" was "capable of being carried into practical operation." Seces-sion over the embarrassing question of slavery would be regarded by onlookers throughout the world "as the first step toward the entire break-down of our whole system of republican government."[20]

Once secession happened, more Northerners began to realize that if the nation was to avoid war, then the North would need to adopt some plan of action. A small fraction of the northern population advised allowing the southern states to depart in peace, but the more general urge in the early part of the secession winter was to search for a compromise. Congress hastily generated and considered piles of compromise proposals, as the public looked on expectantly. The Crittenden Compromise, named for the Kentucky senator who spearheaded the effort, consisted of a series of con-stitutional amendments and Congressional resolutions. It would have guaranteed perpetual noninterference with slavery; extended the Missouri Compromise line permanently across the continent, allowing slavery to spread south of 36° 30′ latitude; forbidden the abolition of slavery in the District of Columbia without the consent of local voters, and only then if Maryland and Virginia had abolished slavery; prohibited Congress from exercising any authority over the interstate slave trade; channeled federal funds into compensation for slave owners whose runaway slaves remained at large in the North; and added an "unamendable amendment" to the Constitution which guaranteed that none of the Crittenden Compromise amendments could ever be amended once passed.[21]

The Crittenden Compromise pleased almost nobody. It fell short of the heightened federal role in the promotion of slavery sought by southern states. Discussed as a series of Senate resolutions on slavery in early 1860 and then substantially adopted as the platform of southern Democratic presidential candidate John Breckinridge in the election of 1860, the desired federal slave code would have expressly forbidden either Con-gress or a territory's own legislature from barring slavery from any U.S.

territory, and it would have committed the *federal* government to the enforcement and protection of slavery in the territories.[22] By sidestepping demands for increased federal involvement with slavery, the Crittenden Compromise fell short of these requirements. At the same time, some northern Democrats found unamendable amendments difficult to square with strict-constructionist constitutional principles, while northern Republicans despised the way in which the compromise repudiated the platform of nonextension on which a candidate had just freely and fairly been elected.[23] To young farmhand Leigh Webber, compromise along the Crittenden lines amounted to allowing "an oligarchy of slaveholders," not the electorate, to "rule our nation." Simultaneously decrying the compromise proposals and chiding friends for not writing to him often enough, Webber announced, "I want no more compromise like the correspondence between you and me, or like a jug handle, all on one side."[24]

Meanwhile, as the U.S. government refrained from making military preparations for fear of alienating the Upper South and the border states that had not seceded, the newly established Confederate government adopted a wartime footing. On March 6, the Confederate Congress authorized the enlistment of 100,000 troops. Seceded states seized federal property such as forts and ports located within state borders, and appropriated the revenue from such properties, including customs duties, a major source of the nation's income in an era that predated the personal income tax. By April, 60,000 Southerners were enrolled in military service and only four federal forts in seceded states remained in U.S. hands. One was Fort Sumter, and its soldiers were about to run out of food. Lincoln sent a ship of foodstuffs to Fort Sumter, despite South Carolina's warnings that the state would regard any attempt to supply the fort as a hostile act.[25] As promised, South Carolina troops fired on U.S. soldiers located on federal property. The federal garrison surrendered, and Lincoln called for 75,000 troops to put down the rebellion. Four more southern states, including the bellwether state of Virginia, seceded, creating an eleven-state Confederacy.[26]

Southern states' seizure of customs duties and federal property had angered members of the northern public, but Fort Sumter proved to be the final straw.[27] After a winter of urging caution, the *Wisconsin State Journal* called the bombardment of Fort Sumter a "crowning act of wanton aggression," which must "sweep at once away all further scruple or hesitation" in favor of a "vigorous policy" to suppress "treason and rebellion."[28] New York City, a metropolis with strong southern ties, had been home to pronounced pro-southern sentiment throughout the winter, but after Fort Sumter, a quarter of a million people gathered to participate in a Union rally. In small towns and villages throughout the North, enthusiastic men, women, and children flocked to patriotic parades and ceremonies.[29]

When President Lincoln called for 75,000 volunteers to put down the rebellion, northern communities responded eagerly. Addressing all "Patriots of Marshall County," an Illinois recruiting poster urged local men to answer Lincoln's call out of duty to "our God and our country."[30] The response overwhelmed makeshift recruiting offices in Illinois and throughout the North. Similarly, white southern men all over the Confederacy rushed to join regiments, worried that the fighting would end before they had a chance to participate.

"If it had not been for . . . abolitionism . . . I would never have been soldiering"

While initially the desire for excitement and adventure may have been enough to propel many young men into the ranks, it did not take long for the novelty to wear off, leaving soldiers in both armies to think more deeply about how matters had come to war. Among other reasons, men on both sides justified the conflict by describing it as a defense of the memory of the American Revolution, although in both cases, the memory was selective. Union and Confederate soldiers alike believed that the republican government inherited from the Revolution derived its legitimacy from the consent of the governed, that it existed to preserve the ideals of liberty and equality, and that self-government could work only as long as the population remained virtuous.[31] Yet beyond these basic principles, they disagreed over whether the Revolution's most worthwhile legacy consisted of the act of rebellion or of the government that the rebellion had created.

Confederates believed that their rebellion against a federal government that inadequately served white Southerners' interest in slavery reenacted the colonies' revolt against Great Britain. As Pvt. Ivy Duggan explained, "our Revolutionary fathers taught us . . . to resist oppression, to declare and maintain independence, to govern ourselves as we think best." The British attempt to tax colonists' tea without colonial representation in Parliament constituted far less of an infringement on colonial rights than hostility toward slavery did on white southern rights. If the revolutionary generation "could not endure a tax on tea because it violated a sacred principle, how could WE submit to be governed by those whose steady determination is to sacrifice our happiness, and even our lives, in the abolition of an institution guaranteed to us by the constitution of our fathers?" Duggan demanded.[32] The actual Union that the Revolution had created mattered less than the reasons for its creation.

Just as the Confederate interpretation of the Revolution's most important legacy downplayed the importance of the government that emerged from the Revolution, so did Confederate soldiers in 1861 pay surprisingly scant attention to the new government that their own rebellion created. The outlines of the new government took shape when a provisional congress drafted a provisional constitution in February and ratified a permanent constitution in March. The Confederate Constitution quoted the U.S. Constitution verbatim in most places. The small number of changes included increased executive power (through a longer presidential term, a line item veto, enlarged presidential control over appropriations and the budget, and other relatively minor provisions), limits on tariffs, prohibitions on most internal improvements, and bans on democratic electoral activities like public statements of party platforms. Most important, the Confederate Constitution contained explicit guarantees for the institution of slavery. The constitution then went to the states where it would be ratified by state conventions. In sum, the creation and ratification of constitutions occupied Confederate politics for the first months of the war.[33] These tasks did not, in contrast, occupy the attention of soldiers, whose letters and diaries virtually never discussed political principles such as states' rights, or political practicalities like the foundation of a new government, despite the fact that the South was engaged in landmark tasks like ratifying a constitution.[34] For the men who filled the Confederate ranks, secession, the Confederacy, and the war were not about state sovereignty or whether the central government could levy a tariff or build a road. Secession, the Confederacy, and the war were about securing a government that would do what government was supposed to do: promote white liberty, advance white families' best interests, and protect slavery.

When Confederate soldiers spoke of liberty, they referred not to a universally applicable ideal, but to a carefully circumscribed possession available to white Southerners. No mere abstraction, liberty had to do with the unobstructed pursuit of material prosperity for white men and their families. As one Virginian put it, liberty consisted of the "good many comforts and privileges" that his family could enjoy without outside interference.[35] While exclusive in terms of race, liberty was inclusive in terms of class. In other words, while liberty applied strictly to whites, it applied to all whites, regardless of present social class or economic condition, because all whites, by virtue of being white, enjoyed the right to individual ambition and aspirations of material betterment through means of their own choosing. To quell rising discontent among recruits, an article in *The Missouri Army Argus* (a Confederate regimental newspaper) appealed to this version of liberty by conflating *every* white man's ambitions, regardless of social status, with the Confederate cause:

> What interest has General Sterling Price or Governor Claiborne Jackson or General or Governor anybody else, in the cause of our common country, that you have not? How are they or the officers more interested than you or I? There is not a soldier in the army who is not a free man. . . . Not a soldier who may not become rich or great. . . . One man has as much at stake—as much to gain or lose as another.[36]

Good government should uphold white liberty; the Confederacy offered a better choice for white Southerners than the Union because it was better for white liberty as Confederates defined it.

In order to retain legitimacy, government must also serve the needs and interests of white families, according to Confederates. Georgia soldier Josiah Patterson explained to his young sons that he must "leave you and become a soldier" to make sure that the boys grew up under a government that would facilitate their "hopes of becoming great and good men."[37] His fellow Georgian, Ivy Duggan, described "[our] homes and the sweet ones there" as Confederate soldiers' main priorities, while Pvt. Thomas Taylor of Alabama agreed that what mattered most were "our dear wives and little children."[38] The presence of Union troops on southern soil could, of course, have made Confederates look to their own homes and families, but to dismiss the Confederate focus on family interests as nothing more than a response to Yankee threats is to miss something central about Confederate soldiers, and also to misunderstand their expectations of the war in 1861. No Union soldiers appeared anywhere near central Georgia or Alabama, or the home of any Confederate soldier who lived any distance from the coast or the Union border, and most Confederate soldiers doubted that the Yankees could fight well enough to penetrate very far into the South before the Confederacy won the war. Therefore, while white southern men cared deeply about their families and feared that emancipation would endanger their safety, few of them viewed the arrival of Northerners in their neighborhood as likely, let alone as the cause of the war. With or without advancing hosts of Union soldiers, ordinary white southern men were most concerned about their own material interests and their families.

Confederates' focus on individualistic and familial concerns endowed their cause with both strengths and weaknesses. On one hand, Confederate calls to arms in 1861 worked in large part because southern white men believed that their personal interests were best served and their families best protected by fighting for a Confederacy more attuned to white Southerners' individual needs and aspirations than the Union was. Further, if at some later date a soldier became disillusioned with President Jefferson Davis, the Confederate Congress, or any other branch of government, he was unlikely to turn against the Confederate cause if that cause had more to do with himself or his family than it did with the Richmond government. This trait gave Confederate patriotism a certain resiliency and imperviousness to political events. On the other hand, soldiers' concentration on personal and family well-being could mean trouble if the needs of the Confederacy ever clashed with family priorities. Since few such conflicts arose in 1861, the potential for trouble remained latent, but it was present from the start.

Because white Southerners' unique understanding of liberty and their inclination toward privileging individual families' interests could make unity elusive, Confederate unity relied heavily on white Southerners' interpretation of the third main function of government: the protection of slavery. In order to wage war against a better-equipped foe, in the name of a government whose form and structure differed little from the enemy's government, Southerners needed to maintain a united front, both for the practical purposes of making war and for the moral purpose of showing that the war was justified because it represented the will of the people.[39] Shared belief in the dangers of abolition powerfully united Confederate soldiers and motivated them to fight, even when they shared little else. An urbane young lawyer and son of a wealthy South Carolina plantation owner recognized the unifying potential of perceived threats to slavery when he urged "the whole South to make common cause against the hordes of abolitionists who are swarming southwards."[40] Joseph Bruckmuller, a German immigrant saloon keeper who fought with the Seventh Texas, had almost nothing in common with the scion of the Palmetto State, yet Bruckmuller also saw the need to preserve slavery as a powerful glue binding all whites in the South. Scoffing at "improve-the-world ideas of emancipation," Bruckmuller urged his fellow "adoption citizens" to stand by "your own countrymen and race" against the "murder and arson, hanging and stealing" that were sure to accompany the "liberation of the half-civilized cannibal."[41]

Slaveholders' commitment to slavery comes as no surprise, but most Confederate troops (including Joseph Bruckmuller) owned no slaves. Nonetheless, like Bruckmuller, they forthrightly depicted the war as a battle to prevent the destruction of slavery. When discussing reasons for the conflict, a Georgia regimental newspaper, *The Spirit of '61,* pointed to personal liberty laws, "those grevious enactments of some of the free state legislatures in regard to fugitive slaves," as evidence that Northerners were "black hearted abolitionists" who must be opposed before they crushed slavery.[42] With less legislative specificity but at least as much passion, James Williams fumed, "confound the whole set of Psalm singing 'brethren' and 'sistern' too. If it had not been for them . . . preaching abolitionism from every northern pulpit," Williams was convinced, "I would never have been soldiering."[43] It is patronizing and insulting to Confederate soldiers to pretend that they did not understand the war as a battle for slavery when they so plainly described it as exactly that. There is no way to understand the Civil War from a Confederate perspective—no way to understand why the war began or why it lasted so long—without understanding why white nonslaveholding men would believe that the preservation of slavery justified a fight.

Slavery was worth fighting for because it served many fundamentally important purposes that white men considered vital to themselves and their families, whether or not they owned slaves.[44] Black slavery in the antebellum South buttressed the ideals of white liberty and equality. It stabilized an otherwise precarious social structure. Slavery undergirded white Southerners' convictions of their own superior moral orthodoxy. In addition, it anchored the individual identity of white southern men as men in a firm conception of their rights, duties, and social roles, and it intertwined with the southern notion of honor. Finally, slavery supplied an unambiguous mechanism of race control in a region where 40 percent of the population was black. Nonslaveholding Confederate soldiers' willingness to fight for slavery grew from a much deeper source than the calculation of economic interest to be expected among those who owned slaves. It grew from white southern men's gut-level conviction that survival—of themselves, their families, and the social order—depended on slavery's continued existence.

Black slavery enabled white liberty and equality because it allowed all whites to pursue property ownership (including slaves) without outside interference, and because it made whites equal in not being slaves.[45] Confederate assumptions about the reliance of white liberty and equality on black slavery appeared in countless ways. To take one example, an Alabama soldier wrote "Run, Yank, or Die," a song that soldiers from other states exchanged and sent home to give loved ones a taste of camp life, and to help explain the war from an enlisted point of view. The song repeatedly portrays "little Northern Yankees," minimized by the absence of slavery in their own society, who run away whenever southern men shouting "Hurrah for slavery" (the first line of the song's chorus) arrive on the scene. One verse specifically identifies and mocks the Tennessee unionist Andrew Johnson, who broke with his state and remained in the U.S. Senate until later appointed military governor of Tennessee by President Lincoln. According to the verse, once "old Andy Johnson . . . join[ed] Lincoln to set the negro free," Johnson revoked his claims to liberty, equality, and even manhood. He no longer counted among the true "Southern boys."[46]

White equality was fragile in an antebellum South characterized by change and growth; slavery helped strengthen it by providing stability and making ambitions seem attainable. The antebellum United States thrived with the growth of a market economy, territorial expansion, and vast increases in wealth. Again and again, southern whites abandoned places of poor soil and disappointing prospects for new locations where land and slave ownership seemed possible.[47] Yet movement did not always bring upward mobility. As white Southerners sought to get ahead, wealth became increasingly concentrated, a pattern with disturbing implications for the idea of white equality.[48] Slavery softened the dislocations by holding out the prospect of slave ownership as an ambition to which all whites were entitled to aspire, and by providing reassurance.[49] No matter how difficult in practice, entrance to slaveholding status remained possible in theory, and it offered white southern yeomen the chance for advancement that counted among the prerogatives of white men. The importance that southern whites placed on the appearance of slaveholding attainability helps explain why the question of reopening the Atlantic slave trade emerged in the 1850s, and also suggests another reason, along with concern for public safety, why the question of slavery's extension to the territories loomed so large. Slaveholding possibilities seemed even greater in the West: while one out of three white southern families living in the states that eventually formed the Confederacy owned slaves in 1860, the proportion rose to as high as one out of two families in southwestern states like Mississippi, giving nonslaveholders real reason to care about slavery's continued expansion westward.[50]

Especially for the economically insecure, the hope of slave ownership staked a claim to white equality in a competitive world that offered few guarantees. Some non-slave-owning soldiers used the war itself as an opportunity to enjoy the benefits of slaveholding as soon as they got the chance. Marching through Missouri in August 1861, for example, yeomen soldiers seized slaves from local plantations for their own use.[51] Meanwhile, slavery steadied an otherwise turbulent and dynamic southern society by promising that southern whites could never fall into the lowest social stratum no matter how far or frequently they moved, geographically or economically.[52]

Slavery also provided stability by securing southern claims to moral orthodoxy. The Second Great Awakening, a period of religious revivals culminating in the 1830s, swept the antebellum North and South. As a result, just over one-third of Northerners and slightly under one-third of white Southerners were church members, principally within the Methodist, Baptist, and Presbyterian denominations, yet the fiery religious fervor glazed the North and South with distinctive casts. In the North, emphasis on perfectibility (the idea that since all people were made in the image of God and God was perfect, individuals and societies could reform themselves into a state of moral perfection) sparked a wave of social reform movements, including abolitionism. In the South, revivals inspired concentration on personal conversion and salvation while discouraging involvement in radical social reform.[53] As the Kehukee (North Carolina) Association of Primitive Baptists plainly put it in 1849, "the Kingdome of Christ is not of this world," which made human attempts to approximate God's kingdom on earth presumptuous and heretical.[54] A South Georgia and Florida Baptist publication made the same point when it criticized New England ministers who had signed an antislavery petition for sinfully seeing themselves as God's "viceregents to act for him on earth."[55] Furthermore, southern evangelical emphasis on biblical literalism cemented the relationship between religion and slavery. As southern clergy and proslavery ideologues had pointed out for decades, slavery appears in the Bible, which meant it must be part of God's divine order.[56]

Since the destruction of slavery defied God's appointed order, abolitionism amounted to sinful heresy. South Carolina soldier Chesley Herbert summed up many white Southerners' conflation of abolitionism with general moral decay when he dismissed Northerners everywhere and unionists in border states as "abolitionist and any other sort of an 'ist' that is not good."[57] Abolitionism worked like an infection, except that instead of sickening the body, it perverted right morals. Georgia soldier A. H. Mitchell, for one, linked abolitionism in the North to other moral patholo-gies like "spiritualism and free love."[58] Allowing infidelity to slavery to creep south would contaminate the moral virtue needed to retain God's favor and to sustain a republic.

Mitchell identified abolitionism with "free love" for a reason: aboli-tionism, according to many white Southerners, would set off a social earthquake sure to rattle every single social relation, right down to the basic units of society, households and families. While most antebellum American families continued to live and work on farms that relied on the labor of all family members, the growth of a market economy facilitated the development of a "separate spheres" ideology that divided the aggres-sive competition associated with the market from the domestic realm of home and family. The task of moral inculcation, on which survival of the republic and the favor of God depended, fell to mothers, who were to train children within the family circle. So important was this ideal of an invio-lable family cemented by bonds between mothers and children that any threats to the family ideal were regarded as a "crisis of the family" by the mid-nineteenth century, according to one historian. Insulating the family from threats secured the moral fiber, guaranteed the safety of republican government, and pleased God, in the minds of many nineteenth-century Americans.[59] To white Southerners, the way to safeguard the family was to preserve a strictly hierarchical household structure within which women played circumscribed roles, subordinate to men and confined to the private sphere. Among abolitionism's many faults, according to numerous proslavery ideologues, was its tolerance of activism among women, who figured prominently among the abolitionist rank and file. As William Drayton explained in an influential pamphlet, women's "interfer-ence with subjects of this character, if sufficiently important to have *any* influence, must have an evil one," because female participation in a public question interfered with women's proper roles, and therefore threatened the family structure.[60]

Disturb slavery, in other words, and even the family fell apart. If the family disintegrated, so did white men's identities as men because of the centrality of the nuclear family to nineteenth-century American culture, and because nineteenth-century Americans regarded marriage and the establishment of one's own household and family as the threshold that ordinarily marked the passage from boy to man. In southern society as white southern men conceived it, adult white males headed households and possessed the right to command all dependents, such as women and children. Slavery meant that white men, regardless of whether they were slave owners, also had the right to exert mastery over African Americans. The loss of slavery would call white men's right to rule over blacks into question, and once right to rule in any sphere was weakened, its legitimacy became suspect in every sphere.[61]

Many Confederate soldiers warned that abolition would obliterate the rights and duties of white manhood, chief among them the protection of white women's virtue, which required control of white women's bodies.[62] Newspapers like the *Richmond Enquirer* reminded readers "where the two races approximate equality in numbers, slavery is the only protection of the laboring classes against the evils of amalgamation."[63] "Amalgamation," later known as miscegenation, was hardly unknown; white men's sexual coercion of female slaves accounted for the high number of mulattoes in the South. But allusion to amalgamation in relation to "laboring classes" was another matter, because it reminded non-slaveowners of slavery's importance to them. Without slavery, the *Enquirer* warned, the daughters of honest white yeomen would be helpless against the sexual advances of black men. Soldiers frequently and emphatically echoed this theme. One Georgia recruit fretted about rumors that slaves who thought the war meant freedom were already discussing "whom they would make their wives among the young [white] ladies."[64] Virginia soldiers expressed similar anxieties in *The Tenth Legion,* a camp newspaper. If the "fanatical marauders" of the North succeeded in eradicating black slavery, intimate relations between white women and black men would occur, and the South would become a place "terrible to contemplate."[65]

By depriving white southern men of the rights and privileges due the white male head of household, abolition would leave white southern men powerless, propertyless, and degraded in real, not simply symbolic, senses. The daily conditions in which they lived made it impossible for white southern men to ignore this danger, because every day white southern men observed adult males (slave men) who did not enjoy the unfettered right to accumulate property, who were subject to the will of others, and who could not protect their families from dangers like punishment or sale. Black slavery constantly reminded white men that in a society where most residents (African Americans, women, and children) were disenfranchised and subordinate to them, the independence that white men enjoyed as adult white males, and the ability to command the labor and fealty of the people in their households, set them apart and identified them as men. Meanwhile, the presence of dependents also forced white men to recognize and dread what subordination and loss of manhood's privileges meant.[66]

While family life was central to many white southern men's assumptions about what it meant to be a man, additional prerogatives of manhood, which the destruction of slavery would also threaten, existed outside the realm of the family. Unmarried as well as married white men had the duty to protect and right to control white women's bodies and morals, as the Georgia volunteer's worries about former slaves *choosing* white wives (rather than already having them) testifies. Men who failed to provide such protection did not deserve the love of a woman, another key hallmark of true manhood.[67] Other indicators of white manhood included personal mobility and the right to bear arms. Women, at least white ladies, did not parade about unescorted, nor did they wield guns. Meanwhile, black slaves required passes signed by whites to justify their movements, and a slave's access to firearms relied on the discretion of his owner rather than on the slave's own free will. Even unenslaved blacks in the South could not travel freely without carrying special papers, signed by whites, certifying their freedom, and black access to firearms was closely governed by law in many locales. The right to handle firearms freely and the ability to go where one pleased in a society where most inhabitants did not enjoy such privileges distinguished an individual as a white man.[68] Complaining that if a soldier "wants to go any where he has to have a pass," Louisiana private Frederick Taber told his parents that he found himself treated more like a "Nigro" than a white man.[69] Taber could afford to exaggerate because his white skin saved him from actually being mistaken for a slave, but if slavery disappeared, it would take with it the clear distinctions between the rights of whites and blacks that Taber and his fellow soldiers relied upon to secure their own masculinity.

White men's ability to exercise authority over others contributed to another quality, honor, which set white men apart and identified them as men. Though difficult to define precisely (and significantly different from what we mean by "honor" today), a specific notion of honor was central to white Southerners' values and culture. It encapsulated white southern men's concern with personal reputation, and rested on acknowledgment by one's peers of attributes like courage, right morals, and masculinity.

Recognition of a man's honor chiefly depended upon his demonstration of authority over subordinates, including women, children, and African Americans, whether or not he owned slaves.[70] Enforced by an elaborate set of rules and rituals (the duel being the most dramatic if least often utilized), honor was a vulnerable quality demanding vigilant oversight, even to the point of touchiness. To many white Southerners, outside reproaches about slavery insulted southern honor by casting aspersions on Southerners' morals. Criticizing slavery questioned one way—and therefore *every* way—in which white men exercised authority over others. Such insults necessitated war, much as questioning a white man's character or authority over his wife could lead to a fight.[71] Charles Trueheart believed secession was unconstitutional, but still supported departure from the Union as the only proper reaction to slurs against slavery. "There is no other alternative left us," he decided, "unless we come down from the high ground that we have taken, and humble our heads in the dust at the feet of Black Republican masters, disgraced in our own eyes and before the whole world."[72]

Finally, nonslaveholding whites believed in the necessity of slavery because they lived in a biracial society, which they assumed would explode into race war without slavery. Much as worries about slave revolt plagued antebellum white Southerners, rumors of slave violence circulated throughout the Army in the early days of the war. A Virginia soldier pretended to scoff at the idea that slaves near his home "were marching through the Country & committing all manner of depredations and outrages," yet gossip to that effect preyed upon him enough that he wrote to his father just in case.[73] When Ivy Duggan warned that abolition by even the most apparently slow and careful measures meant "fire, sword, and even poison as instruments in desolating our homes, ruining us and degrading our children," he invoked the racial fear that strengthened nonslaveholding whites' belief in the necessity of slavery.[74]

So intrinsic was slavery to southern life and culture, pervading everything from white men's individual identities to safety to the structure of society, that many white Southerners simply could not imagine its absence. If the absence of slavery was unthinkable, then abolition would not eliminate the racial hierarchy that slavery enforced; it would reverse it. The *Richmond Enquirer* cautioned that abolition meant "the substitution of the white by the black race in the southern tier of States."[75] To fight in defense of black slavery was to resist white degradation, and the life-and-death necessity of that resistance explained the outbreak of the war to

Confederates who repeatedly proclaimed that they must fight or be made slaves. Alabama private Thomas Taylor, for instance, described the "hellish undertaking" of "Lincoln & his hirelings" as an attempt to ensure that all white Southerners were "doomed to slavery."[76] White men like Thomas Taylor and the countless others who uttered fears of becoming slaves were not speaking in code. They were genuinely afraid of being reduced to the powerless, libertyless, and emasculated lives and conditions occupied by black slaves. Shared white racial anxieties overpowered class tensions, suppressed prospective challenges to slavery, and imparted a sense of unity and common goals among white Southerners who were otherwise inclined to focus on personal and familial interests. Nonslaveholding Confederate soldiers regarded black slavery as vital to the protection of their families, interests, and very identities as men, and they relied on it to prevent race war. Perceived northern attempts to destroy it had to be stopped.

"The rebellion is abolitionizing the whole army"

The outbreak of war led many northern men, like their Confederate counterparts, to describe the war as the defense of the legacy of the American Revolution, but Northerners interpreted that legacy and its importance in distinctive ways. Just weeks after Fort Sumter, a group of African American men who gathered in Cleveland, Ohio, resolved, "to-day as in the times of '76 and 1812 we are ready to go forth and do battle in the common causes of the country."[77] The Cleveland men's offers to serve were rejected by a Union policy that initially restricted enlistment to white men, but their insistence on the connection between the Revolution and the present crisis was sincere and widely shared. Soldiers of the Seventh Iowa similarly instructed one another to "look back to seventy-six" and "remember well that sacred trust our fathers placed in our care."[78] The words used by the men from Cleveland or Iowa could just as easily have appeared in a Confederate regimental paper or a southern soldier's diary, but the words would have meant something different there. Confederates emulated the Revolution through the act of rebellion, but Union troops honored the Revolution by fighting to preserve the American government it created. By rallying "around the star spangled banner to defend the Union of our Revolutionary sires," one camp newspaper explained, Union troops were helping to "protect and perpetuate a Government which the oppressed in every land have looked upon for half a century as the beacon of liberty."[79] That statement contrasted sharply with the Confederate claim (voiced by

Ivy Duggan and countless others) that the Union in 1861 violated its own reasons for being and threatened liberty.

Union troops interpreted the significance of the Union more broadly, and harbored a different vision of liberty. The Union existed, according to northern volunteers in 1861, not simply for limited purposes like facilitating white citizens' pursuit of material interests, but for the grander purpose of proving to the world that republican self-government based on the principles expressed in the Declaration of Independence could work. The destruction of the Union would turn the idea of government based on liberty and equality into an object of ridicule, and dash all hopes for the success of "the experiment of our popular government."[80] One soldier explained to his father that the Union must survive to prove "man is capable of self government," while his regiment's newspaper asked, "destroy this Union and what can republics hope for?"[81]

Union soldiers identified the U.S. government as "our political temple of liberty" rather than a menace to liberty, because Union men's conceptions of liberty did not depend on the existence of slavery (as Confederate troops' definition did), and because Union troops viewed liberty less as an individual possession than as a universally applicable ideal, embedded by the Revolution into the foundation of the American Republic.[82] As far as slavery was concerned, some Northerners believed liberty and slavery were incompatible, but initially most white Northerners did not define liberty in relation to slavery at all. More important (to most Union recruits in 1861), while Confederates associated liberty with the enjoyment of their own families, privileges, and belongings, Northerners assumed liberty transcended personal and family interests. In fact, one Michigan volunteer saw real liabilities in intensive focus on individual "labors to perform and dear friends to greet," because a soldier who concentrated excessively on his own loved ones and their concerns could lose sight of what was at stake, or lose his nerve in the face of danger.[83] Indiana private W. D. Wildman told his former schoolteacher, "the Union is not only the citadel of our liberty, but the depostory of the hopes of the human race."[84] A Wisconsin volunteer struck a similar note when he claimed that the liberty enshrined by the American Union applied to "the friendless and oppressed of every sun."[85] Northern men cared about their families and their material interests as avidly as southern men did, but, unlike white Southerners, they did not intertwine those priorities with the concept of liberty; instead, they understood liberty in less personal, more worldwide terms. As Kansas private Leigh Webber put it, Union soldiers had to fight "for the

Cause of Constitutional Liberty" because "if we fail now, the hope of human rights is extinguished for ages." Webber fought in a regiment from Kansas, a state as threatened by wartime violence as any in 1861, yet he did not describe the war in terms of protecting his loved ones or belongings, as Confederates (including those from areas far removed from danger) did. Like other Union soldiers, he had grown up believing that liberty mattered not simply because it belonged to oneself and one's relatives, but because it applied to everybody.[86]

Soldiers from border states like Kentucky and Missouri might have been expected to connect the Union's struggle more directly to their own homes and families, since more than most Northerners or Southerners in 1861, their neighborhoods and loved ones faced threats of actual violence, and Kentuckians and Missourians did articulate the Union cause in more directly personal terms than Union soldiers from more distant states. Yet even when border state Union soldiers spoke of their interests, they were less likely than their Confederate counterparts to speak in terms of material possessions, and they were also less likely to confine the discussion to their own relatives. Kentucky volunteer Terah Sampson felt that the "priveliges" to "act freely without being molested or harmed" which Americans enjoyed as a birthright were in danger of being "taken away" not just from himself or his mother and brothers, but from the entire "once happy and free people" of the United States.[87] Soldiers from homes farther from the front were more likely to reason that liberty applied to everybody, and that they and their loved ones were part of everybody.

Union soldiers' distinctive understanding of liberty as a universal quality specially entrusted to the United States grew out of a tradition of millennial thought far more prominent in the antebellum North than in the antebellum South. Sunday sermons, schoolbooks, and Independence Day orations had long assured Northerners that God had special plans for the American Republic.[88] When the Second Great Awakening swept Civil War soldiers' parents' generation and singed soldiers' own generation in its youth, northern revivalism's emphasis on perfectibility renewed the United States' special mandate to bring about God's kingdom on earth. Sin, corruption, injustice, and misery plainly demonstrated that the United States remained a long way from perfection, but by banding together into reform societies, many middle-class Northerners believed ordinary citizens could remove obstacles to perfection and establish the United States as a model to the world. An "explosion in voluntary societies" occurred in the North from 1825 to 1850, during which northern middle-class men and women formed organizations dedicated to idealistic causes like temperance, prison and asylum reform, and (less popularly) abolitionism and women's rights.[89] In short, the millennial tradition and the Second Great Awakening encouraged even the majority of Northerners who did not join reform societies to think about ideals like liberty in more collective terms than Southerners were accustomed to, and to view the United States as a specially chosen example that would bring ideals like liberty to the whole world, while simultaneously leading the rest of the globe to a state of moral perfection.

Millennial habits of thought combined with daily habit and local governmental practices to encourage northern men to feel and express more emotional attachments to the government—not just the geographic territory or population or idea—of the United States than Southerners were wont to do. Over and over, new recruits in 1861 referred to the Union not just as their home or their country, but as "the best government on earth." Joseph Scroggs, an Ohioan about to enlist in the 104th Ohio, called the Union the "best government that ever existed"; a Wisconsin sharpshooter wrote about "the best and most honorable Government on the face of God's earth"; and an anonymous enlisted contributor to the camp newspaper *The Ohio Seventh* praised "the justest, freest, most beneficent government on which the sun has ever shone." These men were only a few of the legions who sounded some variation on this refrain, which recurred incessantly among Union soldiers in 1861 but not at all among Confederates.[90] As one historian has explained, daily life in the North gave white northern men more reason than their southern counterparts to believe that "government in the pre–Civil War North was not 'them,' it was us." Differences in northern and southern society offered northern men more opportunities to participate directly in government in ways beyond voting. While dispersed settlement patterns minimized the number of town governments and therefore opportunities to cast ballots on mundane municipal questions or to hold minor office in the South, the northern landscape included more small towns and villages, more local ballot questions, and more prosaic offices, such as that of fence-viewer (a village official who inspected fences and helped neighbors resolve property, livestock, and trespass disputes), which were unnecessary and therefore rare in the South.[91] Recruits who joined the Union ranks in 1861 did not view the U.S. government as a distant abstraction or as a hostile ruling force. Neither did they see it as irrelevant to their lives or dangerous to their liberties. Instead, they viewed government in general and the Union government in particular as a dynamic process in which they expected to take active part.[92]

Because Union troops felt emotionally attached to the U.S. government, many would have perceived any rebellion as a personal insult, but secession from the United States in response to election results amounted to an especially egregious affront to the principles of self-government for which northern whites believed the Union stood. In practical terms, secession undermined self-government and democracy by undercutting the electoral process. Elective government depended upon all parties abiding by the outcome of fair and free elections. If the losing side severed the government whenever it disapproved of the results, electoral government lacked legitimacy and all hopes for self-government were destroyed. As one camp newspaper explained, the United States owed its "powers and its privileges" to its "rules of government," which were based "upon the will of the people fairly and legally expressed" through elections.[93] Lincoln was elected according to procedures outlined in the Constitution, which made reneging on the outcome tantamount to abandoning elections altogether.

Further, as Union troops saw it, Confederates had repudiated the principles of self-government by rejecting not just any undesirable election result; they had specifically rejected an outcome that did not favor the expansion of slavery. Firmly convinced that the rebellion was started by slave owners "to secure the extension of that blighting curse—*slavery*—o'er our fair land," an Iowan volunteered to defend "the Union and *a government*" from destruction by such base motives.[94] Meanwhile, a Vermont soldier claimed that the moral "stigma" of slavery brought "animosities and wranglings" down on the nation and threatened its very existence, while a Wisconsin chaplain emphasized that "radical reform must be had everywhere" or else "a slave Empire" would replace "Republican Government," and then "our country must die."[95] The Union mattered to Union soldiers and to the whole world (by the rank and file's lights, at least), and in 1861 a large and growing number of ordinary soldiers believed that a war endangering that Union had come about because of slavery. White Southerners' willingness to destroy the Union over slavery made the war about slavery whether an individual Union soldier wanted it that way or not, and regardless of how he felt about black Americans.

Widespread recognition that slavery had started the war did not immediately translate into agreement over what the Union should do about it. At first, slavery and emancipation were the most hotly contested issues in the

Union Army, unlike in the Confederate Army, where soldiers shared a belief in the necessity of black bondage. Then as now, racism was a nationwide, not exclusively southern, phenomenon, and it led some Union troops to denounce the idea of a war to end slavery. The regimental newspaper of the Seventeenth Illinois lambasted "the northern fanatic," who awaits "the probable abolition of slavery in the southern States, rubs his hands with delight and rejoices that the day of deliverance has arrived. All the horrors of civil war are of no consequence to him if his darling project is accomplished."[96] Other soldiers concluded that the way to end the war was to quiet southern fears about the safety of slavery by leaving the institution alone.[97]

Right from the beginning, some Northerners rejected the conciliatory approach. Most obviously, black Northerners knew immediately that the war must strike at slavery. As one black New Yorker bluntly put it, "this war . . . is virtually nothing more nor less than perpetual slavery against universal freedom." In his view, the Union would not win until it made up its mind "to put an everlasting end to negro slavery."[98] Just weeks after Fort Sumter fell, the black newspaper the *Anglo-African* predicted that "no adjustment of the nation's difficulty is possible until the claims of the black man are first met and satisfied. . . . If you would restore the Union and maintain the government you so fondly cherish, make way for liberty, universal and complete."[99] Some white Northerners concurred. Andrew Walker, a son of Irish immigrants, was teaching school in Illinois when he heard that Fort Sumter had fallen. He hoped that the crisis would at last allow the United States to "forever set aside Slavery," and before the year was out, he enlisted in the Fifty-fifth Illinois to help.[100]

Disagreement never wholly disappeared from the Union Army, but fighting the war convinced many Union troops early on that slavery was "the exciting as well as the approximate cause of the trouble which now agitates our once proud republic," which meant that winning the war would require the destruction of slavery.[101] If Southerners had not rebelled, a Pennsylvanian insisted, most Northerners would have continued "following their plow, minding their forge, or exerting their talents in the mercantile line" with thoughts of slavery and war far from their minds, but the South had left no choice but to take action against the institution that brought the war.[102] Wartime service reinforced that analysis in two ways. First, early battles like Bull Run and Wilson's Creek dispelled delusions about a short and easy war. One shaken survivor of Bull Run testified to the impact that combat could have when he lamented to his fiancée,

"O Emily you can imagine nothing about the horrors of war. I have read about it but knew nothing what it was untill I experienced it."[103] As soldiers came to grips with the likelihood of a long and difficult struggle, they also looked differently at measures that might once have seemed too radical. Second, soldiers heard over and over from southern civilians that the Yankees were out to destroy slavery, and that the South went to war to save it. Wisconsin Chaplain A. C. Barry spent a lot of time talking to residents of Virginia's eastern shore, where he was repeatedly struck by their insistence that they had gone to war because they believed "the institution of slavery was in danger."[104] Sgt. E. C. Hubbard, a hard-bitten volunteer serving in Missouri, explained to his brother that white men were killing one another "all for a detestable black man."[105] Hubbard hardly qualified as a radical abolitionist, yet his observations convinced him that slavery had caused the war. The longer he served, the more certain he grew that successful war policies would have to strike at slavery.[106]

Men like Hubbard added up to a striking pattern that took shape between August and December of 1861: soldier after soldier began to insist that since slavery had caused the war, only the destruction of slavery could end it. In October, a member of the Third Wisconsin told the *Wisconsin State Journal,* "the rebellion is abolitionizing the whole army." Time in the South forced troops "to face this sum of all evils, and cause of the war," slavery. "You have no idea of the changes that have taken place in the minds of the soldiers in the last two months," the soldier continued, and the changes were not restricted to Republicans. Now that they saw slavery with their own eyes, "men of all parties seem unanimous in the belief that to permanently establish the Union, is to first wipe [out] the institution" of slavery.[107] A Missouri private agreed that since "it was slavery that caused the war," it would take "the eternal overthrow of slavery" to win it.[108] Throughout the rank and file, as enlisted soldiers decided that only elimination of the war's cause could end the rebellion and prevent its recurrence, they championed the destruction of slavery a full year ahead of the Emancipation Proclamation, well before most civilians, political leaders, or officers did.

Union policy toward slaves and slavery evolved out of the interplay between pragmatic practices adopted in the field and official legislation passed by Congress. In May 1861 three slaves fled to Union Gen. Benjamin Butler's lines at Fortress Monroe, Virginia. When the owner, a Confederate colonel, demanded their return, Butler refused, calling the slaves "contraband of war," which he was under no obligation to give back.[109] On

August 6, Congress codified the refusal to return some slaves by passing the First Confiscation Act, which allowed the Union Army to divest disloyal owners of any slaves used to serve Confederate Army officers, build Confederate fortifications, or otherwise aid the Confederate cause. Illinois private Andrew Walker gladly heralded the First Confiscation Act as "something extraordinary in the history of America."[110]

The First Confiscation Act marked an important milestone, because it was the first time the U.S. Congress passed a law injurious to the slave-owning rights of slaveholders; however, many soldiers and even some officers remained dissatisfied with what they regarded as a weak gesture where a vigorous blow was needed. The First Confiscation Act, after all, targeted the property rights of select individuals without dislodging the institution of slavery or affecting all slaveholders. Gen. James Lane, an opportunist already notorious for his fierce activity in the Kansas border wars, paid no attention to official distinctions drawn by the First Confiscation Act, and instead actively liberated slaves and intimidated their owners throughout much of western Missouri.[111] Taking a somewhat less aggressive approach, Gen. John C. Frémont of the Western Department issued a controversial proclamation on August 30, 1861. Frémont's proclamation liberated the slaves of any disloyal residents in Missouri, whether or not masters were using their slaves to aid the rebellion. Statesmen in other border states, especially Kentucky, warned President Lincoln that such a radical policy could shake the loyalty of slave states still in the Union, and Lincoln requested that Frémont bring his proclamation more into line with the terms of the First Confiscation Act. Frémont refused to do so, and then proceeded to lose a series of engagements with Confederate Gen. Sterling Price. Lincoln responded by removing Frémont from command.[112]

Frémont's proclamation and his removal elicited strong reactions. Some Union troops objected to any action against slavery; President Lincoln worried that Kentucky soldiers in particular would balk. Others fretted about the practical implications of Frémont's proclamation. One soldier, E. P. Kellogg, thought the proclamation excessively rash, and feared that it saddled the Union Army with too many jobs to do at once. The "question of the disposal of the negroes after their emancipation" would be complicated, Kellogg warned. Better to "have but one Gordian Knot at a time. If you give us more we shall have to cut them all, and perhaps cut our fingers if not our throats."[113]

Kellogg urged caution from hundreds of miles away in Virginia, but in Missouri itself, many soldiers cheered for Frémont and his bold measure.

A. G. Dinsmore of the Thirteenth Missouri praised Frémont, "whom we all esteem, and in whose integrity, courage, patriotism and good judgment we all have the utmost confidence." Dinsmore reported that "our troops were very much enraged when we heard the news that Frémont was to be Court Martialed and superseded." The countermanding of Frémont's bold stroke "would certainly have a bad effect on the army in the western department."[114] E. C. Hubbard wrote of soldiers' support for Frémont's proclamation and their worry over the general's fate. "Considerable anxiety is evinced here to know whether Frémont will be removed or not," he explained to his brother. "If he is not sustained by the Government and is removed it will be a heavy blow to his department."[115]

Numerous soldiers outside Missouri also took heart from Frémont's actions. Though William Dunham was stationed in the eastern theater, he speculated that Frémont "has done more for to infuse energy into the Western Division of the service than all others together."[116] When he learned of Frémont's removal, Dunham resented that a leader whom he considered to be decisive and effective had "been slaughtered by *fogy* politicians."[117] Pvt. Adam Marty, a Swiss immigrant who fought with the First Minnesota in the Army of the Potomac, wondered why the administration "interfered" with Frémont at all, "who if he could have his way would soon end this war by removing the cause of it."[118] In discussing Frémont, Marty echoed the more general refrain (sounded throughout the Union rank and file) that since slavery caused the war, it would take the elimination of slavery to win the war.

Enlisted Union soldiers came to the conclusion that winning the war would require the destruction of slavery partly because soldiers' personal observations of the South led many to decide that slavery blighted everything it touched. "If it were not for the curse of slavery [the South] could not be beat," one northern corporal told a friend. As it was, southern whites lacked "the thrift and energy that we see in the free States and the baneful effects of slavery are visible everywhere in the lack of enterprise and universal indolence of the inhabitants . . . white men do not work. . . . The land is excellent, but there is little raised."[119] Pvt. Leigh Webber admired the "reddish loam" of Tennessee, which, "if inhabited by Yankees would bloom like Eden." Instead, to Webber's eyes, "everything generally wears an aspect of neglect, *shiftlessness* and decay" thanks to "the blighting effect of slavery and secession."[120] Serving right next door to his own state, Illinoisan E. C. Hubbard determined that Missouri should have been "one of the richest states," instead of "the poorest." It was too close and climatically similar to the Midwest for distance or weather to account for the differences, so the cause, decided Hubbard and others who drew similar conclusions, had to be slavery.[121]

Soldiers who insisted that slavery impoverished southern society did not simply mean that slavery reduced wealth; in 1860, the nation's twelve wealthiest counties were in the South, and one of the country's greatest sources of wealth, slaves, was concentrated almost entirely below the Mason-Dixon line.[122] Soldiers were also commenting on what they saw as poor social health. "Books and newspapers are very rare, and schools and churches are like angels' visit—few and far between," complained one soldier.[123] William Gibson, a chaplain with the Forty-fifth Pennsylvania, wrote to his children about the South's failings as he saw them. For one thing, "Southern refinement does not pay much respect to the difference between male and female," reported Gibson. In Pennsylvania, Germans were sometimes viewed as lacking "due consideration for the female sex" when they "sen[t] their wives and especially their daughters in to the harvest field," but at least among German Pennsylvanians, female labor stayed within the family. On South Carolina plantations, "these Southerners work other men's wives and daughters," Gibson marveled. "Here we have the boasted refinement of America employing [slave] females in all kinds of plantation work, in common with the males." A second failing according to Gibson, who saw the middle class as a repository of social virtue, was that "so far as I can see there has been no middle class" in the South. Instead, "there was the Southern planter having nothing to do for the greater part of the year, but to devise means how he might best enjoy himself." Next came "the overseer," and finally, slaves "but little removed from a state of barbarism." Rather than civic equality, Gibson saw "the extremes of luxury and poverty, refinement and barbarism." Even among nonslaveholding whites, he found "nothing but a set of *toadies* for the rich planters: and what the South wanted to make the whole North—slave catchers for the South."[124]

To some extent, diagnoses (like Gibson's) of southern cultural woes arose from attitudes soldiers brought south with them.[125] While staple-crop commercial agriculture in plantation districts did differ from diversified agriculture on northern family farms, the attribution of all differences to slavery came partly from white middle-class Northerners' own assumptions and from popular travel literature. In *The Cotton Kingdom*, for example, Connecticut-born New Yorker Frederick Law Olmsted depicted a listless South deprived by slavery of virtues prized by white middle-class Northerners, including thrift, self-discipline, and an ethic of civic improvement.[126] Because northern soldiers (especially from New England and the upper Midwest) expected to see certain characteristics, of course they did.[127]

Yet more influential than Union soldiers' preexisting notions, or even their firsthand observations of the South, were their interactions with actual slaves, which led many to view slavery as a dehumanizing and evil institution that corroded the moral virtue necessary for a population to govern itself. Like Southerners, Northerners believed in the power of moral contagion, but where white Southerners identified abolitionism as an agent of moral infection, Northerners pointed to slavery as a poison contaminating the South with "social, intellectual and moral degradation."[128] Nothing made slavery's toxicity more obvious to Union troops than its effect on the fundamental unit of society, the family. For one thing, slave sales separated families. In the Upper South, where many Union soldiers were stationed in 1861, about one in three first marriages was broken by sale, and about half of all slave children were separated from at least one parent.[129] With their own eyes, soldiers saw slavery snap bonds between parents and children. The men of the Seventh Wisconsin were awakened by gunshots one November night. The following day, soldiers "learned, and saw the cause of the alarm in the form of two negro women—a mother and a daughter." The pair had fled to Union lines to avoid the proposed sale of the "goodlooking" daughter into the so-called fancy trade, which soldiers viewed as a form of concubinage. Outraged by the plight and moved by the vulnerability of the mother and daughter, "every private in the ranks" cursed "that system which tramples on the honor of man, and makes merchandise of the virtue of women," according to one member of the regiment.[130] When an Iowan encountered a young child about to be sold by her own father, who was also her master, he vowed, "By G–d I'll *fight* till hell *freezes* over and then I'll cut the ice and fight on."[131]

To be sure, not even the most compelling evidence of slavery's cruelty could persuade every soldier to support emancipation. Pvt. Henry Bandy was not alone when he cheered, "hooraw for the union and not for the nigar," but more common were the soldiers who decided that the Army must either get rid of slavery or prepare to fight the same battle all over again.[132] As a New York soldier put it, "as long as we ignore the fact (practically) that Slavery is the basis of this struggle so long are we simply heading down a vigorously growing plant that will continually spring up and give new trouble at very short intervals. We must emancipate."[133]

Hostility to slavery did not necessarily mean support for racial equality. In fact, white Union soldiers strove mightily to keep the issues of slavery and black rights separate. "I have a good degree of sympathy for the *slave*," one private admitted, "but I like the *Negro* the farther off the better."[134] Many Union troops used demeaning terms like "nigger" and "darky" and trotted out stereotypes such as "woolly-headed, good natured, with a tongue that never stops" to describe blacks.[135] These and other expressions of patronizing views toward African Americans did not necessarily indicate tolerance of slavery (the same soldier who derided a black boy as "woolly-headed" also raised money to help the boy escape to freedom), but neither did they suggest a belief in racial equality. The coexistence of antislavery sentiment and racism among northern troops may seem contradictory from a modern point of view, but many Union soldiers did in fact hold antislavery and racist views at the same time. Proemancipation sentiment did not banish racism; nor did continued racism invalidate support for emancipation. White Union soldiers' assiduous distancing of slavery from more complicated questions of racial equality allowed many to call for an end to slavery regardless of their own ambivalent racial attitudes and therefore heightened support for emancipation in the Union Army; it also limited the rank and file's willingness to face complicated questions about racial justice.

IN SHORT, contact with slaves and southern society convinced many Union troops that the immoral and blighting institution of slavery was antithetical to republican government, and that any republican government that tried to accommodate slavery was doomed to eventual failure. The recognition was not universal among the entire Union Army, nor was it shared by most civilians, political leaders, or high-ranking military officers. Yet clear demands for the destruction of slavery plainly emerged among enlisted Union soldiers, especially those stationed in the slave states who were witnessing slavery with their own eyes for the first time. Even some border state Union soldiers joined the clamor, either because they had witnessed for years the violence that slavery could engender or out of shock and anger that slaveholders in their home states valued the peculiar institution over the Union. Slaves themselves did the most to force emancipation onto the Union agenda, but the first and most important way they did so was by winning over enlisted Union soldiers, who, in the first year of the war, became the first major group after black Americans and abolitionists to call for an end to slavery, and who expected their views to influence the prosecution of the war.[136]

Confederate soldiers noticed the Union Army's actions against slavery, but they regarded them as confirmation of the suspicions that drove the southern states to war rather than as a change or a surprise. Many even derived grim satisfaction from measures like Frémont's proclamation: it cleared things up by crystallizing issues that had long been present, but held in a state of uneasy suspension. Mississippi private John Foster, for instance, wrote to his aunt that "Frémont has done more for us than any General we have save [Sterling] Price," because his proclamation reminded all southern whites that the North wished "to annihilate us by turning loose a servile population with arms in hand to commit the most outrageous acts of cruelty & barbarism."[137] Less than one year earlier, Foster had "hated to give up the idea of the Union," but he changed his mind because the North's true intentions toward slavery were now transparent.[138] Reminders of northern abolitionism should prove just the thing, believed Foster and others, to unite the South into an indomitable fighting force capable of ending the war before another year passed. Yet rather than conclude the war, 1862 would confound expectations for everyone.

Confederate soldiers with visiting family members outside Richmond, Virginia, 1862. *Johnson-Jones Family Portrait, Courtesy of Special Collections, Robert W. Woodruff Library, Emory University*

Confederate dead in front of Battery Robinette, Corinth, Mississippi, 1862. *Courtesy of Library of Congress*

Union soldiers encamped on the Pamunkey River during the Peninsula Campaign, Virginia, 1862. *Courtesy of Library of Congress*

CHAPTER 2

"Richmond Is a Hard Road to Travel":
Gaps Between Expectation and Experience

I N FEBRUARY 1862 in Mobile, Alabama, James Boyd and other Georgia soldiers grew impatient with a war and an army that did not fit their expectations. Boyd's regiment had not been paid, and its weapons were so outdated that the Georgians regarded them as insults. Even worse, officers seemed to think that the pressures of war gave them the right to treat members of the enlisted ranks as less than equal white men. Boyd and his friend Jesse Jones had had enough. One Monday, they persuaded the members of their company to stack the decrepit arms and threaten "to do nothing more until they paid us and gave us other guns." The protest continued until "the Colonel came around and . . . scared them all back but myself and a few others," Boyd reported. He held out stubbornly and refused to drill for half a day, resuming arms only when threatened with the guardhouse. All the while he insisted, "we were only rebelling against those haughty officers for not giving us our rights."[1] Ordinary white southern men like James Boyd had been persuaded of the necessity for an independent South largely by assurances that a southern Confederacy would better serve the interests (including the preservation of slavery) of themselves and their families and better honor their rights and identities as white men. Now many troops faced conflicts between their needs and those of the Confederacy. Meanwhile, the intensification of the conflict turned the war itself into something quite different from what most recruits had anticipated. Boyd's small rebellion showed that the gaps between the war that soldiers expected and the one they experienced

"Richmond Is a Hard Road to Travel," an 1863 song by John Thompson, mocked the Union Army's failure to capture Richmond in 1861 and 1862.

strained but did not dislodge ordinary men's commitment to the war or to the side for which they fought.

In 1862, the war's mounting demands and the steps taken to meet them introduced dissent and disillusionment into both armies, which soldiers withstood chiefly by reminding themselves that the enemy's victory and all it stood for were unthinkable. The gulf between expectation and experience created problems for both Union and Confederate soldiers, but it created bigger ones for Confederates, partly because of the nature of the demands placed on the South, but even more because Confederate patriotism was more centered on white families' self-interest than Union patriotism was. By bringing the requirements of the Confederacy into conflict with the needs of soldiers and their families, the war in 1862 ushered Confederate patriotism's latent tensions to the surface; it also revealed the importance of white Southerners' opposition to emancipation and fears of race war in resolving those tensions.[2]

"I love my country but I love my family better"

In 1862, the experience of warfare bore so little resemblance to most Confederate soldiers' early imaginings that a soldier's "glory" now consisted of "rain, mud, want-wickedness-exposure-danger-death and oblivion," as one Alabama man told his wife.[3] For the first half of the year, the military progress of the war did little to cheer white Southerners. In the West, Confederates suffered defeats in Missouri and Arkansas, surrendered Forts Henry and Donelson (valuable posts on the Tennessee and Cumberland Rivers), and lost major cities like Nashville, New Orleans, and Memphis. Just as devastating, when Confederates moved in April to thwart the Union Army's approach to an important rail junction at Corinth, Mississippi, by striking federal forces in Tennessee, they succeeded only in precipitating the ghastly battle of Shiloh. Shiloh generated more casualties than all previous United States wars combined, but it did not prevent Confederate withdrawal from Corinth on May 25. In the East, Confederates enjoyed springtime victories in Virginia's Shenandoah Valley, but federal movements elsewhere in the Old Dominion gave cause for alarm. The Union General George McClellan's elaborately planned Peninsula Campaign involved sailing the Army of the Potomac to Fortress Monroe at the tip of the peninsula between the York and James Rivers, and then moving it up toward the Confederate capital. After taking Yorktown and Williamsburg, Union forces steadily progressed, arriving within six miles of Richmond by the end of May. Aided by the weather and a new leader, Gen. Robert E. Lee, Confederates stopped the Union advance and saved the capital in a series of battles (culminating in the Seven Days battles) that resulted in even more casualties than Shiloh. Through it all, the intensity of the fighting mounted ferociously. "Manassas . . . was mere child's play compared with those [battles] in which we have been lately engaged," explained one South Carolinian after the Seven Days.[4] Some Confederates responded to the escalation with increased hatred toward the enemy. Hoping to push Union troops out of Arkansas and Missouri, Texas cavalryman John Wall desired to see "the edges of the we[s]thern states be paved with the yankey's and duches [foreign-born soldiers] bons and drenched with ther blud."[5] Displaying his own hardening attitudes in Virginia, a North Carolinian who made a Yankee soldier "acquainted with powder & lead" in his "Thoracic viscera," took particular satisfaction in noticing that his victim's "carcass as also the carcass of his fine steed" were being left to rot in the sun.[6] At the opposite extreme, some troops lost their appetite for fighting. Bone-weary and badly on edge from constant skirmishing around Corinth, an Arkansan lamented, "Oh! What suffering, what misery, what untold agony this horrid hell-begotten war has caused. I wish all the misery . . . might be turned from the mass of humanity and entailed upon the prime movers, the instigators of this war." As for himself, he admitted that he was "awful tired of being a soldier." The war was a "wild Goose Chase," and he wanted Confederate leaders to "dry it up and let us go home."[7]

Instead, pressed by necessity, government authorities consolidated power with remarkable speed and steadily transformed the Confederacy into a nation very different from the one that soldiers expected. In 1862, the Confederate Congress and the Davis administration worked together to impose conscription and martial law, and permitted the Army to commandeer private citizens' crops through practices that would be officially adopted and systematized as impressment and tax-in-kind policies in 1862 and 1863. The strong arm of the Confederacy, in other words, fell much harder on white Southerners than the light hand of the federal government ever had. Voicing a common complaint, an Alabama private grumbled, "we were promised a government of justice and economy but I see neither."[8]

Conscription accounted for part of the problem. In late 1861, the Virginia legislature responded to the most pressing need, the need for soldiers, by introducing a statewide law that automatically extended the enlistments of soldiers whose terms were set to expire. The new measure was designed to prevent the catastrophic reduction in forces that would occur if all soldiers whose enlistments were up went home, but not surprisingly, many men in the Virginia ranks objected to the bill regardless of its purpose. Pvt. George Peebles commented on the "excitement in Camp to night on account of a bill before the Senate of Virginia . . . requiring all the volunteers *now* in service to remain during the war," and even warned, "if the above act is passed, mutiny will ensue."[9] The threatened mutiny did not come to pass, but that did not mean that dissatisfaction went away. Instead, it spread throughout the Confederacy when, on April 16, 1862, the Confederate Congress enacted the first national conscription law in American history.

The Confederate Conscription Act drafted white able-bodied men between the ages of eighteen and thirty-five, and extended the enlistments of soldiers already in the Army. The bill exempted men in a number of categories, including Confederate and state civil officials, laborers in certain war-related industries, state militia officers, teachers, and eventually (because of outspoken opposition to the draft in the press) newspaper editors. It also allowed for substitution, which permitted a man to buy his way out of the Army by paying somebody not subject to the draft to enlist in his stead. The exemptions and substitutions were so badly abused that the law had to be changed repeatedly, eventually resulting in the elimination of substitution in December 1863 (by which time growing manpower needs also argued against allowing anyone to purchase his way out), but anger about loopholes and unfair privileges for the wealthy would come later. In the spring of 1862, the law enraged troops because it violated their rights, as soldiers saw them, by extending enlistments without their consent.[10] Texas private Benjamin Tamplin reported that his regiment was "upon the verge of disbanding" when soldiers learned they must serve two years longer, not necessarily because they no longer believed in the war, but out of anger at a Confederate government that "made a great many fair promises before we volunteers left home," and then turned into a bully that ignored men's rights.[11]

Manpower posed only one of the logistical problems Confederate authorities faced in 1862. In addition to the draft, Davis's administration established taxation and finance systems, instituted socially controlling measures like a travel pass system and prohibition of alcohol in selected locations, and began nationalizing transportation and industry. By 1862, Davis ran a substantially more centralized government than Lincoln did.[12]

While all these measures were new, soldiers and civilians objected only to some of them. Despite sporadic complaints about its irritating inconvenience, the pass system, which curtailed white Southerners' freedom of movement, did not lead to a major outcry. Even prohibition passed with little sustained comment from Confederate troops, while civilians often welcomed the liquor ban as a way of controlling rowdy soldiers.[13]

Policies affecting white Southerners' livelihoods and crop-growing practices, in contrast, stirred up acute discontent. Since supply shortfalls could prove nearly as dangerous as personnel shortages, the Richmond government as well as various state governments enacted policies to convert production of nonessentials (such as cotton for export) into production of necessary items like foodstuffs. In addition, while impressment and tax-in-kind policies would not be formally adopted and uniformly implemented by the Confederate government until 1863, ad hoc appropriation of families' private property by Confederate authorities began in 1862. Impressment took place when army commissary and quartermaster officers obtained food and supplies for soldiers and horses by taking what they needed from farm families unlucky enough to live nearby. In return, families were supposed to receive IOUs in the amount that the army officers (not the farm families) determined to be fair, but the IOUs were always well below market value. In addition, they depreciated so dramatically before families could redeem them that many officers stopped bothering to issue the IOUs altogether. In response to civilians' complaints about impressment, the Confederate Congress tried to curb abuses by passing a regulatory law in March 1863, but by that time, impressment had been taking place for more than a year. On the surface, tax-in-kind looked more orderly, but to ordinary families its results were very similar. Tax-in-kind required farm families to pay taxes in the form of 10 percent of their total crop minus a small amount for subsistence. Thousands of government agents prowled throughout the countryside to collect the tax, literally showing up at families' front doors and driving away with part of the harvest.[14] In adopting measures that told farmers what they could and could not grow, and in allowing for the seizure of individual citizens' crops, the Confederate government and southern state governments touched white Southerners' daily lives far more directly than the Union government ever had, and not in ways that advanced individual white Southerners' interests.

Some soldiers were willing to tolerate new agricultural measures, as long as the strict policies did not directly affect them or their families.

In Corinth, Mississippi, Tennessean George Blakemore approvingly observed that cotton plantations now grew corn and wheat for "feeding the southern army." He also praised a policy that called for the widespread burning of cotton crops in the belief that such action would prevent northern soldiers from helping themselves to the fruits of southern harvests.[15] One Mississippi prisoner of war urged Virginia newspaper readers to "burn and destroy everything that would be of service to the enemy," including lucrative crops like cotton and tobacco. Such destructive measures might sound extreme, but the northern victory they sought to prevent would be even more catastrophic. "If the North is successful, our property is destroyed—all that have Southern proclivities will be confiscated, so the South will be penniless," he warned. Ruthlessness offered the South's "only salvation."[16]

The Mississippi soldier did not speak for everyone. In fact, if the road *to* Richmond was a hard one to travel for Union troops trying to capture the capital, the road to nationhood prescribed *by* Richmond looked downright impassable to many Confederate soldiers. Georgia and Alabama troops cared for little beyond their own narrow horizons, one Louisiana sergeant complained, and would "get out of this trap as soon as they get a chance, and return to their corn hills and potato patches," which suddenly seemed more threatened by Confederate policies than by the Union Army.[17] In Nashville, Tennessee, when Confederate forces under Gen. Nathan Bedford Forrest tried to ship out supplies and burn bridges, civilians resisted so stoutly that the cavalry charged on citizens in the streets. In response, the residents and mayor of Nashville promptly surrendered the city to the Union as soon as the Union General Don Carlos Buell's troops appeared on the Cumberland River.[18] Meanwhile, a soldier noticed that Memphis residents "are lukewarm in the southern cause and if the Yankees will protect their cowardly carcases and save their property, they would give up the Southern cause without striking a blow."[19] Throughout the Confederacy, as troops ran headlong into conflicts between individual interests and Confederate needs, the personal attachments to one's own property, family, aspirations, and identity that led them to support or at least accept the need for an independent Confederacy in the first place could do little to resolve growing tensions.

Virginia sergeant John White summed up the quandary that many Confederate troops faced in 1862. He viewed military service as an extension of his "christian duty" to provide his family with "rescue and protection" against a Union force that would destroy his home and endanger his wife and children by freeing slaves. Now, the will of the Richmond government kept him *away* from his vulnerable family and enacted policies that added to its problems. While White faced danger in the Army, he was powerless to help his family combat food shortages or the frightening prospect of slave uprisings. "How better can I die than defending my family & fireside," he demanded. The Confederate government had presented itself as protector of the best interests of white men and their families. By impinging on those interests, it contradicted one of its reasons for existence, and it presented Confederate soldiers with a dilemma. As White put it, "I love my country but I love my family better."[20]

Clashes between individuals' best interests and the demands of war also eroded unity among white Southerners, aggravated class tensions, and contributed to soldiers' growing impatience with the citizenry as well as the government. Far from behaving more admirably than Northerners, white Southerners quickly showed that traits like greed and meanness were not confined to north of the Mason-Dixon line. Soldiers especially complained about extortion and speculation. Extortion referred to lending at usurious interest rates or to overcharging for necessities in times of need or shortage. Closely related, speculation involved hoarding food or other necessary goods for the purpose of inducing or creating the appearance of shortages, and then charging astronomical prices.[21] Soldiers hated both practices. A South Carolina private railed against extortionary prices charged for bare necessities like a coat and blanket. "The over coat is a swindle," he exclaimed after paying twelve dollars when he was sure any honest man would sell "a better coat for $5.50." Adding the cost of an eight-dollar blanket brought his bill to twenty dollars, nine dollars more than his monthly pay of eleven dollars, even before he bought anything "to keep starvation off," let alone sent a penny home to his family.[22] Meanwhile, annoyed because "the rich men are all leaving the army and the poor men will have to fight for their property" while "the speculators get rich," Alabama soldier Louis Branscomb "sometimes wish[ed] the Confederacy would sink."[23]

To make matters worse, civilians seemed neither to appreciate the troops nor to carry their fair share of war's burdens. When Edward Brown's brother-in-law, Nim, was sick and unable to get a bed in a hospital in Mississippi, Brown tried to find lodging for Nim in a private house nearby. To his request for a room, the woman who owned the house retorted, "I couldn't let you have one if I had a thousand rooms." The sting of the woman's snub, and the ingratitude to soldiers that Brown felt it indicated, did little to rejuvenate Brown's enthusiasm for the war or the Confederacy.[24] A South Carolinian complained that soldiers were "not cared for much more than a Dog. . . . they are scorned by some of the women[;] they say the soldiers stink."[25] Whatever else soldiers had expected when they enlisted, they had not anticipated callous disdain from the population for which they fought.

When the war began, few soldiers envisioned conflicts between the needs of their home communities and the demands of the Confederacy, but now, as such tensions arose, they revealed limitations in a version of patriotism based heavily on defense of home, family, and material interests. White southern men had begun the war in the belief that the Confederacy would serve themselves and their families better than the Union did. Soldiers' wartime service would advance white Southerners' interests and protect the South's superior people and society from corrosive northern influences. In exchange, the Confederate government would respect individuals' rights and advance their families' interests, while all southern whites would rise above class pettiness to support troops' efforts generously. Instead, the government behaved in distasteful ways, armies lost battles, and Southerners on the home front let soldiers down. Many Confederate troops felt betrayed, or, as one Georgia soldier memorably put it, "honey-fuggled."[26]

Honey-fuggled soldiers could suggest that the Confederacy faltered and eventually collapsed because of its own internal fault lines, especially class resentment.[27] In fact, in 1862, some Confederate soldiers (on whom the infant Confederacy relied for its survival) did look for the quickest way out of the Army. Georgia soldier Roderick Harper, for instance, spent the spring of 1862 searching for a substitute to take his place.[28] Taking their discontent to the logical extreme, some soldiers dispensed with the travails of finding a replacement and simply left the ranks. As a result, desertion became a consideration for the Confederate Army for the first time in 1862, although rates varied widely by soldiers' regions of origin.[29] Yet while sparks of disaffection and class resentment undeniably flickered in 1862, they did not engulf the Confederacy or reduce it to ashes, and neither the war nor the Confederate States of America came to an end for several years. Most men stayed in the ranks, no matter how aggrieved they felt, or how little obvious devotion they displayed to the larger Confederacy. Serving in the neighboring state of Mississippi, Pvt. Thomas Warrick of Coosa, Alabama, confided to his wife, "I have heard a heap of talk about the Country But I have Seed as much of it as I wount to see if I was

Jest free I would com Back to old Coosa in a hery." Given the choice, Warrick "wountin Give old Coosa for no Country."[30] When push came to
shove, Warrick might not have been as willing to sacrifice for the Confederate cause as the eager volunteers of the spring of 1861 claimed to be, but
his decision to stay in the Army showed that he was not prepared to abandon the fight, either. Divisions like localism and class fissures certainly
affected the Confederacy and its war for survival in 1862, but they did not
undo it.

Neither the primacy of individual and family interests nor internal
social divisions ruined the Confederacy in 1862, in part because the
strengths of the Confederacy's particular variety of patriotism had not
entirely disappeared. Disheartened as Pvt. Edward Brown was when Mississippi civilians refused to help him take care of his sick brother-in-law,
Brown still insisted to his wife that "the Yankees *must* be whipped, if it
takes every dollar & every man in the Confederate States to do it."[31]
Because soldiers' attachment to the Confederacy had less to do with Richmond or the Davis administration than with their own families, material
interests, and aspirations, troops could withstand some disgust with government authorities or even their fellow white Southerners. In addition,
the insular tendencies of Confederate patriotism limited soldiers' ideological responsibilities. Unencumbered by duties like proclaiming inalienable
human rights or saving republican government for the whole human race,
Confederate troops were free to focus on the more manageable goal of
separating white Southerners from people who were different or did not
share the same interests. Louisiana soldier Thomas Davidson, for example, told his sister, "we should carve out our own destiny ourselves." The
Confederacy should be an independent land for white Southerners, with
"no foreign blood to besmirch our young tree of liberty."[32]

Even more important, all white Southerners knew that what mattered
most was even more endangered by the prospects of Union and abolition
than by the Confederate government or their fellow white Southerners, no
matter how unsatisfactory the latter two entities proved. Confederate
patriotism was interwoven with material interests and private aspirations,
but more than just the barn, corncrib, and hearthstone was on the line, and
soldiers knew it. An entire social order was at stake, and it could be preserved only by isolating it from northern influence. As soldiers like Pvt.
William Bellamy saw things, if white Southerners wanted to achieve
"blessings of independence and prosperity," they had to separate themselves from the North first, and southern flaws could be worked out later.[33]

In short, conflicts between personal interests and Confederate necessities were troubling but resolvable as long as Confederate troops remembered that no matter how disappointing the Confederacy was, the Union under an antislavery president would be worse. Statesmen and clergy had long preached the sinfulness and fanaticism of the North, and while few southern soldiers exactly echoed the words of their civil or religious authorities, they had clearly internalized the assumptions that the South was a better place than the North and that Southerners were better people than Northerners.[34] Pvt. James Manahan feared that Northerners would meddle with the South's "social and political framework." He hated the idea of victorious Yankees dividing "the large estates into ten acre lots with a two story framed house on each with ginger bread and apples in the window." Worse, they would probably try to impose their own "laws morality philosophy and philantropy." Manahan dreaded the northern middle-class order (symbolized in his description by farmhouses of modest equality and his reference to philanthropic reform movements) because he believed that it replaced respect for a proper social order designed by God with an unorthodox, presumptuous, and just plain sinful belief that reform-minded Northerners knew better than God how to make the world a better place.[35]

If Confederate soldiers needed proof of nefarious Yankee intentions to unravel the southern social fabric, the Union general Benjamin Butler's notorious "Woman Order" of May 15, 1862, provided more than enough. In response to the abusive treatment heaped (or, in the case of chamber pot contents, thrown) by New Orleans women on Union soldiers, General Butler issued General Order No. 28, declaring that any woman caught demeaning a Union soldier "shall be regarded and held liable to be treated as a woman of the town plying her avocation."[36] Women who insulted Union troops, in other words, would be assumed to be prostitutes.

Few things could more effectively make nineteenth-century white men, North or South, feel that their society was under attack than questioning the behavior or morality of white women. Americans in the nineteenth century placed great value on the moral sense of women. Ostensibly removed from the competitive values of the marketplace, free women were supposed to safeguard the upstanding moral virtues on which republics relied. At the same time, assumptions that women's true sphere was a domestic one effectively absolved women of responsibility for actions committed in public, since the public was supposedly not the arena in which women really belonged or could be expected to understand the ramifications of their own actions. Female innocence entitled women to immunity and protection by white men when the southern social order founded on male mastery over subordinates like women and African Americans was working properly.[37] New Orleans white women's public displays of contempt for Union soldiers flouted the South's traditional gendered order, but did not jettison it, because white southern men approved of the behavior. In fact, by smiling at the actions as evidence of women's emotionalism or even endorsing them as signs of southern female spirit, white southern men could still claim to be in control of them. But to have white ladies' behavior corrected by northern men was intolerable. By holding women accountable for what they did and said in public, Butler's order discarded the idea of female innocence and made white southern male protectors superfluous. Further, doubting white women's claims to moral goodness challenged the moral righteousness of all of southern society and also announced that white southern men had not been exercising their authority over subordinates properly. On top of all else, Butler's order did not question just any female virtue; it explicitly disparaged white women's chastity, which was supposed to fall under the sole authority of white southern men as hallmarks of their true manhood. An insult of that magnitude could not be taken calmly. Butler's Woman Order blatantly violated the strictly defined gender roles that helped maintain the South's orthodox social order, impugned white southern men's demonstration of authority, and insulted the honor and true manhood of every white southern man. In so doing, it threatened white men's very identities as men.

The immediate result of Butler's Woman Order was that the women of New Orleans stopped spitting on and otherwise mistreating Union troops, but Confederate soldiers felt the impact of the order differently. Union forces never acted on the Woman Order. Anxious to protect their reputations as ladies rather than street women, New Orleans females policed their own behavior and the order enforced itself, but that was hardly the point to Confederate soldiers. When Butler's order cast aspersions on white southern women's moral purity, white southern men's fitness for mastery, and the entire southern social order, it dispelled any lingering doubts about northern moral turpitude or the Union's intention to overthrow the southern social structure. North Carolinian Tristrim Skinner believed that Butler's "devilish order in New Orleans" justified nearly any severe measure the Confederate government saw fit to take. In particular, Skinner wanted Confederates to institute a "policy" of "having such fiends secretly assassinated."[38] Pvt. John Street wrote about how Texas troops were outraged by the "insolent proclamation" which likened "brave, virtuous and patriotic" women to the common "street *whore*," but he also revealed how Butler's order helped unify the Confederate rank and file, which had been sinking into disunity and malaise. Now, every "soldier in the Confederate army," no matter how disgruntled, could rally to the "watch word of '*Our Mothers, our wives, our daughters, our sisters, Our God & our country.*' "[39] As Street's reaction revealed, Butler's Woman Order reminded southern soldiers that they fought for a purer society based on clear social roles and an orthodox social structure which, whatever its shortcomings, had to be better than a society that produced the despicable "Beast" Butler. Losing a war to such a society would be simply intolerable.

Most of all, losing to the Union was unthinkable, according to Confederate soldiers, because it would mean abolition, and abolition would destroy the southern social order even more completely than Butler's Woman Order did. The tautly woven tapestry of southern life had been "rent asunder by fanaticism," according to an Arkansas soldier, merely by northern opposition to slavery's expansion into the western territories. Imagine how much more frayed southern society would become if Northerners succeeded in imposing abolition on the Confederacy itself.[40] If that happened, a Mississippi private predicted, "we would be slaves to the Yanks and our children would have a yoke of bondage thrown around there neck that never could be moved during time."[41] "Lincolns fanatical rule" would bring "abolition laws" that turned the world upside down, warned James Williams. White families would be made to submit to "a master from new England," and wives and sisters throughout the South would be demeaned, as New Orleans women had been by Butler's order, to the level of "town-women."[42]

Abolition would destroy the South's social order, in other words, by reversing it, freeing blacks and degrading whites, and the dread of that certain disaster invigorated Confederate troops no matter how disenchanted they had become with every other aspect of the Confederacy and its war effort. As one soldier put it shortly after the failure of the Union's Peninsula Campaign, if the Yankees had taken Richmond, white Southerners could have expected to see "the Negro population set free and the white population bound by fetters."[43] When John Street received a letter from his wife asking why he could not just come home, he replied that failure to fight the Yankees would be the same as lying "supinely upon our backs" while "we are all bound hand and foot & the fair daughters of the south reduced to a level with the flat-footed thick-liped Negro."[44] If white Southerners stood idly by while abolition dismantled the South's racial hierarchy, the purity of white women would be destroyed and white men's masculine identity would be lost. Unless they resisted, southern whites of all classes could expect to live in degraded circumstances that they recognized all too well as the conditions endured by slaves every day.

With more Yankees making their presence felt among southern whites and blacks, and with wartime conditions disturbing the absolute control white Southerners felt they needed over African Americans, Confederate soldiers confronted constant reminders that the world as they knew it would not be safe until they won the war. A southern poem claimed that once Yankee troops appeared in Williamsburg, Virginia, black slaves dared to walk alongside whites in city streets as if they were equals. The sight of blacks and whites walking side by side "put everything out of order," and left white Southerners "utterly at a loss" as to "how to bear with such a cross."[45] Suddenly, black Southerners acted on alarming ideas about their own independence and status, and they overtly threatened the authority of white southern men. Macon Bonner was furious when he learned from a neighbor that his wife's house had been taken over as "*negro* quarters" for "negroes in town who have left their owners," and that his mother's house could fall prey to the same fate. The turbulence of war churned up new ways for slaves to claim freedom, assert their own wills, and reject the authority of white masters. The slaves who did so by choosing Bonner's wife's house as living quarters made him so angry, he wished his "prayers could consign them in the depths of hell."[46]

Bonner and others felt such rage because a world in which slaves acted assertively, the Confederate Army lost battles, and the Confederacy turned out to be nothing like soldiers had imagined it would be felt like a world spinning out of control. If a soldier owned slaves, he could try to regain some semblance of order by dominating every aspect of his slaves' lives, even from afar. In Tennessee, Robert Snead reacted angrily when a letter from his wife informed him that his slave Ellen wished to get married back home in Virginia. At first, he refused to allow "any one to marry on the place," for fear that the slaves would expect a celebration. As for Ellen, "she ought not to want it nor can I consent for any thing of this kind." Eventually, Snead reluctantly permitted Ellen to exchange her vows as long as she agreed to "not create any fuss or trouble."[47] Just days after the fall of nearby Fort Henry, with Federals poised to capture the supposedly invincible Nashville, a Confederate soldier's world might have seemed to be whirling into chaos, but by retaining mastery over the life of a black slave woman, Snead could keep his own senses of social order and individual manhood intact.

Another way to cope with the turmoil created by the weakening of slavery's strictly enforced racial hierarchy was to blame the Yankees who caused it, and despise them all the more for it. Hatred for the Union soldiers who would destroy life as white Southerners knew it aided the Confederate cause once the war entered its second year by ensuring that even soldiers who were out of sorts with the war in general or the Confederacy in particular directed most of their rage at the enemy. Henry Graves found satisfaction in the thought of "many a Yankee carcass now rotting in the mud of the chickahominy swamp" because of "his pity & love for the poor slave."[48] To Graves, gruesome deaths were fitting recompense for soldiers who threatened the foundation of all southern society by meddling with slavery. No matter how war-weary an Alabama soldier became, he continued to believe that "we are ruined if we do not put forth all our energies & drive back the invaders of our slavery South."[49]

Confederate unity relied so heavily on soldiers' shared commitment to fending off abolition that one soldier worried more about possible lapses in proslavery solidarity than he did about military defeats. Rudolf Coreth, whose family owned slaves, saw the necessity of fighting to keep them, but he worried about what would happen if one day nonslaveholding soldiers no longer shared that view. In February 1862, Coreth mentioned that "there was a report from Washington that the [U.S.] Congress had decided to get rid of slavery," which, if true, would "arouse a little spirit in the Confederate soldier again." Yet he worried that the benefits of abolition rumors might be short-lived if other rumblings of southern dissatisfaction were not addressed soon. The rumors "won't help for long," he warned, because nonslaveholders were "already asking now what they are fighting for anyway."[50] His fears increased in the following months when he heard that the *Houston Telegraph* was circulating rumors about Richmond considering the "founding of a monarchy" in order to protect slaveholders' interests. Coreth noticed that local slaveholders "loudly declared themselves in favor of it, and the kind of shock that a report of that kind ought to call forth was not seen at all." If elites were not more careful, he worried that they would provoke a revolt on the part of nonslaveholding commonfolk.[51]

Coreth need not have worried; non-slave-owning soldiers still regarded all whites' shared interest in preserving slavery as more vital than any class differences. Nonslaveholding cavalryman William Wilson's favorite result of a recent campaign in the Shenandoah Valley was that "many negroes were also taken while attempting to escape with the Yankees."[52] Meanwhile, a Texas corporal believed that the best way to motivate enlisted Confederate soldiers was to entice them with the prospect of slave ownership. He told of a fellow soldier named Barker, who "caught sight of a couple of darkies in blue uniforms, armed and equipped for battle." Since the Union Army had not yet authorized the enlistment of black soldiers, these African Americans probably worked for the Army as laborers or officers' servants, but their exact occupation did not matter to Barker. "Never a slave-owner but always wishing to be, he decided then and there to make use of his opportunities and capture and confiscate both of the likely fellows." Reports that "prisoners taken were to be held as the private property of their respective captors" inspired the "common rank-and-file" to prepare to attack with more than usual "spirit and zeal." As it turned out, the episode did not lead to a battle, but it did emphasize the value of "laurels and ethiopians" as restorers of the proper social order and inducements for Confederates, including those who owned no slaves, to fight.[53] In the face of disappointment in a Confederacy that did not correspond to soldiers' expectations, the Confederate rank and file remained sure of the benefits and necessity of slavery. Even as disaffection about other matters spread, soldiers did not dispute the idea that they must fight to resist abolition, or else lose everything that mattered to them.

"Arguing on the Negro question"

Although the war did not treat the Union as severely as it did the Confederacy in the first half of 1862, the conflict still differed from what troops had first envisioned. Rather than elevating men to glory, it whipped them back and forth between the extremes of boredom and terror. After a day of washing his clothes in a creek, Nathan Parmater quickly learned that soldiering contained more drudgery than heroics. With his hands sore because scrubbing "ware the bark off" his fingers, Parmater reflected, "I should never blame the women for being 'cross' on washing day for it was more of a task than I was aware of."[54] Cyrus Boyd would likely have agreed that camp life lacked glamour, but even dull chores were better than what his Iowa regiment experienced when it was "thrown into this *hell* of battle" at Shiloh in April. Two days of utter confusion, showers of bullets, exploding shells, and murderous cannonballs left "pieces of clothing and *strings of flesh*" hanging from battle-scarred trees. The stench from the piles of dead and dying overwhelmed the fragrance of April blossoms, much as the "pall of death" overpowered romantic notions of war.[55] Shiloh, at least, ended in ostensible Union victory, since federal forces retained the field of battle and eventually pressed on toward the Confederate rail junction at Corinth, Mississippi. The tedium, carnage, and eventual failure of the Peninsula Campaign proved even more demoralizing.

Like their Confederate counterparts, Union troops responded to the unexpected nature of the war in a variety of ways, sometimes developing attitudes they could scarcely have imagined before the war. Cyrus Boyd noted that the relentless violence and confusion that his regiment experienced in the spring of 1862 "brutalizes men and crushes out all human feeling."[56] Some troops grew angry at the military brass, or "shoulder straps" as the enlisted men called officers, especially after costly defeats. When the Peninsula Campaign failed, one volunteer complained that General McClellan's "boasted great military talents consist in old woman like imbecility joined to bombastic self-confidence, and foolish reliance on strategy, and obsolete tactics."[57] Others saved their rage for the rebels. In the tension preceding the Seven Days, the Fifth New York's nerves were worn thin by anticipation of the impending clash, and by Confederate pickets who were "constantly *murdering* our men in cold blood." Finally, when a picket shot a member of the Irish brigade, the dead man's comrades hanged the unfortunate Southerner, bayoneted his body, and left him in the road for wagons to make "a jelly of the remains."[58] Some troops were simply too weary to be outraged at anyone. In the middle of the Peninsula Campaign, Pvt. Moses Parker looked around at "a field strewn with dead and dying men" and "pretty much concluded that I have seen all the rebels all the fighting, war, dead men, etc. that I want to see at present."[59]

The Union government did not disillusion its soldiers as much as the Confederate government alienated its troops, but sometimes it disappointed them. Minnesota soldier George Brookins criticized the Union government for not treating the war seriously enough. Humiliated by the capture of his regiment at Murfreesboro, Tennessee, Brookins had "no great anxiety to be exchanged till our government" replaced its "milk and water" approach to the war and to Confederates with sterner measures designed to break the back of the rebellion.[60] A hot-tempered soldier named Roland Bowen, on the other hand, could not abide what he saw as sniveling and bickering among legislators who seemed to spend all their time criticizing the Army and arguing about slavery. Apologizing to his mother for his harsh language, Bowen wished the "Damned set of Politicians" were "all in hell Rolling and Pitching upon the firey coals."[61]

Northern civilians did not always measure up to soldiers' expectations either. Profiteering accompanies all wars, and the northern experience in the Civil War proved no exception, much to the revulsion of soldiers who assumed that anybody at home making money sinned twice, first in the failure to join the Army and second in the exploitation of war for personal gain. New York private Caleb Beal complained, "I am afraid this is getting to be too much of a money-making war now," and hoped that the property of "the money making and miserly leeches on our government" would be "confiscated."[62] Meanwhile, to soldiers' families relying on the low and unreliable pay of an army private, the war was anything but a money-making opportunity, and hard times frayed tempers. The men of the Seventy-ninth Pennsylvania were distressed to learn that soldiers' wives had appealed publicly to city leaders for free flour since their husbands' army wages had not been paid. After reading about the incident "in one of the lancaster papers," one private wrote to his wife to let her know that "drag[ging] sutch things into poloticks" was "not thought mutch of out hear by the soldiers." Although he agreed to "rite down to the mill for som flour for you," it bothered him that soldiers' families and mill owners had not been able to rise above personal pettiness to arrive at a magnanimous solution.[63] The Pennsylvania wives, like most northern civilians, were sheltered from many of the hardships afflicting southern families, but they still coped with an escalating war, higher casualty counts, and the social disruption caused by the absence of many men from home, and they did not always respond with cheerful selflessness.

Yet for all the ill temper, Union soldiers were not as seriously demoralized as Confederates were, and only partly because northern families suffered less and the war went better militarily for the Union than the Confederacy until the failure of the Peninsula Campaign. The Union rank and file faced fewer challenges than Confederate soldiers did, but more important, their version of patriotism proved more resilient and made weathering setbacks easier. Individual Northerners did not possess inherently more selfless personalities than Southerners did, but they envisioned the function of government differently, and they understood the benefits of the Union to transcend rather than serve self-interest, which equipped them to withstand the challenges of the war's second year more easily.

Far from sharing the Confederate idea of government as an outside imposition, necessary but best kept distant from people's lives, Union troops retained their view of legitimate government in general and the Union government in particular as the creation of the people who composed it. The camp newspaper *Seventh Brigade Journal* summarized this view when it declared, "the President has sworn to sustain the Constitution and enforce the laws. And for this purpose come the thousands of soldiers whom he has called to aid him in the enforcement of the laws they helped to make."[64] The Union government could not betray its citizens, as Confederates suspected their government of doing, because it consisted of those citizens. When soldiers of the Second Delaware received the "acceptable and very timely present" of warm gloves from a knitting society back home, they met as a regiment to express their appreciation in a set of written resolutions to be sent back to the women of the knitting society. The list of resolutions thanked the knitters, but just as important, it identified the women's efforts as contributions to a shared "just and holy cause," and it recognized the women themselves as constituent parts of "this noble Union" that soldiers and civilians made sacrifices to preserve.[65] Union soldiers' conviction that individuals, families, home communities, and the federal government were all parts of the same whole minimized disillusionment with the Union government, even when the war grew more difficult than anticipated.

Union soldiers were also better prepared to withstand the vicissitudes of war because from the beginning they saw the stakes of the war differently from Confederate soldiers. The rebellion must be put down not because it endangered the material welfare or aspirations of individual soldiers and their families, but because the defeat of the Union would lead to "a long farewell to Republican Liberty and self-government throughout the world!"[66] Confederate soldiers fought a war for the benefit of themselves, their families, and white Southerners, but the rest of the world ought to be left to its own devices, according to the Confederate rank and file. Union troops, in contrast, continued to echo the American millennialist tradition that infused much of the nineteenth-century North when they insisted that "the defense of the rights of humanity, and the well-being of unborn generations" depended upon the survival of the American Republic, which made personal setbacks less damaging, because less central, to the Union cause and the point of the war.[67] After a deadly skirmish in Kentucky, a Wisconsin soldier who lost friends there vowed that the blood of the fallen would "flow and mingle . . . to nourish and water the tree of liberty, whose leaves are the healing of the nations." When Confederate soldier Thomas Davidson had summoned Thomas Jefferson's image of blood nourishing the tree of liberty, he insisted that both the blood and the tree be purely southern; the Wisconsin soldier expected the blood and the tree to foster "the healing of the nations," even when it meant personal loss.[68]

Before other nations could be healed, the United States had better save its own republican government, and Union soldiers knew that meant more than beating the Confederate Army or even dismantling the Confederate government in Richmond. If republics survived only among populations of sufficient independence, equality, and virtue, it meant restoring those qualities to a southern society that northern soldiers claimed lacked them.[69] A white slave catcher in South Carolina who tried to seize the Forty-fifth Pennsylvania's cook (a free black from Baltimore) unwittingly embodied many of what enlisted Union men saw as the South's social failings, which were of course far easier to diagnose in the enemy's society than in one's own. The Pennsylvanians assumed that the slave catcher chose to make his living by delivering fugitives to local nabobs in order to curry favor with the wealthy elite, and to exercise power over someone lower than himself on the South's social ladder. Neither motivation was compatible with the ideal of a republican citizenry characterized by independence, equality, and virtue. The hapless slave catcher's fate illustrated the rank and file's enthusiasm for straightening out all they saw as unrepublican about southern society. The colonel in command collared the would-be slave catcher, and, in front of the assembled enlisted men, told him, "if you were treated as you deserve, you would be kicked down the whole line of the regiment." As soon as the colonel turned his back, "first one soldier and then another lifted his foot and give him [the slave catcher] a kick on the posterior and so on till he passed beyond the line of the regiment, every soldier giving him a kick." Soldiers gleefully complied with the officer's thinly veiled order partly because it was not every day they got the opportunity to kick the enemy in the backside, but also because the slave catcher represented the hated cause of the war, slavery, and punishing him gave troops the chance to attack what they viewed as social qualities that had brought the war and threatened to destroy the United States' experiment in republican government.[70]

Union troops saw additional reasons to worry about southern virtue when they observed southern women. Like white Southerners, Union soldiers believed that women's sheltered status and their natural inclinations made them into moral arbiters who safeguarded the virtue on which a republic's survival depended. Yet when soldiers like George Landrum viewed the South, they saw violations of gender roles that were certain to undermine the moral sensibilities of women and therefore of everyone. Once Landrum realized that southern "money comes from the labor of [slave] *women* of all ages, from fifteen to fifty years and upwards, *in the field* hoeing, plowing, and planting," his "opinion of the southern character" began "changing for the worse rapidly."[71] Even white women who did not trudge out to the field every day seemed to have lost the decency on which the survival of republican society depended. General Butler issued his famous Woman Order to curb the spiteful actions of New Orleans women, but reprehensible female behavior was hardly confined to New Orleans. New York private Constant Hanks was distressed by white Virginia women who insulted Union soldiers in such uncouth language that Hanks concluded, "they must have picked [it] up in a fish market. They give a fellow invitations to kiss them in localities that I never thought of applying that token of affection."[72] When women abandoned moral standards, all of society followed suit, and republican government became impossible.

The source of the infection sickening the virtue necessary to sustain a republic was not hard to spot, according to the Union rank and file: it was "that corrupt and festering curse of slavery."[73] Because of slavery, Vermont soldier Rufus Kinsley explained, even respectable men like "merchants, lawyers, and doctors and preachers" were encouraged to indulge their lustful passions by exploiting female slaves, who were in turn robbed of their chastity. Children resulting from such unions could be shamelessly sold for profit, which "the moral sense of the South" placidly regarded as "a matter of course business transaction." Kinsley briefly wondered, "O, womanhood, how art thou fallen so low, as not to be sensitive here," before determining that "no where but to Slavery can we look for the cause" of such "dehumanizing."[74] In short, Union soldiers continued to regard slavery as the gravest threat to the virtue that the United States' experiment in republican government required for its success and, for that and other reasons, as "the prime cause of this great sectional conflict."[75]

Even as Union troops remained quite certain in 1862 that the war happened because of the "perpetuation of human Slavery," and that slavery was "the first last, and only cause of the present rebellious war," they disagreed over what to do about it.[76] In contrast to the Confederate Army, in which the issue of slavery provided the most reliable point of agreement among the rank and file, soldiers in the Union Army were more likely to find themselves "arguing on the Negro question" than about any other issue, and dissent over the slavery question actually increased in the first half of 1862, compared to the last four months of 1861, when a swelling chorus demanded an end to the institution that caused the war.[77] In the camp of the Tenth Massachusetts, Lt. Charles Brewster reported, the men were "divided into two parties on the question, and most bitter and rancourous feelings have been excited," between high-ranking officers who approved of restoring slaves to their owners and men of lower rank who did not. On one side, the captain and major advocated the return of slaves to their masters, but junior officers and enlisted men refused to "be instrumental in returning a slave to his master in any way shape or manner." Tempers flared so badly that the regiment was "almost in a state of mutiny."[78]

Union troops became more divided on the issue of slavery in the first half of 1862 than they had been in late 1861 for several reasons. Except for a break between April and June, when the federal government suspended recruiting in the mistaken belief that the war would end before more troops were needed, new men streamed into the Union ranks. Newcomers influenced the tone of the Army for a number of reasons. The earliest volunteers might have been more likely to come from the most idealistic segment of the northern population, in which men predisposed to favor emancipation might have been overrepresented, although more conservative soldiers insisted that they had been just as quick to enlist as their abolitionist counterparts had been. Most important, the fresh volunteers had not yet witnessed as much of the South or of slavery as the veterans of 1861 had done, and therefore had not yet drawn the conclusion that only eliminating slavery could end the war and prevent its recurrence. Until they saw things for themselves, many of these new recruits diluted, though they did not neutralize, the support for emancipation that had crystallized among the rank and file in late 1861. Further, prospects looked bright for the Union war effort in the first half of 1862. Western armies achieved key victories, and until the Seven Days battles at the end of June, Northerners confidently expected that the Army of the Potomac's Peninsula Campaign would capture Richmond and end the war. With victory in sight, the need for drastic measures like abolition seemed less acute to some soldiers.

Despite skepticism on the part of some newcomers and cold feet on the part of some veterans, slavery policy continued to evolve on the ground and in legislative halls. In May 1862, Gen. David Hunter issued General

Order No. 11, which declared martial law and freed slaves in South Carolina, Georgia, and Florida; President Lincoln revoked the measure on grounds that only the president possessed the authority to issue such an edict, but Hunter's tactic clearly signaled that changes were afoot. Also that spring, Congress abolished slavery in Washington, D.C., and the western counties of Virginia took steps toward ending slavery as part of the process of entering the Union as the state of West Virginia.[79] In July, the Second Confiscation Act became law, allowing for the confiscation of all property, including slaves, held by individuals disloyal to the Union, whether or not that property was being used to aid the Confederate war effort directly.[80] Though clumsy and difficult to enforce, the Second Confiscation Act represented a clear step in the direction of de facto emancipation, even as developments in the District of Columbia and West Virginia signaled important de jure changes.

Union troops reacted in a variety of ways to these transformations, and to the countless other ways the war undermined slavery. Kansas soldier George Mowry, for one, was delighted. "We got the Papers yesterday [reporting] that the Confiscation bill had become a law and that we were to fight the Rebles as if we were fighting for something," Mowry told his sister. "There is nothing that would give the soldiers more joy in this Division than it did to hear that."[81] Meanwhile, from Tennessee, Lt. P. V. Wise reported, "the vote for emancipation in New Virginia and the passage and approval of the bill abolishing slavery in the District of Columbia, are hailed as the greatest victories for the cause of freedom and humanity of the age."[82] Yet others opposed dramatic measures. Sgt. Henry Hubble complained that Hunter's General Order No. 11 was "foolish and can do no good, but will create a great deal of trouble." After all, General Frémont had been deposed just months earlier for issuing a similar order. In Hubble's view, "this sweeping proclamation of Hunters" failed to "do justice to the loyal masters" or to "provide for the future of the slave."[83]

As Hubble, Wise, and Mowry suggest, Union soldiers occupied a broad spectrum of opinion on slavery in the second year of the war. Some impatient souls grew restless because they thought change in slavery policy was coming too slowly. "Some of us were led to take up arms in this contest on the grounds that we were going to fight for the restoration and maintenance of *republican institutions,* menaced by a slaveholding aristocracy in open rebellion," one soldier began. Unless direct action against slavery came soon, the Union Army "had better disband at once, and go home," he advised, because there was no point in trying to win the war without attacking "the manifest and acknowledged cause of the rebellion."[84] In contrast, others cited pragmatic reasons to avoid dramatic changes to slavery. Pvt. Phillip Hacker, whose regiment arrived in the South in time to join the Peninsula Campaign, resented the inconveniences caused by newly freed slaves. "They would eat our bread and ears [of corn] up," Hacker complained, and besides that, fugitive slaves "take up a great deal of time for our hed men," who ought to be concentrating on the war.[85] Beyond practical or strategic considerations, some troops simply despised the idea of abolition out of sheer racism. A Maine soldier who joined the Army in March 1862, for instance, claimed that men in his regiment "hate a 'nig' as they do the great enemy of mankind." Far from freeing a slave, they would "shoot one as quickly as they would a snake."[86] For others, it was a question of priorities, and quibbling about slavery while the Union was in danger was like worrying about a single piece of furniture while the whole house burned. Pvt. Roland Bowen fumed that "here we poor Soldiers are dying by scores from disease and hardships . . . and pouring out our blood like so much worthless water," while Congress wasted its time "everlastingly fighting it out about a Damned Nigger or some General." If Lincoln declared "all Slaves are hereafter Forever Free—Amen. And on the other hand if he says not one shall be freed. Amen. If this can be done then this War will come to a Speedy and Happy termination."[87] Ending the war and saving the Union stood as his primary objectives, and he viewed national unity as more indispensable than slavery policy to those goals.

Yet even while dissent persisted, many troops continued to believe (and others, especially newer recruits, came to the conclusion for the first time) that ending the war and saving the Union required the destruction of slavery. As one Kansan described Confederates, "there is nothing that they seem to feel so much, and care so much about, as to lose their slaves. I honestly believe that many of them would rather have us *kidnap their children,* than to *let* their niggers go off with us." Either wipe out slavery, he insisted, or "the same difficulty in an aggravated form will soon rise again."[88] Anti-abolition sentiment thickened the cacophony in the Army in 1862, but demands for emancipation provided a steady drumbeat amidst the din, even if the strength of its pulse varied in response to the changing progress of the war and composition of the ranks.

Soldiers in 1862 demanded an end to slavery for many of the same reasons as in 1861, including slavery's influence on southern agriculture and its impact on slave families. "The soil has been exhausted by the system of slave labor, which taxes it to the utmost without rendering an equivalent in manure," Massachusetts private Edwin Wentworth reported to his father, while a Wisconsin volunteer added that the availability of an exploitable slave labor force discouraged advances in "agricultural implements" like plows that would lead to healthier harvests.[89] The breakup of slave families moved even more soldiers. Pvt. Constant Hanks believed that the cases he witnessed "would wring the tears out of anyone's eyes." Hanks met an elderly slave grandmother running away with her three-year-old granddaughter because the little girl's mother had been sold, and the grandmother was about to be. The story of the feeble old woman who would rather risk the open road than leave her granddaughter with no family "started the apple sauce out of my eyes," admitted Hanks. How could anyone who missed his own family help but ask himself, "suppose that was your mother and little one, instead of poor miserable niggers?"[90] Abolitionist propaganda had long broadcast the evils of forcible separation of slave families, but witnessing the phenomenon firsthand influenced soldiers more than any sermon, sensationalist pamphlet, or sentimental novel ever could have done.

Soldiers' wartime experiences also gave them additional reasons to turn against slavery. An unpopular policy requiring Union troops to guard the property (including slaves) of southern civilians made many men "tired of fighting the Rebels and guarding and protecting them at the same time."[91] Wasting resources and manpower to safeguard the possessions, including slaves, of the very people whom soldiers identified as architects of secession and instigators of war made no sense, and "still, our Government handles slavery as tenderly as a mother would her first born," one soldier grumbled. "When shall it be stricken down as the deadly enemy of freedom, virtue, and mankind?" he demanded to know.[92] Meanwhile, as the Union Army guarded the belongings of hostile white Southerners who "look as if they would like to kill us," black slaves welcomed and helped the soldiers in blue.[93] "Language cannot express the joy depicted in the countenance of the negroes," Byron Strong told his family when his regiment arrived at Falmouth, Virginia. "One of them afterwards told me he was as happy as if the Lord hisself had come."[94] Slaves provided far more than flattery. One company owed a narrow escape to the alertness of "a slave giving them notice that they were to be attacked early in the morning."[95] It seemed absurd to mollycoddle secessionists while behaving heartlessly toward black Southerners who aided Union troops.

The more time soldiers spent in the South, the more they cited the physical abuse suffered by slaves as a reason to end the institution of slavery. One soldier scathingly listed *"beneficent* effects" of slavery he had seen with his own eyes, including a young boy "all black and blue with red stripes" who couldn't lift his arms over his head because of what his master deemed a *"slight correction,"* a man covered in "great *welts,* and callous stripes . . . [and] great scars" applied by his "perfect *Simon Legree"* of an owner, and a young slave woman who had just given birth to a white man's child and was now starving in the woods in order to escape the deathly flogging she could expect if her master recaptured her. "I have been so saddened by the miseries I have seen that I can hardly enjoy my own blessings," the soldier admitted. In response, he and his fellow soldiers fed and sheltered as many contrabands as they could, spirited slaves to freedom whenever the opportunity arose, and developed great disdain for the Union government's "disgraceful" negligence in allowing slavery to persist. "They may court martial me and be ———," he proclaimed, as he defiantly carried on his aid to runaways.[96] A Pennsylvanian who had little patience with radical abolitionism before the war now assured his brother that anyone who saw the things he had seen in Virginia "will be more of an Abolishnest than any person could make him believe to be posible."[97]

The sexual abuse of slave women by white men also influenced many Union troops' views, though in complicated ways. Walking down the street in Washington, D.C., Pvt. Constant Hanks watched slave and free children playing and reflected, "you can see also the intervening shades, from white to black that would leave one to think that perhaps larger children have *played together* sometime."[98] Lt. George Landrum was haunted by the sight of a young slave boy "as white as ever I was; light curly hair, blue eyes . . . not the first sign of the negro about him except in manner." The unfortunate little boy was about to be sold away from his mother by his master, who was also his father. To make matters worse, the boy was far from unusual. "There are many such here," Landrum continued. "I have seen them in every town we have come through, slaves as white as any white man can be" because they had been fathered by white masters whose complete control over their female slaves left the bondwomen vulnerable to exploitation.[99] As men from a society that prized female chastity, some Union troops were repelled by undeniable evidence that sexual coercion by white men was a fact of life for many slave women. Other soldiers reacted strongly because their own racial sensibilities were offended by the very idea of sexual relationships between whites and blacks. Still others recoiled at the sight of enslaved human beings whose complexions resembled their own. Whatever their rationale, many soldiers regarded racial mixing as inherently wrong; they reasoned that since slavery led to sexual relations between white men and black women, it too was wrong, and toleration of it weakened the American Republic.

While personal interactions with mixed-race slave children might seem to make it hard to ignore the links between the issues of slavery and race, white Union soldiers did their best to overlook those very connections. Confederate soldiers and black Americans north and south knew that slavery and race were woven too tightly together for one issue to be extricated from the other. Nonetheless, white Union troops continued to separate the institution of slavery from the more complicated question of black rights, which could then be brushed aside. William Dunham, for instance, admitted, "it is a matter of great concern to many what disposition will be made with the Colored race" after emancipation, but he did not intend to be "troubled much about that question."[100] His dismissive attitude illustrates the limits of much of the Union Army's pro-emancipation sentiment in 1862. Ending slavery was one thing, but caring for or about freed black Americans was something else altogether. Even Union troops who hated the whole idea of allowing one human being to own another often held their own racist assumptions of black inferiority. One self-congratulatory soldier cheered the fact that "negroes have had more liberties since the army has invaded the State than ever before," but in the same breath he used the derogatory term "coonnesses" to refer to slave women working in the fields.[101] Other soldiers, like Lewis Jones, proved they could be hostile to both slavery and slaves at the same time. Jones hoped for prompt Union victory because "I don't want my cildern to have eney trouble with rebels or niggers," and he assumed that a successful end to the war would shield future generations from having to worry about secessionists or black Americans.[102] Even as soldiers matter-of-factly adopted stances on slavery they would once have considered radical, they continued to hold ambivalent or prejudiced views of black Americans, and therefore preferred to keep the topics of slavery, racial equality, and black rights hermetically separated. As William Dunham expressed it, "*nigger* is a great *bugger boo* to the *delicate* and *refined American*," and most simply tried to sidestep the uncomfortable subject.[103]

Yet both the war's demands and its differences from what soldiers expected began to force some troops to confront their own racist attitudes, which most so fervently avoided facing. Such was the case in Cyrus Boyd's regiment, the Fifteenth Iowa, when soldier Thomas Jeffries, who was "without doubt half *Negro*," enlisted. Boyd profiled Jeffries in the "Sketches of Lives" he compiled about his fellow soldiers in the back of his diary, noting that Jeffries, a twenty-two-year-old born in Orange County, Indiana, had enlisted on January 13, 1862, at Knoxville, Iowa. At the time of Jeffries' death of typhoid fever in June 1862, Boyd remembered:

> considerable prejudice was excited against him when he first came to our Co. But a majority decided to allow him to remain and he in spite of his negro blood was a gigantic and powerful man and proved a good soldier—for he was always willing to do his duty. He was most of the time employed as a Cook. He was in battle of Pittsburgh Landing and fought well. He was very dark. Was also a private.[104]

Boyd's reflections show that at first Jeffries endured hostility and menial service because of his fellow soldiers' racism, but the demands of battle finally overruled the rank and file's animosity. Few regiments had a Thomas Jeffries to influence their thinking quite as directly as was the case for the Fifteenth Iowa, but nonetheless, this striking new direction in the thinking of even a handful of soldiers came about because of the changing nature of the conflict. The war was so different from anything soldiers anticipated that it led some to think in ways that had never occurred to them before.

SOLDIERS in both armies in the first half of 1862 struggled to adapt to a war that differed enormously from their expectations, relying on coping strategies that were shaped by the values and attitudes of their home societies. Union troops remained convinced that responsibility for upholding a nation governed by the people and founded on the core ideals of liberty and equality rested with them. Many also believed that slavery posed the greatest threat to the success of the United States' experiment in republican government, and therefore had to be destroyed in order to save the Union and encourage it to live up to its ideals. Yet antagonism toward slavery rarely meant support for equal rights for African Americans, as most Union troops still sought to separate the issue of slavery from the more complicated questions of black rights and racial equality. At the same time, new arrivals who had not yet witnessed slavery or the South first-hand frequently brought anti-emancipation sentiments with them when they enlisted, which increased Union dissent on the topic of slavery.

Meanwhile, Confederate discord escalated on virtually every topic except slavery. Soldiers and civilians objected vehemently to impress-ment, tax-in-kind, and conscription. Troops' commitment to a Richmond government that conflicted with rather than advanced their interests was weak, and many grew contemptuous of a civilian population that failed to live up to early expectations of a purer, morally superior population. Yet as disappointed as troops were with the Confederacy, they accepted the logic that the Union was worse because it meant abolition, and abolition meant disaster because it would destroy the social order, undermine men's very identities, and unleash race war on unprotected families. As soldiers everywhere coped with a changing (and often disillusioning) war, slavery, a source of dissent in the Union Army, proved more powerful than any other single factor in overriding dissent in the Confederate ranks. It con-tinued to define the war.

CHAPTER 3

"Kingdom Coming in the Year of Jubilo":
Revolution and Resistance

O NE J ANUARY night in 1863, Arkansas soldier James Harrison dreamed of a big dinner at his Aunt Polly's house. Suddenly, the dream turned sour when Harrison realized, "I had too eat by the side of a negro." Even worse, the black man "had a plate to eat on and I had none." Harrison had his dream just days after President Lincoln issued the Emancipation Proclamation, as bondmen and bondwomen continued to chip away at slavery and the Union Army enlisted black soldiers. Harrison's nightmare encapsulated much of what Confederate soldiers feared all those changes would mean. Blacks would not only "eat at table with white folks," but they would also enjoy new rights and benefits at the expense of ordinary whites like small farmer James Harrison, who sat helplessly without a plate while a black man used a plate that Harrison regarded as rightfully his.[1] The Emancipation Proclamation and black enlistment in the Union Army pushed Confederate discontent into the shadows and steeled resolve in the Confederate Army by providing soldiers like James Harrison with fresh reminders of precisely why they must keep up the fight.

Meanwhile, the impact of the Emancipation Proclamation and black enlistment also reverberated among the Union ranks, changing a war to preserve the Union into a war to reform it. That shift revolutionized the American Republic. While the revolution clarified war aims for Confederates, it complicated things for many Union soldiers, because it required them to admit painful truths about the Union they had revered all their

Chapter title from "Kingdom Coming," a song written by Henry Clay Work in 1862.

Emancipation and black enlistment in 1863: "Journey of a Slave from the Plantation to the Battlefield," James Fuller Queen, 1863. *Courtesy of Library of Congress*

lives, confront the uncomfortable reality of slavery as a national rather than sectional issue, and face difficult questions about what the place of former slaves within the Union should be. Yet despite lingering ambivalence and some resistance to the revolution that 1863 constituted, the men of the Union rank and file on the whole continued to serve as advocates of emancipation, partly because they knew that emancipation was necessary to save the Union, but also because they now recognized that it was necessary to make the Union worth saving.

"This peculiar institution . . . has become so deeply rooted that [removing] it will shake the nation"

From the summer of 1862 through the spring of 1863, the men in blue sustained major defeats on the battlefield, just as the Union withstood its most profound revolution since the nation's founding. For the first year and a half of the conflict, Union soldiers had stressed the need to save the republic inherited from the founders in order to demonstrate to the rest of the world that a self-governing republic founded on ideals of liberty and equality could survive and flourish. For over a year, many had identified slavery as the cause of the rebellion and the greatest threat to the success of the American experiment, and therefore demanded the destruction of slavery as the only way to end the war and prevent its recurrence, but before the Peninsula Campaign, most had assumed that eventual Union victory was assured, and emancipation would demand little of northern whites other than their abstract approval. Once the Peninsula Campaign failed to take Richmond, military setbacks forced federal soldiers to re-examine basic assumptions. President Lincoln appointed Henry Halleck general in chief in the hopes that Halleck would be able to coordinate the Army of the Potomac (under Gen. George McClellan) and the Army of Virginia (under Gen. John Pope) into a renewed offensive against Richmond. Instead, rivalry between McClellan, Pope, and their allies led directly to another Union defeat at Manassas at the end of August, which in turn permitted Confederate forces to threaten Washington, D.C. Confederates then seized the momentum to launch an ambitious invasion of Union territory in September. Left with little choice, President Lincoln restored McClellan to command. With Little Mac at the helm, the Army of the Potomac stemmed the invasion at the battle of Antietam on September 17, 1862, but at the cost of the single deadliest day of the war. Grim as it was at the time, Antietam stood out as a relative Union highlight compared to what followed. Under a new commander, Gen. Ambrose Burnside, the beleaguered Army of the Potomac endured a devastating loss at Fredericksburg, Virginia, in December, and then suffered humiliation under yet another commander, Gen. Joseph Hooker, at Chancellorsville in May 1863. Even in the West, things looked bleak. Confederate invasions designed to affect the fall 1862 elections rattled Northerners and cost soldiers' lives, though the Confederate advances were checked at places like Perryville, Kentucky. A bogged-down and disease-ridden campaign for the Mississippi River further weakened confidence. Meanwhile, all the changes in high command combined with discontent on the home front to create more upheaval. By the spring of 1863, Massachusetts private Charles Tubbs was not alone when he feared "the Union is a thing that was and we might as well lay down our armes at once."[2] In short, in 1862 and 1863, some Union soldiers began to suspect that saving the Union might not be possible.

Others decided that merely saving the Union was not enough. In 1863, members of the 102d Illinois still believed that "the best interests of the human race" were at stake, because the failure of the Union would prove "fatal to all human freedom, independent of color or race," but they began to suspect that they could not truly save the Union or vindicate its ideals of liberty and equality until they made sure those ideals meant something.[3] In 1863, soldiers started to realize that turning the nation's ideals into realities would require fighting to reform rather than simply preserve the Union. "If all this untold expense of blood and treasure, of toil and suffering, of want and sacrifice, of grief and mourning is . . . to result in no greater good than the restoration of the Union as it was, what will it amount to?" Pvt. Leigh Webber wondered. All the hardship and heartache would "result in no real and lasting good" unless the war transformed principles like "the rights of human nature and universal human freedom" from hollow platitudes (or worse, blatant hypocrisies) into actual achievements.[4] Fighting for "the Union under the old construction" was just not enough anymore, Pvt. Thomas Covert told his wife. "We now want a new one, that knows nothing about slavery."[5]

From the harvest of 1862 through the 1863 planting season, Northerners struggled to come to grips with a revolution that would ask far more of them than even soldiers who had been demanding emancipation since 1861 had previously supposed. This revolution demanded that white Northerners admit that they had been mistaken about the nature of their beloved Union, which they once assumed was sacred and stainless, but was instead badly marred. It forced them to see slavery not as a sectional oddity, comfortably removed from them by geography, but rather as a national institution. Even more painful, the revolution also forced white Northerners to see that they were partly to blame for the Union's ugliest defects. "Any country that allows the curse of Slavery and Amalgamation as this has done, should be cursed," an Illinois soldier confided to his sister and brother-in-law, "and I believe in my soul that God allowed this war for the very purpose of clearing out the evil and punishing us as a nation for allowing it."[6] In short, white Northerners had been wrong about the Union, and by 1863, it had become much more difficult to deny their mistakes or hide from their culpability.

The revolution of 1862–63 also forced a shift in the relationship between ending slavery and the purpose of the war. In 1861, soldiers saw slavery as something akin to a malignant mole on the body politic: it was an unsightly blemish with the ability to poison the entire nation, but since slavery appeared only in a limited area, Union troops assumed it could be excised with little impact on the rest of the body. After nearly two years of observing slavery, interacting with slaves, and fighting a horrible war, the Union rank and file now recognized slavery as a much more insidious cancer, embedded in the very spine and sinew of the nation. Its elimination amounted to traumatic surgery for the entire organism. Northerners as well as Confederates must help "up root [slavery] and cast it out," Pvt. Orra Bailey insisted, even though he knew that the process would be harrowing. "We of the free states have yielded to this peculiar institution . . . untill it has become so deeply rooted that [removing] it will shake the nation and our institutions to the very center."[7] Like many of his fellow enlisted men, Bailey knew a revolution when he saw one.

Slaves initiated much of the shaking themselves, as Union soldiers continued to observe. Tennessee slaves on an abandoned farm proved to be more than a match for Confederate guerrillas in an episode recounted by a Union Army surgeon. As the guerrilla band's leader rode onto the farm to round up escaped slaves, a black man stepped out from behind a fence and sent a bullet "crashing through his ribs and heart." After watching their comrade fall, the rest of the raiders "thought discreshion the better part of valor and took to a hasty flight, doubtless supressing a whole brigade" of guerrillas, the surgeon surmised. As he saw it, the incident handily illustrated "the way the Blacks will treat . . . the Robbers of their labor[,] of their children[,] and their freedom."[8]

The actions of slaves were crucial in eroding the institution of slavery, but they also asked the least of white Northerners, since the impact of slaves' acts of self-liberation fell primarily on slaves themselves and on white Southerners. The Emancipation Proclamation and the enlistment of black Union soldiers, in contrast, involved everyone. When the preliminary Emancipation Proclamation was issued on September 22, 1862 (just days after Union forces claimed victory at Antietam), it announced that all slaves held in areas still in rebellion against the Union on January 1, 1863, would be free. The document mentioned voluntary colonization of former slaves outside the United States as one possible alternative for freedpeople, while saying nothing about black enlistment, even though blacks had begun joining Union regiments raised in Kansas and South Carolina. The final Emancipation Proclamation of January 1, 1863, freed all slaves in areas still in rebellion, just as the preliminary proclamation had promised. The final proclamation also exempted from emancipation slaves in several areas under Union control, but, unlike the first document, it omitted any mention of colonization and explicitly endorsed the enlistment of black soldiers into the Union Army.

By making abolition a matter of national policy, the Emancipation Proclamation and black enlistment directly implicated all Americans, even though the territory specified by the proclamation included only areas under Confederate control. The proclamation and the arming of black Union troops made it much harder to ignore complicated questions about the place of former slaves and other blacks within the American Republic, which most Union soldiers had resolutely avoided since the war began. Even acknowledging the limited jurisdiction of the proclamation, it is impossible to overstate its magnitude, for it took direct aim at an institution even older than the nation itself. It was issued by a man renowned for the statement, "A house divided against itself cannot stand." The nation must become all slave or all free, Lincoln had famously argued.[9] The proclamation pointed the country in the all-free direction, which was uncharted territory for a nation in which slavery had always existed, and where it had profoundly shaped foreign policy, domestic affairs, and the national character.[10] To destroy the institution was to create a new United States unlike one that had ever existed before.

Given the immensity of the transformation wrought by the proclamation, it comes as no surprise that the measure elicited a wide variety of strong reactions among Union soldiers and civilians, but soldiers' responses were not nearly as negative or simplistic as has long been supposed. The idea that Union troops reacted to the Emancipation Proclamation with fury, throwing down their arms by the regiment and plunging the Army into a morale crisis from which it never fully recovered, has proven both popular and tenacious, but it is based on a set of three assumptions rather than on evidence.[11] The assumptions go like this. First, since Union morale declined in the winter of 1862 and 1863, and since the preliminary Emancipation Proclamation arrived in the autumn of 1862, followed by the final proclamation in January 1863, the proclamation must have caused the dip in morale.[12] Second, since many Union soldiers held racist views, they must have objected to the proclamation.[13] Finally, since anti-war and anti-emancipation Democrats made gains in the 1862 state and Congressional elections, which were held hard on the heels of the preliminary proclamation, the election results amount to soldiers' repudiation of emancipation.[14] None of these assumptions holds up under scrutiny.

Morale in the Union did plummet in the winter and spring of 1862 and 1863, and the preliminary proclamation did arrive in the autumn of 1862, followed by the final proclamation on the first day of 1863. Yet to most Union soldiers, emancipation and declining morale were distinct phenomena, not two halves of a cause-and-effect relationship. Union troops themselves attributed their sagging morale mainly (but not solely) to military factors, although the precise triggers differed between eastern and western armies.

In assessing the mood of the Army of the Potomac, a New Jersey private explained, "patriotism has oozed out through the pores opened by the imbecility of [army] leaders, and the fatigues and disappointments of a fruitless winter campaign."[15] The spirits of the Army of the Potomac began to decline in the summer of 1862, when the Peninsula Campaign failed to take Richmond. Morale perked up in the wake of Antietam, but only temporarily. By November, when Richmond remained as firmly in Confederate hands as ever and the Army of the Potomac seemed stuck in an everlasting rut, a Massachusetts soldier noticed, "I hear nothing but curses both loud and deep even from some of the best men, whom I left at Harrisons Landing full of faith and hope."[16] An equally frustrated President Lincoln identified Gen. George McClellan as the main obstacle to Union progress, and removed him from command of the Army of the Potomac on November 7. However necessary, McClellan's demotion cast a "gloom over [the] army," as one Little Mac supporter put it, because many members remained loyal to the general.[17] It also failed to solve the Union's high command woes, as a string of ill-fated successors and a winter of bad fortune made clear. Tracing low Union morale like a troublesome river, many soldiers located its origins in Fredericksburg, Virginia, where the badly mismanaged December attack achieved nothing but appalling Union casualties. To John Babb, the mere fact of being "whiped, and that severely" at Fredericksburg would have been bad enough, but the humiliation and senselessness of sacrificing "ten thousand lives" all for nothing made it worse.[18] The aftereffects of Fredericksburg and the so-called Mud March that followed lingered for months. In February, Cpl. Adam Muezenberger reported that disconsolate soldiers remained unable to recover from the effects of the battle, some of them so downhearted that only "the thought of their families keeps them from suicide."[19] After a winter of dispiriting inactivity, and the Army of the Potomac's loss and retreat at Chancellorsville in May, one Pennsylvania sergeant claimed he had "never seen the Armey so much demorralised as it is at the Pressent time."[20] Battlefield reverses and leadership woes made the Army of the Potomac feel as if it had been put through a wringer.

Despair took longer to set in among western armies, where morale held reasonably steady through 1862, but by February of the new year, the unique set of challenges facing western regiments took their toll. Soldiers most often attributed their dreary spirits to idleness, soaring disease rates, and the futility of a grand design to regain the Mississippi River by moving it. The scheme entailed digging through swamps and diverting the Mississippi from its riverbed into a new channel to get around the Confederate stronghold of Vicksburg. The absurdity of the task was enough to make digging detail miserable, but even worse, days spent in the unhealthy conditions led to disease rates so high that Iowa private Charles Musser described duty along the Mississippi as "wholeSale murder." Musser warned that his dysentery-plagued regiment was so "tired of the war" and of the fruitless channel digging that "if there is not some great movements made between this and spring, I believe one half of the army will throw down their arms and go home."[21] When spring came, battles at Jackson, Champion's Hill, and Big Black failed to capture Vicksburg, and Union troops settled in for a grim siege.

While Musser, Muezenberger, Babb, and others freely admitted to discouragement, they did not blame the Emancipation Proclamation. Pvt. Dayton Flint, who personally opposed emancipation, listed the proclamation as one of many factors, but even he judged woeful army leadership, battlefield defeats, disease, and the removal of McClellan to be more responsible than the Emancipation Proclamation for poor morale.[22] Furthermore, timing does not support a link between emancipation and demoralization. If soldiers' low spirits resulted from the preliminary or final Emancipation Proclamation, then morale should have dropped at the same time throughout the entire Union Army, right after one or the other of the proclamations. Instead, morale in the Army of the Potomac slid in November and plunged most steeply in December, months after the preliminary proclamation but before the final proclamation. Meanwhile, morale in the West did not drop until February. Demoralization, in short, struck eastern and western armies at different times in response to local circumstances, not as the result of emancipation, which troops everywhere had known was coming since September.

In fact, when the preliminary and final proclamations came, many soldiers regarded them less as unwelcome surprises than as evidence that a tardy federal government was finally catching up to what soldiers had known for more than a year. Three weeks before Lincoln issued the preliminary proclamation, a German immigrant who fought with the Twelfth Missouri argued impatiently that emancipation was "the only proper policy," and without it, "the war will not take a successful turn."[23] Once news of the preliminary proclamation reached the camp of the Third Kansas Cavalry, Joseph Trego announced, "we are rejoiced to learn that Abraham has, at last begun at the bottom of the difficulty to solve it."[24] Gratified though Elijah Penny was by news of emancipation, he could not help but grumble, "if the Presidents *proclamation* had been proclaimed one year sooner than it was I think the war would have been just so much nearer the end."[25]

However much soldiers may have anticipated the destruction of slavery, the final Emancipation Proclamation still amounted to big news. An Iowa regiment gathered for a reading of the document and greeted it with "3 times 3 hearty cheer[s] from the whole regiment, hurrah for the proclamation and old Abe."[26] In Louisiana, the Eleventh Illinois listened to a speech reminding soldiers that "the Negroes was free, as free as the wind that blows, and that they had to be treated as men & women." After the speech, Sgt. William Parkinson admitted that approval of the proclamation was "not a unanimous thing," but he added that overall, "I never in all my days saw such inthusiasm." A "large majority" of the men greeted the proclamation and the speech with "shouts & Hurrahs."[27]

When Parkinson remarked that response to the proclamation was "not a unanimous thing," he rightly noted that soldiers remained individuals with their own, sometimes conflicting, opinions. Yet despite a wide range of outlooks, a predominant view clearly emerged, and it is best summed up by a soldier who explained, "slavery is the primary cause, or the root of the matter"; therefore, the Emancipation Proclamation made good sense, because "to distroy the tree root & branch is the surest way to brake this rebellion."[28] Certain that "the ware never will come to a close while the negros is left where they are," Pvt. Jasper Barney set out to persuade his socially elite brother-in-law (an officer and Barney's superior in rank), who worried that emancipation would upset the social order. "Even if we could suppress the rebellion and leave the main root where it was before," Barney argued, "it wouldent be long before they would try the same game as before. But if we take away the main root of evil and confiscate their property they will have nothing to fight fore hereafter."[29] To soldiers who had been claiming that emancipation was the only way to end the war once and for all, the proclamation seemed like plain old common sense.

Without a doubt, some soldiers bitterly resented the radical transformation that they rightly saw in the Emancipation Proclamation. In July 1862, Gen. George McClellan had warned President Lincoln, "a declaration of radical views, especially upon slavery, will rapidly disintegrate our present armies."[30] General McClellan personally opposed emancipation, and habitually exaggerated the odds against any proposition he himself did not favor, emancipation included. Nevertheless, some individual soldiers shared McClellan's hostility. Nobody could have been more angry than Ohio private Chauncey Welton, who fumed to his father, "I can tell you we don't think mutch of [the Emancipation Proclamation] hear in the army for we did not enlist to fight for the negro and I can tell you that we neer shall or many of us anyhow no never." Welton even agreed with McClellan's prediction that emancipation would deplete the Union ranks. "Already men are deserting evry day from our regment," he reported.[31]

Opponents of the Emancipation Proclamation objected for various reasons, including legality and practicality. Some troops cited constitutional scruples. One Pennsylvania corporal personally opposed slavery, but worried that the proclamation violated constitutional guarantees for the institution, which mattered in a war fought in defense of the Constitution. Stretch the Constitution once, he feared, and Washington's "set of Pollitical demagogues" would begin using the document recklessly to advance their own petty quarrels.[32] Among Chauncey Welton's complaints was his belief that the proclamation was "both illegal and unconstitutional."[33] Welton and others also reasoned that the proclamation would prolong rather than resolve the war, because it would inspire Confederates to fight harder. The measure, according to Welton, "swelled the southern ranks to an alarming extent." Confederates also became so much "more ferocious" that they "fight much better since the 1st of Jan."[34] Another soldier agreed that the proclamation "unite[d] the South almost as a unit," which minimized the valuable asset of internal southern dissent.[35] Meanwhile, some Union troops feared that the proclamation would divide Northerners. Cyrus Boyd had no personal hostility toward emancipation, but fretted that "Rebel sympathizers at home" might use the inevitable disagreement over the issue to stir up antiwar "revolution in the north."[36]

The Emancipation Proclamation created particular dilemmas for soldiers from the border states (especially Kentucky, Maryland, and Missouri), which retained both slavery and their place in the Union, even as the measure turned the war into a struggle to end slavery elsewhere. When secessionists had warned in 1861 that the slaveholding states must choose between slavery and the Union, many border-state unionists had refused to believe they would have to sacrifice either. Now they could not be so sure. Some border-state soldiers called for an end to slavery just as insistently as troops from any other state, but others, like Marylander John Babb, had their doubts. "It really seems to me that we are not fighting for our *country,* but for the freedom of the negroes," Babb grumbled, and that perception was likely to "do more harm than good" to the Union cause in Maryland.[37] David Massey and Phillip Reilly came from the fiercely divided state of Missouri, home to many who had been committed to protecting and expanding slavery since the Kansas border wars of the 1850s. Both soldiers resented the war's transformation into a "negro crusade," as Reilly put it.[38] Massey went further, suggesting, "if old Abe does free the negro I say that the Democrats owt to go in with the south and kill all the Abalitians of the north and that will end this war where nothing else will."[39] The proclamation did not disillusion Kentuckian Terah Sampson quite as badly, mainly because Sampson blamed the Confederacy for starting the war to protect slavery and therefore bringing the proclamation on itself. Nonetheless, the whole idea of being "in the army for to free nigros" did not sit easily with him.[40]

Many soldiers born and raised in free states shared Sampson's racism, and for some of them, dislike of black people was reason enough to oppose the Emancipation Proclamation. Some troops blamed slaves for the existence of the war, and resented the idea of rewarding the culprits with emancipation. Cyrus Boyd saw such scapegoating at work in his Iowa regiment, where he estimated that about one-quarter of soldiers opposed emancipation. Some of them took out their wrath on African

Americans on the grounds that if it were not for slaves, the war never would have happened. "The poor African . . . from no fault of his—save in the fact of his black skin" was subjected to "prejudice," "indignant language," and threats from surly Union troops in the months following the proclamation.[41] No soldier anywhere spoke more angrily or hatefully than Chauncey Welton. In one of his outbursts, he raged:

> When we think it is all for the purpose of raising the poor down troden affrican to a common with an intelligent race of beings[!] My abolition enimys . . . say . . . free the negroe at all hazzards whether the union is saved or not if it takes the last man, yes this is their language. The nigger, nigger, nigger, free him, free him, free him sacrifice money, wealth, treasure, blood, life and country, but free the nigger, and their mottow is emancipation first and the union, afterwards.[42]

For Welton, racism provided reason enough to oppose emancipation, which makes it easy to leap to the conclusion that all northern racists resisted emancipation, but despite obvious exceptions like Welton, Union soldiers by and large proved themselves perfectly able to retain prejudice and support the proclamation at the same time. According to Fred Pettit, "nine tenths of the army" supported the proclamation because "a Negro has rights as a dog has rights and [we] think his rights should be respected."[43] Reassuring his parents that he was "no nigger worshiper," David Nichol affirmed his own racial prejudice even as he praised the proclamation for striking "at the root of the Evil," and helping to "end this war."[44] Sergeant Nichol saw no contradiction between calls to end the institution of slavery and personal bigotry toward black people because, like most white Northerners who so much as glanced at a newspaper in the 1850s but whose prewar lives rarely or never brought them into contact with actual African Americans, Nichol had plenty of practice reading or thinking about the abstract institution of slavery without giving a thought to flesh-and-blood black Americans. For other Northerners, racism even made it easier to support emancipation, because their assumptions of the innate inferiority of black people convinced them that nature would keep African Americans in unthreatening, subordinate positions even without the legal institution of slavery. "This talk about 'putting ourselves *on an equality with niggers,*' is to me, the *boldest nonsense* or rather an *insult* to me as one of the Saxon race," claimed Leigh Webber, an ardent supporter of abolition long before the proclamation. As he saw it, whites' "natural superiority" made any notion of equality an "absurdity."[45] In short, most white Union troops felt that they did not need to believe that black Americans were equal to white Americans in order to support the destruction of the institution that brought the war. Illinoisan Amos Hostetter, who devoted no thought to freeing slaves before the war, admitted that he and many of his fellow soldiers "like the Negro no better now than we did then but we hate his master worse and I tell you when Old Abe carries out his Proclamation he kills this Rebellion and not before. I am henceforth an *Abolitionist* and I intend to practice what I preach."[46]

In fact, many of Hostetter's fellow Midwesterners felt especially pressed to affirm their support for the proclamation in order to salvage the good name of their home states. Exaggerated stories of enraged Indiana, Illinois, and Ohio soldiers stacking weapons rather than fighting for emancipation, along with the denunciation of the Emancipation Proclamation by the state legislatures of Indiana and Illinois, embarrassed and angered many midwestern troops. When James Dodds heard of letters in his hometown newspaper purporting to be from soldiers "on the point of laying down their arms on account of the Proclamation," he angrily dismissed them as "all untrue," and claimed instead that "the army was never more united than now." While Dodds's assessment of unity was exaggerated, his disgust at reports of opposition was sincere.[47] William Lewis insisted that if any antiproclamation demonstrations took place, they must have been the work of officers. "I no that the soldier had nothing to Doo with it it wer sholder straps and no one Elttze," he claimed. Enlisted men were too busy fighting the war to protest a measure that was likely to help win it.[48] When the men of the 105th Ohio "heard that there is also a story going the rounds in the north that the soldiers of Ohio, Indiana, Illinois and other western states that are in the army of the west are willing to throw down their arms and let the cause go as it will," they passed resolutions supporting the proclamation and criticizing its opponents as "traitors to our cause and country."[49]

Some pragmatic troops praised specific benefits of emancipation as a war measure. One soldier wrote to his hometown newspaper to remind readers that emancipation robbed the Confederacy of a valuable war resource. "Any man who comes into, or goes with the army will see that the white men of the South are in the Southern army, and their negroes are at home raising crops to support their families," he pointed out. Free the slaves, and "the white men will be obliged to come home to look after the welfare of their families and go to work themselves or starve."[50] A lifelong Democrat from Ohio, Sam Evans, succinctly explained his reasons for supporting the proclamation to his father, who opposed it: "my doctrine has been any thing to weaken the enemy."[51] Whatever else motivated soldiers, most of them wanted to go home, and they welcomed a measure they believed would help speed their returns.

Other soldiers embraced emancipation because it eliminated an embarrassing source of hypocrisy, and moved the American Republic closer to living up to its own ideals. William White saluted the proclamation because it announced that the flag of the United States "shall triumphantly wave over a free land, which it has never done yet."[52] Until emancipation was achieved, an Indiana private held that "this war has not done its work." He fought to "sustain a principle, to protect a right, and secure the liberties of the oppressed." Emancipation constituted "a check to the tyrany of European monarchs" and a step in "the establishing of free government throughout the earth."[53] If the existence of slavery had mocked the propositions of human equality and universal justice in the United States, then eliminating slavery should strengthen those ideals and certify the success of the United States' republican experiment in the eyes of the world.

Once the proclamation turned the ending of slavery into official war policy, it also alerted many complacent troops who had been advocating emancipation while ignoring the future of freed slaves to the reality that, as Sgt. Maj. Stephen Fleharty put it, *"the status of the negro in the future organization of our government"* was a "vexed question" they could no longer ignore.[54] Few soldiers had clear ideas of how a postslavery, biracial society might function. As Pennsylvanian Jacob Seibert pointed out, "we don't want [former slaves] in the north."[55] Some troops pinned their hopes on labor schemes that kept former slaves in southern fields and at a safe distance from white Northerners. An April 1863 edition of *The Banner of the Ironsides* advocated a solution adopted in Louisiana, in which black workers labored for wages on sugar plantations. According to the *Banner,* "hundreds of negroes" now proved themselves to be "commendable" workers in a free labor system.[56] Others hoped emancipation would pave the way for genuine equality such as had never yet existed in the United States. A black man "is our brother and has God's likeness," Stephen Emerson reminded his mother, even predicting that "prejudice against him will soon begin to wear away."[57] While Emerson's optimism proved to be inflated, he accurately recognized that the Emancipation Proclamation eliminated the comforting luxury of emancipation as an abstract proposition. Just as it forced many federal soldiers to admit the imperfection of the old Union, the proclamation also insisted that even reluctant Northerners begin to envision new roles for black Americans within the American Republic.

Even more than emancipation, the enlistment of black soldiers into the Union Army forced many white Union soldiers to face questions about the standing of black Americans within the nation. African American soldiers had served in early conflicts such as the Revolution and the War of 1812, but they had been barred from the Mexican War, which was the conflict freshest in American memory when the Civil War broke out. Since military service was a long-standing hallmark of citizenship, black enlistment in the Army forced white Americans to reexamine the place of African American men within the American social structure. Moreover, black soldiers bore witness to how revolutionary the war had become by 1863. For these reasons, black enlistment proved more controversial among Northerners than emancipation. James Brewer wholeheartedly endorsed freeing slaves, but he was "awfull mad about Negroe arming," which he regarded as "a burlesk on the white man's Soldiering."[58] Yet by late spring 1863, the discouraging progress of the war was fast convincing many troops that a Union victory would require new measures. Stationed near a black regiment from Arkansas, Leigh Webber noted that soldiers who "less than a year ago would threaten to desert if the Government even enlisted negroes are now among the most earnest in the new policy."[59]

Soldiers grew more favorable toward black enlistment for many of the same reasons they espoused emancipation. "The purpose of employing negroe soldiers is to make them be serviceable to the country," one soldier noted. As a "war measure," arming blacks who were anxious to fight their former masters was simply "the most efficient means that can be brought into action," especially as the North faced the prospect of its first nationwide draft in 1863.[60] Cpl. Charles Musser and his regiment agreed. "The arming of Negroes for Soldiers is now considered by all or a large majority of the boys as a necessity, and they go in Strong for it," Musser maintained.[61] Lt. Anson Patterson, meanwhile, saw potential benefits in black Union enlistment, because the very sight of black soldiers would terrify Confederates and convince them that "the closing scene of the Rebellion" had arrived.[62]

The performance of black soldiers also converted many white troops to the idea of black enlistment, even though it did not wholly dislodge white soldiers' racial prejudices. After a Florida expedition, Pvt. Orra Bailey noticed that black soldiers "whip[ped] the rebels handsomely," fighting "like tigers" and striking horror in the enemy, who regarded no fate as worse than "being taken prisner by a niger."[63] Some members of Samuel Storrow's Massachusetts regiment objected to the prospect of black soldiers before "fighting alongside them" in North Carolina. Witnessing black troops' bravery, according to Corporal Storrow, changed many soldiers' minds.[64] Changing minds did not mean that bigotry disappeared. Henry Kircher was "very much for" arming black soldiers, as long as he did not have to fight next to them and risk being "wounded by the same bullet that first trafficks with a Negro and then pays me a visit." If black and white regiments mixed too closely, "gradually the difference between white and black will show less and less until it has disappeared," warned Lieutenant Kircher. "What is a white who forgets that he stands above the African?" he wondered.[65]

Even though black enlistment did not wholly eliminate white racism, black soldiers like Joseph Williams recognized that it still underscored both how revolutionary the war had become by 1863 and how crucial African Americans' actions had been in that process. Just three years previously, Williams reminded readers of the *Christian Recorder* (a northern black newspaper), "slavery, with all its wrath was upon us." In contrast, emancipation brought "hope, happiness, and enjoyment" by turning the "bondman" into a "freeman." Now black soldiers stood to attain even more. "Determined to hold every step which has been offered to us as citizens of the United States," blacks fought "for our elevation which represents justice, the purity, the truth, and aspiration of heaven."[66] Bitter disappointments like lower pay and a prohibition against black officers would plague black soldiers' aspirations to racial equality, but few of these setbacks were apparent when black regiments first began fighting for what black private William Matthews called the "great and glorious Cause of Union and Liberty."[67]

The determination and performance of black soldiers, the passage of time, and soldiers' experiences in the South and on the battlefield helped to change the minds of some white troops who initially objected to the Emancipation Proclamation. As early as February, Terah Sampson began to reassess his dislike of the measure, and asked for his family's opinions on the matter to help him reformulate his own.[68] By March, an Ohio soldier reported, "the Pres. Proclamation is gaining favor in the army every day," as troops grew to recognize it as "the right move at the right time."[69]

Even Chauncey Welton had begun to reconsider by June. He still disliked abolitionists and blacks, but he had also come to believe that the once-odious proclamation represented a "means of haistining the speedy Restoration of the union and the termination of this war," and he was willing to stand by it as a pragmatic war measure.[70]

Welton also came around partly because he grew disenchanted with the anti-emancipation and antiwar wing of the Democratic Party, known as the Peace Democrats, or Copperheads. A loyal Democrat, Welton did not change his mind all at once, but as the Copperheads stepped up attacks on emancipation and the war, Welton, like many others, began to associate opposition to emancipation with a lack of support for soldiers or the war effort. Far from mirroring the anti-emancipation rhetoric of Copperheads in 1862 and 1863, soldiers increasingly resented it, and shaped their own opinions in direct opposition to it. That progression took time, but it had largely been accomplished by the summer of 1863.

The autumn of 1862 was an eventful political time for the Union. State and Congressional elections took place just weeks after Lincoln issued the preliminary Emancipation Proclamation, which may have guaranteed that slavery and race would dominate the 1862 elections in any event, but a move by Secretary of War Edwin Stanton compounded matters. On September 18, just one day after Antietam and four days before the preliminary Emancipation Proclamation, Secretary of War Stanton ordered that black refugees at Cairo, Illinois, be sent by rail to communities throughout the Midwest, which were to feed, clothe, and employ them.[71] In June, Democratic Congressman Samuel Cox of Ohio, in a widely publicized speech, had raised the specters of labor competition and racial mixing as logical outcomes of emancipation.[72] Racist propaganda capitalized on white voters' prejudice and fear and kept the issue of race at the forefront of political debate during and after the campaign season. An Ohio soldier, for instance, sent his wife a song called "Fight for the Nigger," which he identified as "a specimen of the Trash the damned Copperheads have been sending." Exploiting popular prejudices, the lyrics of the song asked soldiers, "What if with your fighting you all lose your lives? / You help the Abolitionist to get nigger wives."[73] The Emancipation Proclamation and Stanton's order persuaded many civilian voters (especially Midwesterners) that Cox and propagandists like the author of the offensive "Fight for the Nigger" were right about racial threats to whites, just as discouraging casualty lists and malaise kept Republican voters at home.[74] The Republican Party was by no means trounced (in fact, Republicans actually gained

Senate seats), but Democrats picked up key victories, such as the state leg-islatures of Indiana and Illinois and the governorship of New York.

The success of anti-emancipation candidates at the polls in 1862 has often been assumed to indicate troops' dissatisfaction with the Emancipa-tion Proclamation, but the electoral results reveal less about soldiers' stances on the proclamation than enlisted men's reactions to the campaign and elections do. Because most states had not yet made provision for absentee balloting by the 1862 elections, few soldiers in the field voted, but they paid attention anyway. Pvt. Constant Hanks believed that Repub-lican victories were so important that he wrote home to insist that his ill and elderly father "if he lives and can . . . must go & vote for Gen. [James] Wadsworth for Governor" of New York. Wadsworth "is a firm supporter of Lincons policy of cutting Slavery up by the roots in all the Reble States, so that it never can disturb the peace of the country again." The Democratic candidate, Horatio Seymour, supported the idea of the Union as it was before the proclamation, which Hanks felt certain would cause war to "break out again in a few years worse than ever." In fact, the prospect of anti-abolitionists in power so worried Hanks that he wished "women could vote" so that his mother could also cast a ballot for pro-emancipation candidates.[75] After the elections, a Pennsylvania soldier interpreted Congressional victories of anti-emancipation Democrats as better news for Confederates than for loyal Union supporters. "The rebles that we take prisoner tell us with an air of triumph that we are getting divided among ourselves and point to the Democratic majority for proof and they are very much tickled about it," he informed his brother and sis-ter.[76] Union troops felt they had less to celebrate, according to soldiers like Pvt. John Garriott, who found things "mighty glumey" in the wake of "the late lections," or Capt. Maschel Manring, who reported that "the news of the elections in the free states has so discouraged the army that they are almost ready to weigh anker."[77]

In 1863, antiwar Democrats could add dissatisfaction with conscrip-tion to their platform. The U.S. Congress passed its first conscription law in March 1863, scheduling a draft to take place in the summer. It differed from the Confederate law in several ways. First, while the Confederate draft automatically placed every nonexempt able-bodied white man of military age into the ranks, the Union draft created a lottery system. The names of eligible men aged twenty to forty-five were entered, but a man was conscripted only if his name was drawn.[78] Also unlike the Confeder-ate draft, Union conscription did not extend the enlistment terms of soldiers already serving. Finally, the Union draft offered different escape hatches. Whereas the Confederate draft provided only for substitution and various class and occupational exemptions, the Union conscription law contained a controversial commutation clause, which permitted draftees to purchase exemption from the draft for $300 per round. One New Yorker who was "down on" conscription objected to the measure "not because it is a Conscription Law, but because it was framed for the benefit of the rich and the disadvantage of the poor."[79] Pvt. Phillip Reilly complained that commutation transformed the government into a "bold Highwayman [who] says to every man in the loyal states 'three hundred dollars or your life!' "[80] Opposition notwithstanding, commutation was actually more fair than class-based exemptions or substitution alone, which cost far more than $300 and therefore was available only to the wealthy. Further, numerous immigrant, workers', and municipal groups banded together to form "draft insurance pools" to pay the commutation fee of any drafted member. In the end, of 207,000 northern men drafted, only 46,000 actually entered the ranks.[81] Nevertheless, commutation looked unfair, and inequity in a war waged to uphold a government dedicated to the ideal of equality angered many enlisted men. The unrelenting continuation of the war and its incessant casualty lists heightened frustration with a war that now required more soldiers than the number willing to volunteer for it.

The most prominent Copperhead, Ohioan Clement Vallandigham, latched onto racism to tie multiple sources of resentment together and fire up the opposition. In 1862, Vallandigham lost his bid for reelection to Congress, but he did not allow defeat to slow down his larger campaign to repudiate the war and emancipation. On Janaury 14, 1863, Vallandigham made his farewell speech to the House, and later circulated the speech in a pamphlet entitled *The Great Civil War in America,* which for the next two years served as the basic articulation of the Peace Democrat platform. In turning a war for Union into one for emancipation, Vallandigham argued, Republicans sacrificed lives needlessly and turned the North into a despotism heedless of civil liberties. Condemning "the folly and madness of this crusade against African slavery," he demanded an immediate end to the war that would be beneficial to "the welfare, peace, and safety of the white race, without reference to the effect that settlement may have upon the condition of the African."[82]

Among Union soldiers, Vallandigham badly overplayed his hand. On May 1, just as the Army of the Potomac fought desperately at Chancellorsville, Vallandigham recapitulated his platform at Mount Vernon, Ohio,

and soldiers hated him for it. Wilbur Hinman and his friends in the Sixty-
fifth Ohio entertained themselves by imagining Vallandigham "pounding
his head against the wall of Fort Warren instead of preaching his treason."
Upon hearing that the Ohio agitator had in fact been imprisoned by the
Union general Ambrose Burnside, Hinman and his peers suggested that as
additional penance, the prisoner "be fed only on army crackers," and
offered to "donate a few boxes of that loyal food for his use."[83] Chauncey
Welton did not find anything about Vallandigham amusing, especially
when he learned that Vallandigham was out of prison and running for governor of Ohio. According to Welton, that "news fell like a thunderboalt
upon this regiment." Despite lifelong Democratic loyalties, Welton now
believed that Vallandigham and Copperheads like him betrayed "the true
principles of democracy," and wanted his father to "understand that any
man who upholds Vallandingham at all never can be called any thing but
my enimy. . . . There is no one on the face of this earth that is despised and
hated by every soldier as mutch as the copperhead is."[84] Aaron Beck
summed it up best when he wrote, "I don't know which would cause the
most rejoicing in camp, Richmond taken or Val[landigham] hung but I
believe the latter would."[85]

Soldiers' anger at Vallandigham and Copperheads did not amount to
repudiation of Democrats in general, the two-party system, or political
dissent, all of which soldiers continued to regard as aspects of the republican self-government they fought to uphold. "Politics govern this nation," a
Michigan private pointed out to his mother. "Defending the proper politics
in majority" was tantamount to "defending our Nation in fact," but the
only way to determine the majority was to pit two alternatives against
each other at the ballot box and see who won.[86] Many proud Democrats
continued to identify themselves as Democrats, but they also increasingly
viewed two topics, Union and emancipation, as above politics. Partisan
disagreement over economic policy or civil liberties remained perfectly
acceptable, even desirable, but the survival of the intact Union and the end
of slavery became nonnegotiable, because they were national, not partisan
issues in many soldiers' eyes.[87]

The problem with Copperheads was that they overstepped the bounds
of legitimate dissent, and in so doing ran the risk of discrediting the
Democratic Party as the respectable alternative necessary to the proper
functioning of electoral democracy. As one Illinois Democrat grieved,
"the name of Democrats . . . is being sullied and disgraced by demagougs
who are appealing to the lo[w]est prejudice and passion of our people."

Copperhead agitation sent a "keen and fatle pang to the heart" of every loyal Democrat. "There is just as good Democrats as any other partie," but "there are a portion . . . that deserve the name of Copperheads," and "the Democrats in our Regiment are even madder at them than the Republicans."[88] Union troops, in short, saw a real distinction between dissent and disloyal obstruction. They hated Vallandigham and the Copperheads not because they were Democrats, but because they refused to admit the connection between emancipation, winning the war, and saving the Union.

When civilians did not respond as hostilely to Copperheads as soldiers did, a rift deepened between soldiers and the folks at home. After learning of the anti-emancipation leanings of their state legislatures, "the soldiers of Illinois and Indiana are boiling over with rage and indignation," Jacob Behm reported.[89] David James did not know whether to be disappointed or just plain angry when he heard that the citizens of his hometown, Richland Center, Wisconsin, had convened an anti-emancipation meeting. He told his parents about Illinois regiments encamped nearby that had "passed some encouraging resolutions" in support of the administration, the proclamation, and the war effort. The Wisconsin soldiers, assuming that their families and neighbors would never do anything so disgraceful as to denounce emancipation, had not passed similar resolutions, but now James and his fellow troops regretted their misplaced confidence in the home front.[90] Even Chauncey Welton accused his Peace Democrat father of being "mistaken considerable" about the war and politics.[91]

Soldiers regretted disagreements with family members, but their commitment to the war and emancipation could for the most part withstand family disharmony because success or failure of the Union would be proven by its ability to show the world that republican government based on universal principles worked, not by the government's track record in promoting the interests of particular individuals and families. As a Massachusetts private explained, all of "civilization and common humanity" had a stake in the Union's survival, which meant that soldiers must rise above "*family ties*" to "sacrifice something for the common good."[92] When Samuel Storrow's parents objected to his decision to hazard his own life and responsibilities to help save the Union and end slavery, Storrow asked them, "what is the worth of this man's life, or of that man's education, if this great and glorious fabric of our Union . . . is to be shattered to pieces . . . ? If our Country and our nationality is to perish, better that we should all perish with it and not survive to see it a laughingstock for all posterity to be pointed at as the unsuccessful trial of republicanism."[93]

Differences and quarrels with the families and communities that soldiers believed they represented might sadden soldiers, but they did not necessarily undermine the rank and file's faith in the Union or the war, because both the Union and the war were about something important enough to transcend personal aspirations, and even, by 1863, to warrant revolution.

"Any man who pretends to believe that this is not a war for the emancipation of the blacks . . . is either a fool or a liar"

Cpl. Samuel Storrow's questions would have struck many white Southerners as odd. After all, the function of government was to *protect* citizens' property and interests, not diminish them to nothingness. The logic of secession said that when the government came into conflict with the interests of enfranchised citizens, it contradicted its own purpose and relieved citizens of loyalty to that government. One irony of the Civil War was that Union soldiers' way of envisioning the relationship between individuals, families, and the government lent itself to sacrifice better than the Confederate vision of government did, but the war demanded more sacrifices from Confederates than it did from Northerners. In 1862 and 1863, white Southerners and the interests of their families suffered while the Confederate government continued to function in ways that met with severe disapproval from Confederate soldiers. Incidents like the Richmond bread riots demonstrated that disaffection had become a genuine problem for the Confederacy. Yet as powerful as discontent was, it did not amount to rejection of the Confederacy or the war effort because all internal upheaval faded in the face of united opposition to the very ideas of the Emancipation Proclamation and the enlistment of black soldiers into the Union Army.

In October 1862, the Confederate Congress modified the conscription law by exempting one white owner or overseer for every farm or plantation containing twenty or more slaves. To supporters of the provision, the new measure contributed to community safety by protecting white women and children from violence at the hands of slaves left at home with no white men to control them. In reality, the law intensified the conflict between individual or family interests and community well-being that plagued the Confederacy from start to finish. Specifically, the twenty-slave law (more commonly dubbed the "Twenty-Nigger Law") aggravated class tensions, which in turn strained, but did not negate, ordinary Confederates' willingness to fight in two ways.

First, many nonslaveholders concurred with the rationale that race control and home-front safety required the presence of white men to police slaves, but they did not see why nonslaveholders could not provide that community service just as effectively as the wealthy could. After all, many nonslaveholders had experience on antebellum slave patrols.[94] A nonslaveholder from Green County, North Carolina, for example, agreed that unless a white man stayed behind, local "negroes" would be "left hear to plunder an steal . . . an destroy our famely," but he also argued that a poor man with a family to support should be allowed to stay home and do the job for his local community rather than exempting a wealthy man whose family could better afford his absence.[95]

Second, and more broadly, ordinary white Southerners did not begrudge fighting for the security of wealthy slave owners' human property—they accepted the necessity of that—but they did object to the way in which the so-called Twenty-Nigger Law seemed to make them bear the disproportionate brunt of the fight. An angry Georgia soldier challenged, "I cannot for my life see how it is, that because the institution of slavery elevates the social position of the poor man, that therefore the poor man should fight the battles of our country, while the rich are allowed to remain at home and to enjoy ease and pleasure." He did not question that he should fight to defend slavery, but he did question why the wealthy should not also have to pitch in, and he resented elite stay-at-homes who took his suffering for granted. "For God's sake don't tell the poor soldier who now shivers in a Northern wind while you snooze in a feather bed, that it is *just* and *right*" for one class to avoid the war while the rest of the white male population "must fight, bleed, and even die, for their ten [*sic*] negroes," he seethed.[96] Months later, in March, a Texas soldier remained furious at the "trembling lawgivers" who pandered to the wealthy with measures like the twenty-slave exemption. He went so far as to wish the Yankee cavalry would ride into Richmond, if such an invasion would "prevent our Congressmen from continuing their weighty deliberations on the conscript act which was to force every man of the South except themselves and their kind into the army."[97]

In April 1863, the Richmond bread riots heightened the disaffection that many soldiers already felt because of hardships imposed on their families by the war and by oppressive policies like impressment. Thomas Warrick's enthusiasm flagged even before the bread riots. In March, he instructed his struggling wife "to sende me worde if the Goverment has dun Eney thing for you." Warrick knew that the cow was sick and producing little milk, and he worried about his ailing children, along with his farm's prospects for the upcoming growing season. His faith that an independent Confederacy could or would do anything to alleviate his family's woes had all but disappeared.[98] The bread riots further strained that faith. On April 2, 1863, several hundred Richmond women met at a Baptist church and marched to the Virginia governor's mansion to inform the state's chief executive of their families' distress and to demand relief. When the governor rebuffed the women, the crowd began to turn into a mob and headed for Richmond's commercial district. There, the rioters broke into bakeries and shops and helped themselves to food and to thousands of dollars' worth of other merchandise until the governor and the mayor of Richmond organized a militia company and marched it into the fray.

Meanwhile, President Jefferson Davis joined the mayor and governor, climbed on a cart, and tried to get the attention of the rioting women by addressing the crowd calmly, and then throwing a few coins into the mob. The clamor did not die down, and in the midst of the confusion, one of the three officials announced that he would order the militia to fire if the crowd did not disperse in five minutes. After four tense minutes, the mob melted away, and cannons rolled into town to prevent further looting. Smaller riots also began to erupt in other towns throughout the Confederacy, but the riot in the Confederate capital especially intensified ill feeling. Pvt. Daniel Brown was dismayed by a "mob" of famished women swooping in on commissary stores with "bowie nives and swoards," but he was even more horrified when "old jef davis ordred our troops to fiar on them." He reported that even though his regiment never fired, two men and one woman were killed by the very army supposedly fighting for the rights of *all* (even poor) white Southerners.[99] The riots certainly illustrated existing dissatisfaction with a Confederacy that was clearly not furthering white Southerners' best interests, but they did more besides. By creating a situation in which white men endangered rather than controlled and protected white women, they shook soldiers' faith in the Confederacy's ability to uphold its own social order.

In response to developments like the twenty-slave law and the bread riots, soldiers' vocal dissatisfaction with both the government and the population of the Confederacy intensified. The Arkansas soldiers who created a camp paper called *The Reveille* criticized the Confederate cabinet as nothing more than a scribbling menagerie of petty and self-serving "chief clerks." They also lambasted President Davis as a power monger who forgot that the "President of the Confederate States is the creature of the Constitution," not of his own devising.[100] Focusing his own resentment on the Confederate Congress, Sgt. Felix Buchanan sourly concluded that the weak and corrupt legislature did not "reflect much honor upon our government."[101] Confederate civilians did not portray the South in a very flattering light either, complained soldiers like Alabamian Edward Brown. As the pressures of war intensified and the home front grew more jaded, Brown nearly despaired to learn that civilians in his home county insisted on growing cotton rather than food. Nobody could eat cotton, which meant that if farmers insisted on growing it, "we are *whipped.*" The Army would be "starved out," and defeat would follow. Only greed for the profits earned by running cotton through the blockade (or worse, sold north) could explain farmers' blindness to the needs of the South's own army.[102] Sgt. William Chunn grew despondent over what he viewed as civilians' petty profiteering. Instead of proving "willing to make any sacrifice in the cause of their country & for the accommodation of the suffering soldier," everyone he met in Mississippi "from the children up" was on the take. "There is nothing they are willing to do for the cause unless they get the money," Chunn complained.[103]

In short, the Confederate assumption that government existed primarily to allow white individuals and families to pursue their own interests had led to real trouble by 1863. Rule by "ignoramuses at home & bigots in the army . . . has crushed the spirit of liberty," Sgt. Edward Brown claimed.[104] On one hand, a government that imposed impressment, tax-in-kind, and a draft that was widely perceived to be unfair ran counter to the interests of most soldiers and their families. At the same time, when some civilians took advantage of opportunities for personal gain, soldiers interpreted other people's self-interested behavior less as manifestation of sound political ideology than as selfishness at a time when unity was more necessary than ever. The boastful prewar fire-eaters who had been so sure of a quick Confederate victory that they promised to drink all the blood spilled in the conflict could now sit at home if they wished, spared by the twenty-slave law from making the sacrifices demanded of ordinary men. As Pvt. J. C. Daniel expressed it, "the men that was going to drink the blood, Are not the men that wades the mud." In his company, at least, the "[se]cession boys are very scanty."[105] Louisianan John Ellis was so disgusted with the Confederacy that he advocated "a counter revolution . . . another secession, a recall of all the state troops . . . and freedom from Jeff Davis."[106]

Yet as vehemently as they denounced the Confederacy, not even the angriest of Confederate soldiers like John Ellis called for a return to the Union. White Southerners might not share much in the way of affection for the Confederate States of America, but they did share hostility to the North. Even when the war's mounting fury, resentment of seemingly unfair burdens placed on nonslaveholders, and the fierce hardships that culminated in the bread riots provoked John Ellis to call for "counter revolution," the revolution he had in mind bore no resemblance to the one taking place in the Union, nor did it involve abandoning the Confederacy for the Union. Whatever else the Richmond government might do, Confederate soldiers knew it would neither abolish slavery nor introduce measures that hinted at racial equality.

In contrast, when Abraham Lincoln issued the Emancipation Proclamation and endorsed the enlistment of black soldiers, he finally revealed what Confederate soldiers assumed had been Northerners' grand design all along. As a Confederate soldiers' newspaper put it, "Now, any man who pretends to believe that this is not a war for the emancipation of the blacks, and that the whole course of the Yankee Government has not only been directed to the abolition of slavery, but even to a stirring up of servile insurrections, is either a fool or a liar."[107] No internal tensions or political quarrels could outweigh the danger of imminent abolition or the terrifying prospect of armed slaves. That revolution, Confederate soldiers felt sure, would be worse than the Confederacy in spite of its disappointments, and it must be resisted at all costs.

The Emancipation Proclamation might look like a weak and insubstantial piece of paper issued by a government that Confederates did not even recognize as legitimate, but it proposed to do nothing less than destroy the foundation of the only society white Southerners had ever known. The logical implications of emancipation horrified Confederate soldiers. Just weeks after the preliminary proclamation was issued, Antoine Prudhomme was convinced that civilization as white Southerners had known it was falling apart in Union-occupied New Orleans. "A perfect reign of terror pervades all hearts—the negroes have the right of citizenship," he claimed. Rumor also had it that "the colored population have turned traitors to our cause they excite the negroes by public demonstrations to insurrection and destruction."[108] An Arkansas soldier also assumed that emancipation could only lead to violence. He readily believed false rumors that the Union general Samuel R. Curtis "had freed all the negroes in Phillips County [Arkansas]," and that freed slaves immediately began hanging innocent whites, killing livestock, ransacking property, and otherwise destroying every vestige of society.[109] A clever Texas soldier described the logical outcome of the proclamation by writing a song. One verse began:

> *They howl the sin of slavery and curse us for the crime,*
> *Of trafficking in human flesh in this enlightened time*
> *They threaten now to signalize the next new calendar*
> *By setting every bondman free beneath the Southern Star.*

Black freedom would be a disaster, the song went on to say, because it would lead "the blacks to mad revolt to murder and to char / With conflagration every home beneath the Southern Star."[110] Emancipation amounted to a direct attack on every aspect of white southern society, and not a single white household was safe.

Even something so basic as a white man's individual identity seemed to come under siege in the wake of emancipation. Before John Williams became a soldier, he lived on his father's struggling farm and helped raise just enough corn to keep the family afloat. The family owned no slaves. Yet Corporal Williams wholeheartedly believed in the necessity of a war to separate from the Union and prevent the abolition that the Emancipation Proclamation threatened to impose. A story that he told his sister explains why. Two white Virginians, Williams claimed, were arrested by "an armed band of negroes and carried before one whome they styled the President," who had them "condemned to be shot." The murder accounted for only part of the story's horror. After the shooting, the mortification continued when the victims "were striped of all their clothing and thrown into the river."[111] Racial role reversal, humiliation, powerlessness before an authority of a different race, summary and autocratic justice, and the loss of individual identity and basic dignity could all be expected under the black- and Yankee-controlled regime that emancipation was sure to introduce. The Confederate camp newspaper *The Vidette* made this same point more concisely when it called emancipation "Slavery for the White Man!"[112]

In igniting white Southerners' long-smoldering fears, the Emancipation Proclamation roused many Confederate soldiers to fury. "The proclamation of Lincoln has filled every one with indignation, and we are all now in favor of raising the 'black flag' and asking and showing 'no quarter,' " a member of the First South Carolina announced when his regiment learned of the preliminary proclamation.[113] A Texan denounced "the proclamation of Lincoln" as "the crowning infamy of all his diabolical schemes for our ruin."[114]

Confederates might be outraged, but they were not surprised. In fact, Confederate morale actually improved because the Emancipation Proclamation raised troops' hackles, giving them more energy than they had shown in months. By clarifying the war, the proclamation brought the struggle back into focus and reminded soldiers why they had to fight even when scarcity threatened loved ones, or the Confederacy fell short of their expectations.[115] According to Pvt. John Street, the proclamation called the bluff of any remaining Union soldiers who claimed (deceptively, in his opinion) that they fought for the Union and not emancipation. "The cry of Union is now no longer made a pretext for carrying on the war," he argued. "By their resent acts the Lincoln government have shown plainly what they have in reality been fighting for all the time vis: the abolition of slavery."[116] Scathing as *The Reveille* was toward the Confederate government, it rallied around the cause when abolition appeared on the horizon. Nothing motivated the southern soldier in the weeks before the Emancipation Proclamation was due to take effect, according to *The Reveille,* quite like thoughts of "the chains of slaves, forged in a Northern furnace, with which to mangle his free limbs."[117] Because it provided a clear rallying point, the proclamation renewed the resolve of soldiers like Pvt. Jonathan Doyle, who reminded his sister, "we must never despair, for death is preferable to a life spent under the gaulling yoke of abolition rule."[118]

When the final Emancipation Proclamation came in January, it did more than just declare slaves free; it also proposed to arm them against their former masters. As a result of the Haitian revolution of 1791–1804, the Denmark Vesey plot of 1822 in South Carolina, the 1831 Nat Turner revolt in Virginia, and John Brown's raid on Harpers Ferry in 1859, nothing terrified white Southerners more than the specter of armed blacks. When David Ballenger learned that "the Yankees are drilling the negroes to fight us," he warned his wife that the Confederacy now faced "the bloody year of the war." Yankee use of black soldiers, he believed, "will almost surpass anything recorded in the annals of history for war and blood shed."[119] In addition, African American soldiers would carry firearms, just like white men, and would be dressed in the same uniforms as white men. In the minds of Confederates, making soldiers of black men implied racial equality, and that prospect could not be allowed to pass without a fight. James Branscomb had been downhearted and disillusioned with the Confederacy for months, but the news of black Union soldiers propelled him out of his gloom. For the first time in a long while, he predicted "success for our army" because "the negro army of the north is only adding fuel to [the] fire of our soldiers."[120] One Virginian suggested a practical way in which Confederate authorities could use black soldiers to boost the morale of war-weary troops. "If our Congress would only pass a bill giving each soldier all the negroes whom he could capture," new soldiers would flood the ranks and existing soldiers would perk up again. "Opportunities for speculating in 'human flesh,' as the Abolitionists say," would renew the Confederate Army's enthusiasm like nothing else, the private predicted.[121]

As the war, emancipation, and black enlistment continued to grind away at slavery, enslaved men and women took advantage of opportunities the war uncovered to gain freedom any way they could. For some enslaved Southerners, liberation meant fleeing to the Union Army. "Many negroes are lost by . . . desertion to the enemy," one Florida sergeant noticed.[122] A North Carolina soldier learned that friends of his, the Brown family, lost two slaves when their mammy "went to the Yankees carrying with her, one of her grandchildren, one that Mrs. Brown had raised in the house." When Mrs. Brown sent word to have the child returned to the family's possession, the mammy suddenly became an "old hag" who replied that she would "stand a law suit in h–ll first."[123] Actions like these added to Confederates' motivation by stoking white southern fears of assertive blacks who refused to recognize white authority.

Other slaves found ways to assert their growing autonomy without leaving home, which disturbed Confederate soldiers at least as much as the runaways did, because it reminded them that disruptions to slavery disturbed the stable and reliable order of things, even in the domestic sanctuary of white southern homes. When Leander Parker saw slaves in Mississippi dressing themselves in their masters' "best apparels" and "valuables," and parading about town presuming to the status usually associated with such finery, it seemed as if he was living in a nightmare.[124] Texas chaplain Robert Bunting sought to horrify Confederate civilians and soldiers alike with stories of marriages between slave women and white Union soldiers taking place in the homes of the slaves' helpless white mistresses. "It is no unusual thing," Bunting claimed, "for the mistress to be compelled to witness, in her own parlor, the marriage of her likely house-maids to officers and privates of the army." After the ceremony, shameless brides helped themselves to articles from the home, and then departed from their rightful mistress "with the taunt that now they are as free as she."[125]

No evidence suggests that marriages between white Union soldiers and slaves occurred at all, let alone became commonplace, but Bunting's stories were powerful despite their falsehood. In fact, the stories helped explain why the defense of slavery continued to rally nonslaveholding soldiers whose families needed them at home, especially when measures like the twenty-slave law could have soured the rank and file on a war for slavery. The twenty-slave law made plain exactly how little direct material interest nonslaveholders had in an institution that so clearly privileged the wealthy, but tales like the ones Bunting spun revealed that for nonslaveholders, slavery's importance had little to do with its pecuniary benefits. The intimacy and social parity between black and white implied by Bunting's stories of interracial marriages, along with the brazenness displayed by black house servants laying claim to their mistresses' belongings and social status, tapped deeply into white Southerners' fears. For one thing, protecting white women from insults and depredations by blacks ranked high on the list of duties that entitled a white Southerner to honorable status as a true man. Moreover, the women whose servants were (according to Bunting) insulting their dignity enjoyed no political rights that abolition could usurp, yet the erosion of slavery still compromised them. Nonslaveholders might be just as economically distanced from slavery's financial profits as women were marginalized from its political benefits, but they would still lose safety, personal dignity, and identity if slavery disappeared. White men who enlisted in the Confederate Army believed that they and their families needed the institution of slavery to survive, as Robert Bunting's fabrications both demonstrated and shrewdly exploited.

ONE MAJOR source of consolation remained available to Confederates: the Emancipation Proclamation could destroy slavery only if the Union won the war. After the dreary winter and spring of 1862, Confederate military fortunes had improved. By early 1863, a Virginian noticed the "difference in our army now and this time last year." For much of 1862, Confederate troops had been "demoralized, discouraged by repeated defeats and retreats," but after Fredericksburg, he believed "the yankees are getting very tired of [the war] . . . and they are quite willing to get out of it."[126] A Texas private grew increasingly sure that the Confederate Army

would "whip [the Union] at vixburge," and that would only be the beginning. "Their own papers . . . said that we had whipped them in evry big
fight and . . . that they would loos men and cost them a heap and we would
still whip them . . . and now was the time for them to make a proposial to
us."[127] Other troops sought to capitalize on Confederate morale and
momentum with invasions of the North. Autumn incursions into Maryland, Ohio, and Kentucky had not worked out as planned in 1862, but by
the summer of 1863, the Confederacy's star army, the Army of Northern
Virginia, was ready to try again. Looking toward Pennsylvania, North
Carolinian John Kinyoun could hardly wait to repay "that Grand old
Quaker abolisionist State for all that she has caused our Confederacy to
suffer."[128] In short, prospects looked encouraging at the end of June 1863,
when the Army of Northern Virginia took the war to Union territory, intent
on breaking northern will and rolling back the wheels of revolution.

Gettysburg casualties. *Courtesy of the National Archives*

Union soldiers on the lawn of Vicksburg Courthouse after the Union capture of Vicksburg, July 1863. *Courtesy of the Old Courthouse Museum, Vicksburg, Mississippi*

Log church built by the Fiftieth New York Engineers, Poplar Grove, Virginia. *Courtesy of the Library of Congress*

CHAPTER 4

"Mine Eyes Have Seen the Glory":
The War and the Hand of God

O N JULY 4, 1863, Lt. Quincy Campbell of the Fifth Iowa had plenty to "feel good over." The "glorious Fourth" was "made doubly *glorious*" by news that just a few miles away in the city of Vicksburg, Mississippi, "the rebel army marched out and stacked arms and then marched back as prisoners of war." The long campaign for the Confederate stronghold on the Mississippi River finally ended in Union victory on one of the most significant days of the year. "The victory is too important to not be followed by important results," Campbell reflected, "but I cannot recognize the fall of Vicksburg as the fall of the Confederacy." Victory would come eventually but not immediately, he expected, because "the chastisements of the Almighty are not yet ended." Two years of war had convinced Campbell that "the Almighty has taken up the cause of the oppressed and . . . will deny us peace until we 'break every yoke' and sweep every vestige of the cursed institution [of slavery] from our land."[1] Victory at Vicksburg on July 4 was no accident, Campbell concluded, but rather the hand of God at work.

By the Civil War's midpoint, the ferocity of its wrath had stripped away romantic visions, forcing soldiers to explain not only why it began, but also why it became the horrible convulsion that it did. The explanations that seemed to fit increasingly had to do with God. Specifically, from the middle of 1863, many troops in both armies saw the war as God's punishment for "our sins," though Northerners and Southerners differed in who they meant by "our" and what they meant by "sins." The prolonged and punishing nature of the war reiterated the Union's evident failure to

---

Chapter title from "The Battle Hymn of the Republic" by Julia Ward Howe, first published in the *Atlantic Monthly,* February 1862.

comply with God's will, and forced many white Union men to confront what Quincy Campbell called "every vestige" of slavery: northern complicity in the sin of slavery through the widespread racial attitudes that enabled the existence of the institution. Black Union soldiers' belief in God's presence in the war bolstered their hopes that a transformed nation would emerge from the struggle, ready to honor the humanity, dignity, and equality of all Americans. Meanwhile, Confederates struggled to cope with military setbacks, incessant suffering, and growing divisiveness, but most remained certain of the superiority of their own society and its institution of slavery, and assumed that God would reward them with victory as soon as individuals made adjustments in their own behavior. As soldiers everywhere listened for the voice of God, what most Confederates heard confirmed preexisting beliefs, and what black Union troops heard gave them courage to stay the course, but what Union troops heard contained the potential to change the war and the nation.

"The salvation of our country and . . . the removal of an enormous sin"

Celebration and reverence reverberated through many Union camps on the Fourth of July, not just Quincy Campbell's. As news traveled downriver from Vicksburg, an Illinois surgeon in Louisiana greeted it with the biblical acclamation, "Glad tideings of Great joy." Together with his regiment, he gave thanks that "our Grand Nations birth day has been doubly consecrated by the fall of the last stronghold of the so called southern Confederacy[,] Vicksburg."[2] As if victory on the Mississippi on the Fourth of July were not providential enough, troops everywhere learned that Lee's seemingly unstoppable army had been defeated at Gettysburg, Pennsylvania, and had begun its retreat south on the very day that Vicksburg fell. In Virginia, Lewis Bissell watched "rockets and fireworks" herald the news that "the rebel army [is] demoralized and retreating toward Richmond."[3] Large pictures of U.S. flags and the words "GETTYSBURG" and "VICKS-BURG" adorned the front page of *The Union Volunteer,* while every column of the camp paper recounted "the glorious events . . . [which] have sent a thrill of joy to every patriotic heart."[4]

The victories could not have come at a better time. Since late 1862, northern confidence had been eclipsed by the clouds of doubt that settled in with the piles of Fredericksburg dead, clustered around the unhealthy swamps of the Mississippi, and thickened in the humiliation of routs like

Chancellorsville. Now twin rays of light, Vicksburg and Gettysburg, sliced through the gloom. From his hospital bed, one soldier hoped that the "star of the republic may again shine brightly, and become more than ever the luminary of freedom."[5] Another volunteer speculated, "the light of Liberty is soon to shine."[6]

The occurrence of the two signal triumphs on Independence Day struck Quincy Campbell and Union troops everywhere as more than coincidence: July 4, 1863, announced divine intervention and reawakened Union soldiers' millennial understanding of the war.[7] Young men who fought in the Civil War had grown up hearing their parents' generation recount the Fourth of July, 1826, when John Adams and Thomas Jefferson, architects and signers of the Declaration of Independence, both died on the fiftieth anniversary of American independence. The nation had regarded the two founders' passings as an act of the Almighty. In 1863 it looked to Union troops as though God had once again used the Fourth to send a message. More than ever, soldiers had reason to believe that "the hand of *God* is in this" struggle, and the hand would not be stilled until the Union complied with God's will.[8]

While the apparent interest of the Almighty gave Union troops reason to hope, it also reminded them of their personal and collective responsibility to make the United States fit for God's blessing. In fact, as strategically significant as the Gettysburg and Vicksburg victories were, the response consisted more of soul-searching and less of jubilation than might be expected. In many ways, Union soldiers were already behaving admirably, at least by their own lights. They made great sacrifices to defend the legacy of the American Revolution as they interpreted it. In fighting for "this glorious Union," Ohioan Sam Evans explained, the men of the rank and file put their lives on the line for "the Constitution and Law . . . grace and God . . . [and] the majestic images of our revolutionary sires."[9] Further, Union soldiers acted selflessly; they risked their lives and their families' happiness not just for their own advancement, but also for the benefit of humanity. The Iowa soldiers who created the camp paper *The Corinth Chanticleer* insisted that upholding "the eternal principles of justice [and] freedom" mattered, because the "grand results" would be "felt all over the world."[10]

Yet despite soldiers' fidelity to the founders, or even their noble (as they saw it) concern for humanity, God allowed the war to continue. As it intensified, many men could not help but conclude that God had sent the war as punishment. The sin that brought the punishment, many decided,

must be the sin of slavery, for which both North and South were responsible, and for which both North and South must pay until the evil that
brought the war was dispelled. God designed the war as "a curse . . . upon
the country for the toleration of that inhuman practice, Human Slavery,"
James Jessee reasoned, and "not till the last slave is freed need we expect
Peace."[11] Another soldier saw God at work in similar ways. "Where our
nation has failed to act in putting the abomination away from them[,] God
has allowed war and carnage to operate."[12] Robert Winn, an English-born
Kentucky Union soldier, decided that "the Americans are a sort of chosen
people, a people who will ultimately lead the nations in their forward
march toward a kind of millenium," but toleration of slavery halted American progress. "This war brought about by the agent of the Slave Power"
must "in the end emancipate the last slave." Until it did, war would continue.[13]

To soldiers who thought abolition constituted repentance, the Emancipation Proclamation should have persuaded God to end the war, but in the
immediate aftermath of the proclamation, the war not only continued, it
got worse. The first half of 1863 brought little but failure and humiliation
to Union arms. Even when the July 4 victories came, they exacted a high
and horrible cost, especially on the bloody Gettysburg battlefield. One
young farm boy simply could not bring himself to discuss Gettysburg,
leading his parents to fear he had been killed until they prevailed upon his
captain for information about their son's death or capture. When ordered
by the captain to write a letter home, the shaken soldier described the "one
vast slaughter pen" that was Gettysburg. He told of how a dead companion
nearly fell on top of him, and admitted that only dumb luck could explain
how he escaped the "carnage unhurt."[14] Cornelia Hancock, a nurse who
tended the wounded at Gettysburg, emerged from the experience unable to
find "words in the English language to express the sufferings" of soldiers.
Death and agony "robbed the battlefield of its glory," she reflected.[15]
God's plan might guarantee a Union victory in the long run, but apparently it also included a vision for the nation that Northerners had not yet
achieved.

Further evidence that Northerners did not comply with God's vision
seemed to abound in the summer of 1863. Just two weeks after Gettysburg
and Vicksburg, New York City erupted in one of the ugliest riots in U.S.
history. Within New York's crowded streets, many whites, especially
immigrants and workers, resented blacks as labor competitors and as the
cause of the war. The $300 commutation clause brought long-simmering

class resentment to a boil. When the draft began on July 11, New York lacked adequate guards and patrols, since the militia units ordinarily present were at Gettysburg. Although the first day of the draft passed quietly, riots engulfed the city for the rest of the week. Mobs composed largely of Irish immigrants began by sacking draft offices, federal property, and Republican Party buildings and symbols, but soon turned their vengeance on black New Yorkers.[16] Rioters tortured and killed African American civilians, destroyed black homes, and burned the Colored Orphan Asylum to the ground. In all, at least 105 people, including 11 black victims, 8 soldiers, 2 policemen, and 74 rioters died.[17] Throughout the summer, other northern cities experienced draft riots. Although none surpassed New York's, most contained similar combinations of class resentment and racial animosity. If riots were not trouble enough for one summer, Clement Vallandigham resurfaced. After being transported to the Confederacy, Vallandigham had fled to Canada, and from there launched his bid to be elected governor of Ohio, running on a platform that combined opposition to the war with racial propaganda. The vicious summer riots and the reappearance of Vallandigham added to soldiers' worries that the North lacked sufficient virtue and righteousness (and possibly good sense) to earn God's favor.

A backlash of anger at the rioters whipped through the Union ranks. If draft riots had taken place the previous winter, when all looked gloomy for the Union, the riots might have damaged morale even further, and the rioters themselves might even have found sympathizers among a small number of soldiers like Phillip Reilly who disapproved of commutation.[18] Timing made a difference. Because they erupted at a time when Northerners felt that God had clearly indicated divine favor for the Union cause (and while many northern mourners grieved for loved ones who had died in that cause), the riots provoked outrage. If Lewis Bissell and his friends had been allowed to go after the riot instigators, the Connecticut soldier claimed, they "would have used canister shot and (as the boys say) made guts fly about the streets."[19] Most soldiers attributed their anger to one (or both) of two reasons. Many saw the riots as little short of treason. A volunteer from upstate New York frankly called rioters "traitors" in cahoots with the Confederacy.[20] Other troops were horrified by rioters' brutal treatment of black men, women, and children. Wisconsin soldier Chauncey Cooke regarded white rioters' violence against African Americans as a humiliation for the entire North.[21] Some troops were angry about both the perceived disloyalty of the rioters and the vicious attacks on black New

Yorkers. One black soldier railed against the "bloody, atrocious assaults on my countrymen," and at the same time deplored rioters' willingness to "subvert the government by popular violence" at a time when "the services of every citizen or denizen of the country are imperatively required to defend it."[22]

A similar tide of anger and resentment at Copperheads in general and Clement Vallandigham in particular also swelled up in the ranks. Legislative changes since 1862 permitted Ohio soldiers to cast their votes in the 1863 gubernatorial contest from the field. In the weeks before the election, an Ohio private called Vallandigham "that hell born pup of Cerberus," and even Chauncey Welton identified Vallandigham as "a traitor and an enimy to this government," who deserved "a seat in the lowest, darkest, & hottest pit of Hell."[23] Private Welton was not notable for his verbal restraint whatever the topic, but even though few soldiers matched him in intensity of language, many used their ballots to deliver a stinging rebuke to Vallandigham, who lost decisively to his opponent, War Democrat John Brough.[24] As results came in, a Virginia-born Ohio sergeant wrote triumphantly that Vallandigham had not carried a single company in his regiment, not even a company of Irish Democrats from Cincinnati.[25] John Inskeep rejoiced that in the Seventeenth Ohio, only one soldier had voted for Vallandigham. Even better, he judged that "this is a fair index of the vote for the whole army."[26] The results in George Cadman's regiment supported Inskeep's claim: 9 votes for Vallandigham and 530 for Brough.[27] When a telegram announced Brough's victory to the Ninety-seventh Ohio cooped up in Chattanooga, it sent "a feeling of gladness throughout the entire army, and three times three cheers are given with a will by the Ohio boys and are caught up by other regiments until the hills ring with the echo of patriot voices."[28] The lopsided returns and soldiers' reactions testified not to the rank and file's rejection of two-party politics or of the Democratic Party, but rather that soldiers regarded the issues of Union and emancipation as national issues that transcended party and were vital to victory.

Angry as Union troops were at the rioters and Vallandigham, many realized that blame for every northern flaw could not be comfortably assigned to two convenient scapegoats. Instead, many soldiers recognized the ugly urban outbursts and the persistence of Copperheadism as humbling evidence that the whole North had some real soul-searching to do before it could meet God's demands. Many soldiers felt sure that destroying slavery was necessary to gain God's favor, but in the summer of 1863, they ran head-on into the recognition that emancipation was not, by itself, enough to appease the Almighty. Many in the rank and file began to consider the possibility that God cared about the how and the why of emancipation, not simply about slavery's destruction. More soldiers started to insist on full, immediate emancipation rather than a gradual approach that might have proven popular before the war, or even in the early days of the conflict. As Kentucky soldier Robert Winn saw it, "the benefits of the gradual system are a good deal like the benefits accruing to the dog who had his tail condemned to be cut off by the 'Humane Surgeon.' . . . only cut off about an inch per day." Similarly, an "inch per day" approach to slavery merely prolonged the nation's misery. Only immediate, total emancipation would cure the malady of civil war.[29]

Even more striking, many Union troops began to reexamine the reasons why they advocated emancipation. From the time of God's perceived intervention at Gettysburg and Vicksburg through the rest of the war, soldiers dwelt increasingly on the explicitly moral necessity of destroying slavery, not merely because of slavery's blighting effects on agriculture, or its potential to disrupt the political system, or even its ability to excite the ambitions of southern elites to the detriment of ordinary farmers and laborers, but because it was so evil that it destroyed the moral health of the nation and angered God.[30] "As sure as God is God and right is right, so sure may we look for the war to end . . . in the accomplishment of its glorious object," the "liberation of this oppressed and down trodden race," prophesied James Jessee. "To doubt this would Be to doubt God." In fact, Jessee claimed, "I would prefer ten years war yet and no more slavery, than Peace tomorrow, with slavery. Such is my abhorance of that Barberous institution."[31] Some soldiers, of course, had railed against the immorality of slavery from the very beginning, but after Gettysburg and Vicksburg more of them did so, and with more urgency. Pvt. Levi Hines condemned slavery as a "curse" which "hung like an incubus to tarnish" the nation's very soul. Slavery was more than a regrettable or inexpedient embarrassment; it was a sign of the Devil. It needed to be purged as a matter of righteousness, not merely expedience.[32] Emancipation, one Illinoisan explained, constituted "the salvation of our country and in a moral point the removal of an enormous sin."[33]

For many soldiers, slavery's violation of women's virtue and its disregard for slave family relationships continued to provide the most dramatic and affecting proof of the need to destroy the immoral institution. Ransom Bedell wrote passionately about the need to eradicate an institution in which "a slave dealer can complacently sell his own children as chattel property," and a master's white children had the right to "*Barter,* whip, buy and sell, and hold in chains" their own siblings.[34] "Public sentiment is so corrupt," Cpl. James Miller claimed, that nobody in a Virginia town "seems to think that there is anything wrong with" a wealthy, well-respected community leader selling his own child. Miller went on to compare what he saw in the South to the book that Union soldiers mentioned more often than any other except the Bible. "Uncle Toms Cabin bad as it was fell far short of portraying the evils of slavery," Miller claimed.[35] Soldiers like Miller had grown up in a culture that idealized female chastity as sacred and romanticized the family as a sentimental unit that should be impervious to the slings and arrows of the outside world. Meeting slave women who had suffered sexual abuse at the hands of their masters and then suffered again as they watched those same masters sell any children who resulted—to serve the interests of the marketplace from which the family ought to provide safe haven—repulsed many soldiers more than anything they had ever witnessed.[36]

The presence of light-skinned slave children also reinforced Union soldiers' growing moral objections to slavery. Since first arriving in the South, many white northern men had found the sight of mixed-race children unsettling for many reasons, including discomfort with the idea of racial mixing and abhorrence at the sexual coercion of slave women. Now many also saw fair-skinned slaves as evidence of "moral contagion," or the ability of vice and depravity to float through society's atmosphere and sicken the virtue of the upright.[37] Slaves who shared light complexions with Union soldiers made the wickedness of slavery seem so contagious that it would eventually infect everyone in the nation, and they shattered soldiers' comfortable notions that skin color quarantined the evils of slavery. Pvt. Chauncey Cooke experienced an epiphany when a fair-skinned slave woman whose children had been fathered and sold by her master told the young Wisconsin boy that her children looked like him, and that she missed them dreadfully because she loved them "just likes you mammy loves you."[38] Startled, Cooke realized that he physically resembled some enslaved human beings who shared with their mother the same emotions that he and his mother experienced, and suddenly the reassuring boundary between slavery and predominantly white northern society disintegrated. If the color line constituted a weak and permeable barrier to the horrors of slavery (as so many soldiers learned), how could a geographic line between slave and free states contain the moral corrosion that threatened the entire American Republic? And how could any nation earn God's favor until it self-consciously rooted out the moral, not simply political or economic, infection?

Purposeful wrestling with moral aspects of slavery led many troops in two new directions: expanded consideration of what should become of slaves after emancipation, and examination of northern complicity in slavery through white Northerners' racial bigotry. Whereas in the early days of the conflict, most troops had been content to press for the destruction of slavery while giving minimal thought to the fates of former slaves, from the summer of 1863 onward, a number of Union soldiers began to realize that genuine emancipation would mean more than releasing bondpeople to fend for themselves. It would "take years to right the wrongs that slavery has produced," New Englander Edward Bartlett recognized.[39] How could four million men, women, and children systematically deprived of resources and education suddenly make their way in a hostile world? As a Kentuckian put it, emancipation unaccompanied by remedial measures was about as effective as "the Pope's Bull against the Comet" in solving the problems created by slavery.[40]

Recognizing that emancipation alone could not cure the ills of slavery did not mean that white Union troops or white Northerners in general suddenly grew willing to make personal sacrifices for racial justice. "I should be glad if the Union people were able and willing to employ and protect the contrabands one and all," explained Pvt. Leigh Webber, "but we have to deal with facts as they *are,* not as we would wish them." The facts did little to encourage. "I *know* full well," he continued, "that the people are *not willing* to do this, and I doubt some whether they are fully able."[41]

Evidence of the racism that Webber identified within his fellow white Northerners continued to surface in the ranks, as it had done throughout the war. New York sergeant John England was sick of the war, the South, and African Americans. Much as he detested the challenge to U.S. authority posed by the New York draft riots, he took sadistic pleasure in reports of violence against black New Yorkers. He hoped the "dose of physical whipping" would "keep the great darkey within the limits of his own proper sphere, and to let him know at least that he is only a negger."[42] In some cases, racism led beyond vicious thoughts to malicious actions. In Bowling Green, a group of Kentucky Union soldiers destroyed an African American church out of sheer spite.[43] Meanwhile, in Louisiana, a white soldier shot a black man and got away with it because, as a disgusted Union soldier admitted, "a negroes life is little more regarded than that of a dog" by some troops.[44] Continued racism did not mean that most white Union enlisted men were willing to let slavery survive. Pvt. William Lewis wanted "slavery put out of the united states of American and not onley but I want to see those who have bin made slaves of put out also."[45] Like many of his comrades in arms, Lewis viewed both slavery and slaves as burdens that he wished the nation could shed.

Yet for the first time, some Union soldiers began to suspect that attitudes like William Lewis's angered God, and were therefore partly responsible for the continuation of the war. Men who had not previously shown any inclination to examine beliefs and practices predicated on white supremacy now took critical looks at their own habits. In a camp paper, a group of Ohio soldiers noticed that the widespread practice of "calling all negroes boys," which it had never occurred to them to question, "sounds rather strangely."[46] Others increasingly recognized that few white Northerners were innocent of racist attitudes and assumptions. When Pvt. Wilbur Fisk heard about the draft riots, he knew that white Northerners could no longer duck their own sinfulness. By harboring "wholly wrong, unnatural and unjustifiable" racial prejudices, northern whites had kept "the souls of the African . . . down," and now they must face up to their "fearful responsibility" before an angry God.[47]

Especially after Gettysburg and Vicksburg, many Union troops began to interpret the duration and severity of the war as necessary atonement for white Northerners' racist attitudes, which had helped make the survival of slavery possible. The only way to repent, a number of soldiers concluded, was to settle for nothing short of what an Ohioan called "the equal freedom of all men in this country *regardless of color*."[48] Joseph Scroggs agreed, and pledged to do his part by fighting "to assist in removing the unreasonable prejudice against the colored race."[49] Stationed in Vicksburg, Illinoisan J. G. Nind felt confident that "the nation will be purified" and "God will accomplish his vast designs," because "prejudice against color is fast going away" among soldiers who interacted daily with "negroes, anxious to . . . show themselves men" and "prove to the white race that they are not such an inferior race as they been represented to be."[50] With less optimism, but with equal conviction, Pvt. Constant Hanks insisted that the war would be wasted if it did not place the nation firmly "on the broad firm base of eaqual right" for black Americans.[51] Few soldiers could have imagined, let alone advocated, fighting for equal rights for black Americans at the beginning of the war. Yet now, hard fighting and the Fourth of July reminder that God held definite expectations for the

United States led otherwise very ordinary white northern men to conclude that fighting for anything less than Hanks's "broad firm base of eaqual right" would betray soldiers' sacrifices, impoverish the Union cause, and disappoint God.

Important as Gettysburg and Vicksburg were in inspiring white troops to consider northern complicity in the sin of slavery, the performances of black Union troops proved equally central in forcing white soldiers to confront their own racial attitudes. Some white troops remained opposed to black enlistment. William Lewis, who wanted both slavery and slaves to go away, also wished all talk of African American troops would cease. "For the sake of our Children Do not Enlist them in the survis of the United States," he pleaded, because soldiering would "enable them to Come up and Clame the wright of citizenship."[52] Others accepted black soldiers as long as enlistment did not bring social equality. Ohio private Arthur Van Horn was all for the use of black troops, but was disturbed by rumors that black soldiers might receive pay and bounties equal to those of white soldiers.[53] Nevertheless, a "great change" had been "wrought in the public mind," according to a Pennsylvania recruiter who claimed that black enlistment was "the most popular war measure that the administration adopted," rather than the inconceivable pipe dream of radical abolitionists that it had seemed in 1861.[54] For Henry Fike, who was anything but a radical abolitionist, contact with black troops in Tennessee brought increased, if imperfect, respect for African Americans serving the Union. Fike referred to slaves and black noncombatants as "niggers," but he always called soldiers "negroes," "soldiers of color," or "citizens of African descent."[55] Similar changes occurred in other theaters of the war. In South Carolina, a black sergeant admitted that his regiment had "suffered a great deal" early in its tour of duty, when it was "liable to be insulted by any of the white soldiers," but within months he found white troops treating blacks "as men and soldiers, fighting for the same common cause."[56]

Above all, black soldiers' obvious bravery and effectiveness in battle made an impression on white troops at every level of the Army from top to bottom. In his official report following the Battle of Honey Springs, Maj. Gen. James Blunt praised the "coolness and bravery" of black soldiers, which he had "never seen surpassed."[57] Similarly, the reports of Gen. Edward Wild and Col. A. G. Draper praised the "courage and determination" of black troops in the face of deadly guerrilla warfare in North Carolina.[58] Similar impressions reverberated through the ranks. Every time

African Americans came under fire, "the black man has shown . . . that he is worthy" of the title of United States soldier, argued the Rhode Islanders who created *The Port Hudson Freemen*.[59] After a former private in an Illinois regiment became a company officer in a regiment of black Louisiana soldiers, he and his men withstood an attack at Milliken's Bend on the Mississippi River in which only one enlisted man in the whole regiment emerged unharmed. After the battle, the Illinoisan warned his aunt, "I never more wish to hear the expression, 'the niggers won't fight.' Come with me 100 yards from where I sit, and I can show you the wounds that cover the bodies of 16 as brave, loyal and patriotic soldiers as ever drew bead on a Rebel." The fight had been worse than Shiloh, he continued, yet "not one of them offered to leave his place until ordered to fall back. . . . They fought and died defending the cause that we revere."[60]

Black soldiers' bravery at places like Milliken's Bend and Fort Wagner in South Carolina, along with their skill in the day-to-day aspects of soldiering, persuaded some white troops that justice demanded equal treatment for black Americans within the republic they were helping to save.[61] Charles Berry admitted that the Army had adopted black enlistment to fight the war, not out of racial enlightenment. Yet regardless of initial white reluctance, the performance of black soldiers argued for changes in more than just tactics and logistics. The military aptitude of black troops admitted "no doubt now about the efficiency of this new material for fighting purposes," Berry argued. "Mentally," black slaves might be "children," Berry allowed as a bow to the dominant racial prejudice of his readers, but once former slaves became Union soldiers, they achieved "manhood." They learned complicated tactics quickly and drilled with determination. Black regiments in existence for only a matter of months already displayed the "precision of veteran corps." In short, black soldiers had shown themselves to be "equal, on an average," to "the Caucasian race."[62] A just nation could do no less than recognize that equality.

Not every white Union soldier experienced a racial epiphany, but the willingness of a growing number of men who had evinced no interest in racial justice before the war to reexamine their own attitudes, to treat at least fellow soldiers as equals in a shared cause, and to champion increased rights for black Americans marked a fundamental shift in the history of the nation. In July 1863, the Forty-second Massachusetts regimental band provided the music for the funeral procession of André Cailloux, a black soldier killed in the Port Hudson campaign. The white regimental band members took their place as equals in a procession that included black soldiers, members of Cailloux's family, and representatives of New Orleans black voluntary societies.[63] The prospect of white men taking part in a ceremony honoring a black man as an equal compatriot in the cause they also served could hardly have been imagined before the war. Similarly, calls for racial equality would have been so revolutionary before the war that only a tiny number of radical abolitionists would have endorsed them. More than two years of grueling warfare, which many in the rank and file attributed to the work of a just but angry God, changed the minds of otherwise very ordinary white northern men. The events of the summer of 1863 urged many white members of the Union Army to look critically at themselves and their own society, and to act on the impression that they had not yet pleased God by calling for an expansion in the reach of founding ideals like equality beyond the racial limits that had once seemed fixed and intractable. In short, the uneasy belief that Northerners had not yet lived up to God's expectations led growing numbers of white men in the Union ranks to envision a nation few could have imagined in 1861.

"For equal rights with the rest of mankind"

Black Union troops saw God's hand at work in the war even more clearly than white soldiers did. One black orderly sergeant wrote from South Carolina that the war was "a medium through which God is helping us."[64] In fact, some black soldiers expressed outright gratitude to God for sending the war. "We thank God for it," one African American in Tennessee wrote, while another, miles away in South Carolina, echoed with a simple "thank God."[65] Specifically, black troops believed that God would use the war and their participation in it to achieve four main goals: the salvation of the Union and the realization of the legacy of the American Revolution, the destruction of slavery, the attainment of equal rights and justice for black Americans, and the establishment of what black soldiers called the "manhood of the race," by which they meant recognition of both the masculinity of black adult males and the full humanity of all African Americans.

The belief that God was using the war to achieve divine purposes caused black soldiers less anxiety than the same recognition brought to their white counterparts. White Union men struggled to face their own complicity in the wrongs of American slavery and racial prejudice, but black Union men who had suffered rather than inflicted those wrongs could see the war less as punishment than as reason for hope. As a member of the Massachusetts Fifty-fourth put it, the Almighty "cannot take sides with the oppressor," and since black Americans qualified as oppressed more than oppressors, they had nothing to fear from the war's outcome.[66] Because the "God of battles who knows the justice of our cause" was at work in the war, Cpl. Henry Harmon of the Third U.S. Colored Troops could feel assured that the war meant blessings rather than penance for "our brothers in bondage, and the prospects of our race in general."[67]

Much as white soldiers argued that the Union must survive to show the world that a government based on ideals like liberty and equality could work, many black troops insisted that the purpose of the Union and its army was to "carry out this bold idea . . . *Liberty*."[68] It might seem ironic, admitted Cpl. James Gooding, that black men's "blood is now being spilled to maintain" a nation that had "ground them to dust" for all the years of its existence, but the irony did not stop "Decendants of Africs Clime" from "dye[ing] the ground with blood, in defense of Union, and Democracy."[69] An African American man who enlisted as a soldier and then worked as a recruiter in Tennessee knew from experience that former slaves and free blacks "entered the field for 'Liberty,' and are holding the starry emblem, dear to our hearts as a precious jewel, never to trail in the dust." Like white Union soldiers, black soldiers defined liberty as an intangible and broadly applicable ideal, not a privilege or possession restricted to a few. It had little to do with the personal fortunes or material aspirations that Confederate troops saw as central to liberty. Instead, liberty was the "spirit" that made the "occupant" of "the palace or the hovel . . . happy" regardless of all else.[70]

Black troops, especially northern free blacks, also associated liberty with the American Revolution. As Henry Harmon explained, blacks fought to "preserve that glorious Union which our fore fathers had preserved for us," and which guaranteed "our country's rights; our rights, [and] our people's rights."[71] Yet Harmon and black troops did more than defend the memory of 1776 as whites interpreted it; they also sought to make the American Revolution live up to its promises. When men like Sgt. Isaiah Welch evoked the Revolution with the slogan "Give me liberty or give me death," they insisted that African Americans be included within the Revolution's legacy.[72] In arguing for abolition, antebellum northern black leaders had developed the rhetorical technique of appealing to the memory of the Revolution and challenging white Americans to live up to its ideals.[73] Numerous northern black soldiers adopted that device during the war. One member of the Fifty-fourth Massachusetts wrote a poem entitled "Dedicated to the Mass 54th Vols" in which he claimed:

> At last at last each bright star
> On this beautiful field of blue
> Cover this proud nation shining afar
> Burns to the greatest promise true[74]

For him, the war offered the United States a chance to realize the Revolution's full potential.

Many black soldiers also took their interpretations of the war a step further than white soldiers where slavery was concerned. Many white troops insisted that salvation of the Union demanded the destruction of slavery, but black soldiers regarded abolition with even more urgency. When Aaron Mitchell and two other enslaved men from Missouri ran away from their owners to enlist in the Union Army, one of the men was shot and killed while the other two were beaten.[75] To enlistees who ran such dramatic risks in order to volunteer, slavery was no mere abstraction. As a regiment of black Union troops from Virginia sailed down the Mississippi River toward New Orleans, "thousands [of former slaves] who have been made free by the President's Proclamation [came] from all parts of the cotton and sugar fields to the river banks . . . cheering us loudly," Sgt. James Taylor reported. Watching the former slaves and responding to their greetings, Taylor and his fellow black troops did not see policy problems. Instead, they saw peers recently released from the same bonds that had enchained themselves or their loved ones.[76] The end of slavery meant more than the solution to an intellectual contradiction to Sgt. Richard White. It meant that when people who looked like him worked, they would "see the fruits of their labor," and parents who looked like him could realistically envision a day when "no mother weeps for her babe forever doomed to slavery's hell."[77]

Even more emphatically than their white counterparts, many black soldiers insisted that slavery must be destroyed not just out of convenience, but because the evils of slavery soiled the republic and offended God. "Man has bought and sold, beaten, killed, and enslaved his fellow man," reflected one soldier. These sins of slavery had poisoned the nation, making it easy prey for the cancer of war, which consumed the "Republic from centre to circumference," and "carried suffering, want, devastation, death and ruin throughout a once peaceful, prosperous, and happy country."[78]

The litany of "suffering, want, devastation, death and ruin" sounded like a series of plagues, and the resemblance was no accident. Both free northern blacks and many southern slaves had long used the biblical story of Exodus to make sense of the experiences of slavery and racial oppression. The Israelites had suffered in Egyptian bondage, just as African Americans suffered in slavery.[79] The war as God's way of freeing slaves fit naturally into the Exodus narrative. At the same time, the conflict gave the Union a choice between joining the liberation or acting the part of Pharaoh and risking God's wrath. A member of the Fifty-fourth Massachusetts cast President Lincoln as Moses: with the Emancipation Proclamation he "lifted his hands up" just as Moses "raised up his hand" to lead the Israelites to Canaan.[80] Other black troops warned that the Union could not escape the fate of Pharaoh and the Egyptians as long as it cooperated in oppression. By turning a blind eye to the plight of black Americans, the free North was guilty of "forgetting" God, which was why "defeat followed defeat," and nothing would change until the Union purged itself of the evils of slavery.[81]

By serving as soldiers, black men could help dispel one of the most pernicious of those evils, racial inequality. If some white Union soldiers hesitated to link black enlistment and black equality, black troops celebrated that very connection. Joseph Williams fought "for equal rights with the rest of mankind." Just as God sustained "Joshua, when he commanded the sun to stand still until Joshua had won the victory," so too would the Almighty stand with black men in their struggle for equality.[82] In fact, in 1863 black troops could celebrate clear steps in the direction of equal citizenship, ranging from the outlawing of segregation on public streetcars in Washington, D.C., to the holding of a black suffrage convention in Kansas.[83]

Meanwhile, as military governor George Shepley and Maj. Gen. Nathaniel Banks oversaw steps toward the establishment of a unionist state government in Louisiana, African Americans had reason to hope that a former slave state would enfranchise at least some of its black residents. In November 1863, free men of color petitioned Governor Shepley for black suffrage, while an interracial political rally in New Orleans debated the prospect of extending voting rights to black Louisianans.[84] The following month, hopes for equal citizenship in Louisiana received a boost when President Lincoln issued a Proclamation of Amnesty and Reconstruction, designed to bring Louisiana back into the Union as soon as 10 percent of the number of citizens who had voted in the 1860 election proved willing to swear allegiance to the United States. While Lincoln intended the proclamation chiefly as a war measure designed to heighten internal Confederate dissent and hasten the downfall of the Confederacy, advocates of equal rights saw it as an opportunity.[85] On December 15, a unionist group called the Friends of Freedom held an integrated convention that addressed a wide range of concerns, from the progress of antislavery sentiment in Kentucky to suffrage for free blacks and black soldiers. At the convention, state attorney general and meeting chair Thomas Durant praised the gathering as "the first deliberative body in Louisiana that will have proclaimed the freedom of all men. No matter with how dark a hue their skins may be embrowned, beneath the surface there is the soul of a man, and therein we recognize the great principle of equality and fraternity."[86] In light of such developments, it was no wonder that black soldiers such as artilleryman Richard Black could expect serving as "a U.S. soldier, without regard to color," to "vindicate the cause of freedom and equality."[87]

Black soldiers also articulated another, distinctive, goal: the "manhood of the race." While Confederates identified slavery as necessary to their own identities as white adult males, African Americans knew that slavery robbed black men of many of the nineteenth century's hallmarks of manhood, including independence, courage, the right to bear arms, moral agency, liberty of conscience, and the ability to protect and care for one's family. Fighting in the Civil War offered African Americans the opportunity to display those very attributes and reclaim their identities as black men in direct defiance of proslavery ideology's insistence that blacks were children or savages rather than real men.[88]

For one thing, the very act of fighting required black men to bear arms and display courage. Although initially relegated to laboring rather than fighting duties, black soldiers succeeded in procuring combat assignments in the summer of 1863. While operating the artillery gun known as the Swamp Angel in Charleston Harbor, one black farmer from Pennsylvania explained that he "saw men fall around me like hail stones," but that he and his company "stood fast," even as "the enemy fired shell and grape into us like hot cakes."[89] In verse, a black Louisianan memorialized the experience of combat at Port Hudson, in which black soldiers advanced "through ravines of fire . . . to batteries belching forth a hell." Black soldiers' bold charges into "the cannon's mouth" carried the day, and the ground "strewn with hundreds slain" provided eloquent testimony to the men's bravery. The flowing blood of black "martyr-heroes" not only "unlocked" the Mississippi River, it created a national wellspring from which "Freedom [will] arise and bloom," refreshed by black soldiers' courage, the poet-soldier concluded.[90]

Violence for its own sake might dispel misapprehensions about excessive timidity among black men, but it would do nothing to lay claim to other attributes of manhood, such as liberty of conscience and moral agency, or the ability of adult males to make their own moral choices and act with conscious rectitude in the service of worthy causes. As a volunteer in the Fifty-fifth Massachusetts put it, volunteering "made us men when we enlisted," not simply because the Army put guns in black men's hands, but also because the war gave black soldiers an opportunity to choose to defend noble principles.[91] Black soldiers who fought the Confederacy deliberately chose to help the Union "become triumphant over slavery." In helping to lay "the foundation of our liberty," a black volunteer reasoned, African American men displayed "liberty of soul," which constituted one sure way to "sho forth our manhood."[92] Newly recruited Robert Fitzgerald was eager "to go to the front" to "prove our Love of Liberty," which in turn would prove "that we be men."[93]

Many black Union troops saw serving in the Army as a way to reclaim their standing as husbands and fathers, a characteristic of manhood that had been stripped away by slavery. When a black soldier named Pete scouted with his regiment in Tennessee, he also used the opportunity to liberate his wife from a plantation near Memphis.[94] Former Missouri slave Pvt. Spotswood Rice established his manhood through wartime service when he wrote to Miss Kitty, the owner of his two daughters, announcing his intention to free his daughters forcibly as soon as his regiment came through her neighborhood. Insisting that his children were "a God given rite of my own," and that the Union stood on the side of his rights, Rice warned Miss Kitty that she would "burn in hell" if she prevented a man and father from caring for his own flesh and blood.[95]

The institution of slavery denied the full humanity of all African Americans, not just adult males; sometimes when black soldiers talked about the "manhood of the race," they meant the full humanity of all black Americans. Black soldiers, in other words, saw the war as a way for African Americans as a whole to "attain greatness as a type in the human family," as one black soldier noted.[96] By fighting against slavery, black soldiers not only rescued fellow members of their race from the curse of bondage, but they also sought to free all blacks from the risks, legal discrimination, and stigma of inferiority that the existence of slavery applied to all black Americans. Daniel Walker described fighting courageously as the best way to bring about "the elevation of a downtrodden and oppressed race."[97] Similarly, Isaiah Welch felt certain that because black soldiers "labored faithfully amid prejudice and oppression," and because they helped "to fight the battles of their noble country," the "onward move of my race" must be inevitable. Black Americans were sure to be acknowledged as "a nation worthy of the applause of others" after black soldiers served so well in war, Welch concluded.[98] As long as racial slavery persisted, white Americans could regard blacks as childlike, dependent, or otherwise less than full citizens or true men. Soldiering to end slavery could help destroy such assumptions. Furthermore, as long as slavery existed, even free northern blacks faced the danger of kidnapping and sale into bondage, and institutionalized discrimination in northern law remained nearly impossible to combat.[99] By battling against the institution that kept southern blacks in bondage, black soldiers hoped to smash the chains of prejudice and inhumanity that bound all members of the race.

"God is with us & will carry us through safe if we will only prove ourselves worthy"

Confederates experienced the Fourth of July, 1863, much differently from Union troops. Late June had taken on something of a holiday atmosphere for members of the Army of Northern Virginia as they marched into Pennsylvania, where farms and gardens were ripe for the picking. In addition to being able to supplement their rations in ways that depletion in Virginia had long since made impossible, many Confederates took advantage of the opportunity to capture black men and women.[100] One corporal, for instance, reported that a friend had found several runaways and sent them, along with luckless free blacks, into bondage in Virginia.[101] Virginian Isaac Reynolds had also been enjoying the summer jaunt into Pennsylvania, capturing "horses and cattle by the hundreds" and plucking "anything we wanted in the eating line" from the "Dutch" farms that lined the army's route, until Gettysburg's "great slaughter" abruptly changed the mood.[102] As news of the defeat spread, morale soured. Soldiers traveling by train from Lynchburg, Virginia, to Richmond were already in a foul humor thanks to reorganization among companies and the reshuffling of officers. News of Gettysburg compounded their dissatisfaction, and they gratuitously shot at hogs and cattle through open train windows. Every crossroads where they stopped to stretch their legs had its "Fruit Trees & Gardens demolished, [and its] chickens killed," according to one private.[103] Meanwhile, in Vicksburg, "Many Soldiers" sent a letter to Confederate General John Pemberton stipulating, "if you can't feed us, you had better surrender." The alternatives, the starving troops warned, were "desertion" or "mutiny."[104] As his regiment quit Vicksburg, a Georgian confessed that the army was "whipt," and that he "never did wan to leave eny plase half as bad in My life."[105] Another weary soldier decided, "the backbone of our confederacy is broke."[106] As the ensuing two years of additional warfare make clear, July 1863 did not really mark the downfall of the Confederacy, but the mood after Gettysburg and Vicksburg contrasted starkly with the mood the previous spring. Demoralization was not permanent, in other words, but it was serious.[107]

In addition to battlefield setbacks, mitigated only temporarily by a dramatic but short-lived victory at Chickamauga on the border of Georgia and Tennessee, hardship, divisiveness, and conflict among Confederates continued to escalate in 1863. In 1861, President Jefferson Davis had confidently assured listeners that the Confederacy would "have nothing to fear at home, because at home we shall have homogeneity," but such assurances sounded hollow to many soldiers and civilians by 1863, when, as one army surgeon put it, Confederates did not seem "united enough to strike the decisive blows.[108] James Zimmerman, a nonslaveholding farmer born in Georgia who lived in North Carolina before enlisting in the Army of Northern Virginia in July 1862, articulated several concerns shared by many of his fellow enlisted men in 1863. Soldiers worried about letters they received from home telling, as Private Zimmerman put it, of "children . . . crying for bread and . . . not a mouthfull to give them."[109] Far from feeling that the nation was pulling together to weather difficulties, soldiers resented what John Kinyoun called "those *vultures* that have stayed at home and *preyed* on the hearts blood of the best men of the land while communities are shrouded in sackcloth and in ashes."[110] Other troops noted with distaste that the very men who had done the most to bring about the war seemed to do the least to bear its burdens. In Tennessee, Florida sergeant Archie Livingston wished "that men who were so anxious to see rebellion would do as near their duty as the patriot." Rattling off a list of local elite who had breathed fire at the time of the Florida secession convention, Livingston wanted to know why those same men seemed so reluctant to risk their lives and fortunes now that the Confederacy that they had so urgently called for needed them. The ranks, he claimed, consisted instead of "men who acted no conspicuous part in bringing on the troubles."[111] The rancor is easy to understand in the second half of 1863, when suffering mounted everywhere, the war in the West looked grim for Confederates, and not even the trusty Virginia theater could offer white Southerners much reason to celebrate; it did not amount to a desire to return to the Union, but it taxed the Confederate cause and the men who fought for it nonetheless.

Many Confederates (in and out of uniform) continued to blame government authorities for the war's woes, and sometimes even found ways to resist measures designed to prosecute the war, but which individual southern whites regarded as illegitimate breaches of authority. As the war's mounting challenges led the Davis administration to exercise more power in its attempt to meet those challenges, some white Southerners feared that Richmond posed as great a threat to their liberties as Washington, D.C. Even staunch Confederates like Macon Bonner worried that "President Davis . . . is ambitious and ambition knows no bounds." Few "men who ever have had full power gave it back to the people," Bonner warned.[112] More Southerners resented threats to their immediate welfare. Impressment caused Thomas Taylor to rail against the "Military Despotism" that allowed Confederate authorities to demand a share of the livestock and produce upon which his family relied. To Taylor, impressment violated the whole point of government, which was to protect rather than plunder people and property. He urged his wife to sell her cows immediately while she could still reap some personal profit, since "it would be useless to try to keep them," only to have them taken away by the "Military authorities."[113] James Zimmerman felt even more bitterness toward "the tax collector and the produce gathere[r]s [who] are pushing for the little mights of garden and trash patches . . . that the poor women have labored hard and made." He gave his wife precise instructions to resist the authorities by telling them, "you thought your husband was fighting for our rights and you had a notion that you had a right to what little you had luck to make."[114] State leaders also came in for criticism. Georgia soldier Thomas Trammell complained to Governor Joseph Brown that if Georgia "will not protect our helpless families," he was "unwilling to fight longer," and the same was true of "most of the soldiers here from Fannin [County]."[115]

At the same time, the hard edge of class conflict in the Confederacy sharpened, and while it did not become cutting enough to slice the Confederacy into pieces, it did contribute to an increasingly jagged social landscape as soldiers grew angrier with the kind of civilians that James Zimmerman called "rich bigbugs." "[T]oo many poor [are] fighting for the rich," who stayed home "grasping and grabing after what little the poor women have to spair," Zimmerman grumbled.[116] As Marcus Hefner saw things in mid-July, "this is a rich Mans war it is not for the pore," and Hefner was not alone.[117] If there was anyone that John Kinyoun "hate[d] and wish[ed] damned," it was the local men of wealth and influence who avoided military service and stayed home "to see who[se] pocket they may filch in the persons of widows or some little orphaned children."[118] A Texan complained bitterly about the "rising men" at home who "ignobly speculated upon the necessities of the soldier and his family" and allowed soldiers' families "to live like widows and orphans" while they pursued a "position of profit."[119] The extension of conscription to older men along-side the persistence of the exemption for owners or overseers of twenty or more slaves (rather than poor neighborhood men who might equally well have stayed home to provide local race control) continued to aggravate class tensions. Disgusted that poor men up to the age of fifty-five were to be "called out" while affluent men stayed home simply because they owned a sufficient number of slaves, Sgt. John Calton cursed the govern-ment and the war, and advised his brother to take any steps possible to avoid joining the Army. Meanwhile, he did not exert much effort in his regiment's assigned task of rounding up deserters and draft dodgers.[120]

As John Calton's halfhearted performance of his duty shows, alien-ation among Confederate troops could do more than heighten the fre-quency of griping in camp; it could hurt the Confederacy. Alabama private Richard Ledbetter took part in the Confederacy's victory at Chickamauga in September 1863, only to see the gains made there reversed at Lookout Mountain and Missionary Ridge in the weeks that followed. By the end of 1863, Ledbetter went so far as to predict defeat for the Confederacy, not simply because of the setbacks his army suffered, but also because "two thirds of our army" had no heart in the Confederate cause, and it was impossible to "make good contented and fighting soldiers out of a man who is forced to fight contrary to his own belief and against a cause that he wishes to prosper."[121]

Ledbetter's spirits were unusually low compared to most soldiers, and they especially contrasted with morale in Gen. Robert E. Lee's Army of Northern Virginia, where morale stayed higher than anywhere else in the Confederacy. Yet even among Lee's men, troops like James Zimmerman began to condemn the "firebrands" who had started a war for selfish rea-sons.[122] "It is a pity that the Malitia officers and the big fighting men cant be got out to fight as easy as to make speaches," observed Private Zimmerman, as he gave his wife advice about how to hide the family's meager harvest. "How can they think we can fight when they the great leeding fighting men wont?"[123] In some cases, bitterness even led to desertion, just as the Confederate Army desperately needed more, not fewer, men.[124] From the middle of July, one Louisiana soldier began to note new desertions in his diary almost every day.[125] After Gettysburg, William Wagner wished soldiers everywhere would desert down to "the last man" in order to bring the fighting to an end.[126] Some regiments appeared to do their best to comply with Wagner's wishes. According to one member of a regiment stationed nearby, the Fifty-second Georgia simply up and left one night.[127] Neither the Fifty-second Georgia nor the Confederate Army really evaporated overnight, but the confluence of rising home front hardship and bad battlefield luck was enough to "dishearten and drive [even] old Satin mad," as one soldier put it, and numbers in some regiments dwindled as a result.[128]

Popular disaffection also influenced state and local elections, which painted a muddled picture of what kind of nation white Southerners hoped to see emerge from the conflict. Two-thirds of elected freshman members of the Confederate Congress had opposed secession in 1861, and in some states the proportion was even higher. Nearly 40 percent of Confederate congressmen, and almost half of Confederate senators, now opposed the Davis administration.[129] The results rebuked the administration and the war effort by any measure, but they did not translate into a widespread desire to return to the Union, nor did they add up to any kind of consensus. Instead, the results showed that soldiers and other white Southerners did not like the Confederacy they had, but neither did they share a coherent vision of the Confederacy that they wanted in its place. In Georgia, for instance, Governor Joseph Brown, who relentlessly opposed the Davis administration, ran for reelection. Two candidates ran against him. One, Joshua Hill, supported reentry into the Union, while the other, Timothy M. Furlow, remained true to the Richmond administration and had proven himself an ally of capitalists and large slaveholders while alienating workingmen with an antilabor stance in the Georgia state senate. Brown won reelection, but soldiers' votes and reactions showed division and ambivalence more than anything else. For example, because Lofton's Regiment of Georgia Volunteers was stationed in Georgia at the time of the election, its members could vote. In Companies C and K, which voted together, only five soldiers even bothered to cast votes for governor, and they split them almost equally: Brown received two votes, Furlow received two, and

Hill received one. In Companies D and H, Hill did significantly better, garnering many votes and narrowly beating Brown, while leaving Furlow back at the starting gate with a single vote.[130] Georgia lieutenant Josiah Patterson worried that state elections revealed a populace too disjointed to win the war and achieve Confederate independence. "The times call for bold determined men," he observed, not "wishy washy legislation," and he did not believe that the elections answered that call.[131] Overall, the elections of 1863 created state governments and a Confederate legislature full of dissent and often hostile to the Davis administration, but with no agreed-upon alternative to the Confederacy's disappointing path, nor any desire to return to the Union.

In North Carolina, discontent resulted in more than just ambiguous election results; it contributed to a full-blown peace movement led by newspaper editor William Holden in the summer of 1863, which further revealed a divided and uncertain people, but not a people ready to return to the Union. Especially after the defeats at Gettysburg and Vicksburg, Holden determined (and exclaimed in his newspaper, the *Weekly Standard*) that "what the great mass of our people desire is a cessation of hostilities, and negotiations" leading to a "settlement . . . which would leave them in the future in the enjoyment of 'life, liberty, and happiness.' "[132] Since the people were sovereign and they wanted peace, Holden argued, the Confederate government was obligated to negotiate for peace with federal authorities. If the central Confederate government refused, North Carolina should assert its state sovereignty and conduct its own negotiations, which would in turn inspire other states to do likewise, until a settlement could be reached. Sparked by Holden, communities throughout the state held mass meetings where they passed resolutions calling for negotiations to end the war, ideally between Confederate and federal authorities, but through separate state action if necessary.[133] Resolutions passed from the state's eastern tidewater to its western mountains clearly signaled that North Carolinians were not satisfied with the Confederacy as it was, and that they were tired of the depredations of war, but the resolutions did not necessarily imply a wish to go back into the Union.[134] In fact, the published proceedings of a Caldwell County meeting reasoned that overtures toward peace would actually shore up the Confederate war effort, because even if they did not end the war, they would "restore harmony & unite the people" by quieting "dissatisfaction."[135]

Soldiers' reactions to the North Carolina peace movement varied, and revealed a rank and file that matched the home front in its distaste for the

Confederacy coupled with an unwillingness to give up on a Confederacy altogether. Much as Indiana and Illinois troops had felt a special burden imposed by the embarrassment of meetings against the Emancipation Proclamation in their home states, some North Carolinians felt ashamed of the peace movement back home. A few, like Adelphos Burns, believed that if the loyal simply ignored the meetings, the peace movement would not "affect much," but not many shared Private Burns's restraint.[136] George Dewey called anyone "remaining at home and talking about reconstruction" a "Cowardly scoundrel."[137] In September, when a detachment of the Army of Northern Virginia led by Gen. James Longstreet traveled through North Carolina to join the Army of Tennessee in the western theater, a group of soldiers destroyed Holden's press and sent Holden himself fleeing. Such actions horrified some soldiers who worried about military incursions against civil liberties like freedom of the press, but satisfied others who felt that Holden deserved what he got. One soldier was "verry much pleased to hear of the soldiers making a raid upon old Holden's office," but he wished they had "pitched old Holden into the Streets and broke his neck instead of his press."[138] Still other soldiers actually welcomed Holden and his campaign to end the war. At a regimental meeting, Pvt. William Wagner and his fellow North Carolinians discussed the peace meetings and hoped that they would help "stop the war on some fare terms or another." The men then conducted a straw poll in which "the most of the solegers voted for peese" and even took the rare step of expressing "willing[ness] to go back in the union a gain."[139]

In many ways, the tensions of 1863 come as no surprise. Strain was bound to show when the needs of a government like the Confederacy, which white Southerners supported in the belief that it would promote the interests and aspirations of themselves and their families, clashed with the needs and priorities of individual white Southerners. Cavalryman Samuel Cameron wanted the war over "before night" if possible, because hard service was about to kill his prized horse. When the demands of the Confederacy endangered his own possessions (especially his horse), Cameron did not "care a *Copperdam*" about the "so called Confederacy."[140] As conflicts like the one Cameron gave voice to became more and more prominent, they led to specific results, including low morale, political upheaval, and the growth of a formal peace movement.

Yet the pressures and disappointments of the second half of 1863 did not lead to a clamor to rejoin the Union. It would be a mistake to downplay the disunity or the seething distaste with which many soldiers and civilians regarded the Confederacy in the second half of 1863, but it would be equally inaccurate to read the widespread discontent as a willingness to give up on an independent Confederacy or to go back to the United States. In fact, soldiers like Sgt. Edward Brown lambasted the "poor patriotism" of the down-at-the-mouths who declared "they would never fire another gun." "We ought to be more determined and fight the harder," he urged, no matter how discouraging present prospects might seem.[141] Class conflict raged, families suffered, armies faltered, and state and Confederate governments infuriated the public, yet continued belief in the necessity of the war proved stronger than even the fierce combination of reasons for discontent. Understanding the Confederacy in the second half of 1863 requires understanding what forces contributed to that continued belief.

In part, Confederate soldiers' devotion to the material aspirations of themselves and their families, along with the internal logic generated by the war itself, sustained men's convictions of the necessity of the war. A Missouri Confederate who called himself "the lucky owner of a bald-hill in Missouri" worried that federal victory would endanger his personal property rights and allow German immigrants to gain land at his expense. The prospect of "a raw Dutchman who can't speak our language" taking over his land gave the soldier reason enough to stay in the ranks.[142] The worse the war got, the more likely Confederate troops were to describe their enemies with terms like "vandals," "cruel foe," and "brutal horde." "Spoliation and murder committed by Federal soldiers" who turned "stately residences of southern gentlemen" into stables led Robert Bell to declare that Yankee wickedness "exceed[s], if possible, the vandalism of the barbarians."[143] The hatred he and others felt turned into its own variety of war motivation. We have suffered too much, reasoned some soldiers, to give up now. All the sacrifice and loss had to be for something, but to return to the Union with nothing gained would make everything soldiers and their families had endured pointless. As Pvt. John Price succinctly put it, "we have been out in This Thing so long that we don't want to give it up with out we can get what we come out for."[144]

The most powerful motivator remained Confederate troops' certainty that they must fight to prevent the abolition of slavery, the worst of all possible disasters that could befall southern white men and their families. Over and over, soldiers repeated the same refrains about the necessity of fighting for slavery that they had been sounding since the war began. Abolitionist tyrants would "force the yoke of slavery" onto white men and their loved ones if Confederates ever gave up the struggle, one Texas chaplain warned.[145] Similarly, Alabama private Thomas Taylor insisted that his sister recall that if Northerners succeeded in emancipating black slaves, they would "place upon [white Southerners] the chains of slavery."[146] Far from indulging in rhetorical flourish, Taylor genuinely feared that abolition would destroy southern society and his place within it, and, like most of his fellow soldiers, he sincerely believed in the urgency of fighting to avoid such a fate.

As they had done since the war began, Confederates reminded themselves that challenges to slavery undermined the southern social order by defying God and threatening the family. "Contrary to the injunctions of our Savior," Pvt. Ivy Duggan admonished, "servants have been induced to disobey their masters, abuse the family that raised them, take what they wished and run away." Neither families nor property, two of the very foundation stones of society, were safe without slavery.[147] Even the structure of domestic relations, right down to the definition of ideal womanhood, would come undone if anything happened to the South's distinctive domestic institution. As slavery frayed, a southern society that strove to uphold the ideal of the submissive, dependent lady unequipped to take care of herself, and whose hands remained unsoiled by household labor, unraveled along with it. A Louisiana private lamented that the South's image of itself and its women must now center on the figure of a practical, capable manager, skilled in workaday chores like "culinary cience" and less reliant on the control and protection of white men.[148] The change he described marked no change at all in most women's actual experiences, which had always included hard work. Nonetheless, the shift in the way that soldiers idealized the South and the southern women they claimed to defend still mattered, because it testified to forced changes in a whole society's self-definition at the very deepest and most basic levels. Union challenges to slavery amounted to assaults on the absolute rightness of black Americans' prescribed places within the South's social structure; those assaults in turn threatened domestic security and attacked *everybody's* place in society and very identity.[149]

While most Confederate troops remained firm in their commitment to the necessity of slavery, for the first time a small number of nonslaveholders began to question the wisdom of a war to uphold an institution that disproportionately benefited the wealthy. The only Southerners to gain from the war, according to James Zimmerman, were "slave holder[s] or [those who had an] interest in slaves." Since his family owned no slaves, he saw no material advancement to be gained by prolonging the struggle.[150] Zimmerman did not suddenly decide that slavery was morally wrong or that emancipation was a good idea, but he did question the wisdom of fighting for an institution that profited the wealthy and brought no material advantage to his own family. Struggling to survive and worried for her husband's safety, a nonslaveholding Alabama woman named Martha Warrick voiced similar concerns. She urged her husband to avoid fighting any way he could because his death would ruin the family, which "hant got no nigero to fite for."[151] In December 1863, U.S. President Lincoln's "Ten Per Cent Plan" for Reconstruction enticed Alabama Private Richard Ledbetter. "By freeing the negroes we can save our land and other prosperity and go back into the union where we ought to be," Ledbetter theorized.[152]

Zimmerman, Warrick, and Ledbetter resented fighting to protect rich families' property while their own families suffered, but in the end they found themselves in untenable positions. They did not want to free slaves; they were merely tired of making sacrifices so that other people could keep slaves. Yet when it came down to it, neither they nor their fellow Confederates could really envision a South without slavery, and they fell short of proposing any real alternative to continued war. Martha Warrick admitted that former slaves could not simply be freed and then allowed to remain in the South, because they would "sun destero [soon destroy]" the place.[153] Similarly, an Alabama lieutenant worried that a South without slavery would become a "desert waste."[154] Consequently, while the doubts voiced by Zimmerman, Warrick, and Ledbetter contrasted strikingly with the early days of the conflict, when nobody questioned the institution, they did not amount to serious challenges in 1863 because even the discontented could not imagine a South without slavery, and after brief flirtations with the idea of giving up fighting for it, found themselves forced to admit little option but to continue to fight to save the institution.

Doubts about slavery also proved fleeting because in the second half of 1863, Confederates believed they received renewed evidence of Northerners' intent to undermine the southern social structure, white southern men's identities, and safety in the white South. Many reacted with violence. As the number of black Union troops grew, Union authorities stipulated that black Union soldiers captured in the line of duty be exchanged exactly like white soldiers. The demand infuriated Confederate troops, because it equated a white Confederate with a black man. Grant Taylor, a farmer who had never owned a slave, regarded the prospect of equal exchange as unthinkable. When some of his companions were captured at Marietta, Georgia, he expected Confederate authorities to let the prisoners languish in northern prison camps for the duration rather than allow "the Confederates [to] exchange negroes for white men."[155] Alabama soldier Edmund Patterson saw only one acceptable response: the Confederate Army must avoid the possibility of exchange by killing all black soldiers, leaving no African American prisoners of war to be bartered for free white Southerners. "If we lose everything else, let us preserve our honor," he insisted, apparently concluding that implied equality with a black man was more dishonorable than murdering one.[156] After defeating black troops at a fort near Charleston Harbor, a Georgia soldier reported with satisfaction that black prisoners were "literally shot down while on their knees begging for quarters and mercy."[157] Violence against black prisoners of war allowed weary, frustrated Confederate troops to lash out at the literal embodiments of their worst fears, served warning to any local slaves who might consider running away to join Union regiments, and helped reinvigorate soldiers' commitment to the war.

Along with reliable commitment to slavery, Confederates also drew encouragement from a new source in the second half of 1863: religion. Many soldiers had believed in God even before the war began, of course, but their turn to religious reflections increased in the wake of Gettysburg and Vicksburg. While the incessant suffering brought by the war made a resort to religious consolation almost inevitable, the timing in the summer of 1863 resulted mainly from events on the battlefield. The reversal of Confederate fortunes at Gettysburg and Vicksburg had been so startling and sudden that many Confederate soldiers, like their Union counterparts, concluded that God must have played a role. Since the Yankees could not have engineered such a remarkable turnaround, the twin disasters must have been a part of God's plan. Although Gettysburg and Vicksburg were favorable developments for the Union and setbacks for the Confederacy, Confederate troops' convictions about God's role in the war caused them less anxiety than similar realizations brought to Union soldiers. Even after Gettysburg, Thomas Taylor had no doubt that "the tide will turn again in our favor" because "we are in the right & we are bound to prevail as God is true."[158] Meanwhile, a South Carolinian reassured his fiancée, "However dark and gloomy our cause may now appear, I feel assured that the God of Hosts is on our side," which meant that "our struggle must end" in victory as long as we "look to Him for succor."[159] Since God controlled the outcome of the war, all would be well eventually, because God was certain to side with the Confederates.[160]

Yet it was not simply fatalism that led Confederates to feel less anxious than their Union counterparts when contemplating God's role in the war. Much like Union troops, white southern soldiers interpreted the continuation and the intensity of the war (including the losses at Gettysburg and Vicksburg) as God's punishment for "our sins." As a Virginia corporal summed it up, "Man's wickedness is great and our Heavenly Father is determined to punish sin that a nation might be saved."[161] Yet Confederates understood both "our" and "sins" differently from Union troops, and therefore envisioned a different and less radical road back to God's favor than the one imagined by the Union rank and file. Religious reflections forced many Northerners to envision an entirely new and unprecedented United States without its central foundation stone of slavery, and to confront the personal and collective moral implications of recognizing that slavery was a national, not simply sectional, institution for which they must take partial responsibility. No parallel line of reasoning appeared among Confederates like Louisianan Al Pierson, who reflected, "God is with us & will carry us through safe if we will only prove ourselves worthy."[162] Many Union troops thought so too, but they also began to suspect that proving themselves worthy would require them to admit that because they shared the racial attitudes that made slavery possible, both slavery and the war it caused were partly their fault. Confederates thought differently.

Repentance as Confederate soldiers interpreted it in 1863 and beyond had less to do with reorganizing the very foundation of the nation than with individuals modifying their own behavior in ways that neither required nor created fundamental change. As Pvt. John Brightman put it, the beleaguered Confederacy was "cursed by the Supreme Ruler above for miscreant conduct" on the part of individuals, not for deep-seated flaws in its society.[163] The differences in how Union and Confederate troops thought about repentance grew in part from the distinctive impact of the Second Great Awakening on the antebellum South, which encouraged white Southerners to focus on individual salvation more than social or national reform. Much as Confederate troops grounded their interpretations of liberty in the aspirations and well-being of white individuals and their families, they also experienced religion as something primarily concerned with the welfare of individual souls.[164] In fact, white Southerners tended to view most reform movements as heretical, because tampering with social relations that they believed had been ordained by God, such as slavery or the subordination of women to men, amounted to tampering with the will of God.[165] As one Arkansas lieutenant explained, the problem with Northerners was their insistence on "an antislavery Bible and an antislavery God."[166] Confederate troops responded to the events of 1863 by calling for individuals to reform their own daily behavior, but they did not call on white Southerners to examine the very underpinnings of their whole society, as Union soldiers reconsidering their own complicity in the sin of slavery did.

Confederate troops often identified particular sorts of individual wrongdoing that must be corrected before God would favor the Confederacy with victory. Price gouging and predatory lending by "speculators and extortioners," which had infuriated Confederate troops since the first year of the war, had to be stopped. Josiah Patterson despised all "greedy avaricious money makers," and William Stillwell blamed "speculators and extortiorners" whose "grasping behavior" turned the Confederate cause into "a curse and not a blessing."[167] Other soldiers determined that venal habits among the troops accounted for God's displeasure. James Lineberger was troubled because "the men is groing very wicked and thoutless" and seemed to ignore the Ten Commandments.[168] Soldiers courted "the anger & the judgements of an offended God," warned William Davis, through their heedless behavior. Only "our deep & ernist repentanc" for personal weaknesses such as drinking and swearing could soothe God's indignation.[169] Soldiers' tendency to look to individual behavior in need of correction was no short-lived fad, but rather a habit that persisted for the rest of the war. In 1865, Charles Fenton James identified debauchery and frivolity as Confederate transgressions that angered God. "Dancing parties are heard of every where, and the people seem to have lost sight of the fact that a war was going on and given themselves up to pleasure and dissipation," he lectured his sister. Unless Southerners learned "to lay aside present pleasure," they could expect "direst curses upon the nation."[170]

Another way in which Confederate soldiers differed from their Union counterparts in their reflections on the necessity of repentance was that Confederate troops did not include slavery as they contemplated the wrongs for which God demanded atonement. Before the war, some proslavery clergy had counseled white Southerners to curb the abuses that happened within slavery so that the institution lived up to God's civilizing intentions for it. Antebellum movements to spread the Gospel to slaves or to legalize slave marriage grew from such efforts, and during the war itself, a number of clergy or other proslavery spokesmen echoed similar refrains.[171] Yet Confederate soldiers did not share these concerns. They agreed that since God's plan for society included slavery, they ought to fight to preserve it, but for the most part, their religion remained a personal matter, and it did not lead them to question the institution of slavery.[172]

Even as a personal concern, religion *could* have a collective impact (if enough individuals changed their behavior, the Confederacy would eventually benefit), but the focal point remained the individual soul, as a wave of revivals in the winter of 1863–64 made clear. James Lineberger enjoyed the "fine meetins" full of "singing & praying" led by a Methodist preacher.[173] Pvt. Grant Taylor, meanwhile, attended an emotional series of revivals in which "strong men . . . with tears streaming down their cheeks" testified that "they have found the Lord precious to their souls."[174] Soldiers welcomed revivals because they helped individual sinners repent of their sins, and because they provided individuals with comfort and reassurance even when the war looked bleak.[175] John Street decisively located the benefits of revivals in the souls of the believers, not the policy of a nation. After a revival meeting, Private Street spent time with a fellow soldier so "deeply concerned about his soul's salvation" that he was suffering "great mental distress." Street and the anguished soldier regarded the revival as "the providence of God," not because it inspired the reform of the Confederacy, but because it would "aid [the distressed soldier] in finding Christ."[176]

Other soldiers found consolation and renewed personal strength in the face of danger because revivals reminded them that whatever happened to them on earth, God's reward waited for them after death. All around him, soldiers were "getting religion & fitting themselves to die," Edward Brown reported approvingly. Renewed religiosity among the troops could help the cause, he hoped, because "men who are not afraid to die will fight better than those who have dark forebodings of the future." Yet better fighting would be a fortunate side effect, not the driving purpose, of renewed religious enthusiasm. "We are still expecting a fight yet the people seem to care for or dread it far less than ever before," Brown concluded, because revivals reminded them that God's will would be done, and that a better world awaited those who died in God's grace.[177] That better world made the present world seem less important, and encouraged soldiers to look past it rather than try to reform it.

IN SHORT, the distinctive character of white southern religion helped to sustain Confederate soldiers because it admitted no doubts about the rightness of the South's social order, and therefore no doubts about a war to preserve that social order.[178] Whatever twists and turns God's plan took in the meantime, it was bound to end in Confederate victory, many troops assumed, because God was certain to favor the side fighting to preserve a divinely ordained way of structuring society. We are passing through a "fiery ordeal" now, Confederates admitted, but if our faith remains strong and we withstand the test with fortitude, then God will bring us through at a time and in a way that accords with the will of the Almighty.[179] While personal attention to one's individual failings might help hasten the day when God rewarded white Southerners with victory, Confederates certainly need not consider reforming their society or rethinking its basic structures. To do so would tamper with God's will and risk divine wrath. Instead, white Southerners should patiently bear their burdens, trusting that suffering made them worthy, and the rest was a matter of time.

Meanwhile, chastened by the nature and the continuation of the war, many Union troops undertook the very sort of introspection and social reexamination that white Southerners found threatening and heretical. If white Northerners' complicity in the sin of slavery was partly to blame for the war, then repentance for that sin should eventually convince God to bless the Union with victory. While fraught with more anxiety and a heightened sense of obligation compared to white Southerners' religious beliefs, Union soldiers' religious faith also assumed that eventual victory was certain because it was the will of God. Yet despite the assurance of both Union and Confederate soldiers in 1863, the year ahead would remind them all that God worked in mysterious ways.

Confederate troops holding Atlanta, 1864. *Courtesy of the Library of Congress*

Hardship mounted in 1864, especially in the South, as poverty and the movements of both armies drove refugees like these from their homes. Even those who stayed home faced shortages and other difficulties. *Courtesy of the National Archives*

Confederate violence against black Union troops escalated in 1864, as portrayed in this *Harper's Weekly* illustration, "Rebel Atrocities." *Courtesy of the Library of Congress*

CHAPTER 5

"Many Are the Hearts That Are Weary Tonight":
The War in 1864

As 1864 dawned, Charleston Harbor rang with the songs and speeches of black Union Army regiments commemorating the fact that "one year ago a proclamation was issued from the Chief of this land that severed the bonds of thousands of our race and opened a door that had been shut against us for centuries."[1] On Morris Island, Sgt. William Gray had taken great pains to organize his regiment's "first jubilee meeting." Several enlisted men delivered short remarks while others played the drums, but the climax of the day came when Gray himself addressed the gathering. Even as he congratulated black soldiers for the past year's "accumulated testimony of negro patriotism and courage," Gray knew that many of his listeners seethed with resentment over unequal pay and a prohibition against black officers. Still, on this day he asked them to concentrate on the changes that had taken place since the war began, and to remember, "our children will refer with pride to their fathers, who, for the sake of the liberty of the human race, suffered the baptism of fire."[2]

By combining ideas of suffering, pride, and human liberty in a single sentence, Gray's remarks hinted at the paradoxical nature of black Union soldiers' experiences, and the war in general, in 1864. As the conflict took unexpected turns, African American men in the ranks retained hope and fought for continued advances in the face of biting disappointment and emerging dissent. Faced with setbacks, white Union troops held the line on emancipation but backslid on matters of racial equality in the spring

Chapter title from "Tenting Tonight," a song by Walter Kittredge, 1864.

and summer of 1864. Confederate leaders sought to control the political situation at home and influence the upcoming Union presidential election by emphasizing the Lincoln administration's insistence on emancipation as the chief stumbling block to peace. In their letters home, Confederate troops emphasized how necessary they believed the prevention of abolition to be and why they saw it as so crucial. Meanwhile, as the sheer force of the war undermined the very racial distinctions white Southerners thought the Confederacy was supposed to guarantee, Confederate men in the ranks increasingly reacted with desperation and violence. The war in 1864 revealed a vast array of postwar possibilities; it also exposed a broad spectrum of reactions to those possibilities, ranging from enthusiasm to hesitation to violent resistance.

"For liberty—*but not for* equality—*nor* fraternity— *except in the limited sense."*

For much of 1864, a year many Northerners had been sure would bring peace and victory, military affairs ranged from disappointing to disastrous. The spring began auspiciously, when President Lincoln promoted Gen. Ulysses S. Grant, the hero of Vicksburg, to lieutenant general, and brought him east to lead the Army of the Potomac. Grant planned simultaneous campaigns in the East and West, but at first, none of the efforts worked. Instead, telegraph wires that were supposed to proclaim victory began to transmit some of the longest casualty lists of the war. In May and June, the Army of the Potomac lost 50 percent of its fighting forces at places like the Wilderness, Spotsylvania, and Cold Harbor. As the summer advanced, the Army of Northern Virginia entrenched in a long line from Petersburg, Virginia, to the capital at Richmond, consigning the Army of the Potomac to a dispiriting siege. In the West, Union forces under Gen. William T. Sherman had pushed Confederates closer and closer to Atlanta, but the city remained in Confederate hands. The setbacks took their toll, especially in the Army of the Potomac. At Spotsylvania, the normally cheerful Vermont private Wilbur Fisk ran from the battlefield, and afterward admitted that his "patriotism was well nigh used up."[3] Writing from "Cold Harbor and Hell," Pvt. Lewis Bissell reported, "the roar of musketry was terrible but not so awful as the cries of the wounded," which numbered over three hundred casualties in his regiment alone. "If there is ever again any rejoicing in this world," Bissell concluded, it would not happen until the war was over.[4]

To make matters worse, the military downturns happened just as the three-year enlistments of 1861 volunteers were set to expire. Unlike the Confederacy, the Union did not simply extend all enlistments, which meant that soldiers' decisions about reenlisting or going home would be voluntary. To ensure that the ranks would remain full for the spring campaign season, the Army launched its reenlistment drives in the winter of 1863–64, a time when war-weariness and complacent certainty that the war was already won (and therefore would not need men's services any longer) combined to make reenlistment an uphill battle. The U.S. government tried to counter with bounties, alcohol, furloughs, and manipulation of peer pressure and unit pride. Any regiment in which three-quarters of the members reenlisted would be designated a "veteran regiment," while units with lower reenlistment rates would be shuffled together and denied the proud title of "veteran." Illinois sergeant James Jessee noted that even these measures met with only limited success. On the first day of a week-long reenlistment drive, alcohol flowed plentifully, men gave speeches, and soon the regiment lacked a mere sixty-five of its three-quarters goal. The next day, hangovers and doubts descended, and the pace slowed down, leading Jessee to observe that "Lager beere has nearly lost its veteran Power."[5] In the end, the regiment reached its quota, but the effort required showed that eagerness for the fray had waned.[6]

The military downturn, mounting casualty counts, and listless reenlistment drives gave new life to antiwar and anti-emancipation sentiment. No draft riots tore through northern cities as they had the previous summer, but antiwar meetings sprang up throughout the North. Just as the list of Cold Harbor dead and wounded hit northern newspapers in June, Clement Vallandigham returned from Canadian exile to attend a convention condemning this "unnecessary war" and adopting resolutions in favor of an "immediate cessation of hostilities" and a negotiated peace. Twice in the summer of 1864, Presidents Lincoln and Davis used agents to communicate to each other their conditions for peace negotiations, but far from allaying popular dissatisfaction, the failed attempts actually handed antiwar and anti-emancipation Democrats more fodder. While Lincoln's irreducible conditions consisted of both reunion and abolition, his detractors insisted that only the president's stubbornness on emancipation prevented a peaceful settlement, just as President Davis hoped would happen if he kept quiet about a separate Confederate nation as a precondition to settlement.[7] A hardened Kentucky private grumbled, "this is nothing but an abolition war it is for nothing only to free the negros," and if he had his "way at the abolitionist party I would kill every one of them."[8] Forced to downplay emancipation in the 1863 elections, antiwar Democrats looking forward to the 1864 presidential contest now grasped the opportunity to portray the war as a protracted bloodbath carried out by a Republican administration *not* to restore the Union, but simply to destroy slavery. As the outspoken Copperhead newspaper *The Crisis* put it, "Tens of thousands of white men must yet bite the dust to allay the negro mania of the President."[9]

Antiwar and anti-emancipation impulses influenced the Democratic convention, which met in Chicago in August 1864 to select George McClellan as the party's nominee for president in November and to articulate its platform, which soon became known as the Chicago platform.[10] Describing the war as "four years of failure," the platform criticized Republican infringements on civil liberties and condemned emancipation as an unconstitutional trespass on the rights of southern states. It called for an immediate "cessation of hostilities, with a view of an ultimate convention of the States" to negotiate a peace by which the states regained all rights, including slavery, enjoyed before the struggle broke out.[11]

Embittered by the brutality around Richmond or the enervation of the ongoing siege of Atlanta, some troops welcomed the resurgence of the Peace Democrats, especially with the popular Gen. George McClellan heading the party's ticket. Charles Bates still liked McClellan so much that he pledged to vote for his old hero "if it cost me a dollar."[12] Sick of the war, Vermont corporal Peter Abbott felt sure that compromise was out of the question "if oald Abe is elected." McClellan, on the other hand, might bargain with the South and end the fighting, which would achieve Abbott's main goal of going home.[13] Some responded favorably to the anti-emancipation thrust of the Democratic platform. Languishing on the Mississippi River, Pvt. Adin Ballou complained about "the 'nigger' upon whose shoulders I knew the republicans rested their platform . . . and I find I am fighting for him." Compared to "Northern Abolitionists" whose inflexible convictions made "compromise . . . out of the question," Democratic offers to forgo emancipation in favor of peace looked highly attractive to Ballou.[14] Meanwhile, Democrats made even greater gains among civilians.[15]

Yet for most Union troops, even those who considered themselves loyal Democrats, nothing could make a platform that opposed emancipation and the war palatable because the war had established emancipation and Union as national necessities, not legitimate grounds for partisan debate. Despite his family's traditional Democratic identity, E. C. Hubbard insisted, *"Slavery is gone*. Peace propositions to Richmond won't save it," and any person or party incapable of grasping that central point could "think and howl to the contrary" all they liked, the truth remained that "all men who have seen the actual working of the Proclamation" knew "the war could never be ended without [slavery's] destruction."[16] Hubbard did not stop identifying himself as a Democrat, but he did put his partisan identity aside where the issues of war and emancipation were concerned. No stauncher Democrat had joined the Army than Chauncey Welton of Ohio, but when Welton's father asked the young corporal whom he supported for president, Welton was stunned. He could not believe that any "true and loyal man in the North (especially one who had a son in the armey)" would harbor anything other than disgust for an anti-emancipation, antiwar platform that offered "the onely hope that the Rebels now entertain."[17] When news of a deadly scuffle that broke out between local Copperheads and Illinois soldiers home on leave reached Union soldiers encamped in Georgia, Democrat James Connolly reserved all his sympathies for the soldiers, confiding to his wife that "those Illinois copperheads need killing *just a little*."[18] By provoking such hostility, Peace Democrats unwittingly emphasized two points the Union rank and file, including many of its Democratic members, regarded as nonnegotiable even in the grimmest days of 1864: the importance of saving the Union to sustain the whole world's hopes for self-government, and the necessity of emancipation.

Since 1861, countless troops had insisted that they fought to preserve liberty and freedom as universal ideals applicable to all humanity, and to sustain the United States government as a way of proving to a world that desired but doubted its success that an elected republican government could survive. Union soldiers grew less poetic in 1864 (in February, Thomas King described "genuine patriotism" as nothing more glamorous than willingness to put up with cold, mud, and near starvation), but they did not abandon the core of their convictions, or their anger at Confederates for betraying vital principles.[19] In the view of Abraham Irvine, an Irish immigrant in the Army of the Potomac, the war pitted "the defenders of freedom, the champions of Liberty" against "those enemies of humanity, of Liberty, & God, who would tare to attoms . . . the best Government that the world ever new." The United States stood for "the principle of Self-Government" against "despotism & oppression," and anyone who defended it was "a friend to humanity & liberty." Irvine's family lived in Mountnorris, Ireland, unaffected by depredations from Confederate troops. He explained that fighting mattered not to save the lives and property of his loved ones, but because the whole human family, or, as he put it, all "who would be free," stood to benefit from a Union victory. Irvine had little patience for what he saw as suggestions to the contrary, and neither did many of his fellow Union soldiers, black or white, immigrant or native-born, eastern or western. On the whole, they agreed that the world depended on the Union's defeating, not compromising with, any attempt to destroy it.[20] Union troops could retain such an outlook not simply because their families suffered less (even Kansas soldiers whose communities were subject to deadly guerrilla attacks shared similar views), and certainly not because they were naturally more resilient or selfless than Confederates, but rather because their version of patriotism better equipped them to ride out the war's rough spots.

In the main, white Union soldiers regarded emancipation as an equally fixed point by 1864. Insistence on abolition was less true of some border-state soldiers. Kentuckian Benjamin Jones, for example, was "not fore freeing the negros," but he was in the distinct minority.[21] By and large, Union troops had come to consider willingness to barter on the slavery question as a betrayal of the Union cause. "Slavery is the sole cause of the rebellion," insisted Jacob Behm, which made it "the political, civil, moral, and sacred duty of us to meet it." Any "compromise . . . would give but a breathing spell for a renewed struggle."[22] By these lights, the Chicago platform would spell disaster for the Union war effort. Not content with insolently *calling* the war a failure, the Democratic platform appeared willing to *make* it a failure by leaving the root cause in place, ready to sprout back into secession at the first opportunity. As Pvt. Charles Henthorn put it, every soldier who "loves his country and sustains the administration of its laws" must be an "Abolitionist," or he cut the ground right out from under himself.[23]

Soldiers generally gave one of three reasons for their insistence on emancipation. First, Union victory required an end to slavery as a way to weaken the Confederacy, and also because the ideals for which Union troops believed they fought could not coexist with slavery any longer. "Preaching liberty" without "knocking off the band of the oppressed" could never amount to more than empty words, John Moore insisted. Peals of Union victory could only come after "the death knell of slavery."[24] A Vermont lieutenant criticized the Chicago convention for doing "more to prolong the war than almost anything else." Attempts to "patch the matter up with some compromise" on slavery were worse than hopeless; they were "ignoble, base [and] degrading" to the Union war effort.[25] Another Vermonter added that backtracking on slavery was unthinkable because it would displease God. "As well might Jehovah compromise with Satan and give him back part of Heaven" as the Union might advance liberty and please God by compromising on slavery.[26] Finally, the conflict's horrific nature strengthened many soldiers' commitment to emancipation, because no lesser outcome could make the trauma of the war worthwhile. As one soldier put it, only the consolation of a righteous cause could justify the "wondrous price of lives, misery, agony & desolation" exacted by the long and punishing war.[27] Lying in a hospital bed, Ohio private John English received a letter from his anxious wife, who wanted to know what good such a horrible war could possibly achieve. English responded that only with the elimination of slavery would "all our bloodshed and destruction . . . be rewarded by the blessings of liberty, justice and honor."[28] Like so many other men in the ranks, English needed to transform the terror and loss unleashed by the war. The senseless destruction had to be converted to purposeful sacrifice offered for a goal that was large enough to make the carnage worthwhile. Preservation of the Union, though important, was not enough, unless accompanied by the ending of slavery.

Yet even while Union troops refused to retreat on the slavery question or on black enlistment, the ranks began to back away from the radical stances on racial equality that had begun to percolate through camps after the Gettysburg and Vicksburg victories. In contrast to the previous year, when the regimental band from one white New England regiment participated respectfully in a black soldier's funeral procession, now when a black Union regiment cheered a Maine regiment marching by its camp in Louisiana, the white New Englanders refused to return the greetings. "The negros make a neat looking soldier and our Regt has come to the conclusion that they can and ought to fight as well as white folks," one Maine soldier wrote, "but as for cheering them they cant do it."[29] God's apparent July 1863 intervention in the war had pushed many white Union troops to consider more thoughtfully their own obligations to overcome racial prejudice and promote at least some basic rights for black Americans, but new challenges in 1864 undid many of the previous year's advances.

As battlefield news worsened, antiwar Democrats ratcheted up the intensity of racist rhetoric. While anti-emancipation diatribes got nowhere with most Union troops, antiblack themes met with more success among white Union soldiers who grew discouraged by the downturn in Union military fortunes and even more anxious for the war to end. Pamphlets with titles like *Miscegenation, The Theory of the Blending of the Races* and *Miscegenation Indorsed by the Republican Party* were distributed by antiwar Democrats who passed the publications off as genuine Republican campaign literature. The leaflets underscored Copperhead claims that the Lincoln administration was prolonging the war to promote racial mixing and to advance black rights at the expense of whites. The message hit home for many white Union soldiers. Frustrated with the monotonous siege of Atlanta, Kansas private Andrew Harris reacted angrily when he learned of a Kansas state convention on black suffrage. The previous summer, black men's fitness for soldiering had been a main topic in camp; now Harris focused on African Americans' unfitness for suffrage. Here he was, cooped up in the Georgia mud while white men back at home considered devaluing the right to vote by sharing it with people whom Harris now portrayed as inferior. He hoped that every voter who approved the black suffrage measure would "turn to a niger as soon as he casts his vote."[30] Meanwhile, Sgt. Charles Musser and other men in the Twenty-ninth Iowa who were stationed in Arkansas studiously avoided contact with local blacks. Musser had never evinced much enthusiasm for racial equality, but the plight of slaves had at least evoked his limited sympathy in 1863. Now, bored with a war that seemed to be getting nowhere, he emphasized his distaste. "We have nothing to do with him. We don't like the nigger. We wish they were in Guinea," Musser told his father.[31]

The conscious decision to dismantle or at least reduce white Northerners' own racial prejudices that had clearly surfaced among the Union rank and file in 1863 began to resubmerge for a number of reasons. Sometimes troops displayed no commitment to racial progress simply because they had never relinquished their own bigotry in the first place. Illinois sergeant Ondley Andrus resented any hint that Union duties extended to providing for the welfare of black people, whom he disliked. Why should he have to "pick up all the old crippled and helpless nigger women & children & get them off [white Southerners'] hands & on to our own to feed and raise a big howl over," Andrus wanted to know. As far as he was concerned, providing freedpeople with "clothing & vegetable[s] to keep them from having the Scurvy" formed no part of what the Union needed to do to win the war, and certainly no part of how he wanted to spend his own time and energy.[32]

Other soldiers shied away from support for racial advances because they would be difficult to achieve and were unlikely to meet with instant success. In the summer of 1863, when God seemed so clearly on the Union side and all things seemed possible, practical difficulties could be overlooked, but the drearier days one year later made pragmatic matters more difficult to ignore. "The system of Slavery may suffer material change, yet the negro will not be made practically free" without major social changes, Kentuckian Robert Winn predicted. "The possibility of such a result we push off by mere bravado, not by any good reasoning." Winn's resigned tone contrasted with the millennial conviction he had conveyed in 1863 when he boldly called for an immediate (rather than gradual) end to slavery and for measures to remedy slavery's injustices, all of which he portrayed as part of the nation's realization of God's divine plan.[33] Eliminating slavery created a host of new problems for both blacks and whites, Stephen Fleharty realized when he met an elderly African American couple in Tennessee whose plight illustrated the dilemma that many former slaves faced. Approaching their eighties, equipped with no savings and few resources, the man and woman no longer had the youth or energy to try their luck in an unknown world. Still, the old woman's "remarks showed plainly that her mind was imbued with that vague desire which impels these poor creatures to leave their comfortable homes in pursuit of a phantom." Fleharty admired the woman's longing for freedom, but saw tragedy in it as well, fearing that "the negro's dream of liberty will never be realized in this country."[34] New Yorker Morris Chalmers recognized that emancipation might also create new dilemmas that few white Northerners wished to face, especially if freedpeople turned into "the means of throwing the whites out of employment. The Irish population will not stand that," he reasoned.[35]

Sometimes the support that white soldiers had voiced for racial justice and equality faded because whites found it easy and comforting to resent blacks when the war went badly. For example, many white enlisted men in the Army of the Potomac who had not previously fought with African American troops scapegoated black soldiers for the battle of the Crater, a failed attempt to breach Confederate lines around Petersburg by tunneling below them and exploding a mine. Pvt. Alonzo Rich blamed the fiasco and the malicious treatment of white Union prisoners on black volunteers who had participated in the battle. "If it hadn't been for them we should have occupied Petersburg yesterday," he complained. Further, black troops so angered Confederates that the enemy "didn't show white men any mercy at all they even bayoneted & shot our wounded." Rich remained perfectly "willing the niggers should fight," as long as they did so far away from him. After the disaster at the Crater, he vowed, "they never will catch me in a fight with the niggers."[36]

Other white Union soldiers soured on the idea of racial progress out of a mistaken belief that blacks received better treatment than white troops did. "It seames that every bill that is handed in in favor of the privet soldier is put down but any thing that is a benefit to the oficer and negro is past the negro troops is treeted beter than what we ar in every respect and that dont soot me a bit," complained Ohio soldier Arthur Van Horn, though he could provide no specific examples of special treatment.[37] Several white troops at Benton Barracks, Missouri, agreed with Van Horn. When the colonel of a black regiment led his men into the barracks chapel for a prayer service, many white troops stormed out, disgusted that a white man had "marched a whole colm of the wolleyheads into the chaple and seated them when at the same time there was not room hardly for all of the white soldiers." Among the protestors was a white amputee, who sat on the chapel step and refused to budge, despite the insistence of the chaplain "that the niggar was good as he."[38] Chastising white Southerners for their treatment of black slaves was all well and good, but when white Northerners found their own racial privileges, such as preferential seating in the chapel, questioned, especially during a bleak spot in the war, many turned hostile.

Finally, prisoner exchange policy and the personal suffering it brought to many captured white Union soldiers contributed to the notable regression in Union troops' attitudes toward black rights in the spring and summer of 1864. Infested by lice and grown so thin he could make a ring around the widest part of his arm with his thumb and forefinger, Vermont sergeant William Stevens blamed his extended stay in Confederate prisons on black soldiers, because the Lincoln administration had put a stop to prisoner exchanges until Confederate authorities agreed to exchange black Union soldiers on equal terms with white soldiers. Stevens freely admitted that the "*abolition principles*" he harbored before his imprisonment did not stand a chance when he knew "that the only reason our Government has for leaving us in such a condition was a miserable quibble, about the '*exchange*' Negroes." In fact, he announced he "would not willingly endure this again" for the benefit of "every Negro in the Confederacy."[39]

In short, white Union troops remained (for the most part) convinced that ending the war required ending slavery, and even enlisting black soldiers; yet when changes in northern racial attitudes (which had been apparent among the ranks in the summer of 1863) began to seem irrelevant to the Union cause or detrimental to white soldiers' well-being, some abandoned ideals of racial equality and turned away from black rights. Gettysburg- and Vicksburg-inspired calls for white Northerners to erase their own "prejudice against color" so that the "nation will be purified" and "God will accomplish his vast designs" found few echoes in the aftermath of the military setbacks that plagued the Union Army in the spring and summer of 1864.[40] Robert Winn, who in 1863 had seen concrete advances for black Americans as necessary to help the nation fulfill God's plan, now captured the prevailing mood when he observed, "I am for *liberty*—but not for *equality*—nor *fraternity*—except in the limited sense."[41] His remark helps show that change in white soldiers' attitudes toward racial equality could go backward, and it also helps illuminate how a war that soldiers knew was about slavery could glimpse, but fail to achieve, racial justice.

"Reconstruction is not progressing as fast as we would wish"

As black Union troops surveyed the social and political landscape created by the war in 1864, they noted encouraging possibilities for a postwar United States marked by equality and heightened justice, but they also noticed whites' flagging commitment to, or even rejection of, those very possibilities. Meanwhile, disagreement grew among black soldiers themselves over how best to respond to injustice and work for equal rights. Faced with turmoil, black Union soldiers in 1864 clung to gains already made even as they coped with disappointment and dissent, all while continuing to push toward the goals of putting down the rebellion, destroying slavery, and eliminating racial prejudice.

To some extent, black and white Union troops shared a vision of the war: soldiers of both races believed that the Union must be saved for the good of all humanity, and slavery must be crushed in order to save the Union. Despite the fact that there had never been a moment in the existence of the United States when its government had not overseen and sanctioned the enslavement of African Americans, Pvt. Robert Fitzgerald, a descendant of slaves, still believed that the Union must survive "for the wellfare of a good government & to establish a noble principle."[42] *The Black Warrior,* a regimental newspaper written by black artillerists, made the connection between emancipation and preserving the American Republic clear in an article that sounded a lot like Republican campaign literature. In the 1850s, "the tree of slavery had extended her roots, and towering in her deformity, threw her baleful shadow over the whole land, from Maine to Texas." Violence in Kansas proved that "no compromise" would contain slavery or save the Union. Only the destruction of the institution could stem the insurrection that was bound to occur as long as slavery existed.[43]

Like white troops who were beginning to recognize emancipation's limitations, black soldiers also acknowledged that "if every slave in the United States were emancipated at once, they would not be free yet." Yet unlike white soldiers, black soldiers did not see the limits or difficulties as reasons to give up on racial progress. On the contrary, black troops described emancipation as "prepatory . . . for *equality*."[44] Equality meant many different things to individual black soldiers. To some, it involved "the right to vote, and the chance to buy small farms."[45] Others focused on equal treatment before the law, including "legitimate trial[s] under the civil or military law." Dismayed to learn that some black soldiers had been punished by hanging rather than shooting, as would have been the case for whites, a member of the Massachusetts Fifty-fourth did not question that his compatriots should have been punished, but he did "not think a black man should be hung for a crime if a white man is not treated with the same punishment for a like crime."[46] Still other soldiers placed priority on the right to speak out against obvious disparity. When men of the Seventh Corps D'Afrique suspected that their rations were short, two of them lodged a complaint with the commanding general, and the subsequent inquiry revealed negligence in the commissary department. Although the guilty party reportedly deemed it "a *great outrage* for those who had been slaves to complain . . . and talk about their rights," fuller rations resulted, and former slaves demonstrated that regulations could be enlisted to protect them as well as white troops.[47]

For many black soldiers, equality also meant full citizenship within the Union they helped to save. One sergeant explained that he warred against the notion that "we have no rights in the country in which we live."[48] Another soldier agreed that as "heroes and supporters of the Government," black troops had earned the right "to share alike [the] rights and privileges" guaranteed to citizens of the United States.[49] If blacks fought in the names of "Washington, Madison, Jefferson" to "maintain a Republican Government," vowed yet another, then they deserved "Republican privileges," and they ought to be "recognized as citizens."[50]

As black troops everywhere knew, African Americans had real victories to celebrate in 1864. Most obviously, the United States, a country that had built its treasure and might on the backs of slaves and behaved as a slaveholding nation in both its foreign and domestic policies for its entire existence, had fundamentally reversed its course, and now set itself in direct opposition to the institution of chattel bondage. As long as the Union won the war, in the words of one enlisted man, "slavery is dead, its rotten, bloated carcass floats on the dead sea of the past."[51] Whatever its limitations, emancipation's value should not be understated, as he and countless others insisted. Wherever emancipation could be enforced, marriages could no longer be smashed by arbitrary sale, children could no longer be torn from parents to serve the whims or wallets of masters, and owners no longer enjoyed the legal right to beat, disfigure, or sexually exploit human beings whom they owned as chattel property. A Union victory would make that revolutionary state of affairs both permanent and nationwide.

Some African Americans celebrated intangible advances that accompanied the downfall of slavery. On one June day in New Orleans, black soldiers and civilians gathered to celebrate emancipation with music, a parade, speeches, and a review of colored troops, all in Congo Square, a public space described by one participant as "one of the aristocratic parks of New Orleans," formerly reserved for whites. "Only think of it," the same man continued, "colored people marching through the streets of New Orleans on their own holiday with fire-arms." Few could have imagined such a celebration before the war, when rights such as bearing arms or enjoying public facilities like parks were severely restricted for free blacks and forbidden to slaves except with their masters' permission.[52] Another soldier serving in New Orleans noted that he now "walked fearlessly and boldly through the streets of this southern city . . . without being required to take off his cap at every step," and that small victory meant nearly as much as anything that took place on a battlefield.[53] For the first time in history, a Connecticut soldier serving in South Carolina felt, "the time will soon come when every citizen of this great nation without distinction of color shall enjoy" the liberty and equality on which a secure Union must rest, and which "the Almighty has decreed every man should have."[54]

Other soldiers welcomed practical advances. As word of the integration of New York streetcars reached his camp in Florida, one black soldier described the news as "proof that our cause is making progress."[55] When transplanted Northerners and homegrown Louisiana unionists convened to write a new Louisiana state constitution, spirited debate led to breakthroughs that went beyond emancipation to include public education for white and black children, black access to courts, and black enrollment in the militia. The new state constitution even empowered the future state legislature to enact limited black suffrage.[56] Meanwhile, black soldiers like George Delavan and Andrew Johnson seized the opportunity to learn to read and write, skills that they identified as central to the advancement of their race.[57] Elsewhere, a black sergeant remarked, "more than half the men [of the Third U.S. Colored Troops] desire to learn and endeavor to improve their leisure hours" by taking advantage of reading and spelling lessons offered in camps. Like military service, education would place "us on the platform of equality," he confidently predicted.[58]

However justified the public optimism expressed by many black soldiers, in private many could not help but brood over some of the discouraging signs that lurked alongside promising developments. For one thing, soldiering presented unique dangers for African Americans. A disproportionate share of unhealthy fatigue duty, sometimes accompanied by lower-quality rations, contributed to excessive mortality rates among black soldiers. About one of every twelve white Union troops died of disease, while among black Union soldiers the rate approximated one out of five.[59] Meanwhile, the families of northern black troops lived closer to the economic margins than white families did, and therefore suffered economic hardship when a male family member was in the Army rather than at home helping to support the family. The loved ones of southern blacks who enlisted in the Union Army faced even starker dangers in the form of retaliation at the hands of southern whites.[60]

Confederate policy toward black prisoners of war made service especially risky. Few white prisoners in either army enjoyed gentle treatment at the hands of their captors, but by Confederate definition, a black man could not be a soldier; therefore, any black men captured from the Union ranks would be subject to harsher policies, which began taking shape in December 1862. On December 23, President Davis issued a proclamation declaring that captured black Union troops would be treated as runaway slaves. The proclamation applied to black soldiers seized in New Orleans in December 1862, but it set a precedent for the general practice of disqualifying black Union soldiers from wartime prisoner conventions.[61] Davis reiterated the policy in his January 1863 message to Congress, and Congress obligingly enacted a series of orders calling for the sale of black prisoners as slaves, or the trial of black prisoners on charges of insurrection, for which the punishment was death.[62] In practice, any black man captured in a Union uniform knew he faced the likelihood of slavery or death, either as punishment for insurrection or at the hands of Confederate captors who cut through the niceties of policy to murder black captives on the spot. The most famous such incidents included the massacre of black prisoners at Fort Pillow, Tennessee, in April 1864 and at the Crater outside Petersburg, Virginia, at the end of July, but the danger was not confined to a few dramatic episodes. To take just one example of the danger that attended routine duty, Robert Fitzgerald of the Fifth Massachusetts Cavalry wrote of how Confederate soldiers captured a black Union soldier on picket duty and "broke his skull with the butt of their muskets, his brains are scattered over his face and head."[63] Constant danger wore away at black soldiers' morale, especially when black troops doubted the U.S. government would stand up for them. As a black New Yorker warned Secretary of War Stanton, "no soldiers whom the government will not protect can be depended upon."[64] Prisoner of war policy along with other disproportionate risks faced by black soldiers led to growing dissent among northern black civilians about the wisdom of enlisting in the Union Army.[65]

In light of the dangers black Union troops faced from the Confederate enemy, the scorn many of them encountered from white Americans on their own side proved all the more galling. In 1864, prejudice sat like a giant boulder, obstructing the path toward racial justice and causing some black troops to question whether their sacrifices were really worth the effort if the war did nothing more than "serve the comparatively light results of this present state of things."[66] Black troops were not merely impatient for faster changes; they were saddened to see positive advances slip backward. The resurgence of Copperhead Democrats especially dismayed one member of the Massachusetts Fifty-fourth because the whole point of the Copperheads seemed to be "to maintain a line of demarkation between the white and black race, and to deny to the black equal rights and justice as enjoyed by the white."[67] Legal setbacks that spring compounded his gloom. "We cannot ride in the city passenger cars unless they legislate to that effect, we cannot even buy public lands, unless some act or order is promulgated, extending the privilege; we could not be employed upon the public works, unless some provisional law or order was appended to it," he noted.[68] Even the high hopes raised by the Louisiana constitutional convention faded as the new state legislature, composed of southern unionists and northern transplants, rejected even limited black suffrage.[69] As one volunteer summed it up, "prejudice [is] the curse of the North as slavery is the curse of the South."[70] While earlier signs had pointed to the lifting of that curse, progress now seemed to reverse itself.

Inequality in the Army proved an especially bitter pill to black men who had fought determinedly for the right to defend the Union, only to be discriminated against once they joined the ranks. Members of one regiment grew so disillusioned by the treatment they encountered in the Army that one illiterate black soldier dictated a letter to President Lincoln. The men had enlisted "to face thous vile traitors and Rebeles." Yet once encamped in Louisiana, rather than being treated as soldiers, black troops got stuck with unpleasant duties (such as digging in the "stinking" swamps of Louisiana) that whites eschewed, severely diminished rations, and such poor living conditions that they died in droves. The men knew that "the Country is in A hard struggle," and they expected to make sacrifices, but the gap between the treatment of their regiment and nearby, well-fed white units resulted from prejudice, not the exigencies of war. Believing that in times of crisis it was especially important for the Union to live by its ideals of "Justice and Rights," the soldier regretted the willingness of the nation to jettison basic justice and equality in times of difficulty or inconvenience.[71]

Many African American soldiers also objected to the Army's prohibition against black officers. Black men who had initially served as officers in the Louisiana Native Guards resented a questionable ruse used by the Union Army to trick them into surrendering their commissions, while other soldiers objected to the steps taken to prevent them from ever becoming officers in the first place.[72] When a highly qualified black officer candidate, William Dupree, was denied a commission, Sgt. James Trotter mourned the fact that the Union Army intended to "deny a poor oppressed people the means of *liberating themselves*." Even a despot like Napoleon promoted deserving candidates regardless of physical characteristics, which made it all the more "maddening" that in the United States "no such rule is to be adopted because the soldiers are so *blameable as to have their skins dark*."[73] A mass recruiting meeting among Philadelphia's African American community highlighted many blacks' dilemma. At the meeting, black recruits passed a series of resolutions that declared "there could be no neutral ground in this great struggle.... All are alike bound . . . to exert every influence within their reach on the side of liberty and justice." Yet calls to liberty and justice sounded hollow to men "surrounded with heinous prejudice" and forced to listen to the "insulting endorsement of the old dogma of negro inferiority" which barred blacks from earning officers' commissions.[74]

Black soldiers' relationships with their white officers sometimes soured, especially when the war went badly for the Union. Some troops enjoyed mutually respectful relationships with their white leaders, but others were not so fortunate.[75] One private complained that his officers deprived the men of decent food and medical care, and openly claimed, "it would be no difference if all the niggers got killed." Such attitudes contributed to disproportionate death rates among black troops, and also eroded men's confidence in the idea that their country regarded them as equal citizens.[76] John Cajay noticed that hard times often led to deteriorating relations between white officers and their subordinates. In training camp in Rhode Island, officers had scrupulously addressed the troops with the same terms they would use to address white troops, including "boys," "lads," or "men." After exposure to hard duty in the South, officers stooped to insulting phrases like "Come here, d——d nigger, or something worse."[77] The point was not simply that racism faded too slowly to suit black soldiers, but rather that real advances eroded when the going got tough.

No issue better illustrated the gap between black hopes and wartime backsliding than the equal pay issue. White privates received thirteen dollars per month plus clothing and rations. In 1862, Secretary of War Stanton had authorized equal pay and rations for regiments of South Carolina blacks, and in 1863 Governor John Andrew of Massachusetts raised black regiments with the promise of equal pay, but the South Carolina and Massachusetts precedents did not necessarily apply to all black regiments. Recruitment campaigns, especially those aimed at free blacks of the North, often assumed or implied equal pay, but the only law directly addressing black military personnel was the Militia Act of July 17, 1862. The Militia Act enabled the president to receive blacks into service for whatever purpose he found them competent, but did not mention equal pay.[78] A general order issued June 4, 1863, finally set black pay at ten dollars per month, minus three dollars for clothing.[79]

It took time for the reality of unequal pay to filter back into black soldiers' encampments, but once the news sank in, many soldiers in the South Carolina and Massachusetts regiments, who had been promised equal compensation, were stunned and outraged at the cold, hard proof that the U.S. government literally valued them less than white troops.[80] When the

Third South Carolina Volunteers learned of the seven-dollar policy, its members promptly stacked arms, disgusted that "a government that had declared 'freedom to all' as one of the cardinal points of its policy" would exhibit such hypocrisy.[81] Loudon Langley, a black farmer from Hinesburg, Vermont, resented the "injustice" of federal policy. "Let the sin rests where it belongs, on the U.S. government," Langley fumed, for instituting unequal pay measures so "ungodly and cruel," that they nullified any claims to justice.[82]

When the state of Massachusetts offered to make up the difference between white and black federal pay, black men in the Massachusetts ranks objected, explaining that the principle of the American government's commitment to its own ideals, not a few dollars a month, rested at the heart of the issue.[83] A member of the Fifty-fifth Massachusetts thanked the people of the Bay State for their generosity, but urged them to see that no black soldier should renege on "our principle, the one that we came to fight for," which was exactly what would occur as soon as African Americans acquiesced in discrimination.[84] If black soldiers fighting for an American Union dedicated to liberty and equality agreed to fight for a reduced sum, they would admit that the worth of blacks was less than that of whites, which was the very Confederate doctrine responsible for starting the war in the first place. To accept lower pay from the federal government would "acknowledge ourselves the inferiors of our white comrades in arms, and thus by our own actions, destroy the very fabric we originally intended to erect," maintained a member of the Massachusetts Fifty-fifth.[85] Lower pay compromised black soldiers' concerns for the manhood of the black race and the entire Union cause of equality, justice, and republicanism. It also dampened the hopes for racial justice that had seemed so promising just a few months earlier.

The equal pay issue stirred up fury and disappointment among many black troops, but it did not create unanimity. In fact, in contrast to the early harmony that seemed to reign among black troops, the pay question created the first significant dissent in the ranks of black Union soldiers. Some men opposed the focus on monthly wages because they feared creating the public perception that black soldiers only cared about money. Instead, "people of African descent" should present a "union of sentiment" in favor of helping the Union "become triumphant over slavery for the foundation of our liberty."[86] As long as black troops displayed a united front and served well, one black volunteer advised, white Americans would have to "credit" that "truly we have sacrificed much for our country."[87]

Differences of opinion over the equal pay issue were part of a broader pattern of differences emerging among black troops over how best to achieve justice and equality for members of their race. In order to defuse white fears that increased rights for blacks would lead to social upheaval, some black soldiers advocated conciliation. For example, because many whites dreaded the prospect of racial mixing, some black soldiers hastened to reassure white Americans that black Americans who desired "the exercise of our political, free, civil and public rights" did not intend "that the black man's son should marry the white man's daughter."[88] In contrast, other black troops believed that because equality had been so long and brutally denied, it could now only be achieved through violence fierce enough to uproot white Americans' most deeply held attitudes and customs. One black regiment, camped in an area where many in the ranks had formerly been slaves, captured a local slave owner who had once owned Pvt. William Harris as well as several black women currently in the camp. After tying the former owner to a tree, Private Harris and the women took turns flogging the man who had once given them "most unmerciful whipping[s]." To the men of the First U.S. Colored Troops who learned of the incident, such a powerful reversal provided a necessary "mirror," reflecting hard truths back to all whites who "looked upon [African Americans] as an inferior race." It would take force, they suspected, not gentleness, to root out entrenched racist beliefs.[89]

Yet despite strategic differences, black troops agreed that persistent prejudice and, even worse, backsliding in matters of racial justice, mattered because they compromised northern claims to moral authority, and therefore lessened the likelihood that God would reward the Union with victory. Not until the nation had repented of "the enormity of its crimes" of bias and discrimination should it look to "enjoy that peace which the nation has so long lost, and will never again have until made to know that God's image, of whatever hue, is worthy of respect, liberty, and equality."[90] Another soldier warned, "if our merits will not warrant our acknowledgment as men, veterans and soldiers, the hand of God may send forth His destroying angel and slay our enemies," whether those enemies were Confederates or northern whites who perpetuated the crime of racial bias.[91] In short, until the demon of prejudice was as dead as the monster of slavery, Northerners could expect warfare to persist.

By the end of summer 1864, currents of progress and disappointment, vindication and betrayal, agreement and dissension circulated among African American troops, and soldiers like Sgt. Richard White struggled

to come to grips with the storm of emotions. Sadness over the unwillingness of the "government and religion of this country" to treat blacks as
"men and soldiers" mingled with the hope that as long as blacks remained
"true to the cause of justice and liberty," they could expect "better times in
this country." White regretted that "the work of reconstruction is not progressing as fast as we would wish," but he also recognized that emancipation, black enlistment, and the expansion of some black civil rights
constituted enormous, if limited, steps forward, and therefore he remained
hopeful in the face of setbacks.[92] For White and for black soldiers everywhere, the war clearly revealed the power to dash expectations and sow
dissent, even as that very same war continued to create great potential for
a postwar United States vastly different from the nation that had entered
the conflict in 1861.

"Everlasting war in preference to a union with a people who condescend to equalize themselves with the . . . negro"

While 1864 brought battlefield setbacks to the Union, things seemed to
look up for Confederates, at least militarily and politically. Union failures
to take Atlanta or Richmond amounted to successes for the Confederacy.
After turning back yet another federal advance on Atlanta, one soldier
reported, "our Army is in splendid condition," and looked forward to "an
onward march into Tenn. & Ky."[93] By the end of the summer, with the
Army of the Potomac stymied around Petersburg, Virginia, Henry Patrick
told his wife that "our prospects are brightening," because the supposed
"greatest army on the planet" had accomplished nothing in its push for
Richmond other than the loss of "100,000 of their best troops."[94] Confederates also recognized northern Democrats' efforts to outline a platform
and select a candidate for the presidential election of 1864 as reasons for
hope. The Confederacy *could* win the war after all, as long as it could hold
on long enough to convince Union voters in November to choose a new
president willing to negotiate for peace. Camped not far from Richmond,
Pvt. Thomas Kelley was pleased to learn that "the Chicago convention
met yesterday," and "anxiously await[ed] to hear the result of its proceedings," which he felt sure would result in the nomination of a presidential
candidate "greatly to our advantage."[95] Marking time outside Atlanta,
Douglas Cater also welcomed news of the Chicago convention. "My
hopes of peace now rest on a revolution among the people of the North,"

he confided to his cousin Fannie, "or else the election of a peace candidate for the [Union] Presidency."[96]

Yet even with the military success and promising Union political developments, the world seemed to be falling apart for many Confederates. For one thing, the Confederate government, which was supposed to serve white Southerners' needs and aspirations better than the Union government, continued to appear dismissive of the real hardships that the war and the Confederacy imposed on soldiers' loved ones. When Pvt. Peter Cross "stood up to my Country like a man and defended her rights like a soldier," he never dreamed that the authorities would leave his family to starve, but by March 1864 his wife was so desperate that Cross had to ask his parents to plead with the North Carolina state government for money to buy a little salt and grain. As Cross saw it, no white man should have to beg, least of all for basic necessities from a government that should have promoted white families' best interests.[97] To the men of the Forty-sixth Mississippi, the Confederacy seemed willing to sacrifice rather than protect their families' safety. The regiment had been stationed in its own home state, until suddenly it was ordered to Mobile, Alabama, just as Union forces under Gen. William Sherman began campaigning through Mississippi. Filled with "indignation at the entire abandonment of my own state," privates like William Chambers could not help but "distrust" a Confederacy "that gave up their homes to the torch and their families to the tender mercies of the foe."[98]

The Confederacy was also supposed to protect the race and gender hierarchy that white southern men relied on to define their identities as men, but the weight of the war now strained that very social structure. Many Confederate forces complained about not being treated as white men, especially when the Confederate Congress passed a bill dictating mandatory reenlistment for soldiers whose terms of service were due to expire. Required reenlistment inspired several regiments to renew their enlistments early in a show of support for the Confederacy, but other soldiers resented the way that compulsory reenlistment robbed them of control over their own actions, a key attribute of white manhood. As Pvt. Lewis Branscomb explained, since "congress has declared everybody in for the war," the only way to retain influence over the brigade's organization, and to ensure that "we can't be called conscripts" was to sign on before the act of Congress took effect later in February.[99] Daniel Abernethy, in contrast, was an illiterate private so angered by mandatory

reenlistment that he persuaded a messmate to write a letter at his dicta-
tion. Congress or no Congress, Abernethy and others in his regiment
announced that their "time is out this spring," and "the[y] intend to go."
Abernethy claimed he would return to the Union before he would be
forced into the Army without the respect for his own wishes due to him as
a white man.[100]

White civilians further eroded rather than bolstered the proper social
structure when they failed to treat Confederate soldiers as white men. "If a
soldier goes out in the country hear to get something to eat and goes to
some of these big negroes oners he is not so much as asked in the house,
but if they se fit to give you any thing, they will tell you to set down and
they will send it out to you by a Negro," Pvt. John Killian complained,
which especially infuriated him "when I am fiting for their property."
Regardless of wealth, all white men should be treated as equals, and
equals would be invited to eat in the house.[101] Women family members of
white men off fighting the war should also be treated with respect and
decency, but an increasing number of Confederate soldiers learned that the
opposite was true. A Georgia private "shead tears" at the news that local
citizens treated his wife so poorly that she felt as if she lived "like a
neger," and he even threatened to desert the Army and come home to take
care of her if things did not improve.[102] Louis Branscomb grew enraged
when he heard that his neighbor, Mr. Cable, had not punished one of his
slaves when the slave struck Branscomb's sister. The idea that a white
female member of his own family had been touched by a black man and
nobody had done anything about it was almost more than Branscomb
could take. "Just to think that I am off here fighting for my country and
rich peoples property to have a dear sister treated [like] that at home"
made him less inclined to kill Yankees than it did to kill "half the people in
town," including "that negro or Mr. Cable."[103] If the whole point of fighting against the Union was to prevent whites from being put "on an equality with the Negroes," as the rank and file insisted, then Confederate
failures to uphold the racial hierarchy made for serious trouble.[104]

Black Southerners compounded matters. By defying racial boundaries
and treating white Southerners with scorn rather than deference, they provided soldiers with a glimpse of what life might be like without slavery to
enforce the customary social hierarchy. Sometimes African Americans
presumed to the material possessions and status that whites felt should
have been reserved for them. In Charlottesville, Virginia, a Georgia soldier
watched in shock as a group of former slaves insulted their former master

and his family, "took the rings off ladies' fingers[,] slapped their jaws[,] struck them with their sabres" (presumably borrowed from the Yankees or pilfered from southern whites), "and took all their meat[,] corn and horses and acted mean generally." Released from slavery, blacks seemed to enjoy good food, fine things, and the ability to treat whites as whites had treated them.[105] In Norfolk, Virginia, a Confederate soldier under loose Union guard after his capture at the battle of Greentown complained about former slaves who claimed the privilege of mobility, which should have been reserved for whites. "Great crowds of contrabands who had once been carriage drivers for their masters" drove around Norfolk in their masters' vehicles, escorting young black "wenches [who] would scoff and sneer at us as they passed."[106] Most disturbing, black men threatened white men's abilities to protect and control white women. Pvt. John W. Calton shuddered as he listened to a messmate tell a story about a black man who announced plans "too mean for me to repete but in a mild manner to Seduce your Sister." The story confirmed Calton's fears that the war was so destabilizing the world as he knew it, that soon the Yankees would "set [the black man] free, put him on equality with you, [allow him to] et with your Daughter at Church or else whare if she resists it or insults the Black Scoundrel she is arrested by the Same Party & taken to prisen."[107]

Confederates began to meet black Union soldiers in combat more frequently in 1864, which further aggravated white southern men's sense of racial inversion. By bearing arms and mostly holding the same rank (private) held by most of the Confederate Army, black troops literally presumed to equal status with white southern enlisted men. "Damn you, you are fighting against your masters," howled one Confederate as he faced black troops in Tennessee, but mere words could not put things back in their proper order.[108] One young chaplain, Richard Webb, had never seen "any negro troops before," and his first encounter threw him off balance. He was shocked to see "one big buck" of a black Union soldier "walk nearly down to our pickets . . . big as life dressed in his blue cloth" in order to strike up a conversation, without a hint of the deference that Webb expected from African Americans. Worse, that soldier typified black troops, whom he claimed "will jump out and dance and hollow to our men, calling them rebels, saying they are as free as we are."[109] Initially, Texan Charles Trueheart tried to force black troops into the molds carved by his notions of black men's ineligibility for true manhood. Unable to believe that black men had voluntarily chosen to take up arms against the institution of slavery, for which Trueheart assumed God intended them, he claimed that captured black troops "begged that they might be turned back to their masters." By portraying black prisoners as "abjectly submissive" and reporting that they addressed their Confederate captors as "Master," Trueheart tried to drain the image of fighting black soldiers of its credibility and its danger. His efforts did not work for long. Whether he liked it or not, Trueheart had to admit that "some fought with an obstinacy that was really surprising, and held their ground till our fellows came to close quarter and knocked them in the head with muskets, or bayonetted them." Just when Trueheart thought things could get no worse, a black soldier "stood up boldly at a distance of 30 paces, and had a regular duel with the Sergeant Major of our reg't." Duels took place between equals, not between a "highspirited young Southern blood" and a black man, yet the black soldier held his ground, despite being fired at "five or six times," and "plugged the Sgt. in the forehead" before Confederates finally shot him.[110]

Some Confederate troops responded to the topsy-turvy state of things by sticking with the habit of focusing more intently on the needs of their own families than on the good of the whole Confederacy. Even Al Pierson, who remained much more committed to the "wealth, honor & liberties of this Confederacy" than many of his fellow Southerners, recognized that soldiers fought less for a Confederate government, or a set of political principles, or even the idea of a separate Confederacy, than to "protect their homes" from all comers, including other Confederates.[111] Home- and family-centered motivation might prove useful in the short term, but could backfire if the conflict between the demands of families and the Confederacy became too acute, because troops might side with their families and leave the Confederacy to its own devices. A Mississippi soldier illustrated this very danger. Under no circumstances, he directed his sister, should she comply with the authorities' demand that she turn her tanyard over to the government, no matter how badly the Army needed leather goods. Instead, she should save her resources for her own needs.[112] Meanwhile, when President Davis called up the Georgia militia to help defend Atlanta, one of the most important cities and rail hubs in the Confederacy, Pvt. A. T. Holliday refused to go because he lived in a neighborhood with "about 400 negroes minus any one to control them," and he was not willing to risk "the quantity of Negroes above stated turned loose upon our wifes and children for one month." In the face of such an obvious and immediate threat to the loved ones and racial order that a war for the Confederacy was supposed to safeguard, the menace posed by the Union Army at the city limits of Atlanta seemed secondary, and, as Holliday informed Governor Joseph Brown, he had no intention of subordinating his family's safety or racial control for the benefit of the Confederacy, the state of Georgia, or the city of Atlanta.[113]

Amid all the turmoil, President Davis pursued a strategy of trying to influence the northern election by soft-pedaling independence so that emancipation would look like the real impediment to a negotiated settlement. Some advisers feared that the tactic would push nonslaveholding soldiers to desert the Army out of disenchantment with fighting for someone else's slaves while their own families suffered, but the projected explosion in desertions did not occur.[114] Instead, Confederate troops' thoughts and actions in the summer of 1864 highlight how and why prevention of emancipation remained so critical to most of the nonslaveholding Confederate rank and file, even at a time when many felt like the world as they knew it was crumbling away.

Concerns about nonslaveholders who were beginning to question slavery were exaggerated, but not entirely misplaced. A tiny number of Confederate soldiers did begin very cautiously to regard the institution of slavery more critically. Worried that publicly criticizing slavery might lead to trouble for his family at home, Pvt. Noble Brooks confined his doubts to his diary. In the privacy of its pages, Brooks compared the devastation of the war-torn South to Egypt's plagues in the Book of Exodus. As Egyptian "slaveholders and task masters . . . suffered great privation and final overthrow on account of the bondage of the Israelites," so, too, were "the American people suffering all the calamities of war and the scarcity of provisions on account of African slavery."[115] John Killian, a North Carolinian who had gone to California before the war but had come back to fight against the imposition of abolition on his native South, now found himself disenchanted with the very institution that he had returned to defend. "I some times think that this is rong to one a slave for the Bible ses that a man shal eat bred by his swet of his brough," Killian admitted to his sister.[116]

Yet despite their newfound doubts, neither Brooks nor Killian turned against the war or the institution of chattel bondage because neither of them could imagine a South without slavery any more than their fellow soldiers could. Even if slavery was wrong, Killian resisted the prospect of emancipation, because he dreaded the thought of a society in which "we will aul be on an equaliety."[117] Brooks, meanwhile, could not "divine what will be the final issue of all these things" because he could not envision a safe and peaceful way of managing race relations without slavery. If black bondage disappeared, he felt sure that "there will be an awful shaking of the nation."[118] Another private learned to his chagrin just how unwise voicing any doubts about slavery could be. When Edward Brown confided to his wife that he "would not give a hundred dollars for any Negro" while the Confederacy was in such upheaval, Mrs. Brown made the mistake of sharing the letter with a member of Brown's regiment who was home on leave at the time. The soldier returned to camp and broadcast Brown's views, leading the regiment to "condemn" the hapless Brown as "an unsound southern man."[119] In contrast to their northern counterparts, white Southerners always recognized clearly that slavery could not be separated from race, which made any hint of the absence of slavery without definite plans for managing the fate and maintaining the inferior social status of freedpeople a dangerous matter.

Because they could not imagine that the South, their families, or even their own identities as white men could be safe in the absence of slavery, most Confederate troops responded to 1864's preview of a world without a slavery-enforced racial hierarchy not by questioning chattel bondage, but by clinging desperately to it, and to a war to defend it. Alabamian Joseph Stapp worried about the high prices, food shortages, social unrest, and "desolation and ruin" that plagued the Confederacy, but told his mother that white Southerners would have to "bear any hardships" in order to "live independent of old Abe and his negro sympathizers."[120] To a Louisianan, the options were equally stark. His wife wished the Confederacy would surrender, but he could not face the inevitable results of abolition, which would include "all of our property confiscated[,] our liberties taken from us . . . our slaves stationed in every town with guns in their hands to make us do our masters bidding."[121] War-weary as men might be, much of the Confederate rank and file concurred with Al Pierson's desire for "everlasting war in preference to a union with a people who condescend to equalize themselves with the poor, ignorant & only half civilized negro."[122]

In short, by 1864 Confederate troops faced a Confederacy that differed more than ever from their expectations that an independent nation would advance their families' interests and aspirations and uphold a clear social structure based on racial hierarchy, but the Army as a whole continued to fight a punishing war largely because Confederates feared that reunion with the North and abolition would be even worse. The 1864 North Carolina gubernatorial race between incumbent Zebulon Vance and challenger William Holden demonstrates this calculus at work within one state. Neither candidate ran as a friend of the Confederate government. Since his election in 1862, Vance had built his reputation as wartime governor around resisting Richmond. Holden, editor of the North Carolina *Weekly Standard* and leader of the peace movement, ran as an out-and-out peace candidate who proposed ending the war by negotiating with federal authorities, even if North Carolina had to do so separately from the rest of the Confederacy.[123] The campaign boiled down to a contest over what Vance called "the best plan to obtain this consummation so devoutly wished," namely "Peace, blessed peace!"[124]

For a time, Holden posed such a serious challenge to Vance that Holden looked likely to sweep the soldier vote. Encamped in Virginia, Pvt. George Williams depicted Holden as his regiment's choice for governor "by a large majority," while Sgt. Martin Gash predicted that "Holden will get a good shar[e]" of support from North Carolinians in Georgia.[125] Soldiers' reasons for preferring Holden were simple. They were tired of fighting, their families were suffering, and Holden seemed to offer the best chance for ending the conflict that brought so much misery. James Morris, a private who had recently joined the Fifty-seventh North Carolina, personally favored Vance, but feared that the rest of his regiment would go for Holden in a landslide. Morris wrote to tell Vance, "if you wish to be elected govenor you should try to put and end to those depredations that our cavalry has been committing in western North Carolina." Several of Morris's fellow enlisted men were receiving letters from frightened and hungry wives about how Confederate cavalry banged on doors in the middle of the night and rode off with crops, livestock, and whiskey. "It makes them very low spirited to [think] that they are defending the cause of our country and [our] own soldiers are destroying their homes," Morris explained. Unless Vance could convince soldiers that he would do something about families' problems, his electoral prospects looked bleak.[126] Other war-weary troops like Daniel Abernethy had no inclination to support Vance in the first place; after all the "talk of N.C. doing something for pease," Abernethy was tired of "people at home [who] keepe bloing and don't' strike." As governor, Holden looked like someone who might actually do something about ending the fighting, at least for North Carolinians.[127] Adelphos Burns felt sure that "Holden will beat Vance in the Army," because soldiers would rather be "without a Confederacy" than to keep "fighting this war out."[128]

Governor Vance launched his response with an appearance at Wilkesboro, North Carolina, on February 22, 1864, where, accompanied by music from the "Johnny Reb" band, he delivered a speech that he would repeat around the state and to soldiers camped in Virginia all spring and summer. The speech did wonders. In it, Vance assured audiences that he, too, sought an end to the conflict, but most of all he electrified them with his own gritty determination to achieve it *without* bowing to Lincoln and the abolitionists. He began with a joke, and then immediately moved on to acknowledge the hardships facing North Carolinians. "Gallant boys have been slaughtered," he recognized, and women and children "pine for the presence and support of their natural protector." He could understand how some might be tempted to consider reunion with the North: "all are liable to reach out, with the spirit of a drowning man, to grasp any passing straw, which for the moment, may keep their heads above the roaring flood." Yet North Carolinians must resist such temptations for two main reasons. For one thing, it might temporarily look as if the Confederacy was harming rather than advancing families' best interests, but in fact the welfare of the Confederacy was inseparable from that of individual families. "In its destiny are involved the welfare of State, community, home, wife, children, self," Vance argued. Even more important, North Carolinians had better remember that putting their state "into the arms of Lincoln" would destroy the racial order. Good white men from North Carolina would join "the service of Uncle Sam, to fight alongside of his Negro troops in exterminating the white men, women, and children of the South." They would have to "take an oath to support his [Lincoln's] proclamation abolishing slavery, his proclamation inciting the slaves of our State to burn your homes and murder your families!" Meanwhile, black slaves "are all to be turned loose upon us." North Carolina would look like Beaufort, South Carolina, where blacks owned land confiscated from whites. Every "Southern youth" would have to watch meekly while "he saw a Negro officer walking the streets and making his sister give way for him or insulting her." Any white Southerners willing to endure such conditions deserved "the fate of dogs," Vance thundered.[129]

The speech turned things around among North Carolina troops. When Pvt. David Thompson's brother described Vance's speech after the governor visited his brigade, David could hardly wait for "next Tuesday," when Vance was scheduled to speak to his regiment. "I wouldent miss his speech for nothing," Thompson vowed.[130] Some troops remained unmoved by Vance's dramatic performances (Adelphos Burns, for example, remarked, "Governor Vance told us up at Orange to fight until Hell freezes over That's rather longer than I care to fight"), but for the most part, the governor's words about safeguarding the South's racial order hit their mark.[131] Some Confederate prisoners of war were so exhilarated when they read Vance's speech that they formed a committee to draft a letter of praise. The governor was exactly right, the prisoners agreed: reunion would be just the excuse the Republican administration desired "to confiscate the property of our people, both real and person, and to apportion it among their soldiers and freedmen (slaves whom they have liberated)." Worse, "they propose to take the arms from the whites and put them in the hands of the negros, they propose to extend the right of suffrage to the blacks; while among the whites it is to be restricted." In short, "the order of nature would be reversed," and the South would become "one vast ruin," groaning under "a tyranny more revolting than the visage of death."[132] In the field, Vance's spirited platform steeled the resolve of war-weary men like Isaac LeFevers, who admitted that he was "as tired of the War as enny man, but to support Holden I cant." Furthermore, he predicted, "Vance will make a clean sweap in the Armey."[133]

Vance's bid for reelection benefited in April 1864 from the battle of Plymouth, North Carolina, which gave soldiers the opportunity to act on Vance's racially incendiary themes. Located where the Roanoke River met Albemarle Sound, Plymouth was one of the few places in the state to experience occupation. Under Union control since 1862, Plymouth housed a community of escaped slaves who had begun to build new lives and institutions for themselves by 1864. Among the Union troops fortifying Plymouth was a company of locally recruited African American soldiers who served in Wilde's Brigade.[134] On April 17, the town was attacked by North Carolina troops pulled from elsewhere in North Carolina and from Virginia. When the Union General Henry W. Wessells surrendered on the morning of April 20, the Confederate soldiers who captured the town suddenly found themselves presented with the opportunity to lash out at the people whose emancipation they feared and blamed for causing the war. Confederates pillaged Plymouth and unleashed their rage on captured black Union troops like members of the Second U.S. Colored Cavalry. Samuel Johnson, a sergeant in that regiment, survived because he stripped off his Union uniform and passed as a local slave. No "negros found in blue uniform or with any outward marks of a Union soldier" were so lucky, Johnson later testified. Some soldiers were "taken into the woods and hung," while others were robbed of their uniforms, lined up along a riverbank, and shot. Still others "were killed by having their brains beaten out by the butt end of the muskets in the hands of the

Rebels." White officers and some black soldiers were kept alive for one day, only to be humiliated the next when they were dragged through town with ropes around their necks. Then the "remainder of the black soldiers were killed."[135]

The violence at Plymouth was ruthless, but not senseless. Savaging Plymouth gave white Confederate soldiers whose whole world seemed to be spinning out of control the chance to vent their fear and resentment of blacks released from bondage. Former black slaves occupying property that once belonged to white Southerners, in a town where armed black Union soldiers now enforced the law, embodied the threats that Vance's campaign platform insisted the end of slavery would pose. Plymouth not only permitted Confederate troops to strike at the personifications of their racial fears, but it also proved that fighting really could prevent those fears from coming to pass. Newspapers in Virginia and North Carolina promised, "repeat Plymouth a few times and we shall bring the Yankees to their senses."[136]

With help from the battle of Plymouth (and probably from Union military losses in the spring and summer of 1864), Vance's strategy of reminding soldiers how much worse things would be in a South deprived of its customary racial order worked. Just months after Holden's reconstruction platform looked poised for certain victory, Vance handily defeated his opponent with 80 percent of the total vote, including a stunning 87.9 percent of the soldier vote.[137] Even Sgt. Garland Ferguson, initially suspicious of Vance, grew convinced that Holden was "unsound." Ferguson wanted peace, "but I want that peace to be better than war," he told his brother, which was why he was for Vance.[138] Ferguson's companions seemed to agree; on election day seventy-four soldiers in his company voted for Vance, while not one cast a Holden ballot.[139] Vance also swept R. P. Allen's cavalry company, Henry Chambers's infantry regiment, and even several wayside hospitals where North Carolina invalids cast votes for the sitting governor.[140] The decisive results in the Forty-first North Carolina led a gleeful Pvt. Henry Patrick to report, "Holden's stock has gone so far below par that it is impossible to express its present status in figures."[141] When it came down to it, Holden's peace meant surrender and emancipation, and North Carolina soldiers were not yet prepared to confront, let alone concede, either prospect.

Zebulon Vance's successful campaign highlights the importance of racial fear in keeping enlisted Confederates committed to the war effort by 1864, and helps explain why even in times of hardship, men whose chief interests centered on the well-being and aspirations of themselves and their families would continue to fight a war they knew was waged primarily to prevent the destruction of slavery, despite some political strategists' concerns that heightened emphasis on the slavery issue would dampen rather than invigorate the enthusiasm of the rank and file. Although Vance ran for a state, rather than Confederate, office, soldiers from outside North Carolina eagerly followed the race. South Carolina private William Templeton, for instance, heard Vance speak at Orange Court House, Virginia, and called the speech the best he ever heard.[142] Running on a platform that admitted the unsatisfactory nature of the Confederacy, Vance reminded voters that a faulty Confederate States of America was still better than reunion, because Union and abolition would destroy the racial order that protected soldiers' families and defined their identities as white men. The election also provided soldiers with the opportunity to affirm their commitment to a racial hierarchy that helped keep their fears and frustrations under control, and that they believed was vital to life in the South.

Voting for Governor Vance was confined to North Carolinians in 1864, but violence against black Union troops enabled soldiers throughout the Confederacy to channel their fears, frustrations, and hatred. By 1864, Confederate troops welcomed few mandates from Richmond, but one exception was the Davis administration's standing decision that black Union troops were not to be treated as white troops if captured. To enlisted Confederates, that decision issued a license to practice the "black flag" or "no quarter" policy of killing black troops rather than taking them prisoner. Pvt. John Everett was a young shoemaker who had lost his father and his shoemaking business in the war, and had been "out of heart" since 1862. He worried constantly about the privations faced by his mother and younger siblings at home, and he resented the way imperious Confederate authorities failed to treat him as "a white man."[143] In May of 1864, Everett reported that he and his regiment were "in good spirits" and felt eager to fight for the first time in two years when they learned that they were about to face black Union troops, with the "no quarter" policy in effect.[144] Meanwhile, feeling hemmed in and powerless to stop the Yankee advance toward Atlanta, Douglas Cater anticipated the opportunity to kill captured blacks with nothing short of glee, predicting, "those negros will wish they had never left their masters when they face Gilson's Brigade of Louisianans."[145]

The most widely renowned examples of violence toward black prisoners took place at Fort Pillow in Tennessee and outside Petersburg in

Virginia. The Fort Pillow massacre of April 12, 1864, occurred when Confederate troops under Gen. Nathan Bedford Forrest slaughtered black soldiers and some white southern unionist soldiers at a (by 1864) strategically unimportant Mississippi River garrison.[146] Sgt. Achilles Clark reported that he and other Confederates who were "exasperated" by the sight and defiant attitude of black troops took delight in the killing rampage. "The poor deluded negroes would run up to our men fall upon their knees and with uplifted hands scream for mercy but they were ordered to their feet and then shot down." The fort became "a great slaughter pen. Blood, human blood stood about in pools and brains could have been gathered up in any quantity." Once the killing lost its thrall, according to Clark, "thirty or forty" wounded "were thrown in to the trench" where they were buried alive.[147] Even more Confederates wrote of killing blacks captured at the battle of the Crater outside Petersburg, where Pvt. Henry Bird explained with obvious relish that "Southern bayonets dripped with blood" from the bodies of dying black troops. After the failed Union charge, the eerie stillness was soon broken by the order "to kill them all and rapid firing told plainly how well and willingly it was obeyed." The "terrible vengeance" persisted until "our Genl. sickened of the slaughter and ordered that it be stayed," Bird concluded.[148]

Some Confederates also directed racist violence toward black civilians. Hungry and footsore from a long march, Henry Chambers and his regiment were in no mood to respond to the "double quick" order that rang out as they approached Suffolk, Virginia, until they learned that a regiment of black Union troops was camped just on the other side of town. "We were nearly exhausted," Chambers recorded in his diary, "but when told that the hated negroes had been encountered, we received as it were renewed vigor and on we pushed." When the black Union regiment got away, Chambers and the men of his company turned their wrath on local black civilians. Noticing a house that "had Negroes in it," the soldiers set fire to the structure "before the negroes could be gotten out," killing the African Americans trapped inside.[149] The burning served no tactical purpose. Instead, it allowed white Confederate soldiers whose world was in upheaval to vent their hatred of blacks and act on their fury over upsets to the South's racial order caused by the war.

THE WAR in 1864 provided soldiers everywhere with glimpses of a new United States, which a Union victory could make possible. White Union troops envisioned a world of increasing racial equality and black rights, but many pulled back from that possibility as the war stubbornly refused to end or even ease, as most had expected would happen after the summer of 1863. Black Union troops foresaw that same world and continued to push toward it despite disappointments and growing dissent in their own ranks. Confederates saw the same possibilities and resisted ever more violently, for one thing that everyone knew with certainty was that those possibilities would not come to pass without a Union victory. As late as the summer of 1864, such a victory still seemed anything but assured.

Federal soldiers in front of City Hall as the Union Army takes Richmond, April 1865. *Courtesy of the Library of Congress*

As the end neared, these Confederate soldiers were taken prisoner at Five Forks, Virginia, April 1865. *Courtesy of the Library of Congress*

Black Union soldiers from Arkansas mustering out. *Harper's Weekly*, 1866. *Courtesy of the Library of Congress.*

CHAPTER 6

"Slavery's Chain Done Broke at Last":
The Coming of the End

MORNING mail call on February 1, 1865, brought Ohio sergeant John Keirns a letter from a friend in another regiment. When Keirns tore into the envelope, he pulled out the lyrics to "Take Your Gun and Go, John." Written from the perspective of a soldier's wife, the song urged the soldier to fight for his country without stopping to "think of me or the children" because "Ruth can drive the oxen, John, and I can use the hoe." Meant to soothe, the words actually reminded Keirns that nothing—not family life, society, or basic values—remained untouched by war. The verses hit so close to home that even though he had just sent a long letter to his wife, Sarah, and their six children, Keirns sat right down to write another. "The piece is very nice and true in all its parts," he confided, "yet I do think of you and the Children very often, Yes I may say every day." He did not doubt that Sarah could care for the children, and he knew that she could run the farm with the help of Edwin, their oldest boy, but he missed his family terribly. It was hard to bear a war that tore him away from home and turned everything so upside down that women did the work of men and children grew up without fathers. Yet just months earlier, in spite of the relentless pressure of daily fighting around Atlanta, Keirns had chosen to reenlist because he knew that no matter how hard it seemed, the war had to be fought to the right conclusion, or else neither his suffering nor anyone else's would have been worthwhile. He reminded Sarah of what the right conclusion must be when he asked her to "Pray for Freedom."[1]

Set to the tune of "Joshua," an antebellum spiritual, "Slavery's Chain Done Broke at Last" dates to the end of the war. Unlike many antebellum slave spirituals, which saw relief only in death, this song celebrated the end of slavery's grasp on earth.

After nearly four years of warfare, soldiers everywhere suffered, worried about their families, and wanted to go home. The murderous fury of the conflict had turned romance and delusion into dust, compelling Union troops to revisit what the "freedom" that John told Sarah to pray for should mean and whom it should include. Unforgiving warfare had convulsed the South even more completely, forcing Confederate soldiers to give up first one principle and then another, until by 1865 the Confederacy found itself drained of all but the most stubbornly retained of its tenets and resources. Finally, in the spring of 1865, the only remaining reason for Confederate troops to fight would crack, but nobody in 1864 knew when or how or even if that moment would come.

"By war, God is regenerating this Nation"

After a discouraging spring and summer, military matters (and therefore troop morale) started to improve for the Union at harvest time in 1864. Mobile Bay fell to Union forces in August. In Virginia, the Union general Philip Sheridan reversed the Confederacy's victorious battle record in the Shenandoah Valley, a region that had been critical in feeding the Confederate Army and sustaining its morale. On September 19, Federals routed Confederates at Winchester, and for the next three days chased them sixty miles south, delivering the valley into Union hands once and for all.

But the biggest news came from Georgia. On the first of September, after failing to defeat Union troops south of Atlanta at Jonesboro, Confederate forces under Gen. John Hood destroyed everything of military value in the city and vacated Atlanta. On September 2, accompanied by the triumphal strains of army bands, Union troops under the command of Gen. William T. Sherman marched into Atlanta and raised the United States flag over city hall.[2] From the outskirts of the captured city, Ohio captain Thomas Honnoll revealed the significance that Union troops awarded the fall of Atlanta when he reflected, the "rebellion is well nigh crushed now. The Confederacy is tottering. We have pierced its heart. . . . their people and Army are losing confidence in their cause and Leaders."[3] To a black chaplain, "the news of Farragut's glorious triumphs at Mobile and Sherman at Atlanta" inspired "hopefulness of finally achieving the end for which we are battling."[4]

The capture of Atlanta showed that the war *could* be won by fighting, but it did not complete the moral or military work of the war, and the men of the rank and file knew it. However much they welcomed it, many Union troops responded to the fall of Atlanta with surprising somberness. Even with Atlanta in Union hands, soldiers remained surrounded by the grimness of war and detritus of slavery, in which few could fully escape feelings of complicity. Watching Atlanta burn led to mixed feelings for Sgt. Horatio Barrington. He regretted the destruction and believed it reflected badly on both North and South, yet he saw it as morally inescapable. Atlanta "sowed the wind" every time a slave merchant "traded in the souls of men, bought and sold and whipped women and hammered off children on the auction block"; now both it and the nation that had allowed the slave trade "reaped the whirlwind" of immoral behavior.[5] Soldiers like Barrington also realized that Atlanta served as a milepost on the Union road to victory, but it did not mean that the Army had arrived at its destination yet. If Gettysburg and Vicksburg had shown that God moved in mysterious (and not always speedy) ways, Atlanta reminded Union troops that God helped those who helped themselves. Plenty remained to be done before the war could end.

For one thing, according to many Union troops, Abraham Lincoln needed to win the fall election.[6] Running on a platform that supported vigorous prosecution of the war and a constitutional amendment abolishing slavery, Lincoln enjoyed overwhelming support from the men in the ranks. Many troops worried that a Democratic victory would betray the war effort because McClellan would endorse peace negotiations that fell short of the goals for which their comrades had fallen. Anxious though they were to go home, most men in the ranks opposed negotiation because "the blood of our fallen comrades would cry out against us if we did not fight on until we established those principles for which they fought and died."[7] When Democrats tried to counter soldiers' perception that the party undervalued troops' contributions with a platform plank promising care and kindness to the rank and file, enlisted men rejected the effort as a transparent and insipid ploy for votes. Democrats "might as well try to catch fish with a naked hook—just as if all our soldiers wanted was care, protection, regard, and kindness," one wrote with contempt, mocking the Chicago platform's own words to explain why soldiers would be sticking with Abraham Lincoln.[8] A Lincoln victory, on the other hand, would be "Equivalent to a good army in putting down the Rebellion," Nelson Glazier told his parents as he recuperated from a recent amputation.[9] Among other benefits, Lincoln's reelection would demoralize Confederates, whose morale currently remained buoyed by hope of a McClellan victory and compromise. "McClellan for President . . . would be the worst thing that was ever done for the country," Pvt. Oscar Cram admonished his wife, because "the Rebels say that is what they are depending on most." Instead, "if Lincoln is re-elected the war closes this fall, and most of the soldiers think so too."[10] George Hannaford agreed: "if [Lincoln] is elected," Hannaford told his wife, "it will do more to discourage the rebels than to lose a dozen battles."[11]

As many Union troops saw it, Lincoln had to win not only to end the war, but also to end it right by eliminating slavery once and for all. Like many of his compatriots, Pvt. John Brobst regarded Lincoln as "the only man that can settle this war up and do it as it should be settled." To end the war "by letting [Confederates] have their slaves" would cause the war to "end in four months, for ten years only." By insisting on emancipation, Lincoln would end the war "eternally" by eliminating the cause of the conflict.[12] Pvt. Oscar Cram echoed Brobst's reasoning. After telling his wife that the election of McClellan was exactly what Confederates most hoped for, Cram went on to ask, "which would you prefer, to have the war ended & Slavery continue . . . or have the war continue a year longer & slavery abolished & me stay out here?" Whatever course his wife favored, Cram left no doubt that in his opinion, only a vote for Lincoln and the end of slavery could successfully end the conflict.[13]

Naturally, some troops disagreed. McClellan's personal popularity never completely vanished, numerous lifelong Democrats stood by the old party, and a few of the war-weary attributed the conflict's prolonged existence to the party in power. Hermon Clarke, who broke partisan ranks to vote for Republicans in the 1863 state elections, intended to return to his family's Democratic loyalties because he blamed Republicans for delays in soldier pay. "I think some new administration might do better by us," he explained when he wrote home to ask his father to mail him a Democratic ticket.[14] Resentful because he had been drafted, Edwin Horton pledged himself "a McLellan man up to the handle."[15] Also, while Lincoln's commitment to emancipation won the support of most soldiers, it alienated some troops. "Lincolnism and Niggerism is in the ascendant," career cavalryman Charles Bates observed with disgust, "and a poor fellow like me with McClellan in his mind" grew increasingly lonely in the ranks, where nearly everyone else supported Lincoln and an end to slavery.[16]

Black soldiers expressed mixed opinions about Lincoln. Since voting was governed by state laws and most states outside of New England restricted the franchise to white men, most black troops could not cast ballots, but they still took the election seriously. To some, Lincoln qualified as God's instrument chosen to erase the nation's ugliest stain.[17] One man in the Thirty-first U.S. Colored Troops associated "Honest Abe" with "our Year of Jubilee," and many black soldiers wrote to Lincoln personally with their needs and requests.[18] Others despised McClellan and the Chicago platform, but criticized Lincoln's slow pace toward racial justice. Chaplain Henry McNeal Turner thought the framers of the Chicago platform "ought to every one be hung till dead by the neck," but he also regretted that Lincoln had not adopted a firm line on slavery more promptly. "The principles which should have governed him, were those of eternal justice; they were clearly laid down in the Bible. . . . And had these principles been his *modus operandi,* or his compass, to run the national ship by," both the Copperheads and the Confederates would have been beaten much earlier.[19] Yet while many black troops harbored reservations about Lincoln, all preferred him to McClellan.

The election process in the fall was cumbersome, makeshift, and excluded most black troops, but the fact that it occurred at all was noteworthy. Methods and polling dates varied by state. Eighteen states allowed soldiers to vote in the field (if they were eligible to vote at home) and then send the returns to state election officials. The Army granted furloughs to some men in other states so they could go home to vote.[20] Some soldiers, like Cpl. Charles Harris of the 157th New York, sent ballots home and authorized fathers or brothers to cast them on election day.[21] The Twenty-ninth Ohio "elected 'Viva Voce' three judges and two Clerks" to oversee the balloting, ensure that soldiers cast their votes fairly, and count the votes afterward. The following day, the clerks prepared the returns to send back to all seventeen Ohio counties represented in the regiment.[22]

Despite the reservations of some blacks and the McClellan loyalty of a small number of white troops, when the results came in "the soldiers vote [was] like a handle on a jug, all on one side, for Lincoln," as Sgt. Henry Hart put it.[23] In Hart's own battery, soldiers cast sixty-four votes for Lincoln and only twelve for McClellan, even though supporters of both candidates held "good rousing meetings" to get out the vote.[24] Charles Musser's regiment gave 493 of 544 votes to Lincoln, and other regiments in his division posted similar results.[25] In the total popular vote, Lincoln outpolled McClellan 2,219,924 (55 percent) to 1,814,228, and won 212 electoral votes to McClellan's 21, carrying every state except Kentucky, Delaware, and New Jersey. Not every state distinguished between the soldier and civilian vote, but in those that did, soldier support for Lincoln totaled nearly 80 percent.[26]

Although Lincoln would have carried almost every state without the soldier vote, many troops saw Lincoln's landslide among the rank and file as important because it sent the message that "it is not reasonable to suppose that men will fight for, and vote against, the same principles."[27] After all, four out of five white Union troops chose Lincoln, and if all black soldiers had been permitted to vote, the ratio in favor of Lincoln would likely have been higher, since black soldiers showed no support for McClellan. Lincoln's supporters included Democrats who flocked to the Lincoln banner with the zeal of the converted. Even Ohio Democrat Chauncey Welton, who in 1863 had hated Abraham Lincoln and emancipation, supported Lincoln and chided his father to do likewise.[28]

White Union soldiers loved and stood by Lincoln because by the autumn of 1864 they believed that he articulated a vision of the war's causes and purpose that matched their own. Although black Americans had advocated the destruction of slavery even before the war began, most white troops, like Lincoln, had believed before the war that the Constitution forbade federal interference with slavery. Some regarded the institution with indifference or even mild approval. Yet their wartime experiences convinced most white Union troops that slavery must be destroyed, and they appreciated that even though the president's views (or at least actions) evolved more slowly than their opinions did, the pattern of Lincoln's changing attitudes matched their own. Like the Union rank and file, Lincoln knew that slavery had caused the war and must be destroyed in order to end the war, and he also, like the men in the ranks, interpreted the war as punishment and repentance for the shared national sin of slavery. By 1864, countless soldiers agreed with an Iowa man who praised Lincoln as a model of "Loyalty, Liberty, and Union," because the president understood that in order to prove that "this war is *not* a failure, that Slavery must die."[29]

As their views on slavery demonstrated, going to war changed white northern men in ways that folks at home could only imperfectly understand, and placed an ideological as well as geographical distance between white soldiers and their loved ones. Abraham Lincoln seemed to travel that distance with the troops. When Lincoln characterized the war as "a new birth of freedom," he echoed soldiers like Pvt. Justus Silliman, who voiced the hope that the war and emancipation would infuse "new life and vigor" into "our nation." Moreover, he articulated beliefs about the war that hardship, fear, and suffering (unshared by civilians) had led soldiers to embrace.[30] By 1864, Union soldiers everywhere referred to the president in familiar, even familial, terms like "Uncle Abe" and "Father Abraham."[31]

Besides reelecting Abraham Lincoln, Union troops also recognized that winning the war required continued and decisive military steps. As one midwestern soldier reminded his brother, just and lasting peace "with the South" stood no chance "till they are whipped first."[32] More than any other campaign, the march that Gen. William T. Sherman led through Georgia and the Carolinas signified Union soldiers' commitment to completing the military work of the war. On November 15, the week after the presidential election, Sherman's army departed Atlanta for Savannah, more than 280 miles away. Moving in four columns, Sherman's men tore up railroads, destroyed food supplies, and instilled fear in civilians luckless enough to live along the way. The army captured Savannah just in time for Christmas, and early in the new year, troops headed for South Carolina, where they wreaked even more havoc because the men identified that state as the birthplace of secession.[33]

Union troops largely supported Sherman's famous march, and some even reveled in it, because they viewed harsh measures as integral to crushing southern will and extracting a surrender complete enough to obliterate southern visions of independence and slavery.[34] The song "Marching Through Georgia" sang of slaves freed and foodstuffs confiscated by troops who "made a thoroughfare for Freedom and her train / Sixty miles in latitude—three hundred to the main," and celebrated the defeat of "treason" by "the flag that makes you free."[35] Approaching Columbia, the capital of South Carolina, Pvt. Theodore Upson and his fellow Hoosiers "began to sing 'John Brown's body lies a moldering in the grave but his soul is marching on.' " The words to a song that by 1865 was widely associated with the North's most militant abolitionist "rolled up and down the vall[ey]," Upson recounted, and boosted the men's confidence in their ability as well as responsibility to "brush [Confederates] off our path like so many flies."[36] When a Maine soldier stationed in Virginia heard that Sherman's men had overrun "Charleston the hot bed of treason," he spoke hopefully of "deal[ing] the last blow to this unholy Rebellion."[37]

Yet despite the jaunty tune of "Marching Through Georgia," for most Union troops, the stark destruction and cruelty of the Georgia and Carolinas campaign sealed the conviction that all the suffering and horror of the war could be made worthwhile not simply by preserving the American Republic, but by making it better. Soldiers now rarely wrote of restoring the Union; instead, they preached the need to regenerate the American nation. "To have the 'constitution as it is and the union as it was' is an impossibility," declared an Ohio sergeant in Atlanta, where the surrounding rubble made it obvious to him that warfare had irreversibly altered the nation.[38] Writing to his hometown newspaper, Henry Riggs claimed that the Union was "worth contending for" only if it rededicated itself to a higher "standard of 'liberty and Freedom.' "[39] New York private John Foote frequently revisited this theme. "By war, God is regenerating this Nation," Foote counseled his sister in September. Two months later he explained even more clearly that the war was "rescuing our country" not only from rebellion, but also from its own imperfections, by "founding it on truth & Liberty!"[40] After a hiatus in the spring and summer of 1864, the millennial view of the war was back as the hardened Union veterans of the war's final winter concluded that regeneration and redemption had to be the effect and purpose of the war. In response, many turned their attention to what the republic that emerged from the struggle should be like.

For a start, the purified nation must unequivocally eliminate slavery, as soldiers readily pointed out. One sergeant insisted that soldiers and civilians alike must resist "a restoration of this Union upon any other basis than that of the complete and everlasting overthrow of the institution of slavery." If the North settled for less, "we will have gained nothing."[41] To transform the "land of boasted freedom" from mockery into reality, John Moore, a white assistant surgeon, argued that the Union must create a new nation "based upon equality & freedom to all white, black or copper colored."[42] Neither American ideals nor the will of God allowed any less.

By these lights, the punishing nature of the war could be understood as righteous penance meted out by God for the sin of slavery. As southern cities fell to Union forces that left suffering women and children in their wake, one soldiers' newspaper reminded readers of the biblical promise that "thy sin will find thee out," and pointed to ruin in slave states as evidence that "on their sin has the punishment fallen."[43] Many other soldiers reasoned that the war was horrible not because the South was more sinful, but because slavery was horrible, and God ordained that all who colluded in its existence (whether by sins of commission or omission) must feel the awful weight of that truth. "The nation is passing through a terrible revolution," one black chaplain wrote, "such a one as she doubtless needs to purge" the sin of slavery.[44] As war's end neared, John Moore rejoiced that Americans (not just Southerners) were "beginning to see that slavery is and has been a national evil," and he reminded his wife, much as Lincoln would do in the Second Inaugural Address one month later, that "God will not bless a nation who are guilty of such gross evil."[45]

In the winter of 1864–65, several concrete steps against slavery gratified Union soldiers, including emancipation in border states like Maryland and Missouri. Maryland adopted a new state constitution banning slavery on November 1, 1864. Five days later, the camp of the Twenty-ninth Connecticut Colored Infantry rang with the combined shouts of white and black soldiers alike, as troops celebrated "the Emancipation of Maryland from the thraldom of slavery" with speeches, music, and the announcement of the results of the election in which Marylanders voted to eliminate slavery.[46] More good news came in January, after Missouri passed an ordinance abolishing slavery on the eleventh day of 1865, to the satisfaction of many Missouri troops who had voted decisively in favor of eliminating the institution from their state.[47] "I hear that Missouri is a *free* State," exalted white Missourian Francis Audsley. "That is Glorious news, and I think there will be more changes than that yet."[48] Whooping *"Missouri's* gone and did it, boys! Glory! Hallelugerum," a Colorado soldiers' newspaper printed the Emancipation Ordinance in its columns and congratulated the former slave state for "washing away the foul stain of human bondage!"[49] To celebrate Missouri's achievement, the Second U.S. Colored Infantry hosted a "series of entertainments" in Key West, Florida, including a supper with decorations and bouquets on the tables, to which they invited local women.[50]

Even more momentous, Congress passed the Thirteenth Amendment to the U.S. Constitution, forever banning slavery from the nation. Such a constitutional step had been in the making since January 1864, when the Senate Judiciary Committee met to draft an amendment abolishing slavery. Completed on February 10, 1864, the amendment passed the Senate thirty-eight to six on April 8. In June, it won a majority of votes in the House of Representatives, but not the two-thirds required for a constitutional amendment. After the November elections signaled clear public support for the amendment, the House reconsidered, and on January 31, 1865, passed it 119 to 56. The House's packed galleries erupted as men tossed their hats and women waved handkerchiefs and cheered. Rallies and celebrations greeted the news as it traveled throughout the Union. The amendment still had to be ratified by the states, but that detail was temporarily set aside amidst the jubilation engulfing the country.[51]

Soldiers joined in the nationwide elation. "An act was passed by the house of representatives forever prohibiting slavery in the United States or territories," Joel Molyneux noted in his diary, punctuating the news with a hearty "Bully, boys!"[52] Longtime advocates of emancipation such as John Foote rejoiced that "this, heretofore a land of human bondage & oppression, has become the home of freemen and the land of liberty."[53] A member of the Twenty-fifth U.S. Colored Troops who usually wrote with sarcasm allowed himself a rare unjaded moment when he reflected that "America has washed her hands at the clear spring of freedom." Reverting to his more typical tone, he hoped that the amendment meant that the nation would now "make a show at least of carrying out the principles enunciated in that noble State paper—The Declaration of Independence."[54] Even former opponents of emancipation like Chauncey Welton delighted in a "country *free free free* yes free from that blighting curs *Slavery* the cause of four years Bloody Warfare."[55] Edward Bartlett, whose hopes for the death of slavery had strengthened with every enslaved man, woman, and child he had met over his two and a half years of service, pronounced the "Constitutional amendment vote" a "great success." "Now I am ready for the war to be over," he joyfully told his sister, "as the great cause, Slavery, is abolished."[56]

Bartlett's remarks illustrate the real jubilation that many soldiers felt at the passage of the Thirteenth Amendment, but they also reveal one of the war's cruelest ironies: since many white troops believed that the amendment solved the problem of slavery, some felt no further obligation toward African Americans. Theodore Upson, a soldier who marched with Sherman's army, showed that the same men who could sing about the onward march of John Brown's soul could also play mean-spirited tricks on slaves and rudely discourage blacks from joining in the march. "We do not want them," Upson noted in his diary, and "they had better stay on the plantations."[57] Some troops retained harsh racist feelings that translated into cruel or even murderous actions. Charles Brewster told of a quarrel among three white sailors and one black barber in a Norfolk prison, in the midst of which "the sailors very coolly opened the window and pitched the colored man head foremost out on to the pavement and smashed his head all to pieces."[58] In the same week, when a former Confederate deserter, now a Union volunteer in Resaca, Georgia, encountered a black man asleep by the side of the road, the "soldier . . . was so enraged at the poor innocent fellow for taking comfort that he shot him remarking 'Take that you d——d niger and see if you'll sleep again when *I* have to march."[59] In many cases, even soldiers who lacked such fierce bigotry hoped for speedy reconciliation with the South, and viewed the placation of southern whites on racial matters as the quickest way to refasten ties between the two sections. An article in the camp newspaper *The 83rd Illinoisan* argued that now that "the real cause of the war, African Slavery, is no more," the country needed to hasten the process by which "North and South are to return again to their old status as component parts of this great American Republic" by smoothing over the complications "that must necessarily arise from this vital question" of emancipation.[60]

As firmly as most white Union troops agreed on emancipation, they did not share a consensus as to the meaning of black freedom. John English approved of the Thirteenth Amendment because it made "the Negro . . . free forever in this country, as every other race and nation, and on an equality before the law," but he was not so sure about equality "in a social point of view."[61] Nor did white members of the Union rank and file agree about black suffrage, a question that many northern state electorates and legislatures considered in the final year of the war. By April 1865, many troops determined that long-awaited Union victory really was imminent this time, and complacency led soldiers like self-satisfied Illinois private George Hudson to decide that radical measures like black suffrage would not be necessary after all. "You must have a better oppinion of the Negro than I to leav our Government to their Protection," he haughtily wrote to his family after receiving a letter from home that spoke approvingly of extending voting rights to blacks.[62] Uncertainty rather than certainty motivated Kentucky soldier Robert Winn, yet he shared Hudson's opposition to black suffrage. "Talk of elevating them to the suffrage is folly," Winn lectured his sister, which could only be indulged in by those who were guilty of "*overrating the mental capacities and moral conditions of the poor emancipated (semi* I should say) *slaves.*" Convinced "that more than one generation must pass away before the S. Darkey would be fit for Citizenship," Winn deemed "it best not to complicate the question of their being raised from *things* to *men*" by tackling questions that he thought belonged "to a future generation."[63]

While plenty of soldiers agreed with Winn, the experience of war and interactions with former slaves led many others to insist that the generation that fought the war could not just shift responsibility onto its descendants. Instead, after backsliding in the spring and summer of 1864, many soldiers returned to the ideas that had begun to take shape after Gettysburg and Vicksburg, when they had first suspected that white Northerners must adjust their own racial attitudes dramatically before all the suffering of the war would be made worthwhile, and before God would be satisfied and reward the Union with victory. In a newspaper column aimed at northern children, Pvt. Wilbur Fisk argued that white Americans owed black Americans more than an occasional "dollar for the Freedmen's Aid Society." They owed them respect and decency. Whites must abandon the distinctions they drew between themselves and African Americans and treat former slaves as they would treat Christ. Otherwise, God would frown on anyone who "shall unwittingly despise" blacks, and even if the Union defeated the Confederacy, Northerners would not have fulfilled their duty in the eyes of God.[64] Interacting with former slaves did the most to convince white troops—even those who had shown little prior sympathy for black Americans—that white Northerners needed to modify their attitudes. Impressed by slave women who "toiled along day after day, with their children bound on their backs: making the same hard marches that we did," an Illinois sergeant urged "white mothers of the free North" to see that black women "endowed by the Creator with the same love of children and love of freedom that he has given to you" deserved the same respect and dignity that white women expected.[65] After praising black troops who fought at Fort Blakely, Alabama, one white soldier exclaimed, "blistered be the tongue" of the Northerner who would now harp, as he once had, on the dangers of "negro equality." The sight of "5,000 colored . . . soldiers fighting equally . . . for our common country" proved that "the white man is NOT disgraced" by working alongside blacks as equals, and that "the colored man" should be "ELEVATED."[66] In the waning days of the war, some Union troops, even ones who had been hostile to black rights before the war, seemed willing to re-embrace the more positive attitudes toward black equality and civil rights that many had begun to adopt in the summer of 1863. This pattern demonstrated the existence of a real impulse for racial progress, an impulse that would once have been regarded as intolerably radical among otherwise very ordinary white Union soldiers.

Growing numbers of white troops called for tangible steps toward making the ideals of the American Revolution into lived realities for black as well as white Americans. The *Soldier's Letter* of the Second Colorado Cavalry, for example, embraced black suffrage, desegregation of public facilities, and the news that a black lawyer had been accepted to argue before the U.S. Supreme Court.[67] More than any other measure, education for former slaves stood out as the obligation that countless white soldiers felt the United States owed to black Americans, and many troops went beyond bland words of approval to involve themselves actively in the work of the schools. When Vermonter Rufus Kinsley was not helping to build schools in his off-duty hours, he was "teaching soldiers and contraband children." Teaching in the South was not for the faint of heart, Kinsley observed, especially since white northern teachers were subject to kidnapping by Confederate guerrillas, but despite the dangers, he saw the future of his nation, not just a quaint social project, on the school benches of the South. "The schools are spreading, and are destined to save the Nation," thanks to teachers who were "doing for their country a nobler and braver work than has been done on the bloody battle-fields of the war."[68] Black education even gained support from unexpected quarters. When he first arrived in the South, Illinois sergeant William Bradbury viewed blacks with distaste and blamed them for causing the war, but now he enthusiastically solicited teaching materials from home for southern black pupils.[69]

In short, in the final months of the Civil War, a critical mass of white Union troops supported expanded rights for African Americans, and believed that the U.S. government had a duty to work toward equality for black citizens. After the passage of the Fourteenth and Fifteenth Amendments, and especially in the closing decades of the nineteenth century, the opinions of soldiers like Fisk, Kinsley, Bradbury, and others lost ground to the view that white Americans owed no obligation to blacks beyond abolition, much as the summer of 1863's growing support for racial justice had ebbed in 1864. Yet that outcome was anything but inevitable in 1865, as blacks and whites worked together to change laws, build schools, and lay foundations for a more equitable society. Commitment to racial justice was not unanimous among the white rank and file, but neither was a desire for unabated white supremacy. The potential for a radically different United States existed in the waning days of the Civil War, even while consensus on that subject did not.

"Rising step by step to the summit of liberty and equal rights"

Black Union soldiers knew with perfect clarity that breaking slavery's chain meant inaugurating a freedom defined by basic human rights and full citizenship for black as well as white Americans. First of all, freedom meant the right to family relationships, over which slaves had enjoyed little control in the days of bondage because husbands and wives knew that their union could be sundered at the whim of an owner. Now, black men like the Kentucky slave William Jones risked death in order to enlist, in the belief that enlistment would secure the freedom of their wives.[70] Through-out the South, black men and women flocked to have their marriages con-secrated. The chaplain of a black regiment in Arkansas conducted more than twenty-five weddings in the single month of February 1865.[71]

Genuine freedom, in the view of many black soldiers, also required full citizenship, which meant, among other things, equal treatment in the public sphere. One member of the Third U.S. Colored Troops confidently promised African American readers that they could expect to "be admitted into public conveyances in every section of your town" by the time the war ended.[72] Elsewhere, a black soldier welcomed news of the desegregation of Philadelphia streetcars as "another progressive stride" against "the injustice which [whites] have long practiced upon the negro."[73] Recogniz-ing the links that many white Americans saw between property ownership and membership within the body politic, Sgt. George Massey emphasized the importance of new laws designed to allow black Americans to "become owners of homes and property."[74]

Other black troops defined citizenship as recognition of black people's contributions to the past, present, and future of the American Republic. In June 1864, Congress had legislated equal pay for black and white soldiers, and in late 1864 and 1865, black soldiers finally began to receive their equal wages. Shortly after the paymaster arrived at the Fifty-fifth Massa-chusetts's encampment in South Carolina for the first payday since the enactment of equal pay legislation, the men of the regiment, "anxious to take advantage of this and every opportunity of giving expression to our loyalty," and to exercise "the rights of citizenship," passed a set of resolu-tions. The resolutions explained, "even as the founders of our Republic resisted the British tax on tea, on the ground of principle, so did we claim equal pay with other volunteers because we believed our military and civil equality its issue." In drawing parallels between the American Revolution and their own experiences in the Civil War, the black soldiers of the Fifty-fifth wrote themselves into the nation's past *and* into its future as citizens of a regenerated American Republic.[75]

Finally, full citizenship for black Americans also meant the right to participate in government. Zack Burden even wrote to the president to explain that freedom and citizenship should mean equal treatment on very basic levels, such as comparable rations for black and white troops, equi-table policies for granting furloughs to sick soldiers regardless of race, and government assistance for the dependents of black soldiers, but they should also mean the right to participate in the government that black troops fought to defend. A man who would "fite" should be allowed to "vote," Private Burden succinctly told Lincoln.[76]

Fighting for the same cause and in the same way as white soldiers provided black men with a solid claim to full citizenship; after all, as one black artillerist pointed out, men who "fought and bled for their country" had clearly earned the rights of citizenship within it.[77] At the battle of Nashville in December 1864, "the blood of black and white men flowed freely together for the one common cause, for a country's freedom and independence," reflected a black veteran of the fight. "As the result, wherever the flag of our love goes, our hopes may advance, and we may as a people, with propriety claim political equality with our white fellow-soldier and citizen; and every man that makes his home in our country may, whatever be his complexion or progeny, with propriety, exclaim to the world, 'I am an American citizen!' "[78]

In addition, black soldiers fortified their claims to citizenship through collective action on local and national levels. The Twenty-ninth Connecticut, for example, formed the "Douglass and Garnet Young Men's Literary Society," named for two prominent African American figures. One member described the "object" of the "association" to be "the elevation of our race and the advancement and perpetuation of universal liberty, political and social equality, and . . . the establishment of the great principle that all men were created free and equal."[79] The group elected officers, enacted a constitution and bylaws, and instituted a series of regular meetings dedicated to discussing "the great questions of the hour." In addition to providing black soldiers with experience in creating institutions and participating in self-government, the society allowed them to engage issues such as "social equality and the result of the war" and "the future of America and of our race as American citizens." Society meetings relieved monotony while sending a message to "the enemies of our noble country and our race," whether those enemies were Confederate soldiers entrenched a mile away, or northern civilians who were just as firmly entrenched in tired doctrines of black inferiority that looked silly in light of the society's sophisticated activities.[80] From Nashville, black Ohio sergeant major Dudley Asbury hailed the work of local "churches and societies which are fast forming a basis for our elevation."[81] Asbury also praised the National Equal Rights League, a new association organized at the National Convention of Colored Citizens of the United States (also known as the National Convention of Colored Men) in Syracuse, New York, in October 1864. Elected delegates from eleven free states and seven slave states established the league and adopted resolutions, framed by Frederick Douglass, which called for full citizenship for African Americans, including "general suffrage . . . personal liberty, the right to testify in courts of law, [and] the right to hold, buy and sell property." In short, the convention demanded an end to "prejudice," the elimination of "all enactments discriminating in favor of or against any class of its people," and the institution of "one law for the white and colored people alike."[82] One soldier, primed for the upcoming national convention by news of a Philadelphia gathering conducted for similar purposes, looked forward to the Syracuse meeting as an opportunity for blacks to "agitate the question of equality before the law and demand by the law the rights that citizens enjoy."[83] Months after the convention, Moses Foskey still praised the ability of such gatherings "to elevate the race" by using the national stage and the political process to fight for the "honor and equality" of African Americans.[84]

No Pollyannas, black soldiers in 1864 and 1865 recognized that no matter how diligently they might work to secure their own equality, enfranchised whites possessed a power to change laws that disenfranchised blacks did not, and the persistence of bigotry among many of those whites often curbed black hopes. Pvt. T. Pennington of the Twentieth U.S. Colored Infantry did not doubt "the good intentions of the law-makers at Washington," but he was discouraged by the ways in which racist individuals subverted equal policies. The federal government explicitly dictated equal rations for black and white troops, yet a Union major general stationed in Louisiana still ordered vegetables three times a week for white troops, and an unrelieved diet of cornmeal and molasses for black troops. Such unequal treatment of the "energetic, valiant, and faithful" ranks who fought at "Port Hudson, Vicksburg, Olustee, and other places" insulted the very notion of justice, the frustrated Pennington fumed.[85] Small, constant snubs for no greater crime than "be[ing] made black when you should have known that it is an unpopular color" so embittered one black soldier that he believed that it would take God's direct intervention to bring about "equal right and justice to *all* men in the United States."[86] In addition, the continued bar against black officers made it hard for black soldiers like James Trotter to trust that white Americans really intended to apply the "great principle of equal rights" to black Americans.[87]

Yet for all the disappointments, and despite the continued resistance of some whites, astounding changes had taken place on the nation's racial landscape since 1861. For one thing, black soldiers knew better than to underestimate the death of slavery, an institution that predated the foundation of the United States, defined every aspect of society in the South, affected politics and society in the North, and had until recently been rendered inviolate by no less a document than the U.S. Constitution. James Lewis knew the sting of racism. A New Orleans gentleman of color, Lewis had been forced to resign his captaincy of the First Louisiana Native Guards because of the Union's prohibition against black officers, and so he sympathized with a friend who encountered "prejudice" in his new home of New York, but he also counseled against cynicism. *"We prefer a disturbed liberty to a quiet slavery,"* Lewis emphasized, and no matter how many setbacks blacks faced in freedom, slavery was destroyed as long as the Union won the war, because the Thirteenth Amendment would apply nationwide.[88] On New Year's Day, black regiments in Beaufort, South Carolina, staged ceremonies to mark the anniversary of the Emancipation Proclamation, which reminded one chaplain of "Meriam, Moses' sister, and the women of Israel, dancing on the shores of the Red Sea" to celebrate the entrance of the Israelites into the promised land. "What a change in Beaufort," he exclaimed. "Here only a few years ago slavery held undisputed sway."[89] From near Richmond, a black sergeant meditated, "surely this is a mighty and progressive age in which we live. The hydra-headed monster slavery which, a few short years ago, stalked over the land with proud and gigantic strides, we now behold drooping and dying under the scourging lash of Universal Freedom."[90]

Even soldiers impatient with the pace of change acknowledged the dramatic revolution that abolition constituted, and reminded themselves that the United States' transition from a slave nation to a nation committed to emancipation proved that justice willed by God would come to pass eventually. Irritated by northern foot-dragging on racial equality, Henry Hoyle consoled himself by recollecting, "He has struck the chains of bondage from nearly half a million of our race and given new strength and vigor to the doctrine of Universal Freedom and Equal Rights." The barricade of white prejudice might temporarily impede blacks' advancement toward equality, but "God in his own good time will batter down this barrier . . . and open the hearts of the people to the justness of our claim."[91] In the late months of the war, black troops believed that a God who used the Union government to destroy slavery could also eliminate racial prejudice.

The resolution of seemingly intractable issues helped to prop up black troops' faith that a racially just United States would emerge from the trials of warfare. In addition to winning the equal pay controversy, African

Americans were finally granted officers' commissions in the U.S. Army, much to the delight of members of the black rank and file from Kansas to South Carolina. A gleeful John Scott admitted that news of black officers commanding his artillery battery might sound like "a myth" after so much resistance to the prospect of black officers, but it actually was now a "fact." The editor of the *Anglo-African,* to whom Scott addressed his good tidings, added the comment that black officers "foreshdow the good time coming when complexion will form no longer a barrier to promotion."[92] When Capt. Martin Delany, one of the first African American commissioned infantry officers, visited troops stationed in South Carolina, black soldiers lined the streets to salute and cheer as he passed.[93] In Louisiana, John Cajay welcomed the promotion of Sergeant Hamblin, a fellow enlisted man in the Eleventh U.S. Colored Artillery, to the rank of lieutenant as a "great encouragement" to all who labored for "their rights and liberties, some of which we have partially gained." Hamblin's commission reinvigorated Cajay's hope that "sooner or later, we shall gain them all."[94]

In sum, African American soldiers at war's end surveyed advances in racial equality that seemed unimaginable just four years previously, and they saw many reasons to believe that the postwar United States would continue its progress toward the inclusion of black Americans as equal citizens. "When we look at events as they have transpired from year to year, our energies become aroused and our determination strengthened," reflected Moses Foskey. A black lawyer's appointment as "attorney and counsellor to the Supreme Court of the United States" and "the doings of the Syracuse Convention of Colored Men" should "encourage the men in camp to look forward with hopefulness to their advancement," Foskey declared.[95] John Cajay expanded on Foskey's theme. Fewer than four years ago, "no person or person's were allowed to speak in the House of Representatives, unless the blood of the Caucasion race coursed through his or their viens." Ordinary blacks could now "walk through the Chief Executive Hall of the United States, and look any one in the face as a man, and not with that downcast look, which made us think that the predominant race in this country were our superiors." By fighting in the ranks, and by forcing the United States to live up to its professed ideals, African Americans had helped to ensure that the United States "will truly be a free country to us all," Cajay concluded.[96]

Black soldiers at the close of the war cherished high hopes even as they remained guarded in their optimism. They knew that racial progress was fragile and prone to backsliding in times of strain, as fluctuating white attitudes after the military disasters of spring and summer 1864 and unabashedly racist Democratic election rhetoric had made clear. But they also knew that a tumultuous war had done more than threaten the Union; it had forced white Americans to examine assumptions that had long been taken for granted and consider ideas once thought inconceivable, especially where blacks who had helped to save the Union were concerned. "The black arm" was everywhere apparent in the current "stupendous struggle," wrote one African American soldier, and "the contraction of its muscles" was causing "a revolution of opinions."[97] Another soldier added, "the prejudice against color and race is disappearing before liberty and justice, as the mist flees from before the morning sun. The black man has proved himself a patriot, a hero . . . and worthy citizen."[98] Black soldiers at the end of the Civil War had every reason to envision equal citizenship for themselves in a United States that differed radically from the Union that went to war in 1861. In 1865, African Americans believed that they were "rising step by step to the summit of liberty and equal rights," and, based on the experiences of the last four years, they expected to continue the climb.[99]

"If we are to depend on the slaves for our freedom it is gone anyway"

For Confederate troops, too, the autumn of 1864 marked a turning point in the war, but to white Southerners, the fall of Atlanta, Lincoln's reelection, and Sherman's March looked more like disaster than divine plan. It was hard to overestimate the strategic importance of Atlanta, a critical railroad hub and an interior wedge perfectly positioned to cut the Confederacy in two, as soldiers knew all too well. "The loss of Atlanta has been a terrible blow to us," a South Carolinian in the Army of Northern Virginia fretted, "and unless our troops *fight* and our generals do better, Georgia and South Carolina will be *lost*." For the first time, he feared his own storied army could not carry the whole Confederacy on its back. "The Army of Northern Virginia can*not* do everything," he grumbled.[100] Atlanta also meant trouble because it was bound to energize the enemy. "The fall of Atlanta will cause great rejoycing in the North," an Alabamian predicted, "and the Yankees will be so much inspirited by the fall of Atlanta that they will take new interest in the war."[101] For war-weary Confederates, whose one realistic hope was that Northerners would get tired of the conflict, renewed Union vigor was bad news.

Atlanta also mattered because as the Confederate flag slipped down the mast of Atlanta's city hall, it carried with it George McClellan's chances for victory in the federal elections. A Georgia sergeant told his mother, "the fall of Atlanta was truly a great calamity and has cast a deep gloom upon the people and the army," more because of "the influence it will have against us in the Northern elections for President than anything else. . . . The fall of Atlanta will operate against that [Democratic] party and I fear defeat it."[102] When Lincoln beat McClellan, he dashed the hopes for peace that news of the Chicago convention had inspired among Confederates the previous summer.[103] "You need not build any hopes of peace soon for there will be none," Grant Taylor morosely announced once he learned that "old Abe Lincoln is elected again."[104] Upon hearing the election news, Abel Crawford dejectedly resigned himself to "the hardships of another four years war if any of us should survive that long."[105] Hopes for victory vanished along with hopes of peace in E. L. Cox's regiment, where "many long faces" greeted news of the election results because the prospect of four more years of Lincoln erased soldiers' faith "in our ultimat success."[106]

As Sherman's army made its way through Georgia, it spread even more "gloom which now hangs over the country," as one cavalryman put it.[107] Even in the Army of Northern Virginia, where soldiers maintained much higher morale than elsewhere, despondency began to mount as 1864 drew to a close and the biggest war news outside Virginia concerned Sherman's March. Reports that "Sherman's [army] is making his way through Georgia as hard as he can" convinced Pvt. Cornelius Oliver that "the Yankees will whip us. I don't see any other chance and if they are to do it I won't care how quick."[108] Men in another regiment became "so disheartened" by the news that "old sherman had his own way as he went through Georgia & laid every thing to distructions" that they began seriously to suspect that "god is not for us."[109] As 1864 ended, Virginia private Jim Griggs told his cousin, "in my opinion every man killed or wounded after this it will be cold blooded murder. All know that it is useless for the war to be further persisted."[110]

Sherman's March hurt the Confederacy because it destroyed supplies and weakened will, but it also damaged the Confederate war effort by aggravating the internal divisions that grew naturally out of Confederate patriotism's individualistic focus on the best interests of one's self, home, and family. Hunkering down in Savannah as Sherman's troops approached that city, Georgia private Felix Prior hoped that Union forces would pass through the rest of Georgia quickly and then go bother South Carolina so that Georgia men like himself "may be permitted to come home and stay."[111] To Georgia soldiers stationed outside of their home state, the mission of their regiment faded in importance as news of Georgia's troubles made it into camp. Pvt. Robert Jackson cared little about whether his army's attempt to hold Petersburg, Virginia, succeeded, because if it fell, only Virginians (he believed) would suffer. Meanwhile "old Hood is just leting the Vandles envade our own State Georgia," which bothered him considerably more. Jackson wished he was back home, fighting where it mattered.[112] On the other hand, Georgia's woes evoked limited sympathy from many soldiers of other states. A Mississippi man awaiting marching orders was "much elated at the idea of getting out of Georgia," and declared that "Sherman is perfectly welcome to all" of it, especially if it kept Union forces away from Mississippi. "I would not give one acre of our black land" to rescue Georgia, he declared, "but home I want saved."[113]

As reasons for discouragement piled up, including the Army of Tennessee's virtual disintegration after defeats at Franklin and Nashville, the loss of the Shenandoah Valley, and the fall of Fort Fisher, North Carolina (entry point for provisions supplying the Army of Northern Virginia), some Confederate troops rejected the predominant mood of defeatism and redoubled demands for Confederate independence.[114] From south of Richmond, John Kinyoun vowed, "We must and will whip them in the end, [we] can not aferd anything else if it takes us ten years and all the men of the South."[115] Similarly, Ethelbert Fairfax clung to his desire for "the accomplishment of our complete independence."[116]

But to many, talk of independence rang hollow because so many parts of what independence meant and why it mattered had already disappeared. The early conviction that white Southerners were morally superior to Northerners and needed their independence in order to escape contamination had crumbled. "Our country is ruined," Pvt. David Ballenger concluded, because "the morals of the people, both male and female, are ruined." Optimists had predicted that the challenges of war would bring out the best in the Confederate character, but instead, social turmoil and the demands of survival led individuals to behave in ways they never would have countenanced in ordinary times. According to Ballenger, white Southerners had grown "full of vice and crime, unfit to associate with civil people."[117] Belief that a Confederate government would better adhere to principles of good and limited government under the wise guid-

ance of superior leaders had also vanished. Far from selfless dedication to
the common weal, "our leaders" devoted their attention and efforts to their
own "fame and notoriety," grumbled a Florida sergeant.[118] Anyone who
had expected more power to reside with the states than with the nation
also found himself sorely disappointed, in big ways and small. One outraged Georgia soldier wrote to the newspaper to demand an explanation
for an episode involving state sovereignty and socks. The Georgia Relief
Association had sent socks to Richmond, Virginia, where authorities
decided to distribute the footwear to Confederate troops in need regardless
of their state of origin. Infuriated, the Georgia soldier insisted that not a
single sock from Georgia was "intended for other than the Georgians."[119]
The idea that an independent Confederacy best served the interests of
white individuals no longer held any weight for soldiers like Cornelius
Oliver, who condemned a government in the hands of what he called "a
parcel of drunken politicians that care not what becomes of we poor Privates."[120] Most obviously, the belief that an independent Confederacy
would do a better job of furthering the interests of white southern families
looked tragically ridiculous by the fourth year of the war, when men in the
ranks regularly received letters from hungry families, heard accounts of
ravaged farmlands and blacks who refused to show deference, and worried
about the very survival of their loved ones. As Oliver wrote to his wife in a
later letter, "your being in trouble causes me to see trouble." Mrs. Oliver
was pregnant, hungry, unable to procure salt, and tired of selfish neighbors
who cared too much about their own interests to help her, which made it
hard for her husband, Private Oliver, to see what the point of independence was any longer.[121]

With so much of what they loved crushed, and with so much of what
should have made an independent Confederacy worth fighting for in tatters, many Confederate troops almost reached the breaking point between
Lincoln's reelection and February 1865. "The Armey is very much demoralized. I don't believe that the men will fight much," predicted Henry Morgan, while Spencer Barnes sighed, "every thing looks quite gloomy at the
present & prospects don't seem to get no brighter." Barnes even predicted,
"the next campaign will bring [the Confederacy] down."[122] Robert Jackson harbored a similar view, prophesying that the Union Army "will whip
us yet," and Grant Taylor supposed, "this poor little confederacy is about
played out."[123] Despite valiant protestations to the contrary from some
members of the Army of Northern Virginia, defeatism threatened to over-
take soldiers and civilians alike. As Jesse Hill explained to his wife, "it is

of no use to have the men kild up and destroyed for nothing."[124] Through-out the Confederacy, public meetings also added to the clamor for peace. In Georgia, citizens met to debate Governor Joseph Brown's suggestion that Georgia take itself out of the Confederacy and negotiate a separate peace with the Union. Even Richmond, the capital city inhabited by both the Confederate government and the famed Army of Northern Virginia, oozed so much defeatism and peace sentiment that one newspaper editor reported that civilians "have not the heart to do anything but meet together and recount their losses and suffering."[125]

Yet despite the gloom and doom, the war did not end when 1865 began because, grim as things looked, the most important reason to fight still remained. In fact, in February 1865, Confederate morale spiked one last time, in response, ironically, to a failed attempt at peace. On February 3, Confederate vice president Alexander Stephens, Virginia senator R. M. T. Hunter, and Assistant Secretary of War John A. Campbell met with U.S. President Lincoln and Secretary of State William Seward aboard the steamer *River Queen* at Hampton Roads, Virginia.[126] Soldiers like Cpl. William Andrews waited anxiously, hoping that the mission would bring peace.[127] Instead, the conference foundered, sunk by the Union's peace conditions (restoration of the Union and emancipation) and by the news that the U.S. Congress had passed the Thirteenth Amendment. When word of the conference, the conditions, and the Thirteenth Amendment was published in Virginia on February 6, a huge mass meeting assembled in Richmond, a city that just days before had seethed with peace sentiment, to affirm ongoing resistance to Yankee despotism. Meanwhile, newspapers carried word of the unsuccessful conference to Confederate camps.[128]

Some soldiers regretted the failure. Devastated to learn that "peace is all nocked on the head," Cornelius Oliver blamed "Old Jeff" for being too stubborn to give peace an honest chance. Oliver's regiment held a meeting in the wake of the failed conference, and "the vote was put to our com-pany . . . whether we were for carrying this war on or whether we ware for peace. The whole company was for stopping." The company then sent two delegates to brigade headquarters to help "draft resolutions to that effect." When brigade officers learned that "we were for peace," Oliver continued, they "said the dam privates should not have a sayso in it, so they had it publish[ed] that our brigade (Ransom's) was for the war which was an infernal *lie*."[129] Yet despite the sincerity of his regret, Oliver differed from most Confederate troops in his reaction to Hampton Roads.

When most Confederate soldiers heard the conditions for peace and especially when they learned that the U.S. Congress had passed the Thirteenth Amendment, other dissatisfactions faded because no matter how much they hated Richmond, and no matter how tired they were of the war, the Union meant emancipation. As long as the Confederacy stood a chance of avoiding abolition, reason remained to keep up the fight. When Hiram Harding heard that the federal "Congress had passed an act on the 21st ult. abolishing & prohibiting slavery throughout the United States," and that peace would require the South to abide by the act, he was relieved that the Confederate commissioners agreed to "no extended truce or armistice."[130] Many soldiers were more than relieved; they were reenergized. By 1865, Charles James filled most of his letters to his sister with stern lectures about her dissipated character, but he changed the subject once he read about Hampton Roads and the Thirteenth Amendment, which showed that peace would only come if soldiers "submit to the laws of the Washington government: in other words have our property confiscated, our slaves emancipated, our leaders hung, and we become serfs in the land of our fathers." Of the conditions Fenton listed, only adherence to the Union government and emancipation were true, but from those he assumed the rest and determined that the prospect was unthinkable. "The report of our commissioners has gone forth," he reported and now soldiers were "girding on armor afresh," invigorated once again by the "spirit of patriotic devotion which at first roused the country to arms."[131] Robert Bunting agreed that Hampton Roads and the "amendment of the Constitution abolishing slavery" reminded Confederates why they went to war in the first place. "We have been awakened to the solemn reality of the situation," Bunting wrote. The Union meant "Federal bondage" for white Southerners "and their children," and that reminder took Confederates "back again to the point we started at four years ago," steeling the white southern man to refuse "to stretch out his hand for Northern fetters, and bow his dishonored head for the yoke which abolitionism stands ready to place upon him."[132]

By February of 1865, almost every link in the chain connecting ordinary soldiers to the notion of a Confederacy had come unfastened—individual interests had been trampled, homes had been destroyed by advancing armies or by poverty, governmental power had ballooned, and families were suffering—but one last link still held, and the Hampton Roads conference and the Thirteenth Amendment made clear exactly what it was. Whatever else Richmond or the war itself might destroy, as long as it could get free from the Union, the Confederacy would preserve black slavery, the institution that white southern men regarded as vital to their liberties, material interests, families' welfare, womenfolk's virtue, and individual identities as men. The war had weakened slavery, and in some places Union occupation had all but destroyed it, but Confederates still believed that if only they could wrench free from the Union, the institution would survive. After all, it had been adapting to changed circumstances since the seventeenth century, and in areas of the Confederacy untouched by a Union presence, the institution had actually grown more robust. For example, slavery strengthened in western North Carolina, as slave owners from the occupied South fled with their human property to the relative safety of the mountains, while more local nonslaveholders than ever before became able to buy slaves.[133] But all bets were off if the Union won, as Pvt. David Thompson made clear when, echoing the sentiments of countless others, he warned, "If the Yankees conquer us we will be worse than Negroes."[134] As long as the Confederacy offered an alternative to that fate, enlisted men had reason to fight, and they held on.

In March 1865, the Confederate Congress found itself forced to cut that last reliable link. By that time, the pool of available white men simply could not fill the Army's depleted ranks, and without an Army, the Confederacy would cease to exist. To meet the shortfall, on March 13, 1865, the Confederate Congress passed a bill authorizing the enlistment of no more than 25 percent of black male slaves between the ages of eighteen and forty-five. The act did not free slave soldiers, who could be enlisted only with the permission of their masters, but Adjutant General Samuel Cooper issued General Orders No. 14 requiring a black recruit's master to confer "by written instrument . . . as far as he may, the rights of a freedman." The order could be interpreted as approximating manumission, though it purposely left a gaping loophole.[135] The black enlistment question precipitated a social crisis that finally broke the Confederate rank and file.[136]

As radical as the idea of Confederate black enlistment was, it did not come completely out of the blue. Discussion dated back more than a year, to December 1863, when the Confederate general Patrick Cleburne suggested to other members of the Army of Tennessee that the Confederacy consider alleviating its manpower shortage by arming slaves. Cleburne reasoned that unless things turned around, the Confederacy would lose and the Union would impose abolition, so the Confederacy might as well use every resource at its disposal to prevent Union victory. President Davis hushed the proposal partly because it contradicted the basis and spirit of the Confederacy, but also because authorities feared the effect that such a reversal would have on southern morale.[137] As a result, very few ordinary soldiers learned of the plan, but the reactions of the few who did justified Davis's worries. Alabama sergeant Edward Brown told his wife that the black enlistment proposition was "bound to ruin us," and it made him feel "more despondant . . . than ever before."[138] Relieved when the proposal was smothered, Brown still feared that, despite the proposal's "garb of secrecy," leaked rumors about it made the Confederacy's chances look "hopeless." Desertions climbed, and even among soldiers who stayed in the ranks, the "morale of the army is anything but good now," Brown reported.[139]

As Confederate military fortunes brightened in the spring and summer months, the proposition faded, but the outlook changed once again as autumn's military catastrophes and the suddenly likely reelection of Abraham Lincoln threw the Confederacy back into dire straits. A few prominent Confederates, such as Governor Henry Allen of Louisiana, began to urge reconsideration of General Cleburne's proposal in order to address the disastrous shortfall of troops facing the Confederacy.[140] The Confederate Army had, after all, relied on slave and free black teamsters, bridge and fortification builders, hospital workers, and general laborers since the war began.[141] At the behest of officials like Allen, the Confederate Congress began seriously to debate black enlistment in the fall of 1864. This time, news of the proposed bill made it into army camps.[142]

As Congress debated the practical workings of black enlistment, soldiers lashed out at the idea that their own leaders might pass a bill that did such violence to the racial hierarchy the Confederacy was supposed to protect. As with most issues of any importance, differences of opinion arose. One Georgia sergeant who gave the matter serious thought admitted that he preferred using blacks as army laborers, but that if arming slaves proved to be the only way to avoid surrendering to the Yankees, "I say put them in and make them fight."[143] He was an exception. Charles Baughman responded in more typical fashion. "I think it is the worse measure that could be proposed," he fumed, and he hoped Congress would dismiss the notion immediately. The idea of armed blacks serving in an equal station with white men disgusted him. "I never want to see one with a gun in his hand . . . I never want to fight side by side with one," he insisted. His regiment agreed with him. "The army would not submit to it and half if not more than half would lay down their guns if forced to fight with negroes."[144] Peter Cross made the same point more succinctly when he declared, "if the negro will be put in the army then I shall quit."[145]

Shortly after Hampton Roads, the black enlistment bill's chances for success rose dramatically when the most influential Confederate, Gen. Robert E. Lee, endorsed it.[146] On February 18, 1865, Lee wrote to a Congressional supporter of the bill to say that the enlistment of slaves was "not only expedient but necessary."[147] The *Richmond Examiner* responded by wondering if Lee was really a good Southerner after all, but the paper also recognized that Lee's prestige meant that Congress would pass the bill. Some soldiers thought so, too. Virginia lieutenant William Andrews still held that black enlistment was a bad idea, but when he learned that Robert E. Lee advocated black enlistment out of military necessity, Andrews concluded that it would most likely come to pass no matter how much soldiers opposed it, since "Congress will be certain to give [Lee] whatever he asks for."[148]

In the wake of Lee's public approval, Richmond papers like the *Examiner* and *Sentinel* published resolutions from the Army of Northern Virginia in which soldiers reaffirmed their loyalty to Lee and their willingness to fight. A few such resolutions even acquiesced in the enlistment of black soldiers. On February 14, a meeting of the members of the Eleventh, Twenty-sixth, and Forty-second Mississippi concluded, "the time has come when the war material of our country, regardless of color should be fully developed." The meeting resolved, "we are in favor of the introduction of the negro, as a soldier, into the military service of the Confederacy, upon such conditions as Congress and the wisdom of our rulers may see fit to determine."[149] Meanwhile, a meeting of Thomas's Brigade determined that "when, in the opinion of President Davis and General R. E. Lee, it shall become necessary to arm a portion or all of the slaves capable of bearing arms, and make soldiers of them, we will accept it as a necessity and cheerfully acquiesce, preferring, as we do, any and all sacrifices to subjugation."[150]

A small sampling of resolutions passed by regiments in January and February 1865 even made it into *The War of the Rebellion: A Compilation of the Official Records of the Union and Confederate Armies,* from which perch they have convinced many subsequent observers that the Confederate rank and file supported the enlistment of black soldiers as a last-ditch effort to win the war and secure Confederate independence.[151] Yet while the resolutions (which came exclusively from the Army of Northern Virginia) that made it into the *Official Records* certainly signified a marked shift in some soldiers' opinions, they do not provide a very accurate picture of what most of the Confederate rank and file thought about arming black soldiers. For one thing, very few of the resolutions printed in the newspapers made it into the *Official Records,* and the ones that did are not typical, because most of the resolutions passed in camps in January and February avoided any mention of black soldiers altogether.[152] The subject of regimental consolidation claimed more ink and column space than black enlistment did.[153] Further, several regiments and brigades passed resolutions opposing black enlistment, sometimes even offering alternative solutions. The men in Jordan's Battery announced "that we view with the utmost abhorrence the idea of arriving at a settlement of our difficulties by sacrificing slavery," and in February another soldier wrote to say that more discipline among white troops, not the introduction of black soldiers, held the key to Confederate victory.[154] South Carolina soldiers used the pages of the *Charleston Mercury* to declare that they would not "fight beside a nigger—to talk of emancipation is to disband our army. We are free men and we choose to fight for ourselves, we want no slaves to fight for us."[155]

Finally, many soldiers complained that officers and newspaper editors manufactured false resolutions. North Carolina private J. C. Wright told his sister that at Lee's request his brigade had voted on "the negroe question," and that the men were "opposed to bringing them in, or rather a majority of them [are]." But he knew that what Lee said generally reigned, so he and others determined that they had "better keep silent."[156] One member of Wise's Brigade was so annoyed that the *Examiner* had falsely stated that the brigade had voted unanimously in favor of black enlistment that he wrote to the editor to demand correction of the false report. He admitted that "the negro clause" was "the only objectionable part" of the resolutions, which otherwise emphasized continued soldier support for the war effort, but it was an important enough point for him to write to the newspaper requesting that it do "justice" to the actual views of the regiment.[157]

In their personal letters, Confederate troops spoke even more bluntly, often promising to leave the Army if black enlistment passed. The "negrow question [of] whether they will raise them in the army or not" so incensed Daniel Abernethy that the illiterate private dictated a letter in which he informed his parents, "the white men says they wonte stay under such circumstances."[158] The idea of black enlistment appalled Pvt. Joseph Maides because "if they are put in the army the[y] will be on the same footing with the white man." As Maides explained to his mother, "I did not volunteer my services to fight for A free Negroes free country, but to fight for A free white mans free country & I do not think I love my country well enough to fight with black soldiers." Neither did most of his fellow enlisted men. "It is pointedly against the wills of nearly all the soldiers," he claimed, and rather than "submit to such wrongs," men were deserting "every night."[159] Simply put, black enlistment would, according to a Louisianan, deal "the death blow to our cause."[160]

As passage of the black enlistment bill looked increasingly likely, some Confederate soldiers searched for silver linings. If losing to the Yankees would make emancipation inevitable, some enlisted men reasoned, then at least putting black men in the path of Union bullets would reduce the number of blacks left to enjoy freedom after the war. After all, one private told his mother, it would be better to have the war kill "able bodied [black] men . . . than to have them all set free among us, and we be mad to submit to them as our equals."[161] Edward Brown agreed that, repulsive as black enlistment remained to him, at least the measure might lead to "the massacre of the Negro race," which would be necessary for whites' "self defense" once slavery was no longer around to prevent race war.[162]

Faced with the inevitability of black enlistment, a small number of Confederate troops tried to square the idea of black soldiers with the Confederacy's racial assumptions and social order. One slave-owning Georgia private sent an elaborate justification to the *Augusta Daily Constitutionalist*. Recognizing that whites who objected to the bill generally "oppose the measure upon the grounds that we thereby recognize or admit Negro equality," the private argued that putting black slaves into the ranks would do no such thing: "We own him as a slave, we fight with him as a slave, and when his term of service has expired, he returns to his master still a slave. His social status remains unchanged." The private proposed that, rather than being freed, slaves who served well would be rewarded with the privilege of choosing a new master, while old masters would be financially compensated. The plan would provide bondsmen with an incentive because they would be sure to "fight valiantly upon the assurance of being permitted to select a kind and humble master." This soldier did not fear that black enlistment would lead to racial equality, because he simply refused to recognize a "negro as [my] equal."[163] His plan ingeniously addressed the manpower shortage, reaffirmed belief in the fitness of blacks for slavery, confirmed the property rights of slave owners, and saved the racial hierarchy on which whites relied, all at the same time.

Texas chaplain Robert Bunting went even further, arguing that God willed black enlistment as the best way to save the divinely sanctioned institution of slavery. If considered properly, Bunting maintained, slavery was a "repelling power which God has committed to our trust," and it ought to be put to every possible use. It could save "the wealth already acquired" and "lay the basis of yet larger accumulations," if Confederates would only use it "as a fighting institution." Willful blindness to the Army's need for soldiers was "tantamount" to "abolition," because it would lead to Union victory and complete emancipation. Enlisting up to 25 percent of slave men in order to fill the southern ranks and defeat the Union ensured that 75 percent of all adult male slaves (not to mention women and children) remained in bondage. That way, reasoned Bunting, the institution would endure, even if its numbers temporarily shrank. What mattered most was that slavery "survive the war," and that meant that "duty to ourselves, to the negro, [and] to the civilization of the continent, demands of us the immediate arming of our slaves."[164]

But to most of the Confederate rank and file, Bunting missed the point. The purpose of slavery, from the perspective of the nonslaveholding southern soldier, had less to do with the wealth that it generated for owners and more to do with assuring the identity of white southern men and serving what he saw as his family's best, even if nonmaterial, interests. Slavery mattered because it foreclosed racial equality; it preserved for the southern white man his central identity as a protector and controller of dependents and as a free being in a population where most people (African Americans, women, and children) lacked the autonomy and enfranchisement due to white men. Most of all, it mattered to white non-slaveholding men because they believed it was absolutely necessary to the safety and well-being of their families. Numerous white soldiers protested black enlistment specifically because they viewed it as the attempt of the wealthy to rob ordinary Southerners of the only valuable possession left to them, their white skin. Clothing blacks in identical uniforms and placing them in the ranks alongside ordinary white soldiers—presumably at the same rank as the white privates who made up most of the Army— eliminated the only remaining reason for white nonslaveholders, especially those worried about suffering families at home, to fight. "We would have to drill and fight side by side with the stinking things," a shocked Grant Taylor exclaimed when he heard that the "officers are in favor of putting negroes into our brigade as soldiers." "To think we have been fighting four years to prevent the slaves from being freed, now to turn round and" enlist those same slaves as soldiers was "outrageous." Infuri- ated though he was, he knew exactly where to place the blame. "The big bugs say things have changed, that we must bring the negroes in and make them fight or we will be made slaves of ourselves." He made short work of such logic, writing, "well if we are reduced to that extremity . . . stop the war at once and let us come home for if we are to depend on the slaves for our freedom it is gone anyway."[165] To ordinary Confederate soldiers, black enlistment meant that the surrender of the war's purpose had already happened, which made the surrender of its Army nothing more than a matter of time.

BY THE spring of 1865, the war had created a world almost no American could have recognized in 1861. White Union troops who might once have eschewed radical abolitionism now took pride in fighting to redeem the nation from the sin of slavery, and many took seriously the obligation to make ideals like freedom and equality into realities for black as well as white Americans. Black Union soldiers, more than 80 percent of whom had once been slaves, confidently looked to a purified nation that they had helped to save, and in which they expected to continue progressing toward equal rights. Confederates, in contrast, surveyed a world in tatters, and few could any longer convince themselves of any remaining reason to fight, especially once the Confederacy adopted black enlistment. Even though the Confederacy's resources were exhausted and all that its white citizens cherished lay in ruins, to the very end Confederates resisted giving up slavery and the racial hierarchy that black bondage enforced, despite the fact that black enlistment clearly stood out as the obvious and only remaining way to redress the Confederacy's most critical shortage, manpower.[166] It was not until April 3 that North Carolina lieutenant J. G. Sills sighed, "if we intend to carry on the war, we will have to put [black soldiers] in so the sooner it is done the better."[167]

By April 3, "sooner" was not soon enough. Shortly after the black enlistment bill passed on March 13, attrition and rapidly increasing desertions had so crippled Confederate numbers that General Lee knew his depleted lines could not hold Richmond.[168] The only available options were the abandonment of Richmond, Petersburg, and the long line protecting the two cities, or encirclement. On the night of March 24–25, eleven days after Davis signed the black enlistment bill, Lee planned a surprise attack on Fort Stedman, just east of Petersburg, in hopes of forcing the Union to contract its lines and create a hole through which the Army of Northern Virginia could escape. Fort Stedman failed, and what was more, cost the Army of Northern Virginia nearly five thousand troops. Now Gen. U. S. Grant knew his army could break the Confederate lines, and he did so at Five Forks just days later. On April 2, 1865, the Army of Northern Virginia evacuated Richmond. When Union troops entered Richmond the following day, April 3, African American Union soldiers were among the first to march through the streets of the Confederate capital.

Conclusion:
What This Cruel War Was Over

ON APRIL 3, 1865, Richmond, Virginia, reverberated with so many explosions that it sounded as if a battle was raging within city limits. In the earliest hours of the morning, the last vestiges of the Army of Northern Virginia set fire to Libby Prison, blew up stockpiles of ammunition, ignited boats, bridges, and wharves, and exploded an ironclad while the Confederate government evacuated the city. By nine o'clock, detonations continued to shake Richmond, but the entrance of the Fifth Massachusetts Cavalry and the Twenty-ninth Connecticut Infantry, both black regiments, rocked the Confederate capital as surely as any demonstration of firepower could do. The first mounted Union troops to enter the city, the Fifth Massachusetts Cavalry rode through Richmond's thoroughfares as "thousands of citizens, colored and white . . . cheered and cheered as we rode in triumph along the streets."[1] From a Richmond battlement occupied only hours earlier by members of Lee's army, the men of the Twenty-ninth Connecticut hailed the sight of the recent Confederate "Capitol, over which majestically waved the glorious Stars and Stripes." "Thus another link in the chain of anarchy and degradation has been severed; and trembling like an aspen in the wind, over the yawning abyss of misery and oblivion, hangs the remnant of the rebellion," one member of the Twenty-ninth reflected.[2] Charles Beman, a private in the Fifth Massachusetts Cavalry, told his father even more matter-of-factly that "the Confederate States of America have fallen."[3]

Beman's diagnosis was premature, but not by much. As his regiment

---

Chapter title adapted from "When This Cruel War Is Over," by Charles C. Sawyer, the most popular song of the Civil War. Also known as "Weeping, Sad and Lonely," it sold over one million copies of sheet music.

In May 1865, Union Army soldiers from both eastern and western armies marked the end of the war with a two-day parade through Washington, D.C., known as the Grand Review. *Courtesy of the Library of Congress*

paraded through Richmond and President Lincoln reviewed troops in Petersburg, Virginia (also occupied by Union forces on April 3), the Army of Northern Virginia headed west, hoping to turn south and join forces with Gen. Joseph Johnston's army in North Carolina. The Army of the Potomac clashed with the Army of Northern Virginia one last time at Sayler's Creek on April 6, and on Palm Sunday, April 9, 1865, Gen. Robert E. Lee surrendered the Army of Northern Virginia to Gen. U. S. Grant at Appomattox Court House. A handful of additional battles took place throughout the Confederacy before word of Lee's surrender reached the hinterlands, but it did not take long for news to travel. Four years after the first shots at Fort Sumter, the rebellion had run its course.[4] The fall of Richmond and the surrender at Appomattox marked the end, and Confederate and Union soldiers knew it. "No further resistance will be offered," a Texas soldier promised his cousin once he heard the news. "Even if the officers were willing to continue the struggle, they could not possibly gain the support of the troops. . . . It appears that the idle dream of the *independence* of the *Southern Confederacy* has 'vanished into thin air.' "[5] As the victors, Union troops responded with exuberance. "The joy of the boys knew no bounds," related Lewis Bissell from Appomattox Court House. "They gave cheer after cheer, yell after yell. . . . Flags waved, drums rolled, bands played and hats flew up in the air. . . . There was no disputing that now this cruel war was at an end. . . . Beyond a doubt slavery has played out."[6]

The news that President Lincoln was shot by an assassin on April 14 and died the next day brought even the giddiest celebration to an abrupt halt. One after another, Union troops wrote of the "gloom" or the "dismal cloud" that descended on the Army as news of the president's death reached camp.[7] "The soldier feels as though he had lost his best friend and the country her best Statesman," mourned Nathan Parmater.[8] From his post in Florida, a black soldier confirmed that "sorrow and misery fell upon us and was depicted upon the countenance of every loyal heart."[9] Some northern soldiers felt stronger revenge impulses than the grisliest battlefield had been able to stir in them. "Oh I would like that Booth in my power I would chain him fast to some plaice and plaice all of the best victuals all around him just out of his reach and then have four nigers with hot irons to punch him if he offered to go to sleep," vowed a New York sergeant, who emphasized that he had never felt such hatred "since I have been in the Army."[10] The loss of Lincoln pained soldiers so deeply because of the strong attachment they had formed to the president, an attachment made of ideological as well as emotional bonds. Soldiers had grasped early that slavery had brought the war and must die with the war, and that the outcome of the conflict and the fate of the Union mattered to all humanity. They had also come to see the war as punishment levied on the whole nation for the shared sin of slavery, for which Northerners as well as southern slaveholders must atone. Loved ones at home had often seemed not to understand or share the insights that war brought to the Union ranks—but Lincoln had. In his speeches, especially the Gettysburg Address and the Second Inaugural Address, Lincoln had articulated a vision of the war that matched soldiers' own. Now he was gone.

Many in the Union ranks coped by vowing to carry on the work of the fallen president. Members of the Eighty-third Illinois likened Lincoln's assassination just as the war and slavery came to an end to Moses' death within sight of the promised land. As the ancient Israelites proceeded to Canaan, so would Americans continue to labor for the establishment of genuine freedom in the United States.[11] A black navy man shared in the nation's grief over the loss of "a Christian soldier of God's own choice . . . [to] lead the nation out of the dark slough of slavery," but vowed that "the great work of African regeneration or elevation commenced by [Lincoln] as the instrument in the hands of God cannot be fettered, or abate its onward march," as long as the survivors pledged themselves to carrying on that work.[12]

The assassination of the man most white Southerners blamed for making the war unavoidable brought little comfort to the Confederate ranks. Sgt. William Ellis saw poetic justice in the president's "Providential" death, believing that once Lincoln's "fell purpose [was] accomplished, nature and humanity spurned the foul abortion and he was swept from the Earth." Still, Lt. E. L. Cox captured the mood better when he noted, "instead of a general rejoicing . . . there seams to be a settled sadness upon the countenance of almost every man."[13] Having gone to war in part to fend off perceived threats to order, many Confederates could only view the murder of a president, an act of disorder if ever there was one, with dismay. Others feared a backlash from angry Northerners who might hold the South accountable and exact revenge through harsh Reconstruction measures, but whatever the source of anxiety, most Confederates longed for an end to war and regretted the extension of violence into what should have been the beginnings of peace.[14]

With the end of the fighting, Confederate troops found themselves free to concentrate on their own interests and on the well-being of their loved ones. Rudolf Coreth, who wanted to get home in a hurry to check on his family and the state of the farm, feared "that the immediate future will bring terrible events, because the least that will happen is that the Negroes will be freed." Yet "since that would not be prevented anyway by a prolongation of the fight" once Union victory became inevitable, he consoled himself with the thought that "the prospect of personal freedom is really very nice, after all."[15] William Pitt Chambers was "weary of trying to solve the problems that confront us." As a remedy for his "sick and sore" heart, he prescribed that "individually, we must address ourselves to the material problems of life," and then he headed for home.[16]

War had come, believed Coreth, Chambers, and millions of white Southerners like them, because the election of Lincoln in 1860 had posed a threat to slavery, an institution that enlisted Confederate soldiers viewed as necessary to everything they loved and to the world as they knew it, whether or not they owned slaves. Slavery's absence would doom the prosperity of the South and alter the basis of government dedicated to the interests of the governed, but most of all, feared enlisted Confederate soldiers, the disappearance of slavery would endanger their families' safety, welfare, and material aspirations, and undermine their very identities as white men.

Yet aside from white Southerners' widespread antipathy toward the Union and common certainty about the life-or-death necessity of preventing abolition, Confederates shared little common attachment to an entity called the Confederate States of America. Specifically, Confederate patriotism contained an inherent tension between the needs and interests of the Confederacy, and the needs and interests of soldiers and their families, which soldiers went to war to protect from the dangers of abolition, and which they trusted the Confederacy to serve. Initially the tension remained latent, but as the needs of families increasingly conflicted with the demands of the Confederacy, strains became harder to ignore.

Two factors helped keep Confederate troops committed to the fight and to their disappointing new nation, even as the ferocity of the war undid every aspect of government and society that Confederates held dear. In the second half of the war, many turned to religion, sure that God had sent the war as punishment for individuals' venal transgressions, such as drinking, swearing, or price gouging, which, once corrected, would result in an end to the war and an even more godly nation. Confederate soldiers found solace in religion not only because it promised heavenly rewards after death, but also because in demanding individual behavior modifications while discouraging wholesale social change, it reinforced white Southerners' beliefs in the inherent superiority of their own society, including its bedrock institution of slavery.

Even more important, Confederate soldiers reminded themselves that no matter how bad the Confederacy was, the Union was worse because the Union meant abolition and the attendant destruction of everything that mattered. That ironclad conviction compelled enlisted men to keep up the fight long after they grew to despise the Confederate government and disdain the southern citizenry. Then, in the spring of 1865, the prospect of black enlistment destroyed the guarantees provided by slavery, and, in the minds of the rank and file, eliminated any remaining reason to fight.

In 1865, Confederate soldiers knew that their world was destroyed. "This country is ruined, dead," Henry Richardson emphasized as he described the landscape around his home, now left desolate by the departure of the slave labor force that had once caused it to prosper.[17] Southern whites surveyed the world in tatters, and they expected no say in how the threads were to be knit back together.[18] As a Texan put it, Confederates "do not suppose, nor expect to be allowed to vote any more, as long as we live. We also expect that all the lands in the Confederacy, will be taken away from the white people to pay their war expenses then given in small 160 acre lots to the negroes." Confederates certainly did not relish the fate they supposed awaited them, but neither did they yet believe that they had the ability to avoid it.[19] In short, white Southerners expected far more sweeping Reconstruction measures, including disenfranchisement, property confiscation, and redistribution of land to former slaves, than the federal government actually enacted, and they believed themselves in no position to object or obstruct the will of the North.[20]

Obvious to black Americans and to Confederates from the outset, slavery's centrality to the war quickly became apparent to white Union troops, as well. In 1861, the white men who enlisted in the Union Army believed that the Union had to survive in order to prove to the whole world that a representative government founded on the ideals of liberty and equality could work. By setting out to destroy the Union in order to protect slavery, white Southerners had made the war about slavery whether white Northerners liked it or not; therefore, in the late summer and fall of 1861, a full year ahead of the Emancipation Proclamation, the Union rank and file began to insist on the destruction of slavery for a variety of motives that sometimes conflicted with one another, but that in the end distilled down to soldiers' central insight that the only way to end the war and prevent it from happening again was to get rid of slavery, because slavery had caused all the trouble in the first place. Initially, white Union troops strove to separate slavery from the more complicated issues of black rights and racial equality, embracing abolition while evading hard questions about what the nation owed to former slaves.

Yet as the war progressed, white soldiers' interactions with black Southerners and their perceptions of slavery's effect on families, combined with the inspiring example of black soldiers and the fury of war itself, persuaded many that in order to regain God's favor (which would be necessary to win the war), white Northerners must examine and redress how their own racial attitudes made them complicit in the sin of slavery. Especially after Gettysburg and Vicksburg, widely perceived in the Union ranks as God's direct intervention on behalf of Union and true freedom, Union troops found themselves forced to confront the possibility that God had called the North to erase and atone for the national, not merely southern, sin of slavery. Some even believed that God demanded repentance for the more insidious evil of racial prejudice, and in the war's last year, surprising numbers of white Union troops advocated advances (such as legal equality, equal pay for black soldiers, and suffrage) that only the furthest reaches of radical abolitionism broached before the war. Members of the 122d New York, for example, argued in the pages of *The Third Brigade* that the end of slavery must be accompanied by all-out social and moral reform, and criticized President Andrew Johnson for advocating segregation.[21] New York private Haven Putnam also conceded the need for a "social revolution" and congratulated his sweetheart, Mary, who went south to teach former slaves, for serving as a "warrior" in a "campaign" as necessary, as "arduous, and of as much social importance" as the war itself.[22] The Civil War was revolutionary in many ways, none more so than the radical advances that took place in some white Northerners' thinking on race.

Black Americans, meanwhile, immediately grasped that war against secession must also be a war against slavery, and interpreted the war as a struggle for black freedom, equality, and inclusion within the promises of the American Revolution. African American soldiers also envisioned the war as an opportunity to demonstrate the manhood of their race, by which they meant both their own adult male identity and the full humanity of all black Americans. Although their offers to fight were rebuffed for more than a year, before the war was over African Americans enlisted in the ranks, earned equal pay for their military service, and witnessed changes in American society ranging from the integration of public conveyances to the admission of a black lawyer to argue before the U.S. Supreme Court to reunion with family members once thought lost forever. Surveying the ways in which war had remade the racial landscape, black artilleryman David Williamson surmised, "the time has come when liberty is in reach of all men without respect to color."[23]

In short, black Americans at the conclusion of the Civil War evinced justifiable confidence in their ability to reap the benefits and promises of the nation they had helped to regenerate for themselves and for members of their race, just at a moment when white Union soldiers' opinions on the rights of African Americans were malleable, and when Confederates exhibited the least ability or inclination to resist any reconstructive measures, including racial reform. In a nation that had witnessed massive upheaval and vast steps forward that had once seemed inconceivable, there was certainly reason to believe that continued progress toward racial equality was not only possible, but likely. Because we know those hopes were disappointed by the turn of the twentieth century, we have assumed that the reactionary developments of the Jim Crow era in the 1880s and 1890s, when the hard-fought gains of the war and Reconstruction faded, were inevitable.[24] After all, white Union troops' backsliding on questions of black rights and racial equality in the spring and summer of 1864, along with Confederates' savage violence against blacks in those same months, might make the lynchings and legal segregation of the 1890s seem predictable. Yet by the spring of 1865, attitudes among white Union soldiers were shifting once again, black optimism was justifiably high, and initially, at least, white Southerners did not see themselves in any position to resist. In fact, if the spring of 1865 tells us anything, it fairly shouts at us to let go of our notions of inevitability.

In the spring of 1865, the cruel war was over, but the work of reconstructing the American nation had only just begun. Because that work remains unfinished, it places demands on the heirs to the world the Civil War created. Of these demands, three stand out as especially inescapable. First, Confederate soldiers' admirable devotion to their families and abhorrent attachment to the enslavement of other human beings sound a cautionary note because those impulses were so closely related. There is little doubt that most white southern men cared first and foremost about the well-being and material advancement of their loved ones, and the steadfast love so many displayed for their families surely stands among the noblest of human emotions. Yet that very love led otherwise good and ordinary men to embrace and fight for an institution that stole the lives and bodies and families of other human beings. Clearly, the connection between soldiers' attachment to their families and the institution of slavery does not suggest that love of family is to be disparaged, or that it inevitably leads to an atrocity like slavery, but it does raise sobering questions about the ills that human beings will justify when they convince themselves that they owe no obligation to anyone beyond those to whom they are related or who are like themselves.

Second, astonishing changes took place in many white Union men's ideas about slavery and eventually, if more fragilely, about racial equality. When ordinary northern men, many of whom began the war without a single black acquaintance but with plenty of prejudice toward African Americans, actually met black people face to face and often came to rely on the aid, comfort, and military intelligence that former slaves offered to the Union Army, they found reasons to discard old views. Those changes remind historians of the power of events to rearrange even the most seemingly immovable cultural ideas and attitudes among people in the past, and they alert all of us to the dramatic changes in attitude and achievement that can take place when people who think they have nothing in common find themselves thrust into interaction and interdependence.

Finally, the vision of a very different United States could be seen clearly by men like David Williamson in the spring of 1865 but had faded tragically by the turn of the twentieth century. Taken together, the vividness of the vision and its eventual fading challenge historians to investigate more rigorously exactly how the United States could in the crucible of war create such vast potential for change and then, in the end, fail to fulfill it.

NOTES

MOC   Eleanor S. Brockenbrough Library, Museum of the Confederacy, Richmond

MOHS   Missouri Historical Society, St. Louis

NCDAH   North Carolina Division of Archives and History, Raleigh

NYHS   New-York Historical Society, New York

NYPL   Manuscripts and Special Collections, New York Public Library

NYSL   Special Collections, New York State Library, Albany

OHS   Ohio Historical Society, Columbus

PAW   *People at War,* microfilm collection of Library of Congress sources

PRONI   Public Records Office of Northern Ireland, Belfast

Quiner Papers   *E. B. Quiner Correspondence of Wisconsin Volunteers,* microfilm reels available from State Historical Society of Wisconsin, Madison

SCAH   South Carolina Archives and History Center, Columbia

Schoff   Schoff Collection, Clements Library, University of Michigan, Ann Arbor

Schomburg   Schomburg Center for Research in Black Culture, New York Public Library

SCL   South Caroliniana Library, University of South Carolina, Columbia

SHC   Southern Historical Collection, University of North Carolina, Chapel Hill

SHSW   State Historical Society of Wisconsin, Madison

SU   Bird Library, Syracuse University, Syracuse

TSLA   Tennessee State Library and Archives, Nashville

UAR   Special Collections, University of Arkansas, Fayetteville

UMOC   Western Historical Manuscripts Collection, University of Missouri, Columbia

UMOKC   Western Historical Manuscripts Collection, University of Missouri, Kansas City

UMOR   Western Historical Manuscripts Collection, University of Missouri, Rolla

UVA   Alderman Library, University of Virginia, Charlottesville

VHS   Virginia Historical Society, Richmond

VOS   Valley of the Shadow Civil War Project, http://valley.vcdh.virginia.edu

VTHS   Vermont Historical Society, Montpelier

WRHS   Western Reserve Historical Society, Cleveland

Introduction

1. *The Wisconsin Volunteer,* February 6, 1862, Leavenworth, Kans., p. 3, KSHS. *The Wisconsin Volunteer* was the newspaper of the Thirteenth Wis. Infantry regiment. Hereafter, "Infantry Regiment" will be omitted in the names of military units; any regiments not specified as artillery or cavalry may be understood to be infantry regiments.

2. *The Vidette,* November 2, 1862, Springfield, Tenn., p. 3, TSLA. *The Vidette* was the newspaper of Morgan's Confederate Brigade.

3. *The Black Warrior,* May 17, 1864, Camp Parapet, La., p. 2, SHSW. *The Black Warrior* was the camp paper of the Fourteenth R.I. Heavy Artillery, a black regiment.

4. Ibid.

5. Since Maris Vinovskis famously wondered if social historians had lost the Civil War (Maris A. Vinovskis, "Have Social Historians Lost the Civil War? Some Preliminary Demographic Speculations," *Journal of American History* 76:1 [1989], 34–58), studies of the home front, and later the overlap between the battlefield and home front, have flown off the presses. Joseph Glatthaar's "The 'New' Civil War History: An Overview," *Pennsylvania Magazine of History and Biography* 115:3 (July 1991), 339–69, describes how the mounting realization that wars are "cataclysmic" (339) events that offer insight into the societies that wage them has reinvigorated the study of American wars, especially the Civil War. Recent works that attest to this trend include Edward L. Ayers, *In the Presence of Mine Enemies: The Civil War in the Heart of America, 1859–1863* (New York: Norton, 2003); William Blair, *Virginia's Private War: Feeding Body and Soul in the Confederacy, 1861–1865* (New York: Oxford University Press, 1998); Charles E. Brooks, "The Social and Cultural Dynamics of Soldiering in Hood's Texas Brigade," *Journal of Southern History* 67 (August 2001), 535–73; Drew Gilpin Faust, *Mothers of Invention: Women of the Slaveholding South in the American Civil War* (Chapel Hill: University of North Carolina Press, 1996); Joseph Glatthaar, *The March to the Sea and Beyond: Sherman's Troops in the Savannah and Carolinas Campaign* (Baton Rouge: Louisiana State University Press, 1985); Randall Jimerson, *The Private Civil War: Popular Thought During the Sectional Conflict* (Baton Rouge: Louisiana State University Press, 1988); Reid Mitchell, *The Vacant Chair: The Northern Soldier Leaves Home* (New York: Oxford University Press, 1993). *The March to the Sea and Beyond* in particular probes how midwestern cultural mores and the experiences of three years of fighting molded the men who took part in the Union's famous 1864 march through Georgia and the Carolinas, and who in turn influenced the course of one key campaign of the war.

6. See, for example, Blair, *Virginia's Private War*; Gary W. Gallagher, *The Confederate War* (Cambridge, Mass.: Harvard University Press, 1997); Gary W. Gallagher, *Lee & His Army in Confederate History* (Chapel Hill: University of North Carolina Press, 2001); Anne Sarah Rubin, *A Shattered Nation: The Rise and Fall of the Confederacy, 1861–1868* (Chapel Hill: University of North Carolina Press, 2005); Aaron Sheehan-Dean, "Justice Has Something To Do With It: Class Relations and the Confederate Army," *Virginia Magazine of History and Biography* 113:4 (November 2005), 340–77. Rubin in particular labors to portray instances of white southern self-interest as momentary aberrations from "real" patriotism, which prevailed.

7. See, for example, Fred Arthur Bailey, *Class and Tennessee's Confederate Generation* (Chapel Hill: University of North Carolina Press, 1987); Paul D. Escott, *After Secession: Jefferson Davis and the Failure of Confederate Nationalism* (Baton Rouge: Louisiana State University Press, 1978); Armstead L. Robinson, *Bitter Fruits of Bondage: The Demise of Slavery and the Collapse of the Confederacy, 1861–1865* (Charlottesville: University of Virginia Press, 2005); David Williams, *Rich Man's War: Class, Caste, and Confederate Defeat in the Lower Chattahoochee Valley* (Athens: University of Georgia Press, 1998); David and Teresa C. Williams and David Carlson, *Plain Folk in a Rich Man's War: Class and Dissent in Confederate Georgia* (Gainesville: University of Florida Press, 2002).

8. Susan-Mary Grant in *North Over South: Northern Nationalism and American Identity in the Antebellum Era* (Lawrence: University of Kansas Press, 2000) and Peter Parish in *The North and the Nation in the Era of the Civil War* (New York: Fordham University Press, 2003) portray northern patriotism, by which they mean a militant commitment to the aims of the state and government, as the product of the Civil War. Both authors concede that Northerners felt an emotional attachment to the American nation before the war, but

they did not connect it to the U.S. government until after the war. In contrast, Phillip S. Paludan argues in "The American Civil War Considered as a Crisis in Law and Order," *American Historical Review* 77:4 (October 1972), 1013–34, and *"A People's Contest": The Union and the Civil War 1861–1865* (New York: Harper and Row, 1988), esp. part 1, that the daily exigencies of small-town life and its many opportunities for office holding, voting, and other forms of participation in government led antebellum Northerners to feel a strong emotional attachment to the U.S. government before the war, which was why secession prompted such an outpouring of emotion and outrage among ordinary Northerners.

9. On antebellum millennialism in the North, see Robert Bellah, *The Broken Covenant: American Civil Religion in Time of Trial* (New York: Seabury, 1975); Samuel S. Hill, Jr., *The South and the North in American Religion* (Athens: University of Georgia Press, 1981); Richard T. Hughes and C. Leonard Allen, *Illusions of Innocence: Protestant Primitivism in America, 1630–1875* (Chicago: University of Chicago Press, 1988); Stuart McConnell, *Glorious Contentment: The Grand Army of the Republic, 1865–1900* (Chapel Hill: University of North Carolina Press, 1992); Randall M. Miller, Harry S. Stout, and Charles Reagan Wilson, eds., *Religion and the American Civil War* (New York: Oxford University Press, 1998), Introduction; James H. Moorhead, *American Apocalypse: Yankee Protestants and the Civil War 1860–1869* (New Haven: Yale University Press, 1978); and Philip Paludan, "Religion and the American Civil War," in Miller, Stout, and Wilson, *Religion and the American Civil War.*

10. Bell Irvin Wiley, *The Life of Johnny Reb: The Common Soldier of the Confederacy* (Indianapolis: Bobbs-Merrill, 1943) and *The Life of Billy Yank: The Common Soldier of the Union* (Indianapolis: Bobbs-Merrill, 1952). I was hooked from the time I borrowed *The Life of Johnny Reb* from my local library (and only partly because of the thrill of being allowed to check a book out of the adult section of the library at the tender age of about seven), and any time a group of Civil War enthusiasts gets together, chances are good that at least one of them will share a similar experience.

11. For examples of "bottom up" histories of Civil War soldiers, see Larry Daniel, *Soldiering in the Army of Tennessee: A Portrait of Life in a Confederate Army* (Chapel Hill: University of North Carolina Press, 1991); J. Tracy Power, *Lee's Miserables: Life in the Army of Northern Virginia from the Wilderness to Appomattox* (Chapel Hill: University of North Carolina Press, 1998).

12. Ira Berlin, Joseph P. Reidy, and Leslie S. Rowland, eds., *Freedom: A Documentary History of Emancipation, 1861–1867,* series 2, *The Black Military Experience* (New York: Cambridge University Press, 1985); Dudley Taylor Cornish, *The Sable Arm: Negro Troops in the Union Army, 1861–1865* (Lawrence: University of Kansas Press, 1987); Hondon B. Hargrove, *Black Union Soldiers in the Civil War* (Jefferson, N.C.: McFarland, 1988); James G. Hollandsworth, Jr., *The Louisiana Native Guards: The Black Military Experience During the Civil War* (Baton Rouge: Louisiana State University Press, 1995); Edward Miller, *The Black Civil War Soldiers of Illinois: The Story of the Twenty-Ninth U.S. Colored Infantry* (Columbia: University of South Carolina Press, 1998); John David Smith, ed., *Black Soldiers in Blue: African American Troops in the Civil War Era* (Chapel Hill: University of North Carolina Press, 2002); Noah Andre Trudeau, *Like Men of War: Black Troops in the Civil War* (Boston: Little, Brown, 1998); Keith Wilson, *Campfires of Freedom: Black Soldiers During the Civil War* (Kent: Kent State University Press, 2002). In 1994, the DaCapo Press of New York reprinted Joseph T. Wilson's classic *The Black Phalanx: African American Soldiers in the War of Independence, the War of 1812, and the Civil War* (Hartford: American Publishing, 1890).

13. For an example of a World War II study that stresses the nonideological nature of

enlisted soldiers, see Paul Fussell, *Wartime: Understanding and Behavior in the Second World War* (New York: Oxford University Press, 1989). Despite differences in emphasis and interpretation, and despite the valuable insights they offer, works as diverse as Michael Barton, *Goodmen: The Character of Civil War Soldiers* (University Park: Pennsylvania State University Press, 1981); Gerald Linderman, *Embattled Courage: The Experience of Combat in the American Civil War* (New York: Macmillan, 1987); and James Robertson, *Soldiers Blue and Gray* (Columbia: University of South Carolina Press, 1988) all downplay the significance of ideology to the men who fought the Civil War. James McPherson links this tendency to World War II and the Vietnam War in *For Cause and Comrades: Why Men Fought in the Civil War* (New York: Oxford University Press, 1997), 4–5, 90–91.

14. Reid Mitchell, *Civil War Soldiers* (New York: Simon and Schuster, 1988). In a related development, some historians have taken up the associated issue of how soldiers' religious beliefs molded their wartime experiences. See, for example, Steven E. Woodworth, *While God Is Marching On: The Religious World of Civil War Soldiers* (Lawrence: University of Kansas Press, 2001). An older, but still useful, treatment of soldiers' religious views is Gardiner H. Shattuck, Jr., *A Shield and Hiding Place: The Religious Life of the Civil War Armies* (Macon, Ga.: Mercer University Press, 1987).

15. McPherson, *For Cause and Comrades.* McPherson's earlier book, *What They Fought For: 1861–1865* (Baton Rouge: Louisiana State University Press, 1994), which actually began as the Walter Lynwood Fleming Lectures in Southern History, previews many of the themes that appear in *For Cause and Comrades.*

16. Gary Gallagher, J. Tracy Power, and Aaron Sheehan-Dean, for example, concentrate exclusively on soldiers in the Army of Northern Virginia, while Larry Daniel gives the Confederacy's major western army, the Army of Tennessee, its share of attention. Meanwhile, Union soldiers provide the exclusive focus of works like Earl J. Hess, *Liberty, Virtue, and Progress: Northerners and Their War for the Union* (New York: Fordham University Press, 1997); Earl J. Hess, *The Union Soldier in Battle* (Lawrence: University of Kansas Press, 1997); and Steven E. Woodworth, *Nothing but Victory: The Army of the Tennessee, 1861–1865* (New York: Knopf, 2005). For works covering both armies, but treating them as virtually interchangeable, see Joseph Allan Frank and George Reaves, *Seeing the Elephant: Raw Recruits in the Battle of Shiloh* (New York: Greenwood, 1989); and Larry Logue, *To Appomattox and Beyond: The Civil War Soldier in War and Peace* (Chicago: Ivan R. Dee, 1996). Even McPherson's *For Cause and Comrades* often makes it difficult to distinguish between Union and Confederate troops. In fact, the idea for this study took root in class one day when students and I were discussing *For Cause and Comrades.* Discussion remained lively until I asked students what made Union and Confederate soldiers different from each other. Sometimes dead silence in response to a question simply means students have not read the book, but on that day, they had been chatting right along up until that point. The sudden silence led me to resolve that before settling for the notion that 620,000 Americans killed one another because they all agreed on everything, I wanted to take another, more consciously comparative, look.

17. Despite the rich nature of troops' letters and diaries, all sources present problems and challenges, and these are no exception. The written nature of the sources automatically raises the problem of representativeness, especially with regard to illiterate soldiers, who are by definition virtually excluded from a study of soldiers' writings. However, illiterate Civil War soldiers are fewer in number than might be supposed. Over 80 percent of Confederate soldiers could read and write, while over 90 percent of white Union soldiers were literate. Moreover, illiterate soldiers often dictated letters to literate messmates, and the words of some of these men are included here.

18. In a 1943 article, Bell Wiley excitedly reported the discovery of regimental news-papers, and announced his intention to write a book about them. He mentioned them in *Johnny Reb* and *Billy Yank,* but he later conceded that he had found too few to pursue the idea, and concluded that not very many survived. Wiley's failure to find them is not sur-prising, since they are generally hidden in small archives that are unaware of their exis-tence, let alone their location in the stacks. Finding them involves extensive and determined searching, and to the best of my knowledge, no historian has systematically looked for them since Wiley abandoned the hunt. I found them only by looking at every American newspaper published between 1861 and 1865 in the holdings of forty-five archives. See Wiley, "Camp Newspapers of the Confederacy," *North Carolina Historical Review* 20 (1943), 327–35.

19. See, for example, Ira Berlin, Barbara J. Fields, Thavolia Glymph, Joseph P. Reidy, and Leslie S. Rowland, eds., *Freedom: A Documentary History of Emancipation, 1861–1867,* ser. 1, vol. 1, *The Destruction of Slavery* (New York: Cambridge University Press, 1985), 1–56; Ira Berlin, *Slaves No More: Three Essays on Emancipation and the Civil War* (New York: Cambridge University Press, 1992); and Vincent Harding, *The Black Struggle for Freedom in America* (New York: Vintage, 1981).

20. See, for example, LaWanda Cox, *Lincoln and Black Freedom: A Study in Presiden-tial Leadership* (Columbia: University of South Carolina Press, 1981); and James M. McPherson, "Who Freed the Slaves?" in *Drawn with the Sword: Reflections on the Ameri-can Civil War* (New York: Oxford University Press, 1996).

21. See, for example, William C. Davis, *Lincoln's Men: How President Lincoln Became Father to an Army and a Nation* (New York: Free Press, 1999); and Ida Tarbell, *Life of Lincoln,* vol. 2 (New York: McClure, Phillips, 1900), ch. 27, "Lincoln and the Soldiers."

22. What follows is an abbreviated and incomplete overview of rising sectional ten-sions in the years before the Civil War. The best single-volume study of growing antebel-lum conflict remains David Potter, *The Impending Crisis* (New York: Harper and Row, 1976).

23. Peter D. McClelland and Richard J. Zeckhauser, *Demographic Dimensions of the New Republic* (Cambridge, Mass.: Harvard University Press, 1982); Mark V. Wethering-ton, *Plain Folk's Fight: The Civil War and Reconstruction in Piney Woods Georgia* (Chapel Hill: University of North Carolina Press, 2005), 63. For the expansion of slavery from the seaboard to the Deep South, see Adam Rothman, *Slave Country: American Expansion and the Origins of the Deep South* (Cambridge, Mass.: Harvard University Press, 2005).

24. Missouri itself was the one exception: with its southern boundary at 36° 30′ lati-tude, it is actually north of the Missouri Compromise line. For Tallmadge's Amendment, see *Debates of Congress from 1789–1856,* vol. 6 (1817–21) (New York, 1858). Several votes were taken in each House of Congress, all returning the same overall result. The final House vote at the close of the Fifteenth Congress, Second Session (March 1819), was seventy-nine for Tallmadge's Amendment, sixty-seven against it. The Senate's concluding vote was similarly close, but the result was to reject Tallmadge's Amendment. For the return of the issue to Congress, see *Debates of Congress,* 6: 204–372, with voting results on pp. 344 and 372. On the Missouri controversy generally, see Richard Brown, "The Mis-souri Crisis, Slavery and the Politics of Jacksonianism," *South Atlantic Quarterly* 65 (win-ter 1966); Philip F. Detweiler, "Congressional Debate on Slavery and the Declaration of Independence, 1819–1821," *American Historical Review* 63:3 (1958), 598–616; Don E. Fehrenbacher, *The South and Three Sectional Crises* (Baton Rouge: Louisiana State Uni-versity Press, 1980); Kenneth S. Greenberg, "Revolutionary Ideology and the Proslavery

Argument: The Abolition of Slavery in Ante-bellum South Carolina," *Journal of Southern History* 42 (1976), 365–84; Shaw Livermore, Jr., *The Twilight of Federalism: The Disintegration of the Federalist Party 1815–1830* (Princeton, N.J.: Princeton University Press, 1962); Glover Moore, *The Missouri Controversy 1819–1821* (Lexington: University of Kentucky Press, 1953); Robert E. Shalhope, "Thomas Jefferson's Republicanism and Ante-bellum Southern Thought," *Journal of Southern History* 42 (1976), 529–56; Charles Sydnor, *The Development of Southern Sectionalism 1819–1848* (Baton Rouge: Louisiana State University Press, 1948); Sean Wilentz, "Jeffersonian Democracy and the Origins of Political Antislavery in the United States: The Missouri Crisis Revisited," *Journal of the Historical Society* 4:3 (2004), 375–401; and Joshua Michael Zeitz, "The Missouri Compromise Reconsidered: Rhetoric and the Emergence of the Free Labor Synthesis," *Journal of the Early Republic* 20:3 (2000), 447–85.

25. On the Missouri crisis and the emergence of proslavery ideology, see David W. Blight, "Perceptions of Southern Intransigence and the Rise of Radical Antislavery Thought, 1816–1830," *Journal of the Early Republic* 3:2 (1983), 139–64; Chandra Miller, " 'Title Page to a Great Tragic Volume': The Impact of the Missouri Crisis on Slavery, Race, and Republicanism in the Thought of John C. Calhoun and John Quincy Adams," *Missouri Historical Review* 94:4 (2000), 365–88; Sydnor, *The Development of Southern Sectionalism;* Wilentz, "Jeffersonian Democracy and the Origins of Political Antislavery." On proslavery generally, see Drew Gilpin Faust, ed., *The Ideology of Slavery: Proslavery Thought in the Antebellum South, 1830–1860* (Baton Rouge: Louisiana State University Press, 1981); Larry E. Tise, *Proslavery: A History of the Defense of Slavery in America, 1701–1840* (Athens: University of Georgia Press, 1987). On abolitionism see James Brewer Stewart, *Holy Warriors: Abolitionism and American Slavery* (New York: Hill and Wang, 1996); Ronald G. Walters, *The Anti-Slavery Appeal: American Abolitionism After 1830* (New York: Norton, 1984). For political antislavery, see Richard H. Sewell, *Ballots for Freedom: Antislavery Politics in the United States, 1837–1860* (New York: Oxford University Press, 1976).

26. On the gag rule controversy, see William Lee Miller, *Arguing About Slavery: The Great Battle in the United States Congress* (New York: Knopf, 1996). On Elijah Lovejoy, see Paul Simon, *Freedom's Champion: Elijah Lovejoy* (Carbondale: Southern Illinois University Press, 1994). Even though slavery generally remained below the surface in the 1830s, it was rarely absent, as Susan Wyly-Jones shows in "The 1835 Anti-Abolition Meetings in the South: A New Look at the Controversy over the Abolition Postal Campaign," *Civil War History* 47:4 (2001), 289–309.

27. On expansion and slavery in the 1840s through the Compromise of 1850, see William J. Cooper, *Liberty and Slavery: Southern Politics to 1860* (New York: Knopf, 1983); Eric Foner, "The Wilmot Proviso Revisited," *Journal of American History* 56 (1969), 262–79; William Freehling, *Road to Disunion* (New York: Oxford University Press, 1990); Thomas Hietala, *Manifest Design: American Exceptionalism and Empire* (Ithaca, N.Y.: Cornell University Press, 2003); Bruce Levine, *Half Slave and Half Free: The Roots of Civil War* (New York: Hill and Wang, 1992); Stephen E. Maizlish and John J. Kushma, eds., *Essays on American Antebellum Politics 1840–1860* (Arlington: University of Texas Press, 1982); Michael Morrison, *Slavery and the American West: The Eclipse of Manifest Destiny and the Coming of the Civil War* (Chapel Hill: University of North Carolina Press, 1997); Allan Nevins, *Ordeal of the Union,* vol. 1, *Fruits of Manifest Destiny 1847–1852* (New York: Scribner, 1947); Potter, *Impending Crisis.*

28. First appearing serially in *The National Era* in 1851–52, *Uncle Tom's Cabin* was published as a novel in 1852. More than 300,000 copies sold in a single year. To place that

number in perspective, respectable sales enjoyed by authors like Henry David Thoreau and Herman Melville ran in the two thousand range. *Uncle Tom's Cabin* was also performed as a play throughout the North. For more on Stowe and the impact of the book in the North, see Joan Hedrick, *Harriet Beecher Stowe: A Life* (New York: Oxford University Press, 1994). For an example of the southern response, see Louisa McCord's review of *Uncle Tom's Cabin,* first published in the *Southern Quarterly Review,* in Richard C. Lounsbury, ed., *Louisa S. McCord: Political and Social Essays* (Charlottesville: University of Virginia Press, 1995).

29. Ann Walsh Bradley and Joseph A. Ranney, "A Tradition of Independence: The Wisconsin Supreme Court's First 150 Years," *Wisconsin Magazine of History* (winter 2002–2003), 42–49; Michael McManus, *Political Abolitionism in Wisconsin, 1840–1861* (Kent, Ohio: Kent State University Press, 1998); Thomas Morris, *Free Men All: The Personal Liberty Laws of the North* (Baltimore: Johns Hopkins University Press, 1974); Joseph A. Ranney, "Suffering the Agonies of Their Righteousness: The Rise and Fall of the States Rights Movement in Wisconsin, 1854–1861," *Wisconsin Magazine of History* 75:2, 85–117; Albert J. Von Frank, *The Trials of Anthony Burns: Freedom and Slavery in Emerson's Boston* (Cambridge, Mass.: Harvard University Press, 1998).

30. For Stephen Douglas and the Kansas-Nebraska Act, see Harry V. Jaffa, *Crisis of the House Divided: An Interpretation of the Lincoln-Douglas Debates* (Chicago: University of Chicago Press, 1982); Robert W. Johannsen, *Stephen A. Douglas* (Urbana: University of Illinois Press, 1997); Roy F. Nichols, "The Kansas-Nebraska Act: A Century of Historiography," *Mississippi Valley Historical Review* 43 (1956), 187–212; Potter, *Impending Crisis,* 145–76. Born in Scotland, James Redpath wrote for the *New York Tribune* regularly and for the *Chicago Tribune* and *St. Louis Democrat* occasionally. For Kansas in the 1850s see Albert Castel, *Civil War Kansas: Reaping the Whirlwind* (Lawrence: University of Kansas Press, 1997); Nicole Etcheson, *Bleeding Kansas: Contested Liberty in the Civil War Era* (Lawrence: University of Kansas Press, 2004); Thomas Goodrich, *War to the Knife: Bleeding Kansas, 1854–1861* (Mechanicsburg, Pa.: Stackpole Press, 1998); Sarah T. L. Robinson, *Kansas: Its Interior and Exterior Life Including A Full View of Its Settlement, Political History, Social Life, Climate, Soil, Productions, Scenery, Etc.* (Boston, 1856). For the impact of the Lecompton constitution see Allan Nevins, *The Emergence of Lincoln,* vol. 1, *Douglas, Buchanan, and Party Chaos 1857–1859* (New York: Scribner, 1951); and Kenneth Stampp, *America in 1857* (New York: Oxford University Press, 1990). For more information on guerrilla warfare in the bordering state of Missouri, see Michael Fellman, *Inside War: The Guerrilla Conflict in Missouri During the American Civil War* (New York: Oxford University Press, 1989).

31. Speech of Hon. Lucius Gartrell of Georgia, *Congressional Globe,* Thirty-fifth Congress, First Session (Washington, D.C., 1858), 393.

32. *Washington Union,* November 17, 1857, cited in James M. McPherson, *Battle Cry of Freedom: The Civil War Era* (New York: Oxford University Press, 1988): 180. For more on the Dred Scott decision, see Don E. Fehrenbacher, *The Dred Scott Case: Its Significance in American Law and Politics* (New York: Oxford University Press, 1978); and Stampp, *America in 1857,* 68–109.

33. Paul Finkelman notes the existence of unpublished notes and drafts in Roger Taney's papers which indicate that Taney was preparing to write a decision dictating that "all," including the "free states of the union" had "an obligation . . . to respect the institution of slavery" even within their own borders. See Paul Finkelman, *An Imperfect Union: Slavery, Federalism, and Comity* (Chapel Hill: University of North Carolina Press, 1981), 338.

34. For discussion of *Lemmon* v. *the People,* the case of a slaveholder against the state of New York, see Finkelman, *An Imperfect Union,* 312–36; and Fehrenbacher, *The Dred Scott Case,* 444–45. For more on Northerners' fears that Dred Scott would lead to slavery for every state, see William E. Gienapp, "The Republican Party and the Slave Power," in Robert H. Abzug and Stephen E. Maizlish, eds., *New Perspectives on Race and Slavery in America: Essays in Honor of Kenneth M. Stampp* (Lexington: University of Kentucky Press, 1986), 68–69; and Stampp, *America in 1857.*

35. A vast literature exists on the politics of the 1850s, the rise of the Republican Party, and the Slave Power conspiracy. Adam Rothman provides a very useful and concise summary of the idea of the Slave Power in " 'The Slave Power' in the United States, 1783–1865," in Steve Fraser and Gary Gerstle, eds., *Ruling America: A History of Wealth and Power in a Democracy* (Cambridge, Mass.: Harvard University Press, 2005), 64–91. Eric Foner's *Free Soil, Free Labor, Free Men: The Ideology of the Republican Party Before the Civil War* (New York: Oxford University Press, 1970) emphasizes the importance of the dignity of free white labor to Republicans' appeal. Works such as William E. Gienapp's *The Origins of the Republican Party, 1852–1856* (New York: Oxford University Press, 1987), Joel H. Silbey's *The Transformation of American Politics, 1840–1860* (Englewood Cliffs, N.J.: Prentice-Hall, 1967), and Ronald P. Formisano's *The Birth of Mass Political Parties: Michigan, 1827–1861* (Princeton: Princeton University Press, 1971) stress ethnocultural factors such as anti-Catholicism and nativism. David Brion Davis in *The Slave Power Conspiracy and the Paranoid Style* (Baton Rouge: Louisiana State University Press, 1969) and Michael Holt in *The Political Crisis of the 1850s* (New York: Wiley, 1978) present alternative views of the Slave Power conspiracy idea. Both emphasize the suspicions of conspiracies against liberty (discussed, for example, in Bernard Bailyn, *The Ideological Origins of the American Revolution* [Cambridge, Mass.: Harvard University Press, 1967]) bequeathed to subsequent generations from the American Revolution. Davis, as his title suggests, represents the antebellum variation on the conspiratorial theme as an abnormality, while Holt describes fears of the Slave Power conspiracy less as pathology than as politics as usual. In other words, Holt emphasizes linkages between nativism, anti-Catholicism, widespread suspicion of secretive groups like the Masons, and calls for resistance to the Slave Power, because, he argues, Northerners' real fear was for the fate of republicanism, to which foreigners, Catholics, and shadowy organizations could seem as threatening as slaveocrats. Soldiers, however, made no such connections. Though many began the war without being altogether clear as to whether they opposed the institution of slavery itself or the chief practitioners of it, they regarded issues surrounding slavery as uniquely significant, and spent no time pondering the doom of republicanism at the hands of Catholicism, immigrants, or groups like the Masons.

36. On John Brown and reaction to his raid, see Paul Finkelman, ed., *His Soul Goes Marching On: Responses to John Brown and the Harpers Ferry Raid* (Charlottesville: University of Virginia Press, 1995); and Stephen B. Oates, *To Purge This Land with Blood: A Biography of John Brown* (Amherst: University of Massachusetts Press, 1984).

37. For Brown's resolutions, see *Congressional Globe,* January 18, 1860, Thirty-sixth Congress, First Session, 404. For Davis's, see *Congressional Globe,* February 2, 1860, Thirty-sixth Congress, First Session, 658. In the spring of 1860, the Senate took up the question again. See *Congressional Globe,* Thirty-sixth Congress, First Session, 2321–22. For discussion of the resolutions on slavery, and demands for a federal slave code, see David Herbert Donald, Jean Harvey Baker, and Michael F. Holt, *The Civil War and Reconstruction* (New York: Norton, 2001), 117, 657 n. 39; Allan Nevins, *The Emergence of Lincoln,* vol. 2, *Prologue to Civil War 1859–1861* (New York: Scribner, 1951), 178–81.

William J. Cooper disagrees, writing that Albert Brown proposed a federal slave code, but Jefferson Davis merely wanted to discredit Stephen Douglas and did not call for a slave code, but it seems clear from Davis' explicit mention of "the duty of Congress" that he called for a federal role. See William J. Cooper, *Jefferson Davis, American* (New York: Knopf, 2000), 304–306. On the Democrats in 1860, see William L. Barney, *Secessionist Impulse: Alabama and Mississippi in 1860* (Princeton, N.J.: Princeton University Press, 1974); William Gienapp, "The Crisis of American Democracy," in Gabor S. Boritt, ed., *Why the Civil War Came* (New York: Oxford University Press, 1996), 79–124; and Potter, *Impending Crisis*. Johannsen, *Stephen A. Douglas,* also discusses the Democratic breakup in 1860.

38. See, for example, David Blight, "For Something Beyond the Battlefield': Frederick Douglass and the Struggle for the Memory of the Civil War," *Journal of American History* 75:4 (March 1989), 1156–78, esp. 1162–63; and Miller, *Arguing About Slavery,* 3–4.

39. Oliver Wendell Holmes, Jr., "The Soldier's Faith," May 30, 1895, in Richard A. Posner, ed., *The Essential Holmes: Selections from the Letters, Speeches, Judicial Opinions, and Other Writings of Oliver Wendell Holmes, Jr.* (Chicago: University of Chicago Press, 1992), 89. For later suppression of slavery's place in the war, see David W. Blight, *Race and Reunion: The Civil War in American Memory* (Cambridge, Mass.: Harvard University Press, 2001).

1: "Lincoln and Liberty": Why an Antislavery President Meant War

1. Resolutions of Louisiana students at the University of North Carolina, 1861, Chapel Hill, N.C., Thomas Benjamin Davidson Papers, SHC. The undated resolutions followed Louisiana's seizure of forts on January 26, 1861.

2. Resolutions recorded at Cambridge, Mass., by Stephen Emerson, 1861, Stephen G. Emerson Correspondence, MHS. The undated resolutions followed the fall of Fort Sumter.

3. Alfred Green, "The Colored Philadelphians Forming Regiments," *Philadelphia Press,* April 22, 1861, in Alfred M. Green, *Letters and Discussions on the Formation of Colored Regiments* (Philadelphia, 1862), Schomburg.

4. Pvt. John Lyon Hill, Churchville Cavalry (later Va. Cavalry), diary, August 9, 1861, Camp Alleghany, Va., John Lyon Hill Diary, CMM Ser. A, Reel 17.

5. Walthall Robertson to wife, November 25, 1860, Ashton, La., Mary Overton Gentry Shaw Papers, JCHS. Robertson soon joined the (Confederate) Missouri State Guard.

6. Thomas R. R. Cobb, November 12, 1860, Milledgeville, Ga., in William W. Freehling and Craig M. Simpson, *Secession Debated: Georgia's Showdown in 1860* (New York: Oxford University Press, 1992), 5–30. Article IV of the U.S. Constitution permits slave owners to reclaim slaves who ran away to free states, but it does not require free-state officials or individual citizens to aid in the process. The Fugitive Slave Law of 1850 differed from the Constitution in that it *did* require the participation of free-state citizens, as well as dictate an active role for the federal government in the form of federal marshals and commissioners. In response, some northern states in the 1850s passed personal liberty laws. In Wisconsin, the Fugitive Slave Law clashed with the state personal liberty law, leading to the arrest and trial of Sherman Booth for invoking the personal liberty law and helping prevent the capture of Joshua Glover, a fugitive slave taking refuge in Wisconsin. At Booth's trial in 1854, the Wisconsin State Supreme Court, in one of the purest articulations of states' rights doctrine in the years preceding the war, declared the Fugitive Slave Law null and void in Wisconsin due to its unconstitutionality, and defended the rights of

Wisconsin state residents to choose not to participate in slave catching. For Booth's speech at his trial and Justice Byron Paine's decision, see *Unconstitutionality of the Fugitive Act: Argument of Byron Paine, Esq.,* 1854, Miscellaneous Pamphlet Collection, SHSW. For more on the case, see Bradley and Ranney, "A Tradition of Independence: The Wisconsin Supreme Court's First 150 Years," McManus, *Political Abolitionism in Wisconsin, 1840–1861,* and Ranney, "Suffering the Agonies of Their Righteousness." For a famous fugitive slave case in Massachusetts, see Von Frank, *The Trials of Anthony Burns.* It was precisely this declaration of northern states' rights in the matter of slavery that Cobb and others saw as so dangerous.

7. Alexander Stephens, November 14, 1860, Milledgeville, Ga.; Benjamin Hill, November 15, 1860, Milledgeville, Ga.; Herschel V. Johnson's unionist public letter, November 16, 1860, Milledgeville, Ga., all in Freehling and Simpson, *Secession Debated.* The quotation is from Hill's speech, 103.

8. Thomas R. R. Cobb, December 6, 1860, in Freehling and Simpson, *Secession Debated,* xiv.

9. Michael P. Johnson, "A New Look at the Popular Vote for Delegates to the Georgia Secession Convention," *Georgia Historical Quarterly* 56 (1972), 259–75.

10. John Halliburton to Juliet, February 12, 1861, Chapel Hill, N.C., John Wesley Halliburton Papers, SHC. See also Halliburton's letters of February 1, 1861; February 21, 1861; March 1, 1861; March 6, 1861; and March 7, 1861. Halliburton won half of his battle. Juliet agreed to marry him, but did not abandon her secessionist principles.

11. Hodijah Meade to mother, December 9, 1860, Richmond, Meade Family Papers, CMM Ser. A, Reel 27. Meade soon joined the Richmond Howitzers, an artillery unit.

12. Lt. Rufus Cater, Nineteenth La., to cousin, June 26, 1861, Keachie, La., Douglas J. and Rufus W. Cater Letters, *PAW,* Coll. 32, Reel 11. For discussion of southern domination of the antebellum federal government, see Fehrenbacher, *The Slaveholding Republic.* Fehrenbacher shows that even though slaves only lived in the southern states by the mid-nineteenth century, the whole nation behaved as a slaveholding nation in terms of foreign and domestic policy, which was why the election of 1860 came as such a shock to white Southerners. In "The 'Slave Power' in the United States, 1783–1865," Adam Rothman further shows that before the Civil War, southern political leaders, though in the numerical minority, were able to "get their way time after time in an ostensibly democratic polity" by using the United States' political structure to their advantage, but that in the 1850s they grew increasingly nervous that the faster-growing northern population might one day prevent them from doing so (64).

13. The best analysis of slavery's foundation on force and violence, and the tensions generated by that foundation, is Edward L. Ayers, *Vengeance and Justice: Crime and Punishment in the 19th-Century American South* (New York: Oxford University Press, 1984).

14. For examples of proslavery ideologues' contentions of slave happiness, see David B. Chesebrough, ed., *"God Ordained This War"*: *Sermons on the Sectional Crisis, 1830–1865* (Columbia: University of South Carolina Press, 1991).

15. See Sally E. Hadden, *Slave Patrols: Law and Violence in Virginia and the Carolinas* (Cambridge, Mass.: Harvard University Press, 2001).

16. For the best single-volume treatment of antebellum political events that contributed to rising sectionalism, see Potter, *Impending Crisis.*

17. Lucius Brown to father, November 7, 1860, Nashville, Tenn., Brown Family Papers, NYPL. Brown later joined the Eighteenth U.S. Infantry, serving first as an enlisted man, then as a lieutenant.

18. *New York Daily Tribune,* November 28, 1860.

19. *Chicago Tribune,* December 13, 1860.

20. *New York Daily Tribune,* November 27, 1860.

21. *Congressional Globe,* Thirty-fifth Congress, Second Session, 114.

22. *Congressional Globe,* Thirty-sixth Congress, First Session, 658. James McPherson discusses the Senate resolutions in *Battle Cry of Freedom,* 214.

23. Abraham Lincoln communicated the importance of holding the line on the nonextension of slavery in a letter of December 10, 1860, to a fellow Republican, Senator Lyman Trumbull: "the tug has to come, & better now, than any time hereafter." See Roy P. Basler, ed., *The Collected Works of Abraham Lincoln,* vol. 4 (New Brunswick, N.J.: Rutgers University Press, 1953), 149–50. The remark partly referred to party imperative: after all, the Republican Party had built itself from nothing into a victorious party founded squarely on the principle of nonextension of slavery in less than a decade. To abandon that principle as soon as it won at the polls would be to abandon party supporters. Yet more than partisanship was at stake for Lincoln, as well as for many of the voters who had just elected him. Lincoln also believed that a "house divided against itself," as he famously exclaimed in 1858, could not survive indefinitely. See Abraham Lincoln, Speech at Springfield, Ill., June 16, 1858, in Basler, *Collected Works of Lincoln,* 2:461. Failing to face the slavery issue would not prevent disunion, but rather make it all the more inevitable.

24. Leigh Webber, to friend Charly and Charly's father, Mr. Brown, January 31, 1861, Page Co., Iowa, John Stillman Brown Family Collection, Reel 2, KSHS. Webber later joined the First Kans. Infantry as a private.

25. The Confederate Congress authorized an Army Staff on February 25, and passed a bill to raise an Army on February 28. On March 6, Congress approved the 100,000 number, and Secretary of War Leroy Walker sent a request to governors to transfer state troops to Confederate service. See William C. Davis, "*A Government of Our Own*": *The Making of the Confederacy* (Baton Rouge: Louisiana State University Press, 1994), 212–13.

26. Abraham Lincoln, "Proclamation Calling Militia and Convening Congress," April 15, 1861, in Basler, *Collected Works of Lincoln,* 4:32–33.

27. For discussion of the impact of southern seizure of federal property on northern public opinion, see Silvana Siddali, " 'The Sport of Folly and the Prize of Treason': Confederate Property Seizures and the Northern Home Front," *Civil War History* 47:4 (December 2001), 310–33.

28. *Wisconsin State Journal,* April 15, 1861, p. 2.

29. McPherson, *Battle Cry of Freedom,* 274. See also Paludan, "*A People's Contest*": *The Union and Civil War 1861–1865.*

30. Union Broadsides and Ephemera, CHS.

31. Furthermore, both Union and Confederate conceptions of the Revolution were affected by the way in which the meaning of the word "virtue" had changed from the eighteenth to the nineteenth century. When the founders spoke of "virtue" in 1776, they meant something very specific, namely the willingness to subordinate self-interest to the common good. By 1861, "virtue" had taken on a much more diffuse meaning that had to do with general moral goodness. Whereas founders such as John Adams and Thomas Jefferson had meant that the republic would survive only so long as individuals were willing to place the public good above their own material interests when necessary, nineteenth-century Americans meant that the republic's survival depended upon individuals' avoidance of vices like drunkenness, adultery, gambling, etc.

32. Pvt. Ivy Duggan, Fifteenth Ga., to *Central Georgian,* September 13, 1861, Centreville, Va., Ivy W. Duggan Letters, GDAH.

33. For discussion of the Confederate and state constitutions and their ratification

processes, see George Rable, *The Confederate Republic: A Revolution Against Politics* (Chapel Hill: University of North Carolina Press, 1994), chs. 3 and 4; and Davis, *"A Government of Our Own,"* esp. chs. 10–12.

34. White Southerners' desires for more active federal promotion of slavery through a federal slave code or other similar measure, even over the protests of individual states and citizens, might help explain why Confederate soldiers in 1861 did not discuss "states' rights." In many ways, what they wanted was just the opposite.

35. Capt. Robert Snead, Fiftieth Va., to wife, October 18, 1861, Greenbrier Courthouse, Va., Robert Winn Snead Papers, CMM Ser. A, Reel 40. See also Pvt. Thomas Taylor, Sixth Ala., to wife, October 15, 1861, Fairfax Station, Va., Thomas S. Taylor Letters, ADAH.

36. *The Missouri Army Argus,* November 30, 1861, p. 4, Osceola, Mo., MOHS. The *Argus* was the camp paper of the Mo. (Confederate) State Guard.

37. Josiah Patterson to sons, December 13, 1861, Manassas, Va., in Mills Lane, ed., *Dear Mother: Don't Grieve About Me. If I Get Killed I'll Only be Dead: Letters from Georgia Soldiers in the Civil War* (Savannah: Beehive Press, 1977), 89.

38. Pvt. Ivy Duggan, Fifteenth Ga., to *Central Georgian,* September 7, 1861, Manassas Junction, Va., Ivy W. Duggan Letters, GDAH; Pvt. Thomas Taylor, Sixth Ala., to wife, October 15, 1861, Fairfax Station, Va., Thomas S. Taylor Letters, ADAH.

39. Although their interpretations vary in key respects, George Rable, *The Confederate Republic*; William Davis, *"A Government of Our Own"*; and Drew Faust, *Creation of Confederate Nationalism* (Baton Rouge: Louisiana State University Press, 1988), all address the Confederate need for unity throughout the war. In *The Confederate Republic,* Rable argues that the new Confederate government represented a conscious, revolutionary change from the federal Constitution because it eschewed parties and sought to remove influence from the hands of the people and concentrate it in the hands of the "few" of the Revolutionary-era "one, few, and many" triad. While unconvincing in arguing for vast change (Rable admits that the new constitution virtually replicated the old one and in fact was written after only a few days of tinkering), Rable persuasively demonstrates the importance of a "political culture of national unity" to any successful Confederate effort, and shows that Confederate politics placed at least a theoretical "premium" on "internal harmony and white liberty" (see esp. 1–5, chs. 3 and 4, and the epilogue; quotations from 300, 302). In *"A Government of Our Own,"* William Davis emphasizes continuities between the Confederate government and constitution and the American past. Holding that Confederates saw themselves as more faithful heirs of the founders, Davis views those continuities as important sources of unity, since Southerners were accustomed to rallying around the memory of the Revolution. In *Creation of Confederate Nationalism,* Faust treats the need for Confederate national sentiment among the populace at large rather than the creation of a new government. She points out that since the new Confederacy immediately faced a war against a people in many ways identical to the people of the Confederacy, it needed to craft a sense of nationalism quickly, and that sense of nationalism could ill afford anything other than unity and harmony (see esp. 6–21).

40. Lt. Christopher Winsmith, First S.C., to mother, April 24, 1861, Sullivan's Island, S.C., John Christopher Winsmith Papers, MOC.

41. Pvt. Joseph Bruckmuller, Seventh Tex., Address delivered to other prisoners at Ft. Douglas Prison, Chicago, June 1862, Joseph Bruckmuller Notebook, CAH.

42. *The Spirit of '61,* December 25, 1861, Dumfries, Va., pp. 4–5, EU. *The Spirit of '61* was the camp paper of the Eighteenth Ga.

43. Pvt. James Williams, Twenty-first Ala., to wife, December 20, 1861, Fort Gaines,

Ala., in John Kent Folmar, ed., *From That Terrible Field: Civil War Letters of James M. Williams, Twenty-First Alabama Infantry Volunteers* (Tuscaloosa: University of Alabama Press, 1981), 13.

44. For a recent analysis that emphasizes the decision of ordinary white yeomen in a specific region (south-central Georgia) to support slavery for their own reasons, see Wetherington, *Plain Folk's Fight.*

45. The classic exposition of this concept, known as the herrenvolk democracy thesis, remains George Fredrickson, *The Black Image in the White Mind: The Debate on Afro-American Character and Destiny* (Hanover, N.H.: Wesleyan University Press, 1987), 61–71. See also William J. Cooper, *Liberty and Slavery: Southern Politics to 1860* (New York: Knopf, 1983); Lacy K. Ford, Jr., *Origins of Southern Radicalism: The South Carolina Upcountry, 1800–1860* (New York: Oxford University Press, 1988); Edmund S. Morgan, *American Slavery, American Freedom: The Ordeal of Colonial Virginia* (New York: Norton, 1975); and Frank Lawrence Owsley, *Plain Folk of the Old South* (Baton Rouge: Louisiana State University Press, 1949).

46. T. W. Crowson of the Alabama Hickories composed "Run, Yank, or Die." Pvt. Edward Baines, a Louisiana soldier from West Feliciana Parish, so enjoyed sharing the song with his comrades in camp that he wrote a letter home from Columbus, Ky., on November 4, 1861, on the back of a printed copy of the song so that he could share it with his family. Henry Baines Papers, CMM Ser. B, Reel 5.

47. White antebellum Southerners simply did not stay put for long. For discussion of their tremendous mobility, see James Oakes, *The Ruling Race: A History of American Slaveholders* (New York: Vintage, 1982), ch. 3; Donald, Baker, and Holt, *Civil War and Reconstruction,* 3; and Joseph C. G. Kennedy, *Preliminary Report on the Eighth Census* (Washington, D.C., 1862).

48. For the most thorough yet compact treatment of this theme, see Oakes, *The Ruling Race.* See also Cooper, *Liberty and Slavery,* esp. ch. 11; and Ford, *Origins of Southern Radicalism,* 50, 373.

49. For the importance of ambition as an attribute of manhood as white southern men understood it, see Stephen W. Berry II, *All That Makes a Man: Love and Ambition in the Civil War South* (New York: Oxford University Press, 2003).

50. Cooper, *Liberty and Slavery,* 251–53.

51. Robinson, *Bitter Fruits of Bondage,* 92. For analysis of white nonslaveholders' dependence on the hopes of eventual slave ownership to provide stability and bolster equality in the antebellum South, see Oakes, *The Ruling Race,* 37, 39–43.

52. For Southerners' desire for stability in the antebellum world, see William R. Taylor, *Cavalier and Yankee: The Old South and American National Character* (Cambridge, Mass.: Harvard University Press, 1979, first published 1957), esp. 96–101 and chs. 4 and 10.

53. A voluminous literature treats church membership, reform movements in the North and South, and the particular characteristics of southern religion. Some titles that specifically consider the comparative lack of reform movements in the South; southern suspicion of northern churches, religion, and reform; and the higher value placed by Southerners on orthodoxy include: Bertram Wyatt-Brown, "The Antimission Movement in the Jacksonian South: A Study in Regional Folk Culture," *Journal of Southern History* 36 (November 1970), 501–29; John G. Crowley, *Primitive Baptists of the Wiregrass South, 1815 to the Present* (Gainesville: University Press of Florida, 1998); Hill, *The South and the North in American Religion;* Hughes and Allen, *Illusions of Innocence,* 190; John W. Kuykendall, *Southern Enterprize: The Work of National Evangelical Societies in the Antebellum South*

(Westport, Conn.: Greenwood, 1982); Donald G. Mathews, *Religion in the Old South* (Chicago: University of Chicago Press, 1977); Shattuck, *A Shield and Hiding Place,* Introduction; Timothy L. Smith, *Revivalism & Social Reform: American Protestantism on the Eve of the Civil War* (Baltimore: Johns Hopkins University Press, 1981); and Mitchell Snay, *Gospel of Disunion* (New York: Cambridge University Press, 1993). Recent works such as John Quist, *Restless Visionaries: The Social Roots of Antebellum Reform in Alabama and Michigan* (Baton Rouge: Louisiana State University Press, 1998), and Beth Barton Schweiger, *The Gospel Working Up: Progress and the Pulpit in Nineteenth-Century Virginia* (New York: Oxford University Press, 2000), argue that differences between northern and southern religion have been overstated, and point to evidence of pro-temperance sentiment among some southern divines to make a case for southern reform. Yet even allowing for temperance strength in one Alabama county (Quist) and among some Virginia clergy (Schweiger), it remains the case that even reform in the South focused on behavior likely to earn the individual's salvation. Urging individuals to limit personal consumption of alcohol was one thing, but pushing for public schools or increased civil and legal rights for particular groups, movements that addressed society rather than just individual behavior, truly were much more characteristic of the North than the South before the Civil War.

54. Church Records of Kehukee (N.C.) Association of Primitive Baptists, 1849, as cited in Crowley, *Primitive Baptists,* 86.

55. *Signs of the Times* 22 (April 15, 1854), 54, as cited in Crowley, *Primitive Baptists,* 87–88.

56. For biblical sanctioning of slavery see Mark A. Noll, "The Bible and Slavery," in Randall M. Miller, Harry S. Stout, and Charles Reagan Wilson, eds., *Religion and the American Civil War* (New York: Oxford University Press, 1998), 43–73. The sermons of Charles Colcock Jones, James H. Thornwell, Benjamin Morgan Palmer, and J. W. Tucker in Chesebrough, *"God Ordained This War,"* are examples of southern ministers' eagerness to point to the recognition of slavery in the Bible as vindication of the institution. For the conviction of some white Southerners that "slavery and the southern way of life" more closely approximated the "purity of rectitude of first time" than the North with its lack of slavery did, see Hughes and Allen, *Illusions of Innocence,* 188–204.

57. Lt. Chesley Herbert, Third S.C., to wife, July 3, 1861, Fairfax Courthouse, Va., Chesley Worthington Herbert Papers, SCL.

58. Georgia soldier A. H. Mitchell to father, May 17, 1861, Jackson Co., Ga., in Lane, *"Dear Mother: Don't Grieve About Me,"* 11.

59. For the "crisis of the family" in the nineteenth century, see Michael Grossberg, *Governing the Hearth: Law and the Family in Nineteenth-Century America* (Chapel Hill: University of North Carolina Press, 1985). See also Mary Ryan, *Cradle of the Middle Class: The Family in Oneida County, New York, 1790–1865* (New York: Cambridge University Press, 1981). Much of the literature on the nineteenth-century cult of "true womanhood" also treats the centrality of the family. See, for instance, Drew Gilpin Faust, *Mothers of Invention: Women of the Slaveholding South in the American Civil War* (Chapel Hill: University of North Carolina Press, 1996); Julie Roy Jeffrey, *Frontier Women: "Civilizing" the West? 1840–1880* (New York: Hill and Wang, 1998); Barbara Welter, "The Cult of True Womanhood: 1820–1860," *American Quarterly* 18:2 (summer 1966), 151–74.

60. *The South Vindicated from the Treason and Fanaticism of Northern Abolitionists* (Philadelphia, 1836), 180. Although the pamphlet was published anonymously, William Drayton of South Carolina has long been identified as the author. See William Sumner Jenkins, *Pro-slavery Thought in the Old South* (Gloucester, Mass.: P. Smith, 1960, first

published 1935), 319. For many additional examples of proslavery sermons that made this point, see Snay, *Gospel of Disunion*; and John R. McKivigan and Mitchell Snay, eds., *Religion and the Antebellum Debate over Slavery* (Athens: University of Georgia Press, 1998). For a classic exposition of the same argument by a white southern woman, see Louisa McCord's 1852 essay, "Enfranchisement of Women."

61. See Stephanie McCurry, *Masters of Small Worlds: Yeoman Households, Gender Relations, and the Political Culture of the Antebellum South Carolina Low Country* (New York: Oxford University Press, 1995); and Lee Ann Whites, *The Civil War as a Crisis in Gender: Augusta, Georgia 1860–1890* (Athens: University of Georgia Press, 1995). For the application of McCurry's and Whites's ideas to south-central Georgia, see Wetherington, *Plain Folk's Fight*. McCurry emphasizes the tensions between insistence on white male equality and the vast inequality of wealth more than Whites does, but both note that white men were united in what Whites calls a "common social construction of manhood as largely autonomous and self-directing household heads," and therefore regarded northern attempts to interfere with slavery, a facet of many though not most households, as "a challenge to the independence of all male householders, whether or not they actually held slaves" (Whites, *Civil War as a Crisis in Gender,* 17–18).

To some extent, this conception of social order correlates with what Rogers Smith in *Civic Ideals: Conflicting Visions of Citizenship in U.S. History* (New Haven: Yale University Press, 1997) calls the "ascriptive inegalitarian" tradition of American political thought. Smith argues that throughout U.S. history, several ways of thinking about membership in the American nation have vied with each other, including the liberal tradition, the civic republican tradition, and the ascriptive inegalitarian tradition. The ascriptive inegalitarian tradition assumed that traits that people were born with, especially race, gender, and sometimes religion, determined their eligibility for membership within the American nation as citizens, and their proper place within the social order. On page 68, Smith specifically discusses the domination of men over women as a central feature of the ascriptive inegalitarian tradition. It is too simple to say that Northerners adhered to liberal and civic republican traditions while Southerners hewed to the ascriptive inegalitarian tradition. (Southerners also exhibited liberal qualities, such as attachment to property rights, as well as republican ones, such as the insistence that white equality depended upon black slavery, while most northern men also adhered to ascriptivism where women's lack of the right to vote was concerned.) Still, qualities that Smith associates with the ascriptive inegalitarian tradition were much more central to Confederate soldiers' views of their own identity, and of the social order, than was the case for most Union troops. In fact, much of what white Southerners feared about Northerners was Northerners' presumed infidelity to a divinely ordained social order in which everyone's place in the family, society, and nation was permanently fixed by God, and in which racial purity, social harmony, and maintenance of one's manhood depended upon all individuals abiding by their appointed social roles.

62. John G. Crowley shows that church concern with policing women's sexual behavior increased during the Civil War. See Crowley, *Primitive Baptists,* 93.

63. "The Irrepressible Conflict," *Richmond Enquirer,* October 2, 1860, p. 1.

64. Thomas, private in a Ga. regiment, to mother, May 10, 1861, Ringold, Ga., Confederate Miscellany, Officers' and Soldiers' Letters, DU. W. B. Overstreet of Coffee County, Ga., similarly wrote to Governor Joseph Brown, "the negroes is choosing out the young [white] damsel for wives as soon as the war is over." Overstreet to Brown, April 26, 1862, Box 42, Governor's Incoming Correspondence, GDAH, as cited in Wetherington, *Plain Folk's Fight,* 155.

65. *The Tenth Legion,* June 6, 1861, Woodstock, Va., ISHL. *The Tenth Legion* was the camp newspaper of a Virginia militia regiment.

66. Michael F. Holt in *The Political Crisis of the 1850s* claims that slavery meant something "abstract" to Southerners (258). He argues that antebellum Southerners used the language of slavery to dramatize perceived threats to "self-government" and "rule of law," and fears of being made to seem less prestigious than the North. See esp. ch. 8 and pages x and 242. White southern elites may have talked about slavery in the sense Holt describes, but when enlisted Confederate soldiers voiced fears of "enslavement" or worried about what would happen if black slavery were abolished, they were talking about much more basic, gut-level fears. They dreaded that their lives and conditions might come to resemble the lives and conditions of black slave men, who lacked independence, who could not pursue their own ambitions, and who could do nothing to prevent the sale, physical punishment, or even sexual violation of their own family members.

67. For love, especially romantic love, as a characteristic of manhood (along with ambition), see Berry, *All That Makes a Man.*

68. For discussion of the links between firearms, hunting, and white manhood, see Nicolas W. Proctor, *Bathed in Blood: Hunting and Mastery in the Old South* (Charlottesville: University of Virginia Press, 2002), esp. chs. 3 and 6. Exclusion of women from a masculine culture of hunting and arms bearing is discussed on pp. 50–55.

69. Pvt. Frederick Taber, Eighteenth La., to parents, December 9, 1861, near Carrollton, La., Frederick R. Taber Papers, CMM Ser. B, Reel 8.

70. Bertram Wyatt-Brown, Edward L. Ayers, and Kenneth Greenberg, among others, have discussed the importance of the theme of honor to southern society. Wyatt-Brown explicated the concept in *Southern Honor: Ethics and Behavior in the Old South* (New York: Oxford University Press, 1982) and again in *Yankee Saints and Southern Sinners* (Baton Rouge: Louisiana State University Press, 1985). Both volumes emphasize the centrality of individual reputation and right to respect to southern honor and southern society. Wyatt-Brown demonstrates the preferability of violence over slights to honor to many Southerners and shows how sensitivity to insult distinctively characterized the South. Despite its importance, this work has been convincingly challenged or qualified. Although Wyatt-Brown nods toward the link between southern honor and slavery, noting briefly that honor depended upon "the racially elitist concept that all white men were equal in their hegemony over blacks" (*Southern Honor,* 203), he downplays the connection by arguing that the ideal of honor both predated and postdated slavery, and therefore did not depend upon it. One problem with this interpretation is its reliance on the concept of hegemony, which implies consent between dominant and subordinate, whereas slavery rested not on implicit agreement between white and black, but on force and violence, as Walter Johnson in *Soul by Soul: Life Inside the Antebellum Slave Market* (Cambridge, Mass.: Harvard University Press, 1999) and countless others have demonstrated.

Edward L. Ayers provides a more persuasive analysis of the concept of honor in *Vengeance and Justice.* Ayers's depiction of the interdependency of honor and slavery in ch. 1 of *Vengeance and Justice* roots the somewhat amorphous concept of honor within the "economic, ideological, and religious context—especially slavery" that set the South apart from the North. He therefore more compellingly explains why the concept of honor (or one's worth and status in others' eyes) pervaded the South, while the concept of dignity (or the belief in the inherently equal worth granted by God, not other humans) distinguished the North, especially when the two regions were more alike than dissimilar in other cultural, political, religious, and historical aspects. Without the existence of slavery, the concept of honor would have withered in the South, Ayers shows, because "honor presupposes undisguised hierarchy, and a slave society builds an incontrovertible hierarchy into basic human relations" (26). Without this distinctive social ranking, the aggressive white egalitarianism of the South could not have sustained the ideal of honor. In addition, slavery codified honor by granting it to one visually obvious group while denying it to another, and offered it to poor whites who could share in the collective honor of the "master class" as long as a slave class existed to act as an enabling foil to a master class (26). In other words, since "slavery generated honor," taking away slavery took away white southern honor (26–27), or so antebellum white Southerners believed, since they did not yet have the benefit of postwar history to show them that race could replace slavery as an enforcer of honor.

Kenneth Greenberg has also qualified aspects of Wyatt-Brown's interpretation. Although more narrowly focused on the southern leadership class, Greenberg concurs with Wyatt-Brown's focus on a distinctively southern compulsion for personal honor, but lays more stress on the importance of slavery when he defines honor as the coexistence of "personal autonomy and a distrust of power" with "assertion of power over others." See *Masters and Statesmen: The Political Culture of American Slavery* (Baltimore: Johns Hopkins University Press, 1985) and *Honor and Slavery* (Princeton, N.J.: Princeton University Press, 1996). The quotation is from *Masters and Statesmen,* xi.

71. "The Fight," a popular antebellum story by Georgia writer Augustus Baldwin Longstreet, illustrates important points about southern honor among nonslaveholding white men. "The Fight" is about two close friends, Billy Stallings and Bob Durham. One day, Billy unwittingly insults Bob's wife, without knowing who she is. Despite the friendship between the two men, both recognize that the insult cannot be allowed to pass, because it would question Bob's right and ability to control his wife and protect her reputation. Consequently, Billy and Bob engage in an eye-gouging, biting, poking, and kicking brawl, by the end of which Bob has lost his left ear and one of his fingers, and Bill has lost the tip of his nose. See Augustus Baldwin Longstreet, "The Fight," in *Georgia Scenes, Characters, Incidents &c in the First Half Century of the Republic, By a Native Georgian* (New York: Harper, 1851), 53–64. Though fictional, this story commented on a social reality: the incidence of personal violence among white southern men exceeded national rates, and fights often arose from perceived insults or slights. For a scholarly look at the importance of the fight to securing honor among the southern white yeomanry, see Elliott J. Gorn, "Gouge and Bite, Pull Hair and Scratch": The Social Significance of Fighting in the Southern Backcountry," *American Historical Review* 90:1, supplement to vol. 90 (February 1985), 18–43. For the extraordinarily high rates of interpersonal violence in the antebellum South, see Ayers, *Vengeance and Justice,* 9–33. For the connection between violence, honor, secession, and the Civil War, see Christopher J. Olsen, *Political Culture and Secession in Mississippi: Masculinity, Honor, and the Antiparty Tradition, 1830–1860* (New York: Oxford University Press, 2000).

72. Charles Trueheart to sister, March 1, 1861 (misdated: the letter followed Lincoln's Inaugural Address, so must have been written after March 4, 1861), Charlottesville, Va., in Edward B. Williams, ed., *Rebel Brothers: The Civil War Letters of the Truehearts* (College Station: Texas A & M University Press, 1995), 21–22.

73. Lt. James Langhorne, Fourth Va., to father, June 5, 1861, Maryland Heights, Va., Langhorne Family Papers, VHS.

74. Pvt. Ivy Duggan, Fifteenth Ga., to *Central Georgian,* September 13, 1861, Camp Taylor, Centreville, Va., Ivy W. Duggan Letters, GDAH. Duggan was specifically referring to the doctrines of Hinton Rowan Helper, a white North Carolinian who, in his 1857 book *The Impending Crisis,* argued that slavery harmed the economic interests of southern non-

slaveholding whites, who should seek peaceful ways to abolish it gradually. For his trouble, Helper was run out of the South, but as Duggan's comments show, many southern whites remained disturbed by his ideas.

75. "The Irrepressible Conflict," *Richmond Enquirer,* October 2, 1860, p. 1.

76. Pvt. Thomas Taylor, Sixth Ala., to father, December 19, 1861, Manassas Junction, Va., Thomas S. Taylor Letters, ADAH.

77. *Liberator,* May 10, 1861, quoted in James M. McPherson, *The Negro's Civil War: How American Negroes Felt and Acted During the War for the Union* (New York: Pantheon, 1965), 20.

78. "An Appeal to the Seventh," *Lauman's Own,* 1:1, August 21, 1861, Ironton, Mo., CHS. *Lauman's Own* was the newspaper of the Seventh Iowa.

79. "The Advance into Virginia," *The American Union,* July 5, 1861, p. 3, AAS. *The American Union* was the camp newspaper of the First R.I., R.I. Artillery, First Wis., and Second, Third, Eighth, Eleventh, and Twenty-first Pa.

80. "The Results of this War," *The American Union,* July 5, 1861, Martinsburg, Va., AAS.

81. Capt. Alphonso Barto, Fifty-second Ill., to father, May 27, 1862, near Corinth, Miss., Alphonso Barto Letters, ISHL; *The Illinois Fifty-Second,* 1:1, January 15, 1862, Stewartsville, Mo., p. 3, ISHL.

82. *The First Kansas,* 1:1, Oct. 16, 1861, Chilicothe, Mo., p. 1, KSHS.

83. Lt. Charles Haydon, Second Mich., journal, October 20, 1861, near Mt. Vernon, Va., in Stephen W. Sears, ed., *For Country, Cause and Leader: The Civil War Journal of Charles B. Haydon* (New York: Ticknor and Fields, 1993), 112.

84. Pvt. W. D. Wildman, Twelfth Ind., to teacher, Miss Susan Griggs, November 2, 1861, near Sharpsburg, Md., Virginia Southwood Collection, UMOC.

85. Soldier, Third Battery Wis. Artillery, to *Wisconsin Patriot,* November 30, 1861, Camp Utley, Wis., Quiner Papers, Reel 1, vol. 2, p. 77.

86. Pvt. Leigh Webber, First Kans., to friends, the Brown family in Kansas, April 24, 1862, Tipton Mo., John S. Brown Family Papers, Reel 2, KSHS. Wracked by violence during the Kansas border wars, Kansas still experienced internal violence in the early days of the war itself.

87. Pvt. Terah Sampson, Sixth Ky., to mother, December 29, 1861, Camp Siegel, Ky., Terah W. Sampson Letters, FC.

88. As Robert Bellah explains in his classic explication of American millennialism, *The Broken Covenant,* nineteenth-century Americans, like their eighteenth-century forebears, "interpreted their history as having religious meaning" (2). More specifically, Old Testament and New Testament ideas of covenant influenced a particular brand of "strongly social, communal, or collective emphasis" in New England political thought that spread throughout the North in the antebellum era (17). See also Hughes and Allen, *Illusions of Innocence,* 170–87, 205; Stuart McConnell, *Glorious Contentment: The Grand Army of the Republic, 1865–1900* (Chapel Hill: University of North Carolina Press, 1992), esp. 186; Miller, Stout, and Wilson, *Religion and the American Civil War,* esp. the Introduction; Moorhead, *American Apocalypse,* ix–x, chs. 2 and 3; and Philip Paludan, "Religion and the American Civil War," in Miller, Stout, and Wilson, *Religion and the American Civil War.*

89. For Robert Bellah's discussion of reform (including abolitionism) inspired by the Second Great Awakening as "millennial republican idealism," see *The Broken Covenant,* 49–52. Antebellum reform movements in the North have generated an entire subfield of historical literature reaching far beyond Bellah. Some good starting points include Robert

H. Bremner, *The Public Good: Philanthropy and Welfare in the Civil War Era* (New York: Knopf, 1988); Mary Ann Clawson, *Constructing Brotherhood: Class, Gender & Fraternalism* (Princeton, N.J.: Princeton University Press, 1989); Lori Ginzberg, *Women and the Work of Benevolence: Morality, Politics, and Class in the Nineteenth-Century United States* (New Haven: Yale University Press, 1990); and Ryan, *Cradle of the Middle Class.* For the impact of associationist habits on the northern home front's experiences of war, see George Fredrickson, "The Coming of the Lord: The Northern Protestant Clergy and the Civil War Crisis," in Miller, Stout, and Wilson, *Religion and the American Civil War*; Judith Ann Giesberg, *Civil War Sisterhood: The U.S. Sanitary Commission and Women's Politics in Transition* (Boston: Northeastern University Press, 2000); and J. Matthew Gallman, *The North Fights the Civil War: The Home Front* (Chicago; Ivan R. Dee, 1994), esp. ch. 7. Quotation from Gallman, 109.

90. Joseph Scroggs Diary, May 10, 1861, West Point, Ohio, Joseph Scroggs Diary, CWTIC; "Charley of Nimrod," First U.S. Sharpshooters, to *Gazette,* December 31, 1861, Washington, D.C., Quiner Papers, Reel 1, vol. 2, p. 52; "Wherefore are you Here Among Us?" *The Ohio Seventh,* July 4, 1861, Weston, Va., p. 2, WRHS. Some historians, such as Susan-Mary Grant in *North Over South: Northern Nationalism and American Identity in the Antebellum Era,* have argued that neither Northerners nor Southerners felt an emotional attachment to the government, instead feeling sentimentally disposed toward a particular idea of the "nation," which for Northerners merged with the government during but not before the Civil War. Union recruits' own words, however, display considerable emotional attachment to the Union government, as soon as (or in Scroggs's case, even earlier than) they joined the Army, before the war had time to work the transformation for which Grant argues. In contrast, claims about the "best government on earth" are wholly absent from Confederate soldiers' writing; Confederate troops could be just as sentimental as Union soldiers, but not about government.

91. Phillip S. Paludan, "The American Civil War Considered as a Crisis in Law and Order," *American Historical Review* 77:4 (October 1972), 1020–21. For further elaboration on this theme, see Paludan, *"A People's Contest": The Union and the Civil War 1861–1865,* esp. part 1. White northern men's heightened participation in local government should not obscure the important truth that the right to vote was just as widespread among most white Southerners, and that voting rights constituted a critical element of white southern men's identities as men. Nonetheless, a significant distinction remains: participating in government in ways beyond voting was more possible in the North because there were more local governments and therefore more offices with more impact on daily life than in the South, where most seemed to prefer a more hands-off attitude toward local government.

92. For the importance of soldiers' political identities to their wartime service, see Joseph Allan Frank, *With Ballot and Bayonet: The Political Socialization of American Civil War Soldiers* (Athens: University of Georgia Press, 1998).

93. *The Advance Guard,* August 28, 1861, Ironton, Mo., p. 2, AAS. *The Advance Guard* was the paper of the Seventeenth Ill. Leigh Webber made an almost identical point. See Leigh Webber to friend, January 31, 1861, Page Co., Iowa, John Stillman Brown Family Collection, Reel 2, KSHS. Webber enlisted in the First Kans. the following spring.

94. Sgt. John Quincy Adams Campbell, Fifth Iowa, diary, July 9, 1861, Burlington, Iowa, in Mark Grimsley and Todd D. Miller, eds., *The Union Must Stand: The Civil War Diary of John Quincy Adams Campbell, Fifth Iowa Volunteer Infantry* (Knoxville: University of Tennessee Press, 2000), 2–3.

95. Pvt. Jerome Cutler, Second Vt., to fiancée Emily, November 11, 1861, Camp Grif-

fin, Va., Jerome Cutler Letters, VTHS; Chaplain A. C. Barry, Second Wis., to S. C. Tuckerman, Baltimore, published in *Wisconsin State Journal,* July 28, 1861, Quiner Papers, Reel 1, vol. 1, p. 74.

96. "How Will it End?" *The Advance Guard,* August 28, 1861, Fredericktown, Mo., AAS.

97. See, for example, "The Results of this War," *The American Union,* July 15, 1861, (also July 5 and 6 issues), Martinsburg, Va., AAS. See also *The Clinton Journal,* July 4, 1861, Clinton, Mo., KSHS. *The Clinton Journal* was the paper of the First and Second Kans. In addition, see Gen. George McClellan, memorandum to President Lincoln, August 2, 1861, Washington, D.C., in Stephen W. Sears, ed., *The Civil War Papers of George B. McClellan: Selected Correspondence, 1860–1865* (New York: Ticknor & Fields, 1989), 72. In *The Hard Hand of War: Union Military Policy Toward Southern Civilians, 1861–1865* (New York: Cambridge University Press, 1995), esp. ch. 2, Mark Grimsley discusses how Northerners' assumptions that most (or at least many) white Southerners were actually unionists at heart influenced conciliatory policy toward civilians, including noninterference with slavery.

98. *Liberator,* August 30, 1861, in McPherson, *The Negro's Civil War,* 40.

99. *A-A,* May 11, 1861, p. 1. The *Anglo-African,* published in New York, was the most prominent black newspaper in the United States immediately prior to and during the Civil War.

100. Sgt. Andrew Walker, Fifty-fifth Ill., to parents, Henderson, Ill., April 1861, Andrew J. Walker Papers, LC.

101. Capt. John Callis, Seventh Wis., to *Wisconsin State Journal,* October 3, 1861, Camp Lyon, Md., Quiner Papers, Reel 1, vol. 1, pp. 276–77.

102. *The Cavalier,* July 30, 1863, Williamsburg, Va., p. 2, VHS. *The Cavalier* was the newspaper of the Fifth Pa. Cavalry.

103. Pvt. Jerome Cutler, Second Vt., to fiancée, August 17, 1861, Washington, D.C., Jerome Cutler Letters, VTHS.

104. Chaplain A. C. Barry, Fourth Wis., to *Wisconsin State Journal,* November 1861, eastern Va., Quiner Papers, Reel 1, vol. 1, p. 198.

105. Sgt. E. C. Hubbard, Thirteenth Ill., to brother, August 9, 1861, Rolla, Mo., E. C. Hubbard Letters, UAR.

106. See, for example, Hubbard's December 1861 letter to his sister in which he complained that policies that did not strike at slavery were prolonging the war. Sgt. E. C. Hubbard, Thirteenth Ill., to sister, December 3, 1861, Rolla, Mo., E. C. Hubbard Letters, UAR.

107. "Enlisted soldier," Third Wis., to *Wisconsin State Journal,* October 1861, near Harpers Ferry, Va., Quiner Papers, Reel 1, vol. 1, p. 176. This soldier, and the many others who agreed with him, call into question the received wisdom that says that Union soldiers in general either did not care about or opposed the eradication of slavery, and that Democratic soldiers in particular were hostile to the suggestion of emancipation because slavery was viewed as a partisan issue. Certainly, in 1860, the Democratic platform of popular sovereignty (or allowing white male voters in a territory to vote on slavery there) contrasted with the Republican platform of nonextension, and before and during the war Republicans would be more likely to advocate aggressive action against slavery while Democrats would be more likely to resist such actions out of both racism and constitutionalism. Yet the experience of soldiering, more than their party affiliation, began to shape troops' views on slavery from a very early date. Throughout the war, Democratic soldiers would proudly retain their political identification as Democrats, but they would also increasingly see two issues—Union and emancipation—as transcending political party. For this reason, while

Republican and Democratic soldiers would always differ on some points (strict or broad construction of the Constitution, the suspension of habeas corpus, fiscal policy), many Democratic as well as Republican soldiers would push for an end to slavery as the only way to end the war, some from the very beginning of the war and even more as the war progressed.

108. Pvt. John Boucher, Tenth Mo., to wife, December 7, 1861, Camp Holmes, Mo., Boucher Family Papers, CWMC, 2d Ser.

109. For a discussion of Butler's "contraband" policy, see Berlin, Fields, Glymph, Reidy, and Rowland, *Destruction of Slavery,* 70–75.

110. Pvt. Andrew Walker, Fifty-fifth Ill., to father, December 2, 1861, Camp Douglas, Chicago, Andrew J. Walker Papers, LC. For the First Confiscation Act see Silvana Siddali, *From Property to Person: Slavery and the Confiscation Acts, 1861–1862* (Baton Rouge: Louisiana State University Press, 2005), esp. chs. 3 and 4.

111. In September 1861, for instance, Lane burned the town of Osceola, Mo. For Lane's activities during the war, see Castel, *Civil War Kansas.*

112. For the text of Frémont's proclamation, see *War of the Rebellion: A Compilation of the Official Records of the Union and Confederate Armies* (hereafter *Official Records*) (Washington, D.C.: 1880–1901), ser. 1, vol. 3, pp. 466–67. See McPherson, *Battle Cry of Freedom,* 352–54, and Grimsley, *Hard Hand of War,* 123–24, for discussions of Frémont's proclamation.

113. Lt. E. P. Kellogg, Second Wis., to editor of *Wisconsin State Journal,* November 12, 1861, Camp Tillinghast, Va., Quiner Papers, Reel 1, vol. 1, p. 155.

114. A. G. Dinsmore, Thirteenth Mo., to unidentified friend, who had the letter published in the *Wisconsin State Journal,* October 14, 1861, Benton Barracks, Mo., Quiner Papers, Reel 1, vol. 2, p. 11.

115. Sgt. E. C. Hubbard, Thirteenth Ill., to brother, September 18, 1861, Rolla, Mo., E. C. Hubbard Letters, UAR.

116. Capt. William Dunham, Thirty-sixth Ohio, to wife, October 28, 1861, Summersville, Va. William Dunham Letters, CWMC.

117. Capt. William Dunham, Thirty-sixth Ohio, to father-in-law, November 15, 1861, Summersville, Va. William Dunham Letters, CWMC.

118. Pvt. Adam Marty, First Minn., to friend, October 10, 1861, Camp Stone, Va., MNHS.

119. Cpl. S. H. Helmer, Tenth Wis., to a friend, November 1861, Camp Abercrombie, Shepherdsville, Ky., Quiner Papers, Reel 1, vol. 2, p. 32. See also Sgt. C. Frank Shepard, First Mich. Cavalry, to wife, October 14, 1861, Washington, D.C., C. Frank Shepard Papers, Schoff; Pvt. George Baxter, Twenty-fourth Mass., to brother Jim, December 14, 1861, near Annapolis, Md., George H. Baxter Correspondence, MHS.

120. Pvt. Leigh Webber, First Kans., to Brown family, June 27, 1862, Trenton, Tenn., John S. Brown Family Papers, Reel 2, KSHS.

121. Sgt. E. C. Hubbard, Thirteenth Ill., to brother, October 18, 1861, Linn Creek, Mo., E. C. Hubbard Letters, UAR.

122. Oakes, *The Ruling Race,* 39.

123. M., Eighth Wis., to *Wisconsin State Journal,* November 15, 1861, Pilot Knob, Mo., Quiner Papers, Reel 1, vol. 2, p. 22. A Wisconsin soldier similarly claimed that slavery led to a society with "no church bells, no schools, no education," and forced Southerners to live "in a state of mental darkness." C. McD, Eighth Wis., to *Gazette,* November 18, 1861, Pilot Knob, Mo., Quiner Papers, Reel 1, vol. 2, pp. 22–23.

124. Chaplain William Gibson, Forty-fifth Pa., to children, March 25, 1862, Otter Island, S.C., William J. Gibson Letters, HCWRTC.

125. A vast literature exists on the "middle-class culture" of the antebellum and Civil War–era United States, particularly the North. As Mary Ryan has shown in *Cradle of the Middle Class* and historians too numerous to mention have confirmed, a middle class that encompassed much more than simply the middle-income brackets was imbued with what Ryan and others depict as "middle-class values." These values included literacy, self-discipline, domesticity and family life, and especially the value of work. As Charles Sellers put it, "The so-called middle class was constituted not by mode and relations of production but by ideology. . . . A numerous and dispersed bourgeoisie . . . mythologiz[ed] class as a moral category. Scorning both the handful of idle rich and the multitude of dissolute poor, they apotheosized a virtuous middle class of the effortful." See Charles Sellers, *The Market Revolution: Jacksonian America, 1815–1846* (New York: Oxford University Press, 1991), 237. That middle-class ideology and values pervaded even western and frontier states in the North is demonstrated by Jeffrey, *Frontier Women,* esp. the Introduction and chs. 1 and 4. For the applicability of northern middle-class ideology to Union soldiers, see esp. Mitchell, *Civil War Soldiers* and *The Vacant Chair*; and Hess, *Liberty, Virtue and Progress.*

126. For example, Olmsted described pigs wandering around a southern neighborhood because dissipated owners could not be bothered, as he saw it, to build a respectable pen. Frederick Law Olmsted, *The Cotton Kingdom: A Traveller's Observations on Cotton and Slavery in the American Slave States* (New York: Knopf, 1953), first published as installments in the *New York Times,* and then as three volumes: *A Journey in the Seaboard Slave States* (1856), *A Journey Through Texas* (1857), and *A Journey in the Back Country* (1860). The pig passage appears in *The Cotton Kingdom,* 31. For the impact of travel literature, especially that of Olmsted, on northern readers, see Grant, *North Over South,* ch. 4.

127. Jonathan Wells has shown in *The Origins of the Southern Middle Class 1800–1861* (Chapel Hill: University of North Carolina Press, 2004) that a southern middle class that shared many attributes of the northern middle class, but differed in its staunch support of slavery, did in fact exist and had been growing stronger since the 1850s, especially in towns and cities. Yet Union troops in 1861 proved more inclined to comment on the aspects of southern society that looked most unfamiliar to them, but that they had been most conditioned to look for in the "exotic South."

128. M., Eighth Wis., to *Wisconsin State Journal,* November 15, 1861, Pilot Knob, Mo., Quiner Papers, Reel 1, vol. 2, p. 22. For the theme of moral contagion, see Karen Halttunen, *Confidence Men and Painted Women: A Study of Middle-Class Culture in America, 1830–1870* (New Haven: Yale University Press, 1982); and Charles E. Rosenberg, *Cholera Years: The United States in 1832, 1849, and 1866* (Chicago: University of Chicago Press, 1962).

129. Peter Kolchin, *American Slavery, 1619–1877* (New York: Hill and Wang, 2003), 126. Soldiers might not have had the statistical information available, but observation of and conversation with slaves told them that family separation was a common fact of slave life.

130. W.D.W., Seventh Wis., to his hometown newspaper, December 16, 1861, Arlington Heights, Va., Quiner Papers, Reel 1, vol. 2, pp. 4–5. On the "fancy trade" aspect of the slave market, see Johnson, *Soul by Soul.*

131. Sgt. Cyrus Boyd, Fifth Iowa, diary, February 10, 1863, Providence Lake, La., Cyrus F. Boyd Collection, KCPL.

132. Pvt. Henry Bandy, Ninety-first Ill., to brother and sister, January 12, 1862, Ky., Henry Bandy Letters, ISHL.

133. Q.M. Sgt. Thomas Low, Twenty-third N.Y. Artillery, diary, March 29, 1862, Washington, D.C., Thomas Low Papers and Diary, DU.

134. Pvt. Adelbert Bly, Thirty-second Wis., to Anna, November 9, 1862, Memphis, Tenn., Adelbert M. Bly Correspondence, SHSW.

135. Chip, Eleventh Wis., to hometown newspaper, December 21, 1861, Sulphur Springs, Ky., Quiner Papers, Reel 1, vol. 2, p. 47.

136. The discussion here contributes to the long-running debate about "who freed the slaves." Ira Berlin and his coauthors have argued that slaves themselves were primarily responsible for linking emancipation and the Union war effort, ensuring that a war for Union also became a war for freedom. See Berlin, Fields, Glymph, Reidy, and Rowland, *Destruction of Slavery,* 1–56. James M. McPherson has countered with "Who Freed the Slaves?," where he emphasizes Abraham Lincoln's key role in shaping slave policy, a slightly different proposition from freeing individual slaves. I argue that enlisted Union soldiers proved to be the crucial link between the two halves of the emancipation equation. Enlisted Union soldiers provided the mechanisms slaves used to push the phenomenon of individuals freeing themselves into the accomplishment of emancipation as war policy, which required the cooperation of military leaders and policy makers, all under the leadership of President Lincoln. Slaves convinced enlisted soldiers, who modified both their beliefs and their behavior. Meanwhile, enlisted men used letters, camp newspapers, and their own actions to influence the opinions of civilians and political authorities. These civilians, lacking soldiers' direct contact with slaves, the South, and the experience of living on the front lines in a war that most people wanted over, lagged behind soldiers in their stances on emancipation. Enlisted troops also often outpaced their superior officers in the speed with which they came to oppose slavery. The point is not really that slaves convinced soldiers, and then soldiers turned around and dutifully repeated their new views to officers. Instead, through a series of overlapping experiences and interactions with slaves, enlisted men changed their ideas and then their behavior, leaving their officers with little choice but to sanction the new behavior with policy shifts. In a similar fashion, as Mark Grimsley has argued in *The Hard Hand of War,* interactions with white Southerners led Union soldiers to change their attitudes and behavior regarding property policy, which in turn required officers to implement policy shifts. I would like to thank Aaron Sheehan-Dean for pointing out the parallel with Grimsley's argument.

137. Pvt. John Foster, Second Miss. Battalion Cavalry, to aunt, October 14, 1861, Richmond, John Foster and Family Correspondence, CMM Ser. B, Reel 5.

138. John Foster to father, January 11, 1861, New Orleans, John Foster and Family Correspondence, CMM Ser. B, Reel 5. In May 1861, Foster enlisted as a private in the Second Miss. Battalion Cavalry.

2: "Richmond Is a Hard Road to Travel":
Gaps Between Expectation and Experience

1. Georgia soldier James Boyd to brother, February 16, 1862, Mobile, Ala., in Lane, *Dear Mother: Don't Grieve About Me,* 98.

2. Analyses of the composition of Confederate nationalism include Escott, *After Secession: Jefferson Davis and the Failure of Confederate Nationalism*; Faust, *The Creation of Confederate Nationalism: Ideology and Identity in the Civil War South*; John McCardell,

The Idea of a Southern Nation: Southern Nationalists and Southern Nationalism, 1830–1860 (New York: Norton, 1979); and Rubin, *A Shattered Nation: The Rise and Fall of the Confederacy, 1861–1868.* McCardell focuses on the writings of elites to argue that a separate southern cultural nationalism predated the war. Faust depicts Confederate patriotism as a work in progress, forced to respond to events (especially the travails of wartime), but expressed mainly through cultural expressions such as print media and symbols. The relationship between self-interest and Confederate patriotism is not a central concern of McCardell's or Faust's work. Escott sees the diverging interests of elite and nonelite Southerners as strong factors that militated against the development of an effective Confederate patriotism. Rubin's work, the most recent, struggles to explain self-interested behavior by white Southerners as aberrational and much-regretted exceptions to an emotional commitment to the Confederacy that always existed but sometimes got momentarily eclipsed by self-interest. This analysis differs in its emphasis on self-interest, or more specifically, commitment to the needs and interests (both material and ideological) of white southern families, as *central to* (and not a detraction from) Confederate patriotism.

3. Lt. James Williams, Twenty-first Ala., to wife, June 20, 1862, Gun Town, Miss., in Folmar, *From That Terrible Field,* 81.

4. Pvt. Charles Kerrison, Second S.C., to cousin, July 19, 1862, Camp McLaws, Va., Kerrison Family Papers, SCL.

5. Pvt. John Wall, Eleventh Tex. Cavalry, to brother, January 7, 1862, Washington Co., Ark., John Wall Letters, CWMC.

6. Pvt. William Bellamy, Eighteenth N.C., diary, June 10, 1862, near Richmond, Va., William James Bellamy Papers, SHC.

7. Lt. James Harrison, Fifteenth Ark., to brother, May 26, 1862, near Corinth, Miss., James M. Harrison Letters, UAR.

8. Pvt. James Branscomb, Third Ala., to sister, April 11, 1862, in Va., Branscomb Family Letters, ADAH.

9. Pvt. George W. Peebles, Prince George Rifle Rangers, diary, January 7, 1862, near Hardy's Bluff, Va., George W. Peebles Diary, CMM Ser. A, Reel 39. Peebles noted the near accuracy of his predictions the following month, after the "unjust drafting" law passed. "Stirring times abound[ed]" among his fellow soldiers, with several of them defying the law and "refusing to re-enlist," he reported. See Peebles, diary, February 11–12, 1862, near Hardy's Bluff, Va., George W. Peebles Diary, CMM Ser. A, Reel 39.

10. Predictably, loopholes led to fraud; state militias were suddenly filled with suspiciously high numbers of officers, while the number of Confederate teachers immediately multiplied. Draft dodgers would anger soldiers later in the war, but in the spring of 1862, the enlistment extension aspect bothered them the most. On the draft, see Albert Burton Moore, *Conscription and Conflict in the Confederacy* (Columbia: University of South Carolina Press, 1996), esp. ch. 2. Later drafts eventually extended the age range of conscription to seventeen to fifty-five.

11. Pvt. Benjamin Tamplin, Eleventh Tex., to wife, March 28, 1862, Houston, and Tamplin to wife, May 5, 1862, Camp Lubbock, Tex., William Tamplin Letters, CMM Ser. B, Reel 18. George Peebles, who had described the impact of conscription in Virginia on soldiers from the Old Dominion, noted that Confederate conscription was similarly "denounced by all." See Pvt. George W. Peebles, Prince George Rifle Rangers, diary, April 13, 1862, Strong Wharf, Va., George W. Peebles Diary, CMM Ser. A, Reel 39. Peebles's comments are important because they show that soldiers' dissatisfaction was with the enlistment extension itself, rather than with the source of the extension. Virginia troops had objected just as strongly to state as to Confederate conscription, revealing that to them the

matter was not one of states' rights, but of their own rights, which they did not want violated by Virginia any more than by a national government.

12. Emory Thomas, in *The Confederate Nation* (New York: Harper & Row, 1979), demonstrates that 1862 was a "revolutionary" year for the Confederate government. He credits "the creative efforts of Davis' government" and "the statecraft of the Richmond government" with building a strong centralized government, and (less convincingly) equates the construction of such a government with the emergence of a strong, clear Confederate nationalism (ch. 7, esp. 165). Paul Escott details Davis's attempts to build a stronger government (*After Secession,* ch. 3), but portrays the results as less successful, attributing Davis's "failure" to his own imperious personality, his inept dealing with state leaders, and to social divisions within the southern population (detailed in chs. 4, 5, 7). In *The Elements of Confederate Defeat: Nationalism, War Aims, and Religion* (Athens: University of Georgia Press, 1988), Beringer, Hattaway, Jones, and Still find that the Confederate government achieved remarkable success in its nationalization of railroads and industries, all of which contributed logistically to the war effort, but that the steps required to do so exerted a "debilitating effect on public morale" (22).

13. In *Southern Rights: Political Prisoners and the Myth of Confederate Constitutionalism* (Charlottesville: University of Virginia Press, 1999), Mark Neely challenges the characterization of white Southerners as "obsessive about liberty" (79). He also demonstrates that a strong desire for social order pervaded southern society, as evidenced in civilians' request for the imposition of martial law to control the use of alcohol among rambunctious soldiers (ch. 2) and the lack of outcry at infringements on liberties such as the passport system requiring passes, ordinarily required only of blacks, of southern whites who wished to travel (pp. 1–6). Neely effectively shows that white Southerners did not place a high priority on universal civil freedoms or strict constructionist constitutional principles, and persuasively demonstrates that they seceded in part to uphold rather than undermine good order, but he does not address citizens' resentment of policies that directly affected their own welfare. Specifically, he does not examine responses to impressment, tax-in-kind, or conscription, all of which Confederates did protest.

14. For discussion of policies adopted by southern state governments and the Confederate government regarding the burning of cotton crops, stipulation that farmers grow food crops, impressment, and tax-in-kind, see Thomas, *The Confederate Nation*; Escott, *After Secession*; and Georgia Lee Tatum, *Disloyalty in the Confederacy* (Lincoln: University of Nebraska Press, 2000; first published in 1934), 17–20, 74.

15. Lt. George Blakemore, Twenty-third Tenn., diary, June 2, 1862, Bowling, Miss., George Blakemore Diary, TSLA.

16. Mississippi soldier taken prisoner at Fort Donelson, to *Richmond Enquirer,* April 1862, Camp Chase, Ohio, *Richmond Enquirer,* April 29, 1862, 1.

17. Sgt. Frank Richardson, Second La., to mother, October 8, 1862, Hospital No. 2, Knoxville, Tenn., Frank Liddell Richardson Papers, ser. 1, SHC.

18. Thomas Lawrence Connelly, *Army of the Heartland: The Army of Tennessee, 1861–1862* (Baton Rouge: Louisiana State University Press, 1967), 134–38, esp. 136.

19. Pvt. James Williams, Twenty-first Ala., to wife, March 9, 1862, Fort Pillow, Tenn., in Folmar, *From That Terrible Field,* 45. Lawrence N. Powell and Michael S. Wayne emphasize elite slaveholding planters' calculations of their best interests as factors in the shifting loyalties of residents of the Mississippi Valley in 1862 and 1863 in "Self-Interest and the Decline of Confederate Nationalism," in Harry P. Owens and James J. Cooke, eds., *The Old South in the Crucible of War* (Jackson: University of Mississippi Press, 1983), 29–45.

20. Sgt. John French White, Thirty-second Va., to wife Martha, November 30, 1862, Fredericksburg, Va., John French White Papers, CMM Ser. A, Reel 42.

21. See Faust, *The Creation of Confederate Nationalism,* ch. 3, esp. pp. 44–45.

22. Pvt. Theodore Honour, Twenty-fifth S.C., to wife, October 6, 1862, Camp Stono, S.C., Theodore Augustus Honour Papers, SCL.

23. Louis Branscomb, Third Ala., to sister, December 2, 1862, near Fredericksburg, Va., Branscomb Family Letters, ADAH.

24. Pvt. E. N. Brown, Forty-fifth Ala., to wife, June 9, 1862, Chickasaw Co., Miss., Edward Norphlet Brown Letters, ADAH.

25. Lt. Marcus Willis, Thirteenth S.C., to parents, October 15, 1862, Danville, Va., Willis Family Papers, SCL.

26. Georgia soldier James Boyd repeated Jesse Jones's colorful remark in a letter to his brother, February 16, 1862, Mobile, Ala., in Lane, *Dear Mother: Don't Grieve About Me,* 92.

27. Books making the argument that class conflict led to the downfall of the Confederacy include Bailey, *Class and Tennessee's Confederate Generation*; Escott, *After Secession*; Robinson, *Bitter Fruits of Bondage*; Williams, *Rich Man's War: Class, Caste, and Confederate Defeat in the Lower Chattahoochee Valley*; and Williams, Williams, and Carlson, *Plain Folks in a Rich Man's War: Class and Dissent in Confederate Georgia.*

28. See Roderick Henry Harper Letters, GDAH. Harper never did succeed in finding a substitute; his efforts to do so were cut short when he was killed in the Seven Days battles in June 1862.

29. Confederate soldiers began to comment on desertion in 1862. See, for instance, Pvt. George Warfield, Seventeenth Va., to mother, May 29, 1862, near Richmond, George Warfield Letters, SHC. Although comparatively few secondary sources on desertion exist, later scholars have verified soldiers' observations, showing that by 1862 bands of deserters roamed through parts of western North Carolina, northwestern South Carolina, northern Georgia, northeastern Alabama, and eastern Tennessee. In *Desertion of Alabama Troops from the Confederate Army: A Study of Sectionalism* (New York: Columbia University Press, 1932), Bessie Martin demonstrates that the first of three periods of high desertion among Alabama troops began in February 1862 and lasted until February 1863. The other two periods ran from June 1863 through April 1864 and from the autumn of 1864 through April 1865. According to Ella Lonn's *Desertion During the Civil War* (New York: Century, 1928), factors like physical hardships and anxiety for families inadequately provided for led many northeastern Georgia soldiers to desert, even before the enforcement of the Conscription Act. Mark Weitz's discussion of desertion among Georgia troops, *A Higher Duty* (Lincoln: University of Nebraska Press, 2000), focuses on desertion after 1863 when the Union Army–generated "Register of Deserters" came into existence, and therefore adds little to Lonn's discussion of 1862, but Weitz's more comprehensive *More Damning Than Slaughter: Desertion in the Confederate Army* (Lincoln: University of Nebraska Press, 2005) argues that both threats to home and a persistent undercurrent of southern localism contributed to making desertion a problem for the Confederacy in 1862 (see esp. chs. 4 and 5). Concern over the desertion rate prompted the Arkansas legislature to declare any discouragement of military service a crime in March 1862. In April, the Confederate War Department generated explicit measures for the arrest and return of deserters for the first time, as Moore discusses in *Conscription and Conflict in the Confederacy,* esp. 129.

30. Pvt. Thomas Warrick, Thirty-fourth Ala., to wife, June 15, 1862, Thomas Warrick Letters, ADAH.

31. Pvt. E. N. Brown, Forty-fifth Ala., to wife, July 1862, near Tupelo, Miss., Edward Norphlet Brown Letters, ADAH.

32. Sgt. Thomas Davidson, Nineteenth La., to sister, July 24, 1862, Tupelo, Miss., Thomas Benjamin Davidson Papers, SHC.

33. Pvt. William Bellamy, Eighteenth N.C., diary, July 1862, near Richmond, William James Bellamy Papers, SHC.

34. Southern clergy in particular decried sins like greed, avarice, and extortion as Yankee sins from which only southern independence could provide immunity. See, for example, Chesebrough, *"God Ordained This War"*; Faust, *Creation of Confederate Nationalism,* chs. 2 and 3; and Snay, *Gospel of Disunion.* Ironically, in 1862 Confederate soldiers began to complain about extortion and greed among Southerners, and such complaints would grow as the war progressed. Nonetheless, Confederate soldiers believed that southern society was superior to northern society, and Southerners were superior to Northerners; they based these convictions on the belief that southern society was more orthodox and respectful of a social order ordained by God than freewheeling northern society, where all manner of dubious reform movements reigned and where citizens seemed to evince little respect for the proper order of things.

35. Pvt. James Manahan, Fourth Tex., to friend "Miss Willie," April 4, 1862, Camp Wigfall, Va., James H. Manahan Letters, CAH.

36. For the text and a discussion of General Order No. 28, Butler's "Woman Order," see Chester G. Hearn, *When the Devil Came Down to Dixie: Ben Butler in New Orleans* (Baton Rouge: Louisiana State University Press, 1997), 101–09; and Faust, *Mothers of Invention,* 207–13.

37. For an introduction to the literature on "woman's sphere" and women's role in guarding the morals of the republic, which emerged in the wake of the American Revolution and which grew as the "market revolution" encouraged the development of an ideology (if not always reality) of "separate spheres," see Nancy Cott, *The Bonds of Womanhood: "Woman's Sphere" in New England, 1780–1835* (New Haven: Yale University Press 1977); Jeffrey, *Frontier Women;* Linda Kerber, *Women of the Republic: Intellect and Ideology in Revolutionary America* (Chapel Hill: University of North Carolina Press, 1980); Mary Beth Norton, *Liberty's Daughters: The Revolutionary Experiences of American Women, 1750–1800* (Boston: Little, Brown, 1980); Ryan, *Cradle of the Middle Class;* Sellers, *The Market Revolution;* Barbara Welter, "The Cult of True Womanhood, 1820–1860," *American Quarterly* 18 (1966), 151–74. In *Southern Lady, Yankee Spy: The True Story of Elizabeth Van Lew, A Union Agent in the Heart of the Confederacy* (New York: Oxford University Press, 2003), Elizabeth Varon examines the impact of the Civil War on the idea of female innocence, esp. on pp. 60–61. For a discussion of how all these ideas applied to white elite southern women during the Civil War, see Faust, *Mothers of Invention.*

38. Capt. Tristrim Skinner, First N.C., to wife, May 25, 1862, Goldsboro, N.C., Skinner Family Papers, SHC.

39. Pvt. John Street, Eighth Tex., to wife, May 20, 1862, Corinth, Miss., John K. and Melinda East Street Papers, SHC.

40. Lt. James Harrison, Fifteenth Ark., to brother, September 5, 1862, Camp Priceville, Miss., James M. Harrison Letters, UAR.

41. Pvt. W. H. Williams, Miss., to family, May 19, 1862, Corinth, Miss., W. H. Williams Letters, TSLA.

42. Capt. James Williams, Twenty-first Ala., to wife, June 28, 1862, near Tupelo, Miss., in Folmar, *From That Terrible Field,* 92–93.

43. Pvt. Willilam Bellamy, Eighteenth N.C., diary, July 1862, near Richmond, William James Bellamy Papers, SHC.

44. Pvt. John Street, Eighth Tex., to wife, February 25, 1862, Tishomingo Co., Miss., John K. and Melinda East Street Papers, SHC.

45. Confederate poem found by Union soldiers at Williamsburg, Va., reprinted in *The Cavalier,* July 16, 1862, Williamsburg, Va., p. 2, VHS.

46. Lt. Macon Bonner, Co. B, N.C. Artillery, to wife, May 23, 1862, Fort Fisher, N.C., Macon Bonner Papers, SHC. The phenomenon Bonner described has been well documented by scholars since the 1980s, who have shown the central role that slaves played in using the circumstances created by Lincoln's election and the war to free themselves. See, for example, Steven Hahn, *A Nation Under Our Feet: Black Political Struggles in the Rural South from Slavery to the Great Migration* (Cambridge, Mass.: Harvard University Press, 2003), 13–115; Berlin, Fields, Glymph, Reidy, and Rowland, *Destruction of Slavery*; and Berlin, *Slaves No More.*

47. Capt. Robert Snead, Fiftieth Va., to wife, February 11, 1862, Clarksville, Tenn., Robert W. Snead Papers, CMM Ser. A, Reel 39.

48. Pvt. Henry Graves, Macon (Ga.) Volunteers, to mother, June 13, 1862, Drewry's Bluff, Va., Graves Family Correspondence, SHC.

49. Pvt. Thomas Taylor, Sixth Ala., to parents, March 4, 1862, Manassas Junction, Va., Thomas S. Taylor Letters, ADAH.

50. Pvt. Rudolf Coreth, Seventh Tex. Cavalry, to family, February 22, 1862, Camp Winston, Tex., in Minetta Altgelt Goyne, ed. and trans., *Lone Star and Double Eagle: Civil War Letters of a German-Texas Family* (Texas Christian University Press, 1982), 43.

51. Pvt. Rudolf Coreth, Seventh Tex. Cavalry, to family, March 20, 1862, Camp Winston, Tex., in Goyne, *Lone Star and Double Eagle,* 48.

52. Pvt. William Wilson, Twelfth Va. Cavalry, diary, May 25, 1862, between Newtown and Winchester, Va., in Festus Summers, ed., *A Borderland Confederate* (Pittsburgh: University of Pittsburgh Press, 1962.)

53. Cpl. Joseph Polley, Fourth Tex., to "Charming Nellie," April 5, 1862, near Fredericksburg, Va., in Harold Simpson, ed., *A Soldier's Letters to Charming Nellie By J. B. Polley of Hood's Texas Brigade* (Gaithersburg, Md.: Butternut Press, 1984), 28–30. No battle occurred, according to Polley, because Union forces fled before the Texans reached their camp.

54. Cpl. Nathan Parmater, Twenty-ninth Ohio, diary, February 25, 1862, Winchester, Va., Nathan Parmater Papers, OHS.

55. Sgt. Cyrus Boyd, Fifteenth Iowa, diary, shortly after April 6, 1862, Pittsburg Landing, Tenn., in Mildred Throne, ed., *The Civil War Diary of Cyrus F. Boyd, Fifteenth Iowa Infantry 1861–1863* (Millwood, N.Y.: Kraus Reprint, 1977), 27–39. For an account of the severity of Shiloh and an analysis of soldiers' reactions to it, see Joseph Allen Frank and George A. Reaves, *Seeing the Elephant: Raw Recruits at the Battle of Shiloh* (New York: Greenwood, 1989).

56. Sgt. Cyrus Boyd, Fifteenth Iowa, diary, May 24, 1862, Corinth, Miss., in Throne, *Civil War Diary of Cyrus F. Boyd,* 52.

57. Pvt. Leigh Webber, First Kans., to Miss Brown, August 12, 1862, Gibson Co., Tenn., John S. Brown Family papers, Reel 2, KSHS.

58. Sgt. Felix Brannigan, Fifth N.Y., to sister, June 17, 1862, Fair Oaks, Va., Felix Brannigan Papers, *PAW,* Coll. 22, Reel 4.

59. Pvt. Moses Parker, Third Vt., to Friend Eliza, May 26, 1862, seven miles from

Richmond, in Jeffrey D. Marshall, ed., *A War of the People: Vermont Civil War Letters* (Hanover N.H.: University Press of New England, 1999), 80.

60. Cpl. George Brookins, Third Minn., to brother, July 30, 1862, Benton Barracks, Mo., Brookins Family Letters, MNHS.

61. Pvt. Roland Bowen, Fifteenth Mass., to mother, July 19, 1862, near Harrison's Landing, Va., in Gregory A. Coco, ed., *From Ball's Bluff to Gettysburg . . . and Beyond: The Civil War Letters of Private Roland E. Bowen, 15th Massachusetts Infantry, 1861–1864* (Gettysburg: Thomas Publications, 1994), 115.

62. Pvt. Caleb Beal, Fourteenth N.Y. Militia, to parents, February 4, 1862, Upton Hill, Va., Caleb Hadley Beal Papers, MHS.

63. Pvt. Lewis Jones, Seventy-ninth Pa., to wife, February 12, 1862, Bar[r]en Co., Ky., Lewis Jones Papers, CWMC.

64. *Seventh Brigade Journal,* 1:2, April 8, 1862, Columbia, Tenn., p. 1, TSLA. Soldiers from many regiments contributed to this newspaper, including soldiers of the First Wis. and the Twenty-ninth Pa.

65. *The Regimental Flag,* 1:1, January 16, 1862, Accomac Co., Va., p. 3, UVA. *The Regimental Flag* was the camp newspaper of the Second Del. A similar incident occurred the following month among Indiana soldiers. When the soldiers of the Twelfth Ind. received socks and gloves from the Woldcotville Knitting Society, Pvt. A. W. Cummings wrote a thank-you note from the regiment linking civilians and soldiers in a shared struggle for "Liberty and Union." See Pvt. A. W. Cummings, Twelfth Ind., to Knitting Society, Woldcottville, Ind., February 10, 1862, Washington, D.C., Virginia Southwood Collection, UMOC. For discussion of ties between northern men and their communities, see Mitchell, *The Vacant Chair.*

66. "State Sovereignty, National Union," *The Federal Scout,* 1:1, March 11, 1862, Columbus, Ky., p. 3, ISHL.

67. Pvt. Jerome Cutler, Second Vt., to fiancée, January 5, 1862, Camp Griffin, Va., Jerome Cutler Letters, VTHS.

68. Pvt. L.C.N., First Wis., to the *Motor,* September 9, 1862, Bowling Green, Ky., Quiner Papers, Reel 1, vol. 2, p. 181; Sgt. Thomas Davidson, Nineteenth La., to sister, July 24, 1862, Tupelo, Miss., Thomas Benjamin Davidson Papers, SHC.

69. Although most white southern families worked their own modest farms, many northern soldiers perceived differences between their homes and the South, and claimed that nonwealthy southern whites were treated as inferior. George Landrum, for example, described Alabama poor whites as "really more enslaved than the negroes," and "nearly in a starving condition, can get no work nor pay for what little they do." Lt. George Landrum, Second Ohio, to sister, April 23, 1861, Huntsville, Ala., George W. Landrum Letters, WRHS. As Oakes in *The Ruling Race* and Wells in *The Origins of the Southern Middle Class* have shown, southern society was not as stratified as Northerners interpreted it (at least among whites), but Union soldiers' perceptions of differences nonetheless influenced the conclusions they drew about the South and the War.

70. Chaplain William Gibson, Forty-fifth Pa., to children, March 25, 1862, Otter Island, S.C., William J. Gibson Letters, HCWRTC.

71. Lt. George Landrum, Second Ohio, to sister, April 23, 1862, Huntsville, Ala., George W. Landrum Letters, WRHS.

72. Pvt. Constant Hanks, Twentieth N.Y. Militia, to wife, May 13, 1862, Camp Stink near Fredericksburg, Va., Constant Hanks Papers, DU.

73. Lt. P. V. Wise, First Wis., to hometown paper, April 4, 1862, Columbia, Tenn., Quiner Papers, Reel 1, vol. 2, p. 154.

74. Cpl. Rufus Kinsley, Eighth Vt., diary, August 25, 1862, New Orleans, Rufus Kinsley Diary, VTHS.

75. "R.," First Wis., to hometown paper, April 21, 1862, Mt. Pleasant, Tenn., Quiner Papers, Reel 1, vol. 2, pp. 159–60.

76. Pvt. Constant Hanks, Twentieth N.Y. Militia, to wife, May 1, 1862, Fredericksburg, Va., Constant Hanks Papers, DU; *The Illinois Fifty-Second,* 1:1, January 15, 1862, Stewartsville, Mo., p. 3, ISHL.

77. Pvt. James H. Hougland, First Ind. Cavalry, diary, January 24, 1862, Pilot Knob, Mo., James H. Hougland Diary, JCHS.

78. Lt. Charles Brewster, Tenth Mass., to mother, March 5, 1862, Washington, D.C., in David W. Blight, ed., *When This Cruel War Is Over: The Civil War Letters of Charles Harvey Brewster* (Amherst: University of Massachusetts Press, 1992), 92. Officers in many regiments were slower to embrace emancipation than enlisted men. Their reluctance could have arisen from several sources. More likely to come from the elite of society than enlisted men were, some officers may have distrusted disruptions to hierarchy. Officers may also have had to face more directly the practical complications of emancipation, such as what to do about the bands of freedmen and freedwomen who entered camps or tried to join in on marches. Gen. Henry Halleck, for example, fretted about the military burden that freedpeople would impose (see McPherson, *Battle Cry of Freedom,* 498). Enlisted men themselves sometimes, especially in 1863 and later, grumbled that officers dragged their feet more than enlisted men because it was enlisted men who bore the brunt of the war, and who therefore were quickest to champion steps to end it.

79. Congress ended slavery in the District of Columbia in April 1862. West Virginia's state constitutional convention came within one vote of enacting gradual emancipation on May 23, 1862, and submitted a state constitution to Congress without mention of emancipation. Congress added emancipation as a condition of admission, and West Virginians accepted the condition in December 1862. West Virginia entered the Union on July 4, 1863. See Richard Orr Curry, *A House Divided: Statehood Politics and the Copperhead Movement in West Virginia* (Pittsburgh: University of Pittsburgh Press, 1994); and McPherson, *Battle Cry of Freedom,* 297–304.

80. The Second Confiscation Act was signed into law on July 17, 1862. See "An Act to Suppress Insurrection to Punish Treason and Rebellion to Seize and Confiscate Property and for Other Purposes," July 17, 1862, *U.S. Statutes at Large,* 12: 589–92. For more on the Second Confiscation Act, see Siddali, *From Property to Person,* esp. ch. 6 and the Conclusion.

81. Pvt. George Mowry, Seventh Kans. Cavalry, to sister, July 22, 1862, near Corinth, Miss., Webster Moses Letters and Diaries, KSHS.

82. Lt. P. V. Wise, First Wis., to hometown paper, May 1, 1862, Mt. Pleasant, Tenn., Quiner Papers, Reel 1, vol. 2, pp. 161–62. Wise's celebration regarding West Virginia was a little premature, since West Virginia did not complete its emancipation process for almost a year, but he was sure he saw the direction the new state was heading.

83. Sgt. Henry Hubble, Seventy-sixth N.Y. Militia, to father, May 22, 1862, Edisto Island, S.C., Henry Hubble Papers, NYHS.

84. "Boone," First Wis., to the *Sentinel,* January 3, 1862, Munfordsville, Ky., Quiner Papers, Reel 1, vol. 2, p. 137.

85. Pvt. Phillip Hacker, Fifth Mich., to father, April 17, 1862, Yorktown, Va., Hacker Brothers Papers, Schoff.

86. Pvt. Adin Ballou, Tenth Maine, to parents, November 7, 1862, Camp Berlin, Md., Adin Ballou Papers, ISHL.

87. Pvt. Roland Bowen, Fifteenth Mass., to mother, July 19, 1862, near Harrison's Landing, Va., in Coco, *From Ball's Bluff to Gettysburg,* 115–16.

88. Pvt. Leigh Webber, First Kans., to Miss Brown, August 30, 1862, Gibson Co., Tenn.; and Leigh Webber to Brown family, July 24, 1862, Gibson Co., Tenn., John S. Brown Family Papers, Reel 2, KSHS.

89. Pvt. Edwin Wentworth, Thirty-seventh Mass., to father, September 17, 1862, Arlington, Va., Edwin O. Wentworth Papers, LC; "Marion," First Wis., to *Daily Wisconsin,* May 1, 1862, Mount Pleasant, Tenn., Quiner Papers, Reel 1, vol. 2, p. 162.

90. Pvt. Constant Hanks, Twentieth N.Y. Militia, to mother, August 8, 1862, Fredericksburg, Va., Constant Hanks Papers, DU.

91. Cpl. James Jessee, Eighth Ill., diary, August 16, 1862, Jackson, Tenn., James Jessee Diary, KU.

92. Lt. P. V. Wise, First Wis., to *Wisconsin State Journal,* January 20, 1862, Camp Wood, Ky., Quiner Papers, Reel 1, vol. 2, pp. 139–40. See also Pvt. J, First Wis., to *Times* (in Wisconsin), March 18, 1862, Nashville, Quiner Papers, Reel 1, vol. 2, p. 150.

93. Sgt. Major Elisha Hunt Rhodes, Second R.I., diary, May 20, 1862, Gaines Mills, Va., in Robert Hunt Rhodes, ed., *All for the Union: The Civil War Diary and Letters of Elisha Hunt Rhodes* (New York: Orion, 1991), 66.

94. Pvt. Byron Strong, Twenty-fourth N.Y., to family, April 22, 1862, Falmouth, Va., Byron Strong Papers, NYSL. See also Cpl. Newton Perkins, Thirteenth Conn., to parents, May 3, 1862, Ship Island, Miss., Montgomery Family Papers, LC.

95. Pvt. "M.," First Wis., to *Times,* March 23, 1862, Nashville, Tenn., Quiner Papers, Reel 1, vol. 2, p. 151.

96. Pvt. Leigh Webber, First Kans., to Brown family, July 11, 1862, Gibson Co., Tenn., John S. Brown Family Papers, Reel 2, KSHS.

97. Pvt. James Miller, 111th Pa., to brother, August 17, 1862, near Culpeper, Va., Miller Brothers Papers, Schoff.

98. Pvt. Constant Hanks, Twentieth N.Y. Militia, to wife, April 14, 1862, Hospital, Washington, D.C., Constant Hanks Papers, DU.

99. Lt. George Landrum, Second Ohio, to sister, April 23, 1862, Huntsville, Ala., George W. Landrum Letters, WRHS.

100. Capt. William Dunham, Thirty-sixth Ohio, to wife, June 3, 1862, Meadow Bluffs, Va., William Dunham Letters, CWMC.

101. "Marion," First Wis., to *Daily Wisconsin,* May 1, 1862, Mt. Pleasant, Tenn., Quiner Papers, Reel 1, vol. 2, p. 162.

102. Pvt. Lewis Jones, Seventy-ninth Pa., to his wife, March 12, 1862, near Nashville, Tenn., Lewis Jones Letters, CWMC.

103. Capt. William Dunham, Thirty-sixth Ohio, to wife, January 14, 1862, Summersville, Va., William Dunham Letters, CWMC.

104. Sgt. Cyrus Boyd, Fifteenth Iowa, "Sketches of Lives," in the back of his diary, vol. 1, which he kept in 1862, mainly in Tenn., Cyrus F. Boyd Collection, KCPL.

3: "Kingdom Coming in the Year of Jubilo": Revolution and Resistance

1. The dream disturbed Harrison so deeply that he wrote about it to his parents, describing it in detail and explaining how much it upset him, even though he could not imagine that his Aunt Polly would ever allow such a scene to take place in her home. Lt.

James Harrison, Fifteenth Ark., to parents, January 13, 1863, Grenada, Miss., James M. Harrison Letters, UAR.

2. Pvt. Charles Tubbs, Twenty-seventh Mass., to wife, May 18, 1863, Newbern, N.C., C. H. Tubbs Letters, NCDAH.

3. "Resolutions adopted by the 102d Ill. in camp," transmitted by Cpl. Stephen Fleharty to the *Chicago Times, Chicago Tribune, Galesburg Democrat, Knox Republican, Aledo Record, Monmouth Atlas, Keithsburg Observer, Rock Island Argus,* and *Cambridge Chronicle,* March 17, 1863, Tenn., in Philip J. Reyburn and Terry L. Wilson, eds., *"Jottings from Dixie": The Civil War Dispatches of Sergeant Major Stephen F. Fleharty, U.S.A.* (Baton Rouge: Louisiana State University Press, 1999), 11–12. The *Rock Island Argus* refused to print the resolutions, which caused Fleharty to stop corresponding with that newspaper.

4. Pvt. Leigh Webber, First Kans., to Brown Family, July 24, 1862, Gibson Co., Tenn., John S. Brown Letters, Reel 2, KSHS.

5. Pvt. Thomas Covert, Sixth Ohio Cavalry, to wife, January 11, 1863, Stafford Co., Va., Thomas Covert Papers, WRHS. In *Lincoln at Gettysburg: The Words That Remade America* (New York: Simon and Schuster, 1992), Garry Wills makes the eloquent and persuasive case that in the 272 words of the Gettysburg Address, Abraham Lincoln revolutionized the relationship between the Declaration of Independence, the Constitution, and the American nation. By writing that each listener to the address "was having his or her intellectual pocket picked" (38), Wills depicts Lincoln as ahead of the public in his new understanding of a nation that must reform rather than merely preserve itself, and he may well have been ahead of the bulk of the civilian population. In contrast, soldiers' words in late 1862 and 1863, months ahead of the Gettysburg Address, show that Lincoln was not ahead of much of the rank and file in his vision of the Union transformed.

6. Capt. Amos Hostetter, Thirty-fourth Ill., to sister and brother-in-law, January 29, 1863, Murfreesboro, Tenn., ISHL. Orra Bailey agreed that "God is punishing this nation for letting this great sin to exist amongst us." See Pvt. Orra Bailey, Seventh Conn., to wife, February 16, 1863, Fernandina, Fla., Orra B. Bailey Papers, *PAW,* Coll. 10, Reel 2.

7. Pvt. Orra Bailey, Seventh Conn., to wife, February 16, 1863, Fernandina, Fla., Orra B. Bailey Papers, *PAW,* Coll. 10, Reel 2.

8. Surgeon Thomas Hawley, 111th Ill., to parents, January 17, 1863, LaGrange, Tenn., Thomas S. Hawley Paper, MOHS.

9. Abraham Lincoln, Speech at Springfield, Illinois, June 16, 1858, in Basler, *Collected Works of Lincoln,* 2:461.

10. See Fehrenbacher, *The Slaveholding Republic.*

11. For a long time, popular assumptions about soldiers' resistance to the Emancipation Proclamation have gone largely unchallenged by scholarship. Even Allan Guelzo's recent book *Lincoln's Emancipation Proclamation: The End of Slavery in America* (New York: Simon and Schuster, 2004) repeats the received wisdom about the proclamation nearly "triggering a military coup d'état by General George McClellan and the Army of the Potomac" (6, 187–89). This claim inaccurately conflates McClellan's views with those of ordinary soldiers, who expressed much different sentiments, but very few of whose writings Guelzo cites.

Many other key works on the Emancipation Proclamation dedicate their attention to aspects other than soldiers' reactions. John Hope Franklin's *The Emancipation Proclamation* (Garden City, N.Y.: Doubleday, 1963) examines the creation of the document and its impact on the war, but concludes that "it is not possible to know the prevailing reaction of the average soldier" (127), and speculates that the ordinary soldier's reaction was probably "not very important anyway," as long as he spread the news of the proclamation to slaves in the South (128). Louis Gerteis in *From Contraband to Freedman* (Westport, Conn.: Greenwood, 1973) assesses official union policy toward former slaves, and evaluates its impact on postwar conditions for African Americans, but does not examine soldiers' responses to the proclamation. In "From Preliminary to Final Emancipation Proclamation: The First Hundred Days," *Journal of Negro History* 48:4 (October 1963), 260–76, Roland McConnell notes the proclamation as a turning point for both Union and Confederate armies, but devotes little attention to soldiers' responses.

Studies of soldiers often discuss soldiers' views of slavery, but generally do so over the course of the war as a whole, rather than scrutinize opinions at any one time. James McPherson finds a significant degree of Union support for emancipation and explains its origins sensitively in *Battle Cry of Freedom* and *For Cause and Comrades*. McPherson does devote a little space to soldiers' reactions to the proclamation, finding a broad array of opinion in the Union rank and file. He notes that the proclamation "intensified a morale crisis in Union armies" (123), but also argues that a significant portion of the troops endorsed the proclamation, mainly on utilitarian grounds. Reid Mitchell offers a brief but balanced assessment, writing that when the proclamation "made the war an antislavery war, some soldiers were jubilant, others horrified, and still more accepted the war's transformation with troubled minds" (*Civil War Soldiers*, 126). Useful as the insights of McPherson and Mitchell are, they have thus far made little dent in the popular view; each year students come into my class confident in the assumption that Union soldiers hated emancipation.

12. See, for instance, Bell I. Wiley, *The Life of Billy Yank;* and Wiley, "Billy Yank and the Black Folk," *Journal of Negro History* 36:1 (January 1952), 25–52.

13. The most thoroughgoing treatise on racism among Union soldiers is Leon Litwack, *Been in the Storm So Long: The Aftermath of Slavery* (New York: Knopf, 1979). Bell Wiley lays heavy emphasis on what he calls "an enormous amount of antipathy toward Negroes" in "Billy Yank and the Black Folk" (35). *The Life of Billy Yank* also recounts anecdotes of soldier animosity and even cruelty toward blacks. Litwack never addresses soldiers' responses to the proclamation, and Wiley does so with only two fleeting sentences. One asserts that "the issuance of the Emancipation Proclamation aroused opponents of a 'Negro War' to the highest level of bitterness" (*Billy Yank*, 42). The other suggests that the proclamation had an uplifting effect on Union morale in the long term by ennobling the northern cause, but exerted a dispiriting influence in the short run of January 1863 (*Billy Yank*, 281).

14. Frank Klement, "Midwestern Opposition to Lincoln's Emancipation Policy," *Journal of Negro History* 49:3 (July 1964), 169–83, examines the negative response of Democratic newspapers to the Emancipation Proclamation, and links that response to deep-rooted midwestern racial prejudice. W. Sherman Jackson's "Emancipation, Negrophobia, and Civil War Politics in Ohio," *Journal of Negro History* 65:3 (July 1980), 250–60, shows opposition among Ohio civilians and state government to the Emancipation Proclamation based on antiblack attitudes and fears of "amalgamation," but indicates that the opposition had faded by the 1863 gubernatorial election. Other works demonstrate northern racism, but show that such racism did not necessarily lead to opposition to emancipation. Eugene Berwanger's *The Frontier Against Slavery: Western Anti-Negro Prejudice and the Slavery Extension Controversy* (Chicago: University of Illinois Press, 1967) makes antiblack feeling among Midwesterners clear, but also shows how that feeling could also lead to opposition to the institution of slavery, since the absence of slavery meant the absence of black slaves. In *Free but Not Equal: The Midwest and the Negro During the Civil War* (Chicago:

University of Chicago Press, 1967), V. Jacque Voegeli convincingly details racism among Midwesterners, but also shows that, though most midwestern civilians opposed the Emancipation Proclamation at first, racial prejudice often coexisted with support for the proclamation, and that condescending attitudes did not always preclude favor for vigorous antislavery policies. Neither Jackson, Berwanger, nor Voegeli addresses soldiers' views of the proclamation. T. Harry Williams briefly discusses soldiers and the proclamation in "Voters in Blue: The Citizen Soldiers of the Civil War," *Mississippi Valley Historical Review* 31:2 (September 1944), 187–204. He portrays the proclamation as a source of much discussion, but does not characterize the discussion as pro- or antiproclamation. He does reveal that Copperhead newspapers in strongly Democratic southern Illinois circulated fabricated (or at least highly exaggerated) reports that Illinois soldiers mutinied or deserted in response to the proclamation, but notes that such reports had little basis in fact.

15. Pvt. Dayton Flint, Fifteenth N.J., to father, January 27, 1863, near White Oak Church, Va., Dayton Flint Letters, CWMC, Ser. 2.

16. Lt. Charles Brewster, Tenth Mass., to mother, November 5, 1862, near Uniontown, Va., in Blight, *When This Cruel War Is Over,* 189.

17. Lt. Benjamin Ashenfelter, Thirty-fifth Pa., to mother, November 12, 1862, near Rappahannock Station, Va., Benjamin Ashenfelter Letters, HCWRTC.

18. Sgt. John Babb, Fifth Md., to mother, December 18, 1862, Harpers Ferry, Va., John D. Babb Family Papers, EU.

19. Cpl. Adam Muezenberger, Twenty-sixth Wis., to wife, February 16, 1863, between Stafford Courthouse and Brooks Station, Va., Adam Muezenberger Letters, SHSW.

20. Sgt. Thomas Smith, Sixth Pa. Cavalry, to brother, May 8, 1863, near Chancellorsville, Va., in Eric J. Wittenberg, ed., *"We Have It Damn Hard Out Here": The Civil War Letters of Sergeant Thomas W. Smith, 6th Pennsylvania Cavalry* (Kent, Ohio: Kent State University Press, 1999), 88.

21. Pvt. Charles Musser, Twenty-ninth Iowa, to father, February 3, 1863, near Helena, Ark., in Barry Popchock, ed., *Soldier Boy: The Civil War Letters of Charles O. Musser, 29th Iowa* (Iowa City: Iowa University Press, 1995), 28, 25. Just as desertion had become a problem for Confederates in 1862, it plagued the Union Army in 1863. While most historians regard its figures as too high, Ella Lonn's *Desertion During the Civil War* remains the most extensive treatment of the topic. Lonn estimates that as many as 25 percent of Union troops were improperly absent from the Army of the Potomac on January 26, 1863. In the West, there were about half as many unaccounted-for soldiers. Despite these high figures, Lonn regards most 1863 absences as temporary (some men left and returned; others had been captured and were later exchanged or paroled), and shows that as 1863 progressed, desertion and straggling dramatically declined in the Union Army. See Lonn, *Desertions During the Civil War,* 145–46, 152, and Tables 3 and 5 in the Appendix. Desertion rates varied by region. Lonn reveals comparatively high rates for Illinois and Indiana as well as Wisconsin, and reports "the height of the Copperhead sympathy in 1863" as a time when "absenteeism" was especially "brazen" among Indiana and Illinois troops (152, 204).

22. Pvt. Dayton Flint, Fifteenth N.J., to father, January 27, 1863, near White Oak Church, Va., Dayton Flint Letters, CWMC, Ser. 2.

23. Pvt. Freidrich Ledergarber, Twelfth Mo., to uncle, September 2, 1862, Helena, Ark., Engleman-Kircher Papers, ISHL.

24. Lt. Joseph Trego, Third Kans. Cavalry, to wife, September 30, 1862, Helena, Ark., Trego Collection, KSHS.

25. Cpl. Elijah Penny, Fourth N.Y. Artillery, to wife, November 30, 1862, Penny Family Papers, NYSL.

26. Pvt. Robert Pitts, Twenty-first Iowa, diary, January 5, 1863, Houston, Mo., Robert Pitts Diary, Union Army Boxes, NYPL.

27. Sgt. William Parkinson, Eleventh Ill., to wife, April 13, 1863, Providence Lake, La., William Parkinson Papers, EU.

28. Cpl. Mitchell Thompson, Eighty-third Ill., to wife, April 10, 1863, Ft. Donelson, Tenn., Mitchell Andrew Thompson Letters, TSLA. Statements like Thompson's contradicted what I had expected to find, since like many others, I had been taken in by McClellan's (and later historians') claims about soldiers' antipathy to emancipation. Surprised when I continued to read soldiers repeating Thompson's point, I decided to see if I was spotting a reliable pattern, or if I was just taking more notice of what I had not expected. To determine if there really was a predominant view, I categorized the statements of the first approximately one hundred (actually, 104, reason below) Union soldiers I encountered who explicitly mentioned the Emancipation Proclamation and clearly expressed an unequivocal opinion about it between September 1862, when the preliminary proclamation was issued, and June 1863, six months after the final proclamation. Of these, seventy-nine actively supported the proclamation while twenty-five opposed it. Subsequent soldiers did not change the proportion established by this set, so I saw no further need to inflate the numbers. While I make no pretense of having created a statistically valid sample, these first 104 soldiers consisted of ordinary enlisted men and junior officers who came from every region of the Union and served in every theater of the war. In other words, they were average soldiers, not men preselected on the basis of likely views. The idea was to look for a pattern in the full knowledge that a perfect statistical ratio is impossible (or at any rate, of dubious validity) at this remove; that is why I have not expressed the pattern in falsely precise-sounding terms such as "75.96 percent of soldiers supported and 24.04 percent opposed the proclamation." Nonetheless, the proportions are decisive enough to establish a convincing pattern of support (though certainly not unanimity) for the Emancipation Proclamation among the rank and file. Obviously, many more soldiers wrote about slavery, mainly to demand its destruction as the only way to end the war, and many others treated the related topic of black enlistment, but only these 104 individuals who specifically named the Emancipation Proclamation (or an obvious synonym, such as "the President's Proclamation") in their writings in this specific time frame and took a stance on it are included in this total. Other troops mentioned or noted the proclamation with no objections, but they are not included in the total. Most of the 104 wrote about the proclamation more than once, and many claimed to express the views common to their whole regiments. No matter how many times an individual brought up the proclamation, he is only counted in this total once, except if he changed his mind, in which case he is counted once in both columns. That is why the number is 104 rather than 100.

29. Pvt. Jasper Barney, Sixteenth Ill., to brother-in-law, October 24, 1862, Mound City Hospital, Kans., John C. Dinsmore Letters, ISHL.

30. Gen. George McClellan to President Abraham Lincoln, July 1862, Harrison's Landing, Va., in Sears, *The Civil War Papers of George B. McClellan,* 344–46.

31. Pvt. Chauncey Welton, 103d Ohio, to parents and siblings, January 13, 1863, near Frankfort, Ky., Chauncey B. Welton Letters, SHC.

32. Cpl. John Ellis, 111th Pa., to nephew, February 1863, Acquia Creek, Va., Ellis-Marshall Family Papers, HCWRTC.

33. Pvt. Chauncey Welton, 103d Ohio, to uncle, March 5, 1863, Benson Bridge, Ky., Chauncey B. Welton Letters, SHC.

34. Ibid.

35. Pvt. Edwin Wentworth, Thirty-seventh Mass., to *Argus,* April 4, 1863, near Falmouth, Va., Edwin O. Wentworth Papers, LC.

36. Sgt. Cyrus Boyd, Fifteenth Iowa, diary, February 9, 1863, on steamer *Maria Downing,* La., Cyrus F. Boyd Collection, KCPL.

37. Sgt. John Babb, Fifth Md., to parents and siblings, October 3, 1862, near Harpers Ferry, Va., John D. Babb Family Papers, EU.

38. Pvt. Phillip Reilly, Twenty-ninth Mo., to brother, March 31, 1863, before Vicksburg, Miss., Philip A. Reilly Letters, UMOR.

39. Pvt. David Massey, Thirty-third Mo., to father, January 11, 1863, and to sister, January 26, 1863, near Helena, Ark., David T. Massey Letters, MOHS.

40. Pvt. Terah Sampson, Sixth Ky., to mother, January 9, 1863, near Murfreesboro, Tenn., Terah W. Sampson Letters, FC.

41. Sgt. Cyrus Boyd, Fifteenth Iowa, diary, February 9, 1863, on board steamer *Maria Dowling,* La., Cyrus F. Boyd Collection, KCPL.

42. Pvt. Chauncey Welton, 103d Ohio, to parents, March 7, 1863, Benson Bridge, Ky., Chauncey B. Welton Letters, SHC.

43. Pvt. Fred. Pettit, One Hundredth Pa., to parents and siblings, March 12, 1863, Newport News, Va., in William Gavin, ed., *Infantryman Pettit: The Civil War Letters of Corporal Frederick Pettit, Late of Company C 100th Pennsylvania Veteran Volunteer Infantry Regiment, "The Roundheads"* (Shippensburg, Pa.: White Mane, 1990), 65. Despite the title of this collection, Pettit was not promoted to corporal until June 23, 1864, just before his death.

44. Sgt. David Nichol, Pa. Light Artillery, to parents and siblings, January 4, 1863, near Fairfax Station, Va., David Nichol Papers, HCWRTC.

45. Pvt. Leigh Webber, First Kans., to Brown Family, July 24, 1862, Gibson Co, Tenn., John S. Brown Letters, Reel 2, KSHS.

46. Capt. Amos Hostetter, Thirty-fourth Ill., to sister and brother-in-law, January 29, 1863, Murfreesboro, Tenn., ISHL.

47. Sgt. James Dodds, 114th Ill., to friend Miss Lake, March 18, 1863, Helena, Ark., John L. Harris Papers, ISHL.

48. Pvt. William Lewis, Twenty-sixth Mo., to wife and children, March 18, 1863, near Helena, Ark., William Emmerson Lewis Letters, UMOC.

49. Pvt. John Nesbitt, 105th Ohio, to family, February 18, 1863, Murfreesboro, Tenn., James Nesbitt-Isaac Raub Papers, WRHS.

50. A private in the Ill. Cavalry, to Editor, March 26, 1863, Germantown, Tenn., *Quincy Whig and Republican,* November 11, 1863, ISHL.

51. Sgt. Sam Evans, Seventieth Ohio, to father, February 8, 1863, Lagrange, Tenn., Evans Family Papers, OHS.

52. Sgt. William White, Tenth Vt., to friend Jacob, January 14, 1863, Whites Ford, Md., William White Civil War Letters, VTHS.

53. Pvt. John Strayer, Twelfth Ind., to Miss Griggs, March 23, 1863, Camp Bayard, Va., Virginia Southwood Collection, UMOC.

54. Sgt. Maj. Stephen Fleharty, 102d Ill., to *Rock Island Argus,* January 23, 1863, Gallatin, Tenn., in Reyburn and Wilson, *"Jottings from Dixie,"* 100.

55. Pvt. and clerk Jacob Seibert, Ninety-third Pa., to father and all, January 10, 1863, near Falmouth, Va., Seibert Family Papers, HCWRTC.

56. *The Banner of the Ironsides,* 1:1, April 4, 1863, Thibodaux, La., p. 1, WRHS. *The*

Banner of the Ironsides was written by the 176th N.Y. to be "the official journal of the parish of Lafourche."

57. Pvt. Stephen Emerson, First Mass., to mother, March 24, 1863, Falmouth, Va., Stephen G. Emerson Correspondence, MHS.

58. Pvt. James Brewer, Twenty-eighth Ill., to brother-in-law, April 16, 1863, Memphis, Tenn., Alley-Brewer Family Letters, UMOC.

59. Pvt. Leigh Webber, First Kans. Cavalry, to Brown Family, May 10, 1863, Providence, La., John S. Brown Family Collection, Reel 2, KSHS.

60. Pvt. John Benson, Fifth Kans. Cavalry, to Editor, April 15, 1863, Helena, Ark., *Rock Island Weekly Union,* May 6, 1863, p. 1, ISHL. Lt. Peter Eltinge, 145th N.Y., used similar logic in a letter to his father written from Port Hudson, La., on May 30, 1863 (Eltinge-Lord Family Papers, DU). A Michigan soldier claimed that western troops looked more favorably than the Army of the Potomac did on the use of black soldiers because Westerners, in his view, were generally more practical than Easterners. See Capt. Charles Haydon, Second Mich., journal, June 20, 1863, near Jackson, Miss., in Stephen W. Sears, ed., *For Country, Cause and Leader: The Civil War Journal of Charles B. Haydon* (New York: Ticknor & Fields, 1993), 333.

61. Cpl. Charles Musser, Twenty-ninth Iowa, to father, June 29, 1863, Helena, Ark., in Popchock, *Soldier Boy,* 58.

62. Lt. Anson Patterson, One Hundredth Ill., to aunt, June 8, 1863, near Murfreesboro, Tenn., Anson Patterson Papers, ISHL.

63. Pvt. Orra Bailey, Seventh Conn., to wife, March 13, 1863, Fernandina, Fla., Orra B. Bailey Papers, *PAW,* Coll. 10, Reel 2. The importance of black soldiers in battle in changing whites' opinions on black soldiers is a main argument of Dudley Cornish's classic study, *The Sable Arm: Black Troops in the Union Army, 1861–1865* (Lawrence: University of Kansas Press, 1987), esp. ch. 13; and of two works by Joseph Glatthaar. Glatthaar's *Forged in Battle: The Civil War Alliance of Black Soldiers and White Officers* (New York: Free Press, 1990) documents changing attitudes among white officers of black regiments, while *The March to the Sea and Beyond* notes the views of enlisted men in Sherman's army in 1864 and 1865.

64. Cpl. Samuel Storrow, Forty-fourth Mass., to parents, April 13, 1863, Washington, N.C., Samuel Storrow Papers, MHS.

65. Lt. Henry Kircher, Twelfth Mo., to father, April 19, 1863, Young's Point, La., Engleman-Kircher Papers, ISHL.

66. Joseph Williams, First N.C. Colored Volunteers, to Editor, June 23, 1863, Camp Wild, N.C., *CR,* July 4, 1863, p. 1. Published in Philadelphia, the *Christian Recorder* was an influential African American newspaper put out by the African Methodist Episcopal Church.

67. Pvt. William D. Matthews, First Kans. Colored Infantry, to James Lane, January 12, 1863, Leavenworth, Kans., in Berlin, Reidy, and Rowland, *Black Military Experience,* 70.

68. Pvt. Terah Sampson, Sixth Ky., to mother, February 19, 1863, Readyville, Tenn., Terah W. Sampson Letters, FC.

69. Pvt. Lucius Wood, 121st Ohio, to parents, March 5, 1863, Franklin, Tenn., E. G. Wood Family Papers, WRHS.

70. Pvt. Chauncey Welton, 103d Ohio, to parents, June 15, 1863, Camp Stirling, Ky., Chauncey B. Welton Letters, SHC.

71. See Voegeli, *Free but Not Equal,* for an account of this event.

72. Samuel Cox, "Emancipation and its Results—Is Ohio to Be Africanized?" June 3,

1862, *Congressional Globe,* Thirty-seventh Congress, Second Session, 1862, Appendix, 242–49.

73. Pvt. George Cadman, Thirty-ninth Ohio, April 5, 1863, Corinth, Miss., George Hovey Cadman Letters, TSLA. Continuing in the same vein, Cadman later sent a copy of a poem he called "Ode to Copperheads." The poem lists among Copperheads' sins their efforts to provoke disquiet among soldiers by reducing the war effort to one purpose, and then impugning that purpose. He wrote, "Then to the soldiers they appealed / And tried to make them see, Sir, / That they were only in the field, / To set the Nigger free, Sir." See Cadman to wife, April 12, 1863, Corinth, Miss.

74. Philip Paludan attributes Republicans' lackluster performance in 1862 to "wartime malaise," (*"A People's Contest,"* 101), much as the *New York Times* did in an editorial of November 5, 1862, and as Abraham Lincoln did in a letter of November 10, 1862, to Carl Shurz, in Basler, *Collected Works of Lincoln,* 5:493–95.

75. Pvt. Constant Hanks, Twentieth N.Y. Militia, to mother, October 18, 1862, hospital in Washington, D.C., Constant Hanks Papers, DU. See also Lt. Henry Hubble, Fortieth N.Y., to mother, October 22, 1862, Lexington, Ky., Henry Hubble Papers, Folder 5, NYHS; Pvt. Theodore Skinner, 112th N.Y., to parents, November 2, 1862, Suffolk, Va., Theodore Skinner Letters, CWMC.

76. Pvt. James Miller, 111th Pa., to brother, November 24, 1862, Harpers Ferry, Va., Miller Brothers Papers, Schoff.

77. Pvt. John Garriott, Eighteenth Mo., to sister, November 1, 1862, in Mo. awaiting exchange, John Garriott Letters, UMOC; Capt. Maschel Manring, Fifty-sixth Ohio, diary, November 6, 1862, Helena, Ark., Maschel Manring Papers, UMOKC.

78. When men registered for the Union draft, they fell into one of two categories. Class One consisted of all single men aged twenty to forty-five and all married men aged twenty to thirty-five. Class Two consisted of married men over thirty-five. No names would be drawn from Class Two until Class One had been exhausted. In practice, that meant that Class Two was virtually never called upon, because Class One was never completely emptied. See Peter Levine, "Draft Evasion in the North During the Civil War, 1863–1865," *Journal of American History* 67 (1981), 816–34; McPherson, *Battle Cry of Freedom,* 600–01; and Eugene C. Murdock, *One Million Men: The Civil War Draft in the North* (Madison: University of Wisconsin Press, 1971).

79. Pvt. John England, Ninth N.Y., to friend, March 28, 1863, Newport News, Va., John England Letters, Union Army Boxes, NYPL. See also Sgt. David Nichol, Battery E, Pa. Light Artillery, to folks at home, March 28, 1863, Acquia Landing, Va., David Nichol Papers, HCWRTC; Pvt. William Pedrick, 115th N.Y., to parents, June 1, 1863, Hilton Head, S.C., Benjamin Pedrick Papers, DU.

80. Pvt. Phillip Reilly, Twenty-ninth Mo., to brother, March 31, 1863, before Vicksburg, Miss., Phillip A. Reilly Letters, UMOR.

81. For figures on the draft, see McPherson, *Battle Cry of Freedom,* 601; and Levine, "Draft Evasion in the North."

82. "The Constitution-Peace-Reunion," Speech of Hon. Clement L. Vallandigham in the House of Representatives, January 14, 1863, *Congressional Globe,* Thirty-seventh Congress, Third Session, Appendix, 52–60, quotations from 57, 56. The speech was also reprinted as *The Great Civil War in America* (Washington, D.C.: no publisher, 1863).

83. Sgt. Wilbur Hinman, Sixty-fifth Ohio, to friends, May 20, 1863, near Murfreesboro, Tenn., Wilbur F. Hinman Papers, WRHS. See also Sgt. Sam Evans, Seventieth Ohio, to father, February 8, 1863, Lagrange, Tenn., Evans Family Papers, OHS. President Lincoln commuted Vallandigham's prison sentence to transportation to the Confederacy. Soon

after being escorted under flag of truce to Confederate lines, Vallandigham discovered that the Confederacy did not suit him after all, and he headed for Canada, from which he launched his campaign to be elected governor of Ohio in 1863.

84. Pvt. Chauncey Welton, 103d Ohio, to parents, June 15, 1863, Camp Stirling, Ky., Chauncey B. Welton Letters, SHC.

85. Sgt. Aaron Beck, First Ohio, diary, April 5, 1863, Murfreesboro, Tenn., Aaron Beck Diary, KSHS.

86. Pvt. Rohloff Hacker, Second Mich., to mother, January 6, 1863, near Falmouth, Va., Hacker Brothers Papers, Schoff.

87. Sam Evans, for example, insisted to his father that emancipation was not a Republican or Democratic issue, but rather one that good Democrats should support just as heartily as Republicans, though they remained free to disagree on other points. See Sgt. Sam Evans, Seventieth Ohio, to father, February 8, 1863, LaGrange, Tenn., Evans Family Papers, OHS. Joseph Glatthaar discusses the evolving political views of and relationship between Sam and his father, Andrew Evans (both Democrats), in "Duty, Country, Race, and Party: The Evans Family of Ohio," in Joan E. Cashin, ed., *The War Was You and Me: Civilians in the Civil War* (Princeton: Princeton University Press, 2002), 332–57. In " 'A Viler Enemy in Our Rear': Pennsylvania Soldiers Confront the North's Antiwar Movement," in Aaron Sheehan-Dean, ed., *The View from the Ground* (Lexington: University of Kentucky Press, 2006), Timothy Orr examines soldiers' hardening attitudes toward Copperheads, but Orr interprets such sentiments as evidence of troops' rejection of partisan politics generally. Men like Evans and many others suggest that soldiers actually retained a more sophisticated view of Democrats and of politics than Orr allows.

88. Pvt. Jacob Behm, Forty-eighth Ill., to sister and brother-in-law, February 18, 1863, Bethel, Tenn., Jacob Behm Correspondence, CWTIC. See also Pvt. Ed Griswold, First Conn. Light Artillery, to brother, March 24, 1863, Beaufort, S.C., Edward, Charles, and Joel Griswold Papers, DU; Capt. R. M. Lyons, 126th Ohio, to friend, March 22, 1863, Martinsburg, Va., Shotwell Family Papers, OHS.

89. Pvt. Jacob Behm, Forty-eighth Ill., to sister and brother-in-law, February 18, 1863, Bethel, Tenn., Jacob Behm Correspondence, CWTIC.

90. Pvt. David James, Sixteenth Wis., to parents, March 23, 1863, Lake Providence, La., David Goodrich James Correspondence, SHSW.

91. Pvt. Chauncey Welton, 103d Ohio, to parents, June 15, 1863, Camp Stirling, Ky., Chauncey B. Welton Letters, SHC.

92. Pvt. Edwin Wentworth, Thirty-seventh Mass., to father, fragment from summer 1862, Papers of Edwin O. Wentworth, LC.

93. Cpl. Samuel Storrow, Forty-fourth Mass., to father, October 12, 1862, Boston, Samuel Storrow Papers, MHS.

94. See Hadden, *Slave Patrols*.

95. James Hemby to Governor Vance, September 4, 1863, Green Co., N.C., Zebulon Baird Vance Papers, Governor's Papers, Box 6, NCDAH.

96. A Soldier, Jonesboro, Ga., to *Atlanta Southern Confederacy,* October 30, 1862. Later, the number of slaves required for the exemption did drop to ten, but at the time the Georgia soldier wrote this letter, the exemption applied only to plantations holding twenty or more slaves.

97. Sgt. Joseph Polley, Fourth Tex., to Nellie, March 20, 1863, Falling Creek, Va., in Simpson, *A Soldier's Letters to Charming Nellie,* 99–100.

98. Pvt. Thomas Warrick, Thirty-fourth Ala., to wife, March 4, 1863, Tenn., Thomas Warrick Letters, ADAH. See also Warrick's letter of June 23, 1863.

99. Pvt. Daniel Brown, Third N.C., to wife, April 12, 1863, Camp Roil, Va., Isaac Brown Collection, NCDAH. Most accounts claim that Davis threatened to order troops to fire on the crowd, but the most thorough recent biography of Davis, William J. Cooper's *Jefferson Davis,* identifies the governor rather than Davis as the source of the threat (p. 448). As Private Brown's remarks show, soldiers assumed the president had given the order, and they resented him for it.

100. *The Reveille,* December 4, 1862, Shelbyville, Tenn., p. 1, TSLA. *The Reveille* was the paper of the Eighth Ark.

101. Sgt. Felix Buchanan, First Tenn., to father, March 13, 1863, Richmond, Buchanan-McClellan Family Papers, SHC.

102. Sgt. E. N. Brown, Forty-fifth Ala., to wife, February 27, 1863, Shelbyville, Tenn., Edward Norphlet Brown Letters, ADAH.

103. Sgt. William Chunn, Fortieth Ga., to wife, January 17, 1863, Vicksburg, Miss., William A. Chunn Letters, EU.

104. Sgt. E. N. Brown, Forty-fifth Ala., to wife, February 21, 1863, Tullahoma, Tenn., Edward Norphlet Brown Letters, ADAH.

105. Pvt. J. C. Daniel, Thirtieth Ga., June 29, 1863, Miss., Confederate Miscellany, EU.

106. Capt. John Ellis, Sixteenth La., to sister, December 12, 1862, Eaglesville, Tenn., E. P. Ellis and Family Papers, CMM Ser. B, Reel 5.

107. *The Vidette,* November 2, 1862, Springfield, Tenn., p. 3, TSLA.

108. Antoine Prudhomme, Second La. Cavalry, to father, October 11, 1862, Camp Vincent, La., Prudhomme Family papers, CMM Ser. B, Reel 15. For a good survey of white fears of black violence see William F. Messner, "Black Violence and White Response: Louisiana, 1862," *Journal of Southern History* 41:1 (February 1975), 19–38.

109. Lt. James Harrison, Fifteenth Ark., to brother, August 2, 1862, Camp Priceville, Miss., James M. Harrison Letters, UAR.

110. I. A. Dodge, Tex. Cavalry, "The Southern Star," Public Information Files, ADAH.

111. Cpl. John Williams, Tenth Va., to sister, November 1, 1862, Battery 2 near Richmond, John A. Williams Letters, VHS.

112. *The Vidette,* November 2, 1862, Springfield, Tenn., p. 4, TSLA.

113. Capt. Christopher Winsmith, First S.C., to father, October 4, 1862, near Winchester, Va., John Christopher Winsmith Papers, MOC.

114. Chaplain Robert Bunting, Eighth Tex. Cavalry, to *Houston Telegraph,* February 2, 1863, near Shelbyville, Tenn., Robert Franklin Bunting Papers, TSLA.

115. In "Reaction in North Carolina to the Emancipation Proclamation," *North Carolina Historical Review* 44 (January 1976), 53–71, Harold Moser argues that the Emancipation Proclamation divided public opinion in North Carolina, alienating many ordinary Confederates by making the war explicitly about slavery rather than "states' rights" (undefined by Moser). The analysis here, which comes to the opposite conclusion, is based on soldiers' responses to the proclamation, while Moser included no testimony from soldiers.

116. Pvt. John Street, Eighth Tex., to wife, October 2, 1862, Miss., John K. and Melinda East Street Papers, SHC.

117. *The Reveille,* December 4, 1862, Shelbyville, Tenn., pp. 1–2, TSLA.

118. Pvt. Jonathan Doyle, Fourth La., to Maggie, May 27, 1863, Jackson, Miss., Josiah Knighton Family Papers, CMM Ser. B, Reel 11.

119. Lt. David Ballenger, Twenty-sixth Ala., to wife Nancy, March 22, 1863, Caroline Co., Va., David Ballenger Papers, SCL.

120. Pvt. James Branscomb, Third Ala., to sister, March 8, 1863, Branscomb Family Letters, ADAH.

121. Pvt. Hodijah Meade, Richmond Howitzers, to brother, February 12, 1863, near Harrison's Crossing, Va., Meade Family Papers, CMM Ser. A, Reel 27.

122. Sgt. Archie Livingston, Third Fla., to mother, October 27, 1862, Knoxville, Tenn., Livingston Family Letters, MOC. Livingston also noted that sickness carried off some slaves. See also Capt. John Ellis, Sixteenth La., to sister, October 29, 1862, Knoxville, Tenn., in which Ellis reported that "a good many negroes have gone to the Yankees" (E. P. Ellis and Family Papers, CMM Ser. B, Reel 5). In another instance, Capt. Christopher Winsmith, First S.C., received a letter of July 25, 1862, reporting that a favorite slave had run off (John Christopher Winsmith Papers, MOC).

123. Lt. Macon Bonner, Co. B, N.C. Artillery, to wife, October 20, 1862, Ft. Fisher, N.C., Macon Bonner Papers, SHC.

124. Pvt. Leander Parker, Thirtieth Ga., to mother, May 23, 1863, Vaughan Station, Miss., Leander Parker Letters, AHC. See also James Harrison's fears of equality finding expression in his dream of eating alongside a black man at his Aunt Polly's house, Chapter 3, note 1, above.

125. Chaplain Robert Bunting, Eighth Tex. Cavalry, to *San Antonio Herald,* November 19, 1862, Murfreesboro, Tenn., Robert Franklin Bunting Papers, TSLA.

126. Cpl. John Williams, Tenth Va., to sister, February 11, 1863, near Richmond, John A. Williams Letters, VHS. See also Capt. William Pegram, Purcell's Light Artillery, to sister, January 8, 1863, near Port Royal, Va., Pegram-Johnson-McIntosh Papers, VHS.

127. Pvt. J. W. Gambill, Twenty-first Tex. Cavalry, to wife, January 10, 1863, Des Arc, Ark., J. W. Gambill Letters, UAR.

128. Surgeon John Kinyoun, Sixty-sixth N.C., to wife, September 15, 1862, Hinder Hospital, Va., John Kinyoun Papers, DU.

4: "Mine Eyes Have Seen the Glory ":
The War and the Hand of God

1. Lt. J. Q. A. Campbell, Fifth Iowa, diary, July 4, 1863, near Vicksburg, Miss., in Grimsley and Miller, *The Union Must Stand,* 110.

2. Surgeon Thomas Hawley, 111th Ill., to parents, July 5, 1863, Young's Point, La., Thomas S. Hawley Papers, MOHS.

3. Pvt. Lewis Bissell, Second Conn. Heavy Artillery, to brother, July 4, 1863, Fort Lyon, Va., in Mark Olcott and David Lear, eds., *The Civil War Letters of Lewis Bissell* (Washington, D.C.: Field Educational School Foundation, 1981), 132.

4. *The Union Volunteer,* July 10, 1863, Louisville, Ky., ISHL. Quotation from p. 2. *The Union Volunteer* was the camp newspaper of Illinois soldiers in Louisville.

5. Pvt. Joseph Scroggs, 104th Ohio, diary, July 4, 1863, Marine Hospital, Cincinnati, Joseph Scroggs Diary, CWTIC.

6. Cpl. Rufus Kinsley, Eighth Vt., diary, July 19, 1863, New Orleans, Rufus Kinsley Diary, VTHS.

7. For more on the application of antebellum northern millennialism to the Civil War, see Robert Bellah, *The Broken Covenant,* 53–56; Miller, Stout, and Wilson, *Religion and the American Civil War,* esp. the Introduction and ch. 1, "Religion and the American Civil War," by Phillip Paludan; and Moorhead, *American Apocalypse,* ix–x, chs. 2 and 3. Bellah in particular argues that the Civil War made the long-developing "fusion" between "Protestant covenant theology and republican liberty . . . complete" and cites "The Battle Hymn of the Republic" and Abraham Lincoln's Second Inaugural Address as evidence (53).

8. Lt. J. Q. A. Campbell, Fifth Iowa, diary, November 12, 1863, near Winchester, Tenn., in Grimsley and Miller, *The Union Must Stand,* 131.

9. 2d Lt. Sam Evans, Fifty-ninth U.S. Colored Troops, to father, September 15, 1863, LaGrange, Tenn., Evans Family Papers, OHS.

10. *The Corinth Chanticleer,* July 31, 1863, Corinth, Miss., p. 2, MNHS. *The Corinth Chanticleer* was the regimental newspaper of the Second Iowa. See also "No Failure for the North," *Stars and Stripes,* 1:1, December 1, 1863, Jacksonport, Ark., UAR. *Stars and Stripes* was the newspaper of the Third Mo. Cavalry (Union).

11. Sgt. James Jessee, Eighth Ill., diary, December 31, 1863, Helena, Ark., James W. Jessee Diaries, KU. A New Hampshire soldier agreed that God had sent a "durstructive war" as a rebuke to all who, through sins of commission or omission, allowed slavery to woo them away from "the side of truth and rite." See Pvt. Roswell Holbrook, Fourteenth N.H., to cousin, January 11, 1864, Washington, D.C., Roswell Holbrook Letters, VTHS.

12. Pvt. Ransom Bedell, Thirty-ninth Ill., "American Slavery," an original essay written for his cousin, summer 1863, Ransom Bedell Papers, ISHL.

13. Pvt. (acts as Assistant Surgeon) Robert Winn, Third Ky. Cavalry, to sister, November 20, 1863, and December 11, 1863, Bowling Green, Ky., Winn-Cook Papers, FC.

14. Pvt. Henry Matrau, Sixth Wis., to parents, July 29, 1863, and August 16, 1863, Rappahannock Station, Va., in Marcia Reid-Green, ed., *Letters Home: Henry Matrau of the Iron Brigade* (Lincoln: University of Nebraska Press, 1993), 59–62. I am indebted to Jim Reid for first drawing my attention to Matrau's reaction to Gettysburg.

15. Cornelia Hancock to sister, July 14, 1863, Gettysburg, Pa., and Hancock, undated essay, in Henrietta Stratton Jaquette, ed., *South After Gettysburg: Letters of Cornelia Hancock from the Army of the Potomac, 1863–1865* (New York: Crowell, 1956), 10, 7.

16. On the draft riots, see Iver Bernstein, *The New York City Draft Riots: Their Significance for American Society and Politics in the Age of the Civil War* (New York: Oxford University Press, 1990); and Adrian Cook, *The Armies of the Streets: The New York City Draft Riots of 1863* (Lexington: University of Kentucky Press, 1974). On pp. 196–97, Cook details the class and occupations of the rioters, and notes that two-thirds of the rioters whose place of birth is known were born in Ireland. Some Northerners interpreted the riots mainly as one more reason to distrust the Irish. A Protestant immigrant from the northern Irish county of Derry was disgusted but not surprised by reports that "the Irish papist has raised a great roit in new york." He wished that all Irish Catholics would be "sent out of this Country." Pvt. William McSparron, Fifty-first Pa., to niece, July 30, 1863, New Vernon, Pa., recovering from wound to jaw, in William McSparron Letters, PRONI. Upper-class New Yorkers in particular exploited the opportunities presented by the draft riots to vent long-standing hatred of the Irish. Elite lawyer George Templeton Strong maintained that "every brute in the drove [of rioters] was pure Celtic-hod-carrier or loafer," and claimed that he would "like to see war made on Irish scum." George Templeton Strong diary, July 13, 1863; July 30, 1863. Some newspapers, such as the *New York Evening Post* and the *New York Times,* also characterized the rioters as Irish rabble. In fact, hostility between Irish and native-born ran so high in New York that Catholic Archbishop John Hughes was compelled to deliver a public address calling for peace, restraint, and good behavior. For many Irish Catholic Union soldiers, the riots constituted a gigantic embarrassment. Peter Welsh was mortified that "the Irish men of New York took so large a part in them disgracefull riots," in part because he regarded the riots as hateful and disloyal, and in part because such behavior provided Americans who harbored anti-Irish prejudice "an opportunity to malighn and abuse" the entire ethnic group. See Sgt. Peter Welsh, Twenty-eighth Mass., to wife, July 17, 1863, Pleasant Valley, Md., and July 22, 1863, Bloomfield,

Va., in Lawrence Frederick Kohl and Margaret Cosse Richard, *Irish Green and Union Blue: The Civil War Letters of Peter Welsh, Color Sergeant, 28th Regiment Massachusetts Volunteers* (New York: Fordham University Press, 1986), 115. Although Adrian Cook's account is thorough and largely persuasive, his interpretation of the riots as primarily instances of lashing out at government authority does not seem quite complete, since attacks on nongovernmental institutions such as churches, and on private homes, indicate that mobs were striking out against many forms of authority, not simply at governmental authority.

17. Although sources at the time counted the death toll as high as 1,462, Cook, in *Armies of the Streets,* shows that 105 riot-related deaths can be documented with certainty, and 14 more might have been attributable to the riots (193–94). In *The New York City Draft Riots,* Bernstein does not materially dispute Cook, though he leaves more room for uncertainty and posits between 100 and 150 deaths (288 n. 8). The number of wounded was much higher, and harder to establish. Cook estimates the number of seriously wounded at 128, and admonishes that there is no way to determine the number of slightly wounded (195). Finally, he notes that the names of 352 rioters can be positively identified, but the actual number of rioters was many times that number (195). As Bernstein points out, a "precise body count" of rioters or their casualties is "impossible to draw up," but the riots can still safely be called "by far the most violent civil disorder in nineteenth-century America" (288).

18. Reilly was the Missouri private who in March had accused the federal government of turning into a "bold Highwayman [who] says to every man in the loyal states 'three hundred dollars or your life!' " thanks to commutation (see Chapter 3). Pvt. Phillip Reilly, Twenty-ninth Mo., to brother, March 31, 1863, before Vicksburg, Miss., Phillip A. Reilly Letters, UMOR.

19. Pvt. Lewis Bissell, Second Conn. Heavy Artillery, to father, July 26, 1863, Fort Lyon, Va., in Olcott and Lear, *The Civil War Letters of Lewis Bissell,* 139. Hermon Clarke agreed that soldiers felt "anything but friendly" toward riot-inciting troublemakers. See Sgt. Hermon Clarke, 117th N.Y., to brother, July 23, 1863, Camp Haskins, Va., in Henry F. Jackson and Thomas F. O'Donnell, eds., *Back Home in Oneida: Hermon Clarke and His Letters* (Syracuse, N.Y.: Syracuse University Press, 1965), 94.

20. Lt. Peter Eltinge, 156th N.Y., to father, August 5, 1863, Baton Rouge, La., Eltinge-Lord Family Papers, DU.

21. Pvt. Chauncey Cooke, Twenty-fifth Wis., to mother, July 25, 1863, Snyder's Bluff, Miss., in "A Badger Boy in Blue: The Letters of Chauncey H. Cooke," *Wisconsin Magazine of History* 4:4 (June 1921), 454.

22. G.E.S., Fifty-fourth Mass., to Editor, August 7, 1863, Morris Island, S.C., *A-A,* August 24, 1863, p. 1.

23. Pvt. Joseph Scroggs, 104th Ohio, diary, October 12, 1863, hospital in Cincinnati, Joseph Scroggs Diary, CWTIC; Pvt. Chauncey Welton, 103d Ohio, to parents, October 13, 1863, near Knoxville, Tenn., Chauncey B. Welton Letters, SHC. See also *The Knapsack,* September 3, 1863, Gauley Bridge, W.Va., p. 2, DU. One column predicted that Vallandigham would not get a single vote from anyone in the regiment, and elsewhere the paper instructed Ohio soldiers on how to mail their ballots properly.

24. For more on soldier animosity toward Vallandigham, which the author maintains was much stronger than civilian antipathy, see Frank L. Klement, *The Limits of Dissent: Clement L. Vallandigham and the Civil War* (Lexington: University of Kentucky Press, 1970), 234–35, 240–43. See also Allan Nevins, *The War for the Union,* vol. 3, *The Organized War* (New York: Scribner, 1971), 177. John Brough's party affiliation defied easy cat-

egorization. A lifelong Democrat, he broke with the Peace Democrats, but never officially joined the Republicans. For a while he called himself a member of the "Union Party," which included Republicans and War Democrats. After the war some Republicans claimed him, but Brough himself died in 1865 before the collapse of the Union Party coalition, and therefore before having any reason to identify himself as a Republican. Keeping his affiliation fluid in 1863–65 served his purposes. Historians who identify Brough as a War Democrat include John Niven in *Salmon P. Chase: A Biography* (New York: Oxford University Press, 1995) and Eugene H. Roseboom and Francis P. Weisenburger in *History of Ohio* (Columbus: Ohio State Archaeological and Historical Society, 1954). Thank you to Christine Dee for helping me sort through Brough's convoluted political identity.

25. Sgt. John Baldwin, Seventy-fourth Ohio, to wife, October 18, 1863, Stevenson, Ala., John W. Baldwin Papers, OHS. Brough won with 61 percent of the total vote, including 94 percent of the soldiers' vote. See Klement, *Limits of Dissent;* and McPherson, *Battle Cry of Freedom,* 688.

26. Lt. John Inskeep, Seventeenth Ohio, diary, October 18, 1863, Chattanooga, Tenn., John Inskeep Diary, OHS. Isaac Raub of the 105th Ohio claimed that Vallandigham "did not get a vote in our regiment," while Julius Wood reported results in the Ninety-sixth to be 230 for Brough to 5 for Vallandigham. See Pvt. Isaac Raub, 105th Ohio, to wife, October 25, 1863, Chattanooga, Tenn., James Nesbitt-Isaac Raub Papers, WRHS; Pvt. Julius Wood, Ninety-sixth Ohio, to family, October 17, 1863, near Vermillion, La., E. G. Wood Family Papers, WRHS. *The Chattanooga Army Bulletin* reported that among Ohio soldiers in Libby Prison, Richmond, who mailed their ballots to Columbus, Ohio, Vallandigham had not received a single vote. *The Chattanooga Army Bulletin,* December 25, 1863, Chattanooga, Tenn., p. 3, WRHS.

27. Cpl. George Cadman, Thirty-ninth Ohio, to wife, October 18, 1863, Memphis, Tenn., George Cadman Hovey Letters, TSLA. Cadman was an immigrant who had not yet attained citizenship status or voting rights, and he claimed that the same was true of many in his regiment. If he and other nonvoters had a say, he maintained, "Brough's vote would have been much larger."

28. Ordnance Sgt. John Marshall, Ninety-seventh Ohio, journal sent to wife, October 15–17, 1863, John Wesley Marshall Papers, OHS. Civilians also opposed Vallandigham (though by a narrower margin); as Frank Klement and Allan Nevins have shown, soldiers were more emphatic in their opposition.

29. Pvt. (acts as Ass't Sgn.) Robert Winn, Third Ky. Cavalry, to sister, October 28, 1863, Bowling Green, Ky., Winn-Cook Papers, FC. The necessity of emancipation to end the war and prevent its recurrence by rooting out the cause stands out as the most common theme (aside from personal topics) in soldiers' letters in this time period. In addition to soldiers cited above, see (among others) Pvt. Frederick Pettit, One Hundredth Pa., to father, August 15, 1863, Camp Nelson, Ky., in Gavin, *Infantryman Pettit,* 106; "Death of Slavery," an original poem by Pvt. John Hamer, Fifty-fourth Pa., for his sister, August 23, 1863, Romney, Va., John and Samuel Hamer Papers, HCWRTC; Pvt. Samuel Richards, Sixteenth Conn., to friend, August 31, 1863, Portsmouth, Va., Samuel F. Richards Letters, CWTIC; Sgt. Adelbert Bly, Thirty-second Wis., to sweetheart, November 1863, Memphis, Tenn., Adelbert M. Bly Correspondence, SHSW; Capt. James Lawrence, Sixty-first Ill., to wife, December 19, 1863, Little Rock, Ark., James Lawrence Letters, UAR; Sgt. James Jessee, Eighth Ill., diary, December 31, 1863, Helena, Ark., James W. Jessee Diaries, KU; Pvt. Constant Hanks, Twentieth N.Y. Militia, to mother, January 4, 1864, near Brandy Station, Va., Constant Hanks Papers, DU; Sgt. E. C. Hubbard, Thirteenth Ill., to brother, January 17, 1864, Woodville, Ala., E. C. Hubbard Letters, UAR; Sgt. Hervey Howe,

Eighty-ninth N.Y., to brother, January 30, 1864, Folly Island, S.C., Hervey Lane Howe Letters, SU.

30. In *Free Soil, Free Labor, Free Men: The Ideology of the Republican Party Before the Civil War,* Eric Foner discusses the concern of northern Republicans with the threat that slavery posed to the status and advancement of white farmers and laborers. A wide array of Union troops, Republican and Democrat, voiced similar concerns in the first year of the war. While some soldiers still made similar observations when Sherman's army marched through Georgia and the Carolinas in late 1864 and 1865, the theme of slavery's blighting effects on free white labor captured comparatively less attention than it had in the early part of the war.

31. Sgt. James Jessee, Eighth Ill., diary, December 31, 1863, Helena, Ark., James W. Jessee Diaries, KU.

32. Pvt. Levi Hines, First Vt. Artillery, to parents, May 10, 1864, Fort Slemmer, D.C., Levi Hines Papers, Schoff. Hines was especially sensitive to the effect of name tarnishing; he had grown up in an otherwise upright Vermont farming family that suffered humiliation as a result of the exploits of one black-sheep brother. Maj. James Connolly, an Illinois former Democrat, also referred to the need to relieve the nation of "its incubus of slavery." See Connolly to wife, June 9, 1864, near Acworth, Ga., in Paul M. Angle, ed., *Three Years in the Army of the Cumberland: The Letters and Diaries of Major James A. Connolly* (Bloomington: Indiana University Press, 1959), 217.

33. Sgt. E. C. Hubbard, Thirteenth Ill., to brother, April 12, 1864, Woodville, Ala., E. C. Hubbard Letters, UAR. Hubbard is especially interesting because he explicitly admitted that the war had changed his views on slavery. In this same letter he told his brother that before the war, he "respected slavery," and saw "a negro [as] a parallel case of a dog," but that by spending time in the South and witnessing slavery, he had "seen its practical workings," and had been *"forced* to change my opinion." For more on emancipation as a moral imperative, see Pvt. John Cate, Thirty-third Mass., to wife, March 20, 1864, and April 24, 1864, Lookout Valley, Tenn., in Jean M. Cate, ed., *If I Live to Come Home: The Civil War Letters of Sergeant John March Cate* (Pittsburgh: Dorrance, 1995), 266, 269–70; Pvt. Edwin Wentworth, Thirty-seventh Mass., to wife, May 3, 1863, Brandy Station, Va., Edwin O. Wentworth Papers, LC; Pvt. Jacob Behm, Forty-eighth Ill., to sister and brother-in-law, February 1, 1864, Scottsboro, Ala., Jacob Behm Correspondence, CWTIC. Similarly, Charles Henthorn wrote to influence his sister, whose resolve on the slavery question was faltering: "We cannot hope for a permanent change until the fruitful cause of all this evil that is so vividly apparent all around and about us throughout all our land is removed." See Pvt. Charles Henthorn, Seventy-seventh Ill., to sister, March 7, 1864, on furlough in Quincy, Ill., Charles Henthorn Letters, Schoff.

34. Pvt. Ransom Bedell, "American Slavery," an essay written for his cousin, summer 1863, Ransom Bedell Papers, ISHL.

35. Cpl. James Miller, 111th Pa., to brother, September 7, 1863, near Ellis Ford, Va., Miller Brothers Papers, Schoff. Outrage at the sight of light-skinned slave children at the mercy of their master-fathers persisted as a popular theme during this period. For other examples see Capt. Alphonso Barto, Fifty-second Ill., to father, July 7, 1863, Corinth, Miss., Alphonso Barto Letters, ISHL; Pvt. Constant Hanks, Twentieth N.Y. Militia, to mother, August 5, 1863, near Warrington, Va., Constant Hanks Papers, DU; Sgt. Henry Crydenwise, Ninetieth N.Y., to parents and all, October 22, 1863, Bayou Boeuf, La., and June 2, 1864, Port Hudson, La., Henry Crydenwise Papers, EU; Sgt. Adelbert Bly, Thirty-second Wis., to sweetheart, October 29, 1863, Memphis, Tenn., Adelbert M. Bly Correspondence, SHSW; *The Corinth Chanticleer,* July 31, 1863, Corinth, Miss., p. 1, MNHS.

References to *Uncle Tom's Cabin* (usually claiming that Harriet Beecher Stowe's 1852 novel did not go far enough in portraying the evils of slavery) abounded in late 1863 and early 1864. See, for example, Pvt. Constant Hanks, Twentieth N.Y. Militia, to mother, September 13, 1863, eastern Va., Constant Hanks Papers, DU; Q.M. Uberto Burnham, Seventy-sixth N.Y., to parents, October 29, 1863, Bristoe Station, Va., U. A. Burnham Papers, NYSL; Pvt. James Horrocks, Fifth N.J. Artillery, to parents, November 26, 1863, Washington, D.C., in A. S. Lewis, ed., *Dear Parents: An Englishman's Letters Home from the American Civil War* (London: Victor Gollancz, 1982), 48–49; Pvt. Edwin Van Cise, Forty-first Iowa, diary, July 30, 1864, between Moscow and Memphis, Tenn., Edwin Van Cise Diary, LC; Pvt. Justus Silliman, Seventeenth Conn., to mother, May 30, 1864, St. Augustine, Fla., in Edward Marcus, ed., *A New Canaan Private in the Civil War. Letters of Justus M. Silliman, 17th Connecticut Volunteers* (New Canaan, Conn.: New Canaan Historical Society, 1984), 72.

36. For a succinct treatment of nineteenth-century ideas about the family as a haven from the marketplace and women as upholders of morality within that haven, see Barbara Welter, "The Cult of True Womanhood: 1820–1860," *American Quarterly* 18:2 part 1 (summer 1966), 151–74.

37. The moral contagion theme proliferated in antebellum periodicals, popular literature, and even church sermons. For discussion of the theme of "moral contagion," see Halttunen, *Confidence Men and Painted Women*; and Rosenberg, *Cholera Years.*

38. In response, Cooke fumed, "to think that these slave-holders buy and sell each other's bastard children is horrible"; he then compared life in the South to *Uncle Tom's Cabin.* Pvt. Chauncey Cooke, Twentieth Wis., to sister, September 10, 1864, western Ga., *Wisconsin Magazine of History* 5:1, 98.

39. Edward Bartlett, formerly private in Forty-fourth Mass., now recruiter of black troops, to sister, November 19, 1863, Nashville, Tenn., Edward J. Bartlett Correspondence, MHS.

40. Pvt. (acts as Ass't Sgn.) Robert Winn, Third Ky. Cavalry, to sister, October 2, 1863, Bowling Green, Ky., Winn-Cook Papers, FC.

41. Pvt. Leigh Webber, First Kans. Cavalry, to Sarah Brown, July 12, 1863, Lake Providence, La., John S. Brown Family Papers, KSHS.

42. Sgt. John England, Ninth N.Y., to fiancée, July 24, 1863, Fort Monroe, Va., John England Letters, Union Army Boxes, NYPL.

43. Robert Winn, full of disgust and shame, reported on this event to his sister. Pvt. (acts as Ass't Sgn.) Robert Winn, Third Ky. Cavalry, to sister, July 15, 1863, near Russellville, Ky., Winn-Cook Papers, FC.

44. Lt. Henry Crydenwise, Seventy-third U.S. Colored Troops, to parents and all, December 22, 1863, Bayou Boeuf, La., Henry Crydenwise Papers, EU. Bell Wiley in *The Life of Billy Yank* and Leon Litwack in *Been in the Storm so Long* both emphasize Union Army cruelty to blacks. While mean and hateful acts were committed, the evidence suggests that they were not as widespread, nor were the attitudes that gave rise to them so uniformly dominant, as Wiley and Litwack suggest. In ch. 5 of *Forged in Battle: The Civil War Alliance of Black Soldiers and White Officers,* Joseph Glatthaar discusses instances of racism and cruelty toward black soldiers on the part of some white officers, but he also shows that cruelty was not universal. Instead, treatment varied widely.

45. Pvt. William Lewis, Twenty-sixth Mo., to wife, July 11, 1863, Big Black River, Miss., William Emmerson Lewis Letters, UMOC. While Lewis did not specifically mention colonization, or schemes for the transportation of African Americans outside of the United States to a colony in Africa or Latin America, such plans did circulate in the 1860s,

as they had for much of the nineteenth century, and may have been what Lewis had in mind.

46. *The Mail Bag,* March 28, 1864, Lexington, Ky., Private collection of Donna Casey. *The Mail Bag* was the newspaper of the Seventy-ninth Ohio and Fifth Ohio Battery. Sometimes also called *The Army Mail Bag.*

47. Pvt. Wilbur Fisk, Second Vt., to *Green Mountain Freeman,* August 13, 1863, near Warrenton, Va., in Emil and Ruth Rosenblatt, eds., *Hard Marching Every Day: The Civil War Letters of Private Wilbur Fisk, 1861–1865* (Lawrence: University of Kansas Press, 1992), 135. That Fisk wrote this letter to a public forum, his hometown newspaper, suggests that he may have hoped to help change the attitudes he wrote about so dolefully.

48. Capt. Carlos Lyman, One Hundredth U.S. Colored Troops, to sister, February 12, 1865, Camp Foster, Tenn., Carlos Parsons Lyman Papers, WRHS.

49. Lt. Joseph Scroggs, Fifth U.S. Colored Troops, diary, March 30, 1864, near Norfolk, Va., Joseph Scroggs Diary, CWTIC.

50. Sgt. J. G. Nind, 127th Ill., November 1863, Vicksburg, Miss., in Lydia Minturn Post, ed., *Soldiers' Letters from Camp, Battle-field and Prison* (New York: Bruce and Huntington, 1865), 291.

51. Pvt. Constant Hanks, Twentieth N.Y. Militia, to mother and sister, April 1, 1864, near Brandy Station, Va., Constant Hanks Papers, DU.

52. Pvt. Willliam Lewis, Twenty-sixth Mo., to wife, July 11, 1863, Big Black River, Miss., Willliam Emmerson Lewis Letters, UMOC. New York soldier Haven Putnam commented that many Irish troops opposed black enlistment because "it makes the 'd——d,' dirty black nagur as good as a white man." Since to Putnam that was exactly the point of black enlistment, he merely noted that he could make "no reply." Pvt. G. Haven Putman, 176th N.Y., to Mary Loines, August 23, 1863, Bennet Carre, La., Papers of the Low-Mills Family, LC.

53. Pvt. Arthur Van Horn, Seventy-eighth Ohio, to wife, December 31, 1863, Coliersville, Tenn., Arthur Van Horn Family Papers, LC.

54. Recruiter Thomas Webster to Secretary of War Edwin Stanton, July 30, 1863, Philadelphia, in Berlin, Reidy, and Rowland, *Black Military Experience,* 96–98. Webster exaggerated when he called black enlistment the most popular measure, but it was certainly more popular than it had been a year previously.

55. Lt. Henry Fike, 117th Ill., to wife, see letters of May 16, 1863, May 25, 1863, August 28, 1863, all from Memphis, Tenn., Henry Fike Correspondence, KU.

56. Commissary Sgt. Richard White, Fifty-fifth Mass., to editor, January 27, 1864, Folly Island, S.C., *CR,* February 13, 1864, p. 2.

57. Berlin, Reidy, and Rowland, *Black Military Experience,* 104. Excerpts from Blunt's report also appeared in recruiting posters targeting black volunteers. See Berlin, Reidy, and Rowland, *Black Military Experience,* 104.

58. Edward Augustus Wild, Report on raid against guerrillas on December 5, 1863, in N.C., written December 18, 1863, from Norfolk, Va., and Col. Draper's Report of December 24, 1863, HQ N.C. Colored Volunteers, Portsmouth, Va., Edward Augustus Wild Papers, SHC.

59. *The Port Hudson Freemen,* July 15, 1863, Port Hudson, La., p. 2, MOC. *The Port Hudson Freemen* was the paper of the Second R.I. Cavalry. Other references to growing support for black soldiers due to African Americans' performance in battle include recruiting posters praising black valor reprinted in Berlin, Reidy, and Rowland, *Black Military Experience;* Sgt. Hermon Clarke, 117th N.Y., to father, August 9, 1863, Folly Island, S.C., in Jackson and O'Donnell, *Back Home in Oneida,* 100. The role of black performance in

battle as an agent in changing white opinion is a major theme of Dudley Cornish, *The Sable Arm,* and also appears in ch. 7 of Glatthaar, *Forged in Battle.*

60. Capt. M. M. Miller, Ninth La. Volunteers of African Descent, to aunt, June 10, 1863, above Vicksburg, Miss., published in *The Galena* (Ill.) *Advertiser,* reprinted in the *Anglo-African,* July 11, 1863, p. 1.

61. For more, see Glatthaar, *Forged in Battle,* esp. 81–84.

62. Capt. Charles Berry, Tenth La. Volunteers of African Descent, to citizens of Bath, Mason Co., Ill., November 9, 1863, Goodrich's Landing, La., *Peoria Daily Transcript,* December 19, 1863, p. 2. See also Pvt. Leigh Webber, First Kans. Cavalry, to Miss Brown, July 12, 1863, Lake Providence, La., John S. Brown Family Papers, KSHS. Webber was angry with the U.S. government because it had "not kept faith or been honest with the negroes." The fact that black soldiers who performed comparable duties were paid less than white soldiers bothered Webber, who, after nearly a year of serving near black regiments, regarded the discrimination as disgraceful. See Chapter 5 for discussion of black soldiers' equal pay struggle. See also Lt. Henry Crydenwise, First Corps d'Afrique, to parents and all, November 28, 1863, Bayou Boeuf, La., Henry Crydenwise Papers, EU.

63. Ten Tunnell, *Crucible of Reconstruction: War, Radicalism, and Race in Louisiana, 1862–1877* (Baton Rouge: Louisiana State University Press, 1984), 71–73.

64. Orderly Sgt. Isaiah Welch, Fifty-fifth Mass., to Editor, December 2, 1863, Folly Island, S.C., *CR,* December 19, 1863, p. 2.

65. H. J. Maxwell, soldier turned recruiter, to Editor, January 30, 1864, Gallatin, Tenn., *A-A,* April 27, 1864, p. 4; Commissary Sgt. Richard White, Fifty-fifth Mass., to Editor, January 27, 1864, Folly Island, S.C., *CR,* Feb. 13, 1864, p. 2.

66. G.E.S., Fifty-fourth Mass., to Editor, August 7, 1863, Morris Island, S.C., *A-A,* August 24, 1863, p. 1.

67. Cpl. Henry Harmon, Third U.S. Colored Troops, to Editor, October 23, 1863, Morris Island, S.C., *CR,* November 7, 1863, p. 1.

68. H. J. Maxwell to Editor, January 30, 1864, Recruiting office, Gallatin, Tenn., *A-A,* April 27, 1864, p. 4.

69. Cpl. James H. Gooding, Fifty-fourth Mass., to President Lincoln, September 28, 1863, Morris Island, S.C., in Berlin, Reidy, and Rowland, *Black Military Experience,* 385.

70. H. J. Maxwell to Editor, January 30, 1864, Recruiting office, Gallatin, Tenn., *A-A,* April 27, 1864, p. 4. See also Sgt. Isaiah Welch, Fifty-fifth Mass., to Editor, December 2, 1863, Folly Island, S.C., *CR,* December 19, 1863, p. 2.

71. Cpl. Henry C. Harmon, Third U.S. Colored Troops, to Editor, October 23, 1863, Morris Island, S.C., *CR,* November 7, 1863, p. 1.

72. Sgt. Isaiah Welch, Fifty-fifth Mass., to Editor, December 2, 1863, Folly Island, S.C., *CR,* December 19, 1863, p. 2, and Sgt. Isaiah Welch to *A-A,* January 12, 1864, Folly Island, S.C., in Noah A. Trudeau, ed., *Voices of the 55th: Letters from the 55th Massachusetts Volunteers* (Dayton, Ohio: Morningside, 1996), 60.

73. See, for instance, Patrick Rael's argument that northern black leaders "sought not to revolutionize the existing discourse but instead to appeal to its core values in changing the public mind" on slavery and racial matters. *Black Identity and Black Protest in the Antebellum North* (Chapel Hill: University of North Carolina Press, 2002), esp. chs. 1 and 7; quotation from p. 5.

74. "Morgan," Fifty-fourth Mass., to Esther Hawks, no place, no date, but with 1864 papers, Esther Hill Hawks Papers, *PAW,* Reel, 46 Coll. 18.

75. Affidavit of a Pike County, Mo., slave, Aaron Mitchell, January 4, 1864, Louisiana, Mo., in Berlin, Reidy, and Rowland, *Black Military Experience,* 237–38.

76. Sgt. James Taylor, Second U.S. Colored Troops, to Editor, January 1, 1864, Ship Island, Miss., *A-A,* January 30, 1864, p. 1.

77. Sgt. Richard White, Fifty-fifth Mass., to Editor, May 1, 1864, Folly Island, S.C., in Trudeau, *Voices of the 55th,* 102–03.

78. *The Black Warrior,* May 17, 1864, Camp Parapet, La., p. 4, SHSW.

79. See Eddie S. Glaude, Jr., *Exodus! Religion, Race, and Nation in Early Nineteenth-Century Black America* (Chicago: University of Chicago Press, 2000), for discussion of the uses (including political uses) of the Exodus theme among both antebellum northern black thinkers and southern slaves.

80. "Barquet," Fifty-fourth Mass., to Editor, March 24, 1864, near Jacksonville, Fla., *A-A,* April 16, 1864, p. 1.

81. *The Black Warrior,* May 17, 1864, Camp Parapet, La., p. 2, SHSW. See also Sgt. James Trotter, Fifty-fifth Mass., to Edward Kinsley, March 13, 1864, Palatka, Fla., Edward Kinsley Papers, DU.

82. Joseph E. Williams, formerly of the First N.C. Colored Volunteers, now a recruiter, September 7, 1863, Nashville, Tenn., *CR,* September 19, 1863, p. 1.

83. On streetcar desegregation, see James McPherson, *The Negro's Civil War: How American Negroes Felt and Acted During the War for the Union* (New York: Vintage, 1965), 261. For the text of an "Address of the Colored Convention to the Citizens of Kansas" issued by the Kansas convention on black suffrage, see McPherson, *The Negro's Civil War,* 274–75.

84. Tunnell, *Crucible of Reconstruction,* 36; Peyton McCrary, *Abraham Lincoln and Reconstruction: The Louisiana Experiment* (Princeton: Princeton University Press, 1978), 181.

85. On Lincoln's Proclamation of Amnesty and Reconstruction, also known as the Ten Percent Plan, see LaWanda Cox, *Lincoln and Black Freedom: A Study in Presidential Leadership* (Columbia: University of South Carolina Press, 1981); William C. Harris, *With Charity for All: Lincoln and the Restoration of the Union* (Lexington: University Press of Kentucky, 1997); McCrary, *Abraham Lincoln and Reconstruction;* and Tunnell, *Crucible of Reconstruction.* Harris disagrees with the assessment (shared by the others) that Lincoln intended the plan largely as a war measure, and contends instead that the very lenient terms, including restoration of all rights and property for nearly all Confederates with no penalty or waiting period, were Lincoln's actual blueprint for how all of Reconstruction should work after the war. During the war itself, the proclamation stirred up even more disagreement: many radical Republicans in particular were dismayed by the plan, seeing it not as a chance for expanding the rights of black Americans, but rather as assurance that no such expansion would ever happen because it would simply restore the old power structure that brought about secession in the first place. See William Frank Zornow, *Lincoln and the Party Divided* (Norman: University of Oklahoma Press, 1954).

86. McCrary, *Abraham Lincoln and Reconstruction,* 197.

87. Richard H. Black, Third U.S. Colored Troops, to Editor, October 24, 1863, Morris Island, S.C., *CR,* November 21, 1863, p. 1.

88. For discussion of the relationship between soldiering and manhood for white soldiers, see Reid Mitchell, *Civil War Soldiers,* esp. ch. 3 and pp. 17–18, 42. See also Stephen Berry, *All That Makes a Man.* For the relationship between manhood and the Civil War (including, though not exclusively, soldiering) for black men, see Kathleen Ann Clark, *Defining Moments: African American Commemoration and Political Culture in the South, 1863–1913* (Chapel Hill: University of North Carolina Press, 2005), 13–24, 56–60.

89. Sgt. Isaiah Welch, Fifty-fifth Mass., to Editor, October 15, 1863, Folly Island, S.C.,

CR, October 24, 1863, p. 2. Black Union regiments frequently included men from many states, not just the state that raised the regiment, because the various states authorized the enlistment of black soldiers at different times. Massachusetts began to raise black regiments earlier than many of its neighboring states; therefore, many black men (including Pennsylvanian Isaiah Welch) from all over the Northeast and Ohio joined the Massachusetts Fifty-fourth and Fifty-fifth Infantries, as well as the Fifth Massachusetts Cavalry.

90. A. T. Smith, La. Native Guards, in *A-A,* August 15, 1863, p. 4.

91. "Wolverine," Fifty-fifth Mass., to Editor, December 1863, *CR,* January 2, 1864, p. 2.

92. Joseph Williams, recruiter, formerly of the First N.C. Colored Volunteers, to Editor, September 7, 1863, Nashville, Tenn., *CR,* September 19, 1863, p. 1.

93. Pvt. Robert Fitzgerald, Fifth Mass. Colored Cavalry, diary, May 4, 1864, Readville, Mass., Fitzgerald Family Papers, SHC.

94. Pvt. Edwin Van Cise, Forty-first Iowa, diary, July 30, 1864, between Moscow and Memphis, Tenn., Edwin Van Cise Diary, LC. Van Cise was a white soldier who befriended Pete when their regiments scouted together.

95. Pvt. Spotswood Rice, Sixty-seventh U.S. Colored Infantry, to Miss Kitty Diggs, September 3, 1864, Benton Barracks, Mo., in Berlin, Fields, Glymph, Reidy, and Rowland, *Destruction of Slavery,* 689–90.

96. Joseph Williams, recruiter, formerly of the First N.C. Colored Volunteers, to Editor, September 7, 1863, Nashville, Tenn., *CR,* September 19, 1863, p. 1.

97. Pvt. Daniel Walker, Fifty-fourth Mass., to Editor, January 15, 1864, Morris Island, S.C., *CR,* January 30, 1864, p. 1.

98. Sgt. Isaiah Welch, Fifty-fifth Mass., to Editor, December 2, 1863, Folly Island, S.C., *CR,* December 19, 1863, p. 2.

99. At the end of the war, journalist Whitelaw Reid noticed free blacks' equation of the end of slavery with the security of their own rights. In New Orleans, for example, one free black man told Reid, "we have no rights which we can reckon safe while the same are denied to the field-hands on the sugar plantation." Whitelaw Reid, *After the War: A Tour of the Southern States, 1865–66,* quoted in Tunnell, *Crucible of Reconstruction,* 66–67.

100. General Longstreet's orders issued during the Gettysburg campaign encouraged the capture of African Americans, on the premise that they could be escaped slaves, for enslavement in the South. *Official Records,* ser. 1, vol. 51, part 2, pp. 732–33.

101. Cpl. John Williams, August 4, 1863, near Richmond, John A. Williams Letters, VHS. For more on Confederate soldiers' enslavement of Pennsylvania blacks in the summer of 1863, see Ted Alexander, "A Regular Slave Hunt: The Army of Northern Virginia and Black Civilians in the Gettysburg Campaign," *North and South* 4:7(2001), 82–89; David G. Smith, "Race and Retaliation: The Capture of African Americans During the Gettysburg Campaign," in Peter Wallenstein and Bertram Wyatt-Brown, *Virginia's Civil War* (Charlottesville: University of Virginia Press, 2005), 137–51; and Peter C. Vermilyea, "The Effect of the Confederate Invasion of Pennsylvania on Gettysburg's African-American Community, *Gettysburg Magazine* 24 (January 2001), 112–28.

102. Sgt. Isaac Reynolds, Sixteenth Va. Cavalry, to wife, July 20, 1863, Page County, Va., Isaac Reynolds Letters, DU. "Dutch" (from *deutsch*) meant German. While the jovial atmosphere of the raids quickly changed for Reynolds, the practice of capturing African Americans did not. As late as August 9, he was still writing to his wife about capturing "negroes and horses," but by that time the mood had become grim and retaliatory rather than celebratory.

103. Pvt. Robert Mabry, Sixth Va., to wife, July 7, 1863, Winder Hospital, Richmond,

Robert C. Mabry Papers, NCDAH. Mabry attributed the uncharacteristically bad behavior to inept officers who were unable to manage the ranks' demoralized mood induced by the discouraging war news.

104. "Many Soldiers" to Gen. John C. Pemberton, June 28, 1863, *Official Records* (Navy), ser. I, vol. 25, p. 118.

105. Pvt. Andrew Edge, Fifty-second Ga., to wife, July 10, 1863, Enterprise, Miss., Andrew Edge Correspondence, EU.

106. Sgt. George M. Dixon to sister, July 16, 1863, Jackson, Miss., George M. Dixon Papers, CMM Ser. B, Reel 4. See also Pvt. John Fryar, Thirty-fourth Ga., diary, July 4, 1863, Vicksburg, Miss., John H. Fryar Letters and Diary, MOC.

107. In "Lee's Army Has Not Lost Any of Its Prestige: The Impact of Gettysburg on the Army of Northern Virginia and the Confederate Home Front," in Gary Gallagher, ed., *Lee and His Army in Confederate History* (Chapel Hill: University of North Carolina Press, 2001), 83–114, Gary Gallagher argues that historians have exaggerated the damaging impact of Gettysburg on Confederate morale. While it is true that Confederate morale recovered and Gettysburg did not mark the beginning of the end in Confederate eyes, it is equally true that the concurrence of Gettysburg and Vicksburg struck white Southerners as a definite, though not permanent, change in Confederate fortunes. As explained below, white Southerners did not give up after July 1863, but their thinking did evolve, especially in religious directions that had not been nearly so evident earlier in the war.

108. Jefferson Davis, "Speech of 16 February 1861," in *Jefferson Davis, Constitutionalist: His Letters, Papers, and Speeches* (Jackson: Mississippi Department of Archives and History, 1923–32), 5:48. Surgeon John Kinyoun, Sixty-sixth N.C., to wife, October 4, 1863, in N.C., John Kinyoun Papers, DU. For the best discussion of the necessity of "organic unity" within the Confederacy, see Faust, *Creation of Confederate Nationalism,* esp. ch. 1. For the Confederacy's image of itself as distinctively (and necessarily, if it was to survive) above the fray of petty internal divisions, see Rable, *The Confederate Republic.*

109. Pvt. James Zimmerman, Fifty-seventh N.C., to wife, August 16, 1863, Orange Court House, Va., James Zimmerman Papers, DU.

110. Surgeon John Kinyoun, Sixty-sixth N.C., to wife, July 31, 1863, Kinston, N.C., John Kinyoun Papers, DU.

111. Sgt. Archie Livingston, Third Fla., to brother, November 6, 1863, near Missionary Ridge, Tenn., Livingston Family Letters, MOC.

112. Lt. Macon Bonner, N.C. Artillery, to wife, December 28, 1863, Fort Fisher, N.C., Macon Bonner Papers, SHC.

113. Pvt. Thomas Taylor, Sixth Ala., to wife, August 5, 1863, Orange Court House, Va., Thomas S. Taylor Letters, ADAH.

114. Pvt. James Zimmerman, Fifty-seventh N.C., to wife, August 16, 1863, Orange Court House, Va., James Zimmerman Papers, DU.

115. Lt. Thomas Trammell, Eleventh Georgia, to Joseph Brown, June 23, 1863, Inspector General's Correspondence, GDAH, quoted in Weitz, *A Higher Duty,* 117–18.

116. Pvt. James Zimmerman, Fifty-seventh N.C., to wife, August 2, 1863, Orange Court House, Va., and October 21, 1863, Brandy Station, Va., James Zimmerman Papers, DU. Zimmerman made similar points in letters of August 16 and August 30, 1863.

117. Pvt. J. Marcus Hefner, Fifty-seventh N.C., to wife, July 19, 1863, near Clarkson, Va., Marcus Hefner Papers, NCDAH. William Wagner also resented that ordinary men like himself had to "keepe on fiteing" while the "Big fellows" benefited. See Wagner, Fifty-seventh N.C., to wife, August 2 and August 4, 1863, near Rapidan Station, Va., in William

F. Hatley and Linda B. Huffman, eds., *Letters of William F. Wagner, Confederate Soldier* (Wendell, N.C.: Broadfoot's Bookmark, 1983), 62, 63.

118. Surgeon John Kinyoun, Sixty-sixth N.C., to wife, July 31, 1863, Kinston, N.C., John Kinyoun Papers, DU.

119. Q.M. Theophilus Perry, Second Brigade, Army of the Trans-Mississippi, to wife, July 12, 1863, near Trenton, La., Person Family Papers, DU.

120. Sgt. John Calton, Fifty-sixth N.C., to brother, December 30, 1863, Concord Church, N.C., John Washington Calton Letters, NCDAH. See also Capt. Theophilus Perry, Twenty-eighth Tex. Cavalry, to wife, January 15, 1864, near Marksville, Ark., Person Family Papers, DU.

121. Pvt. Richard Ledbetter, Fortieth Ala., to wife, December 25, 1863, near Dalton, Ga., Fortieth Ala. Infantry File, CNMP.

122. Gary Gallagher and others have argued that soldiers in the Army of Northern Virginia maintained consistently high morale, even when the war was going poorly for the Confederacy, and that these troops retained a high degree of commitment to the war. (See *The Confederate War*.) ANV soldiers were the least likely to berate secessionists for instigating (and then refusing to do their share in carrying out) an unpopular war. Nonetheless, the theme arose frequently in other Confederate armies, and even among some ANV soldiers, especially North Carolinians, most likely because North Carolina had been lukewarm on the secession issue in the first place and remained a hotbed of dissent throughout the war.

123. Pvt. James Zimmerman, Fifty-seventh N.C., to wife, August 2, 1863, near Orange Court House, Va., James Zimmerman Papers, DU. Firebrands and secessionists were also favorite targets of Theophilus Perry.

124. The phenomenon of desertion continued to vary by region in and after the summer of 1863. In *Conscription and Conflict,* Moore notes that "the baleful practice of skulking and deserting" grew in the second half of 1863, and attributes the rise to dissatisfaction with conscription, especially with how exemptions were administered (202). The picture varies a bit from state to state. Summer 1863 was a time of high desertion among North Carolinians, according to Moore (203). In *Desertion of Alabama Troops from the Confederate Army,* Bessie Martin identifies July and August 1863 as the crest of one of the highest waves of desertion among Alabama troops (27). Writing about Georgia troops (and counting only Confederates who fled to Union camps), Mark Weitz cites late 1863 and especially 1864 as the time of Georgia's highest desertion rates, and argues that desertion occurred not in response to the battlefield, but rather to home front concerns. Specifically, he denies that the fate of the Army of Northern Virginia played a significant role in instigating Georgia desertions (*A Higher Duty,* 119, 175). Aaron Sheehan-Dean, in contrast, shows that among Virginia troops serving in Virginia, desertions actually declined in the summer of 1863 after peaking in 1862, a conclusion that makes sense for several reasons that set Virginians serving in the ANV apart. First, the relative quiet of the Virginia theater after Gettysburg saved soldiers posted there the demoralizing battlefield defeats that soldiers serving elsewhere experienced. Second, Virginians serving in their home state were spared the anxiety of non-Virginians, who worried about their distant loved ones and were fighting far from home. Finally, as Sheehan-Dean points out, by 1863 the Emancipation Proclamation provided Confederate troops with a vivid reminder of the need to keep fighting. See Aaron Sheehan-Dean, "Justice Has Something to Do with It: Class Relations and the Confederate Army," *Virginia Magazine of History and Biography* 113:4 (November 2005), 340–77. The important point is that soldiers who spoke of a desertion flood in the

summer of 1863 overestimated the scale of the phenomenon, but their comments matter because they show that soldiers, especially soldiers outside of the Army of Northern Virginia, and even some non-Virginians in the ANV, *perceived* a spike in desertions, and linked it to both military defeats and home front struggles in the second half of 1863, a time of difficulty, though not mass abandonment of the cause, for many Confederates.

125. Capt. Arthur Hyatt, Sixteenth La. Consolidated Infantry, diary, Alexandria, La. For the days July 16–27, every entry mentions desertion. Arthur Hyatt Papers, CMM Ser. B, Reel 10.

126. Pvt. William Wagner, Fifty-seventh N.C., to wife, July 30, 1863, near Madison Court House, Va., in Hatley and Huffman, *Letters of William F. Wagner,* 59. In his demoralized state, Wagner surely exaggerated the number.

127. Pvt. Oliver Strickland, Forty-third Ga., to mother, December 18, 1863, near Dalton, Ga., Oliver Strickland Letters, EU. Like Wagner, Strickland exaggerated. Although the Fifty-second Ga. was what Weitz has identified as a "high desertion regiment," from which many troops had deserted and would continue to do so, the whole regiment did not leave in December 1863 (*A Higher Duty,* Table 3, 71).

128. Pvt. John Forman, Sixteenth La., to sister, August 7, 1863, near Morton, Tenn., Robert A. Newell Papers, CMM Ser. B, Reel 14.

129. In the reconfigured Congress, 41 out of 106 representatives openly opposed the Davis administration, while twelve out of twenty-six senators were anti-administration men. The North Carolina delegation provides an even more extreme example: 90 percent of its members were "Union Whigs." See Beringer et al., *Elements of Confederate Defeat,* 116, 132; Thomas, *Confederate Nation,* 257–58; McPherson, *Battle Cry of Freedom,* 691–92.

130. Lofton's Regiment of Georgia Volunteers, October 7, 1863, near Atlanta, CSA Archives, State Government Papers, 1861–65, DU. The State Government Papers include the voting returns for many companies and regiments, among which Lofton's Regiment's returns are fairly typical. In other words, there is little obvious voting pattern in any of them, but if nothing else, the results make clear that no widespread endorsement of the Confederate authorities existed among Georgia troops in 1863.

131. Lt. Josiah Patterson, Fourteenth Ga., to sons, October 31, 1863, Rappahannock River, Va., Josiah Blair Patterson Letters, GDAH. Other state elections also yielded divided results. In North Carolina, the main issues centered on the peace movement, and the mixed results showed the division that existed among the troops on that topic. See Lt. Macon Bonner, N.C. Artillery, to wife, November 1, 1863, Ft. Fisher, N.C., Macon Bonner Papers, SHC; and Capt. Henry Chambers, Forty-ninth N.C., diary, Suffolk, Va., Henry Chambers Papers, NCDAH. Other states revealed just as many divisions, but the issues in question were as likely to be local matters as they were Confederacy-wide matters. See Capt. Christopher Winsmith, First S.C., to father, October 10, 1863, near Chattanooga, Tenn., John Christopher Winsmith Papers, MOC.

132. "Peace—When shall we have Peace?" North Carolina *Weekly Standard,* July 22, 1863, p. 1.

133. Holden's newspaper, the *Weekly Standard,* reported over one hundred peace meetings in the summer of 1863 and reprinted the resolutions adopted at the meetings. Although the *Standard* characterized the meetings as spontaneous upswellings of native sentiment, the resolutions adopted at each of them were nearly identical, and borrowed phrasing directly from the *Standard* editorial pages. The Zebulon Baird Vance Papers, Governor's Papers, Box 10, and Private Collections, vol. 3 (both at the NCDAH), contain peace resolutions from many locations, including Henderson, Forsythe, Rutherford,

Cabarrus, and Caldwell Counties, N.C. The North Carolina *Weekly Standard* also includes several sets of peace resolutions. The issue of August 5, 1863, for example, includes on pp. 1–3 resolutions from public meetings held in Wake, Moore, Gaston, Iredell, Buncombe and Sampson counties. For more on *Standard* editor William Woods Holden and his role in the peace movement, see William C. Harris, *William Woods Holden: Firebrand of North Carolina Politics* (Baton Rouge: Louisiana State University Press, 1987), esp. chs. 6 and 7. For more on the peace movement, see Marc W. Kruman, *Parties and Politics in North Carolina 1836–1865* (Baton Rouge: Louisiana State University Press, 1983), 241–52. For an account of the meetings and examples of reactions to them, see Buck Yearns and John G. Barrett, eds., *North Carolina Civil War Documentary* (Chapel Hill: University of North Carolina Press, 1980), 291–306.

134. While most resolutions did not express willingness to go back to the Union, there were a few exceptions. A "Humble Citizen" of Forsythe County, for example, wrote to tell Governor Vance that "the people of Bethania, Salem, and the surrounding country are riding about with petitions getting every person they can to sign them, deceiving the ignorant by telling them just sign it, the Governor will call a convention, we will send delegates that will vote us back into the Union, and we will have peace in less than three months." See Humble Citizen to Governor Vance, February 1, 1864, Forsythe Co., N.C., Zebulon Baird Vance Papers, Governor's Papers, Box 10, NCDAH. This citizen's letter about rumors he had heard of peace meetings suggests that some meetings discussed or even supported reentry into the Union, but the resolutions in Governor Vance's papers and published in North Carolina newspapers generally do not explicitly endorse returning to the Union.

135. Proceedings of Caldwell County meeting, February 8, 1864, Caldwell Co., N.C., Zebulon Baird Vance Papers, Governor's Papers, Box 10, NCDAH.

136. Pvt. Adelphos J. Burns, Forty-eighth N.C., to father, August 1863, Talorsville, Va., Adelphos J. Burns Papers, NCDAH.

137. Pvt. George Dewey, First N.C. Cavalry, to sister, July 31, 1863, Culpeper, Va., George Stanley Dewey Correspondence, SHC.

138. Pvt. Jacob Hanes, Fourth N.C., to brother, September 16, 1863, near Rapidan River, Va., Catherine Hanes Papers, SHC.

139. Pvt. William Wagner, Fifty-seventh N.C., to wife, August 15, 1863, near Orange Court House, Va., in Hatley and Huffman, *Letters of William F. Wagner,* 65. Wagner further noted the outrage of the troops when the "Big men," meaning the senior officers, reported to the newspapers that the men had voted to carry on the war. "We never voted that a way we voted to have pease on some terms," the angry Wagner told his wife. See also Pvt. Francis Poteet, Forty-ninth N.C., to family, November 22, 1863, Kinston, N.C., Poteet-Dickson Letters, NCDAH.

140. Samuel Cameron, Second Ala. Cavalry, to brother-in-law, December 15, 1863, Cameron Collection, Hoole.

141. Sgt. Edward Brown, Forty-fifth Ala., to wife, July 8, 1863, near Chattanooga, Tenn., Edward Norphlet Brown Letters, ADAH.

142. Pvt. Albert Allen, First Mo. (CSA), to friend, December 3, 1863, near Meridian, Miss., Civil War Letters 1862–64, UMOC.

143. Surgeon Robert Bell, Tenth Mo. (CSA), diary, July 7, 1863, near Helena, Ark., Bell Diaries, MOHS.

144. Pvt. John Price, Tenn. (CSA), to father, January 4, 1864, near Dalton, Ga., John F. and William Price Letters, EU. Even the ebullient Robert Bunting could resort to this sort of logic when he sensed that his typically hearty tone was getting nowhere. "After all the blood and treasure—after the struggle which has made our name immortal among the

nations," he pleaded, how could anyone even consider "kiss[ing] the scepter of our invaders?" Chaplain Robert Bunting, Eighth Tex. Cavalry, to *Houston Telegraph,* July 30, 1863, near Rome, Ga., Robert Franklin Bunting Papers, TSLA.

145. Chaplain Robert Bunting, Eighth Tex. Cavalry, to *Houston Telegraph,* August 11, 1863, near Rome, Ga., Robert Franklin Bunting Papers, TSLA. Al Pierson also spoke of the impossibility of Confederates allowing themselves to become "enslaved" to the Union government, as long as they kept determined eyes on the goal of "separation from and freedom of the yanks." See Sgt. Reuben Allen ("Al") Pierson, Ninth La., to father, August 22, 1863, Orange Court House, Va., in Thomas Cutrer and T. Michael Parrish, *Brothers in Gray: The Civil War Letters of the Pierson Family* (Baton Rouge: Louisiana State University Press, 1997), 210.

146. Pvt. Thomas Taylor, Sixth Ala., to sister, August 15, 1863, near Orange Court House, Va., Thomas S. Taylor Letters, ADAH.

147. Sgt. Ivy Duggan, Forty-ninth Ga., to *Central Georgian,* November 7, 1863, near Culpeper Court House, Va., Ivy W. Duggan Letters, GDAH.

148. Pvt. Jonathan Doyle, Fourth La., to friend's sister, August 18, 1863, near Jackson, Miss., Josiah Knighton Family Papers, CMM Ser. B, Reel 11.

149. For an extended discussion of the impact of disruptions in the domestic and social order on Confederate ideology, and the Confederacy itself, see Faust, *Mothers of Invention.* For specific treatment of shifting relations between and images of women and slaves, see esp. ch. 3. Ch. 4 details the transformation alluded to by Pvt. Jonathan Doyle above. See also Whites, *The Civil War as a Crisis in Gender,* ch. 2, for analysis of how the war disrupted a social order based on independence of white males and dependence of everyone else, in part by "empower[ing] the domestic labor of Confederate women."

150. Pvt. James Zimmerman, Fifty-seventh N.C., to wife, October 21, 1863, Brandy Station, Va., James Zimmerman Papers, DU.

151. Martha Warrick to husband, Pvt. Thomas Warrick, Thirty-fourth Ala., October 9, 1863, Coosa, Ala., Thomas Warrick Letters, ADAH.

152. Pvt. Richard Ledbetter, Fortieth Ala., to wife, December 25, 1863, near Dalton, Ga., Fortieth Ala. Infantry File, CNMP.

153. Martha Warrick to husband, Pvt. Thomas Warrick, Thirty-fourth Ala., October 9, 1863, Coosa, Ala., Thomas Warrick Letters, ADAH. Southerners who maintained strong loyalty to slavery also expressed doubts about how to control freed slaves. According to Missouri soldier Walthall Robertson, who had once made his living as a slave trader, "turning [slaves] loose to shift for themselves" guaranteed further disruption to the South, since he assumed that most former slaves would either "starve or steal." See Robertson to sister, October 25, 1863, Miami, Mo., Mary Overton Gentry Shaw Family Papers, JCHS.

154. Lt. Edmund Patterson, Ninth Ala., diary, August 18, 1863, Johnson's Island Prison, in John G. Barrett, ed., *Yankee Rebel: The Civil War Journal of Edmund DeWitt Patterson* (Chapel Hill: University of North Carolina Press, 1966), 130.

155. Pvt. Grant Taylor, Fortieth Ala., to wife, December 6, 1863, hospital, Marietta, Ga., in Ann K. Blomquist and Robert A. Taylor, eds., *This Cruel War: The Civil War Letters of Grant and Malinda Taylor, 1862–1865* (Macon, Ga.: Mercer University Press, 2000), 205.

156. Lt. Edmund Patterson, Ninth Ala., diary, August 4, 1863, Johnson's Island Prison, in Barrett, *Yankee Rebel,* 128.

157. Jefferson DeVotie, Ga., to father, July 20, 1863, Charleston, S.C., in Lane, *Dear Mother: Don't Grieve About Me,* 253. See also Pvt. John Brightman, substitute in the Eighteenth Tex., to brother, August 23, 1863, St. Landry's Parish, La., John Claver Bright-

man Papers, CAH; Lt. James Lineberger, Forty-ninth N.C., to wife, August 20, 1863, near Weldon, N.C., in H. O. Pitts, ed., *Letters of a Gaston Ranger: 2nd Lt. James Wellington Lineberger* (H. O. Pitts, 1991), MOC.

158. Pvt. Thomas Taylor, Sixth Ala., to sons, July 20, 1863, Martinsburg, Va., Thomas S. Taylor Letters, ADAH. Similarly, John Street proclaimed the certainty of Confederate victory: "Will not God favor the rights? I believe he will." See Pvt. John Street, Ninth Tex., to wife, September 26, 1863, Camp Lauderdale Springs, Miss., John K. and Melinda East Street Papers, SHC. To Newton Davis, a simple syllogism explained all. Since God was both "omnipotent & just" and the southern cause was "just," then "doubtless He in his own good time will give us the victory." See Newton Davis, Twenty-fourth Ala., to wife, December 11, 1863, Dalton, Ga., Newton N. Davis Papers, ADAH.

159. Pvt. Richard Jacques, S.C., to Tutes, October 20, 1863, Richard Jacques Letters, CAH.

160. Jason Phillips discusses Confederate soldiers' religious conviction that they could not lose because God favored their side in "Religious Belief and Troop Motivation: 'For the Smiles of My Blessed Saviour,' " in Wallenstein and Wyatt-Brown, *Virginia's Civil War*, 101–13, esp. 106–09.

161. Cpl. William Andrews, Tenth Va. Battalion, to father, January 11, 1865, Darbytown Road, Va., William B.G. Andrews Papers, DU.

162. Sgt. Reuben Allen Pierson, Ninth La., to father, January 30, 1864, Orange Co., Va., in Cutrer and Parrish, *Brothers in Gray*, 226.

163. Pvt. John Brightman, Eighteenth Tex., to brother, June 1, 1863, Washington, La., John Claver Brightman Papers, CAH.

164. For discussion of this theme, see Steven E. Woodworth, *While God Is Marching On: The Religious World of Civil War Soldiers* (Lawrence: University of Kansas Press, 2001).

165. For more on southern religion and its general distaste for reform movements, see John Boles, *The Great Revival: Beginning of the Bible Belt* (Lexington: University Press of Kentucky, 1996); Wyatt-Brown, "The Antimission Movement in the Jacksonian South; Crowley, *Primitive Baptists of the Wiregrass South*; Hill, *The South and the North in American Religion*; Hughes and Allen, *Illusions of Innocence*; Kuykendall, *Southern Enterprize;* Mathews, *Religion in the Old South*; Shattuck, *A Shield and Hiding Place*; Smith, *Revivalism & Social Reform;* and Snay, *Gospel of Disunion.* Kuykendall and Shattuck especially emphasize the antireform ethos of the South, and explain that it was based on the belief that reform assigned to humans a role that belonged to God, and also because it flirted with heresy. See Kuykendall, *Southern Enterprize,* esp. ch. 4; and Shattuck, *A Shield and a Hiding Place,* 2–8. While John Quist (*Restless Visionaries: The Social Roots of Antebellum Reform in Alabama and Michigan*) and Beth Barton Schweiger (*The Gospel Working Up*) have modified the picture of antebellum southern religion by showing some temperance activity among Alabama Whigs in one county and among Virginia clergymen, temperance still involved individual behavior, and their findings do not change the central point that white Southerners by and large looked with great suspicion on attempts to remake society.

166. Lt. Frank Peak, Byrne's Infantry Battery (Ark.), diary, December 1863, prison, Alleghany City, Pa., Frank P. Peak Narrative, CMM Ser B., Reel 5.

167. Lt. Josiah Patterson, Fourteenth Ga., to daughter, August 14, 1863, Orange Court House, Va., Josiah Blair Patterson Letters, GDAH; William Stillwell, Ga., to wife, August 13, 1863, Fredericksburg, Va., in Lane, *Dear Mother: Don't Grieve About Me,* 260.

168. Lt. James Lineberger, Forty-ninth N.C., to wife, September 11, 1863, near Weldon, N.C., in Pitts, *Letters of a Gaston Ranger,* MOC.

169. Pvt. William Pemberton Davis, Sixty-third Ga., diary, December 27, 1863, GDAH. For the particular significance of concern over profanity, and for claims that profanity was a collective issue among southern leaders and churchmen, see Drew Faust, "Christian Soldiers: The Meaning of Revivalism in the Confederate Army," *Journal of Southern History* 53:1 (February 1987), 79–80. Soldiers remarked on widespread swearing, but they did not attribute the same social significance to it.

170. Charles James addresses this theme repeatedly in letters to his sister; for the fullest treatment, see Lt. Charles James, Eighth Va., to sister, February 13, 1865, near Richmond, Charles Fenton James Letters, VHS.

171. For the importance of church leaders' and prominent white Southerners' beliefs that God had appointed the slaveholding South as an earthly model of Christian order, orthodoxy, and benevolence, see Edward R. Crowther, *Southern Evangelicals and the Coming of the Civil War* (Lewiston, N.Y.: Edwin Mellen Press, 2000), esp. ch. 5 and the Conclusion; Eugene D. Genovese, *A Consuming Fire: The Fall of the Confederacy in the Mind of the White Christian South* (Athens: University of Georgia Press, 1998); Jack P. Maddex, Jr., "Proslavery Millennialism: Social Eschatology in Antebellum Southern Calvinism," *American Quarterly* 31:1 (spring 1979); Snay, *Gospel of Disunion*. For the emphasis on slave marriage, see Genovese, *A Consuming Fire*, 23–32, 51–54, 59–61. For just a few of many sermons making these points, see "Practical Considerations Founded on the Scriptures, Relative to the Slave Population of South Carolina," by "A South Carolinian who is a D.D." (Charleston, 1823); James A. Thornwell, "The Rights and Duties of Masters" (May 26, 1850), in Chesebrough, *"God Ordained This War,"* 177–92; and J. B. Thrasher, "Slavery a Divine Institution" (November 5, 1860) (Port Gibson, Miss., 1861), Widener Library, Harvard University.

172. Steven Woodworth also makes this point in *While God Is Marching On*.

173. Lt. James Lineberger, Forty-ninth N.C., to wife, September 11, 1863, near Weldon, N.C., in Pitts, *Letters of a Gaston Ranger*, MOC.

174. Pvt. Grant Taylor, Fortieth Ala., to wife, October 12, 1863, near Demopolis, Ala., in Blomquist and Taylor, *This Cruel War*, 184. See also Pvt. Thomas Osborne, Sixth Ky. (CSA), to sister, January 27, 1864, near Dalton, Ga., Thomas D. Osborne Letters, Eastern Kentucky University, transcripts at MOC.

175. Revivals among Confederate troops (especially the Army of Tennessee and the Army of Northern Virginia) have been well documented by historians Larry Daniel, Bell Wiley, and Drew Faust, among others, and as Reid Mitchell points out, references to revivals appear in soldiers' letters and diaries throughout the Confederacy. Faust attributes the timing of the revivals in part to the discouraging progress of the war, explaining that revivals "directly reflected the stresses of the soldier's life and death situation: the strains of life in the ranks of a mass army; the pressures of daily confrontation with death—and with a rate of mortality unmatched in any American war before or since." In addition, Confederate soldiers received poorer rations and fewer furloughs than their Union counterparts, which rendered them even more in need of spiritual consolation. See Faust, "Christian Soldiers: The Meaning of Revivalism in the Confederate Army," 64, 68. For revivals in the West, see Larry Daniel, who counters the supposition that revivals began in the Army of Northern Virginia by arguing that revivalism emerged first in the Army of Tennessee, which suffered from considerably worse luck and fewer victories than its eastern counterpart. *Soldiering in the Army of Tennessee*, ch. 8. Wiley, in *The Life of Johnny Reb*, first examined the revival phenomenon and attributed Confederate revivals to a more religious character among Southerners than Northerners. Reid Mitchell shows that religion was important to Confederate armies, but that Union soldiers, who also experienced a

wave of revivalism, were equally devout, though they were more likely to be church members before entering the Army than were Confederates, and so a smaller proportion was available to "convert" or join a church as members. See Mitchell, *Civil War Soldiers*; and Mitchell, "Christian Soldiers? Perfecting the Confederacy," in Miller, Stout, and Wilson, *Religion and the American Civil War,* 297–309.

176. Pvt. John Street, Ninth Tex., to wife, September 26, 1863, Camp Lauderdale Springs, Miss., John K. and Melinda East Street Papers, SHC.

177. Sgt. Edward Brown, Forty-fifth Ala., to wife, May 1, 1864, Dalton, Ga., Edward Norphlet Brown Letters, ADAH.

178. John Crowley notes that part of the appeal of the Primitive Baptist faith among its adherents in the Wiregrass South was and is that it provides moments when "doubts cease." It is not hard to see why that aspect of religious faith would be appealing to Confederates in 1863. See Crowley, *Primitive Baptists of the Wiregrass South,* 190.

179. "Fiery ordeal" was a pet phrase among Southerners in this time frame. For just two of many examples, see Lt. Edmund Patterson, Ninth Ala., diary, July 4, 1863, Gettysburg, Pa., in Barrett, *Yankee Rebel,* 119; and Sgt. Thoms Ragland, Ninth Tenn. (CSA) to father, August 1, 1863, near Chattanooga, Tenn., Ragland Family papers, TSLA.

5: "Many Are the Hearts That Are Weary Tonight": The War in 1864

1. Sgt. Richard Black, Third U.S. Colored Troops, to Editor, Jan. 4, 1864, Morris Island, S.C., *A-A,* January 30, 1864, p. 1.

2. G.E.S., Fifty-fourth Mass., to Editor, January 5, 1864, Morris Island, S.C., *A-A,* January 23, 1864, p. 3.

3. Pvt. Wilbur Fisk, Second Vt., to *Green Mountain Freeman,* May 9, 1864, Spotsylvania, Va., in Rosenblatt and Rosenblatt, *Hard Marching Every Day,* 217. Fisk then revealed that once the battle subsided and he was able to attend to his own, rather than Uncle Sam's, constitution (i.e., he got something to eat), his resolve returned, but his demoralization, even if temporary, indicates the discouraging effect that the spring 1864 battles could exert on soldiers' morale.

4. Pvt. Lewis Bissell, Second Conn. Heavy Artillery, to father, June 2–4, 1864, Cold Harbor, Va., in Olcott and Lear, *The Civil War Letters of Lewis Bissell,* 245–49.

5. Sgt. James Jessee, Eighth Ill., diary, March 13–16, 1864, Vicksburg, Miss., James W. Jessee Diary, KU.

6. Only soldiers who had signed on for three-year enlistments in 1861 approached the end of their terms in 1864, so anyone who enlisted in 1862 or later did not figure into the reenlistment drive. In the end, of soldiers whose enlistments expired, about 136,000 soldiers reenlisted, while almost 100,000 did not (McPherson, *Battle Cry of Freedom,* 720). The Army of the Potomac generally suffered from lower morale than the western armies did, and it also had the lowest reenlistment rate, 50 percent. In *Embattled Courage,* Gerald Linderman has pointed out the need to resist the easy conclusion that the voluntary reenlistment of the majority of the Army signified patriotic zeal, and has argued instead that reenlistment had more to do with soldiers' fatalistic belief in the certainty of their own deaths and consequent desire to take advantage of the reenlistment furloughs to say goodbye to loved ones. Soldiers' own words similarly caution against an overly romantic view of patriotic zeal in 1864, but otherwise they present a different picture than Linderman asserts. Soldiers who did not reenlist generally explained that they believed that they had fulfilled their commitment and now thought that stay-at-homes should do their part before

three-year veterans signed on for more; they did not write that the war didn't matter any-more, or that its outcome was unimportant. Soldiers who did reenlist described the deci-sion neither in terms of romance and glory nor of resignation and cynicism, but rather in terms of their desire to get the job of victory done, and see to completion the task they had started. In short, the decision to reenlist or go home should not be oversimplified into an up-or-down vote on the war effort.

7. For the peace conference, and for Davis's strategy of soft-pedaling independence in hopes of encouraging the northern electorate to see emancipation as the major issue of the war and impediment to peace, see Larry E. Nelson, *Bullets, Ballots, and Rhetoric: Confed-erate Policy for the United States Presidential Contest of 1864* (Tuscaloosa: University of Alabama Press, 1980); and Edward Chase Kirkland, *The Peacemakers of 1864* (New York: Macmillan, 1927).

8. Pvt. Benjamin Jones, Twenty-first Ky., to brother, March 9, 1864, Chattanooga, Tenn., Union Soldiers Letters, FC. See also Pvt. Joseph Fardell, Invalid Corps (formerly 111th Ill.), to parents, February 6, 1864, Benton Barracks, Mo., Joseph A. Fardell Papers, MOHS.

9. *Columbus Crisis,* August 3, 1864, quoted in McPherson, *Battle Cry of Freedom,* 768–69.

10. The Republicans also held their convention in the summer of 1864. Assembling in Baltimore in June, they renominated Abraham Lincoln, though the more radical and more conservative wings of the party both vetted alternative candidates. Although a faction of the party broke away to run John C. Frémont on a platform that first promised, and then repudiated, greater rights for African Americans than the Republican Party explicitly advo-cated, Frémont's candidacy eventually withered. Soldiers were aware of the convention, but to most of them, Lincoln was so obviously the right choice that they voiced few sur-prising or controversial views on the matter. Soldiers' support for Lincoln in the summer of 1864 was consistent with prevailing opinion in the ranks since 1862, and received even stronger and more vociferous (though not qualitatively different) expression in the autumn of 1864, as the election approached. See Chapter 6 below.

11. "Democratic Platform of 1864," Kirk H. Porter, compiler, *National Party Plat-forms* (New York: Macmillan, 1924), 59–60.

12. Sgt. Charles Bates, Fourth U.S. Cavalry, to parents, June 20, 1864, Big Shanty, Ga., Charles Edward Bates Papers, VHS.

13. Cpl. Peter M. Abbott, Third Vt., to parents, August 15, 1864, on Shenandoah River, Va., in Marshall, *A War of the People,* 253–54.

14. Pvt. Adin Ballou, Tenth Maine, to parents, May 29, 1864, Morgan's Bend, Miss., Adin Ballou Papers, ISHL.

15. See Jean H. Baker, *Affairs of Party: The Political Culture of Northern Democrats in Mid-Nineteenth Century America* (New York: Fordham University Press, 1998); David Long, *Jewel of Liberty: Abraham Lincoln's Reelection and the End of Slavery* (Mechanics-burg, Pa.: Stackpole Books, 1994); and Joel Silbey, *A Respectable Minority: The Democ-ratic Party in the Civil War Era, 1860–1868* (New York: Norton, 1977).

16. Sgt. E. C. Hubbard, Thirteenth Ill., to brother, January 17, 1864, Woodville, Ala., E. C. Hubbard Letters, UAR.

17. Cpl. Chauncey Welton, 103d Ohio, to father, July 28, 1864, near Atlanta, Chauncey B. Welton Letters, SHC.

18. Inspector James Connolly, Third Division, Fourteenth Corps, to wife, April 5, 1864, Ringold, Ga., in Angle, *Three Years in the Army of the Cumberland,* 187–88. The

incident in Charleston, Illinois, took place March 28, 1864, killing nine and wounding twelve. *The Volunteer* also published an article entitled "Copperhead Massacre of Union Soldiers in Illinois," *The Volunteer,* 1:6 (April 2, 1864), Athens, Ala., p. 3, MOHS. *The Volunteer* was a camp newspaper written by members of the Sixteenth Army Corps.

19. Q.M. Thomas Clark King, Second Division, Ninth Army Corps, to brother, February 9, 1864, Knoxville, Tenn., King Family Papers, ISHL.

20. Abraham Irvine, Army of the Potomac, to brother, June 14, 1864, Wilderness, Va., Abraham Irvine Letter, T. 2135/1, PRONI. This theme recurs frequently in 1864, as it had done throughout the war. Cpl. George Cadman, Thirty-ninth Ohio, instructed his wife to remember that if he was hurt or killed, "it will be not only for my Country and my Children but for Liberty all over the World . . . for if Liberty should be crushed here, what hope would there be for the cause of Human progress anywhere else?" (Cadman to wife, March 6, 1864, Athens, Ala., George Hovey Cadman Letters, TSLA). Similarly, Charles Henthorn, Seventy-seventh Ill., wondered "where are the oppressed and down-trodden millions of the earth to look for hope" if the Union's "experiment of self-government by the people shall fail?" (Henthorn to sister, March 7, 1864, recuperating in hospital in Quincy, Ill., Charles Henthorn Letters, Schoff). Richard White, a black sergeant in the Fifty-fifth Mass., also envisioned the Union as a guarantor of "justice and liberty" for "the oppressed and down-trodden" everywhere, despite its record of oppressing and trodding on black slaves since its inception as a nation (White to Editor, May 1, 1864, Folly Island, S.C., *A-A,* June 4, 1864, p. 1). See also Capt Henry Crydenwise, Seventy-third U.S. Colored Infantry, to family, May 8, 1864, Port Hudson, La., Henry Crydenwise Letters, EU; Cpl. Louis Rowe, Twelfth N.H., to Abbie, May 27, 1864, Pointrock, Va., Louis Rowe Letters, CWMC, Ser. 2; Sgt. John Brunt, Thirty-third Iowa, to wife, June 1, 1864, Little Rock, Ark., John M. Brunt Papers, KSHS.

21. Pvt. Benjamin Jones, Twenty-first Ky., to brother, March 9, 1864, Chattanooga, Tenn., Union Soldiers' Letters, FC. For a border state soldier who felt differently, see Robert Winn of the Third Ky. Cavalry, who was pleased to learn of a border slave state emancipation convention in Louisville, and hoped it would mean a prompt end to slavery in Kentucky. See Pvt. Robert Winn to sister, February 21, 1864, near Edgefield, Tenn., Winn-Cook Papers, FC.

22. Pvt. Jacob Behm, Thirty-eighth Ill., to sister and brother-in-law, February 1, 1864, Scottsboro, Ala., Jacob Behm Correspondence, CWTIC.

23. Pvt. Charles Henthorn, Seventy-seventh Ill., to sister, March 7, 1864, recuperating in hospital in Quincy, Ill., Charles Henthorn Letters, Schoff. See also Pvt. Joseph Lester, Sixth Wis. Battery, to father and sisters, August 16, 1864, near Cartersville, Ga., Joseph Lester Collection, *PAW,* Coll. 160, Reel 58.

24. Assistant Surgeon John Moore, Twenty-second U.S. Colored Troops, to wife, May 12, 1864, Wilson Landing, Va., James Moore Papers, DU.

25. Lt. Nelson Newton Glazier, Eleventh Vt., to parents, August 31, 1864, in hospital in Annapolis, Md., recovering from arm amputation, Nelson Newton Glazier Letters, VTHS.

26. Pvt. Wilbur Fisk, Second Vt., to *Green Mountain Freeman,* April 7, 1864, Brandy Station, Va., in Rosenblatt and Rosenblatt, *Hard Marching Every Day,* 206–07.

27. Ibid.

28. Pvt. John English, Ohio soldier in Ninety-second Veteran Reserve Corps, to wife, August 28, 1864, hospital in Evansville, Ind., John English Letters, EU. See also Sgt. Horatio Barrington, Fourteenth Ill., to *Bloomington Pantagraph,* July, 1864, near Resaca,

Ga., *Bloomington Pantagraph,* August 4, 1864, p. 1. See also Capt. Henry Crydenwise, Seventy-third Colored Infantry, to parents, June 2, 1864, Port Hudson, La., Henry Crydenwise Letters, EU.

29. Cpl. Abial Edwards, Twenty-ninth Maine Veterans, to Anna, February 23, 1864, Teche, La., in Beverly Hayes Kallgren and James L. Crouthamel, eds., *Dear Friend Anna: The Civil War Letters of a Common Soldier from Maine* (Orono: University of Maine Press, 1992), 80. On the Massachusetts Forty-second's band at black soldier Andre Cailloux's funeral, see Tunnell, *Crucible of Reconstruction,* 72.

30. Pvt. Andrew Harris, Eighth Kans., to parents, July 22, 1864, eight miles from Atlanta, Isaiah Morris Harris Journal and Correspondence, KU. Compare this letter to Harris's letter of August 1863.

31. Sgt. Charles Musser, Twenty-ninth Iowa, to father, September 12, 1864, Little Rock, Ark., in Popchock, *Soldier Boy,* 150. Compare this letter to Musser's letter of February 1863, in which he hardly shone forth as a radical egalitarian, but in which he at least admitted that slaves "needed pity," p. 26.

32. Sgt. Ondley Andrus, Ninety-fifth Ill., to home, April 1864, Vicksburg, Miss., in Fred Albert Shannon, ed., "The Civil War Letters of Sergeant Ondley Andrus," *Illinois Studies in the Social Sciences* 28:4 (1947), 75.

33. Pvt. (acts as Ass't Sgn.) Robert Winn, Third Ky. Cavalry, to sister, May 3, 1864, Ringold, Ga., Winn-Cook Papers, FC. Compare this letter to Winn's letters of October 2, October 28, November 20, and December 11, 1863.

34. Sgt. Maj. Stephen Fleharty, 102d Ill., to *Rock Island Union,* February 6, 1864, Lavergne, Tenn., in Reyburn and Wilson, *"Jottings from Dixie,"* 157.

35. Pvt. Morris Chalmers, 132d N.Y., to sister, September 26, 1864, Bachelor Creek, Va., Morris Chalmers Letters, CWMC, Ser. 2. For the particular antipathy of working-class immigrants, including Irish immigrants, to African Americans, see David R. Roediger, *The Wages of Whiteness: Race and the Making of the American Working Class* (New York: Verso, 1991).

36. Pvt. Alonzo Rich, Thirty-sixth Mass., to father, July 31, 1864, in front of Petersburg, Va., Alonzo G. Rich Papers, CWMC, Ser. 2. In Atlanta a little more than a week later, Sgt. Charles Bates heard "about the affair at Petersburg," and showed even more eagerness to blame the disaster on black soldiers and to view the incident as reason for racial backtracking. "If Sherman does try to blow up anything I hope he will have sense enough to keep the nigger troops out of the way," he remarked. See Sgt. Charles Bates, Fourth U.S. Cavalry, to parents, August 9, 1864, near Atlanta, Charles Edward Bates Papers, VHS.

37. Arthur Van Horn, Seventy-eighth Ohio, to wife, February 3, 1864, Camp near Memphis, Tenn., Arthur Van Horn Family Papers, LC.

38. Pvt. Joseph Fardell, Invalid Corps, to parents, February 6, 1864, Benton Barracks, Mo., Joseph A. Fardell Papers, MOHS.

39. Sgt. William Stevens, Fourth Vt., to sister, March 26, 1864, "Camp Parole," Annapolis, Md., in Marshall, *A War of the People,* 219. Stevens wrote this letter immediately after his release from a Richmond prison, as he awaited the opportunity to go home. For more on prisoner exchange stoppages in light of Confederate policy toward black soldiers, which ironically ended up damaging the Confederate Army more than the Union Army because the Confederacy needed its exchanged soldiers more desperately, see Michael Fellman, *The Making of Robert E. Lee* (New York: Random House, 2000), 205–209.

40. Sgt. J. G. Nind, 127th Ill., 1863 post-Vicksburg reflections, November 1863, Vicksburg, Miss., in Post, *Soldiers' Letters from Camp, Battle-field and Prison,* 291.

41. Pvt. (acts as Ass't Sgn.) Robert Winn, Third Ky. Cavalry, to sister, July 13, 1864, Connestaula River, near Resaca, Ga., Winn-Cook Papers, FC.

42. Pvt. Robert Fitzgerald, Fifth Mass. Cavalry, diary, June 8, 1864, near Petersburg, Va., Fitzgerald Family Papers, SHC. Another volunteer added that ending slavery would help defend the Union because "the war for slavery and secession could be vigorously met only by war for the Union against slavery." See G.E.S., Fifty-fourth Mass., to Editor, May 26, 1864, Folly Island, S.C., *A-A,* June 18, 1864, p. 1.

43. *The Black Warrior,* May 17, 1864, Camp Parapet, Louisiana, p. 2, SHSW.

44. Cpl. John H. B. Payne, Fifty-fifth Mass., to Editor, May 24, 1864, Morris Island, S.C., *CR,* June 11, 1864, reprinted in Trudeau, *Voices of the 55th,* 147; L. S. Langley, Thirty-third U.S. Colored Troops, to Editor, July 1864, Folly Island, S.C., *A-A,* August 6, 1864, p. 2.

45. Sgt. Andrew King, First U.S. Colored Troops, to Editor, June 15, 1864, City Point, Va., *CR,* July 16, 1864, p. 3.

46. G.E.S., Fifty-fourth Mass., to Editor, March 6, 1864, Jacksonville, Fla., *A-A,* April 2, 1864, p. 4.

47. David D. Frances, Seventh Corps d'Afrique, to Editor, March 11, 1864, Port Hudson, La., *A-A,* April 9, 1864, p. 1.

48. Sgt. John Brock, Forty-third U.S. Colored Troops, to Editor, June 5, 1864, near Hanover, Va., *CR,* June 18, 1864, p. 3.

49. E.W.D., Fifty-fourth Mass., to Editor, June 9, 1864, Morris Island, S.C., *CR,* June 25, 1864, p. 1.

50. J. H. Hall, Fifty-fourth Mass., to Editor, August 3, 1864, Morris Island, S.C., *CR,* August 27, 1864, p. 1.

51. "Barquet," Fifty-fourth Mass., to Editor, November 18, 1863, Morris Island, S.C., *A-A,* January 2, 1864, p. 1.

52. Sgt. John Cajay, Eighth U.S. Heavy Artillery, to Editor, June 25, 1864, New Orleans, *A-A,* July 16, 1864, pp. 1–2. Cajay claimed that the celebration, held on June 11, honored "the day Gen. Benjamin F. Butler emancipated the slaves in Louisiana," but the precise event or order to which he was referring remains unclear. Butler's record on slavery in Louisiana was decidedly mixed. Convinced that nonslaveholders were already loyal to the Union, Butler wooed the loyalty of slaveholders with soft policies on slavery for much of 1862, though his actions were not consistent; sometimes he aided the replacement of slavery with free labor. Butler's successor, Nathaniel Banks (who was in charge of New Orleans by June 1864, and according to Cajay, even put in a brief appearance at the festivities in Congo Square), proved even more sympathetic to slaveholders, so possibly Butler had started to look appealing to antislavery Northerners in retrospect by June 1864. For more on Butler and Banks in New Orleans, see Ira Berlin, Thavolia Glymph, Steven Miller, Joseph Reidy, Leslie S. Rowland, and Julie Saville, eds., *Freedom: A Documentary History of Emancipation 1861–1867,* series 1, vol. 3, *The Wartime Genesis of Free Labor: The Lower South* (New York: Cambridge University Press, 1990), 345–77.

53. James Jones, Fourteenth R.I. Heavy Artillery, to Editor, May 8, 1864, Camp Parapet, La., *CR,* May 28, 1864, p. 2.

54. A. H. Newton, Twenty-ninth Conn., to Editor, June 8, 1864, Beaufort, S.C., *CR,* June 25, 1864, p. 1.

55. Joseph Walker, Fifty-fifth Mass., to Editor, March 26, 1864, Yellow Bluff, Fla., *A-A,* April 16, 1864, p. 1.

56. The black suffrage in question would be limited mainly to freeborn blacks. For more on the Louisiana state constitutional convention, see Cox, *Lincoln and Black Free-*

dom, 97–102; McCrary, *Abraham Lincoln and Reconstruction,* 237–70; and Tunnell, *Crucible of Reconstruction,* 60–61.

57. Cpl. George Delavan, Fifty-fourth Mass., to Mrs. Esther Hawks, November 29, 1863, Beaufort, S.C.; and Pvt. Andrew Johnson, First N.C., to Mrs. Esther Hill Hawks, January 4, 1864, Beaufort, S.C., Esther Hill Hawks Papers, *PAW,* Coll. 18, Reel 46. Because reading, like soldiering, had been out of the reach of many black Americans before the war, many troops regarded it as a route by which the entire race could advance. In his history of black soldiers in American military history, *The Black Phalanx,* Joseph T. Wilson, a former soldier in the Second La. Native Guards and the Fifty-fourth Mass., devoted part 3, ch. 1, to "The Phalanx at School." Articles that address the importance of the Union Army in teaching blacks to read include Dudley Taylor Cornish, "The Union Army as a School for Negroes," *Journal of Negro History* 37:4 (October 1952), 368–82; and John W. Blassingame, "The Union Army as an Education Institution for Negroes," *Journal of Negro Education* 34:2 (spring 1965), 152–59. For the links that African Americans traditionally perceived among literacy, power, and independence, see Janet Duitsman Cornelius, *"When I Can Read My Title Clear": Literacy, Slavery, and Religion in the Antebellum South* (Columbia: University of South Carolina Press, 1991), esp. chs. 1 and 6. Cornish and Blassingame detail the logistics of regimental policies on black education, while Cornelius discusses what literacy meant to African Americans.

58. Sgt. Richard H. Black, Third U.S. Colored Troops, to Editor, January 4, 1864, Morris Island, S.C., *A-A,* January 30, 1864, p. 2.

59. Berlin, Reidy, and Rowland, *Black Military Experience,* 633.

60. Berlin, Reidy, and Rowland, *Black Military Experience,* 656–67.

61. Davis's proclamation of December 23, 1862, appears in Wilson, *The Black Phalanx,* 317.

62. See Wilson, *The Black Phalanx,* 316–19. For one example of this policy at work see Brig. Gen. L. S. Ross to Brig. Gen. W. H. Jackson, March 5, 1864, HQ of Tenn. Brigade near Yazoo City, Miss. Ross explained that when he demanded the surrender of the last redoubt held by Union troops in Yazoo City and learned that some black troops were among the units holding the redoubt, he and the Union commander "squabbled about the terms of the capitulation as I would not recognise Negroes as Soldiers." Ross would not offer protection to them or their officers. In this case, the protracted bickering gave other black Union troops time to regroup and return to drive the Confederates from the redoubt, leading to a much happier ending than usual for black soldiers in time of surrender. Ross's correspondence to Jackson is in Berlin, Reidy, and Rowland, *Black Military Experience,* 438–39.

63. Pvt. Robert Fitzgerald, Fifth Mass. Cavalry, diary, May 16, 1864, City Point, Va., Fitzgerald Family Papers, SHC. References to the massacre at Fort Pillow abound throughout black soldiers' writings. For instance, see *The Black Warrior,* 1:1, May 17, 1864, Camp Parapet, La., p. 3, SHSW. According to the Fourteenth R.I. Heavy Artillery soldiers who wrote the *Warrior,* it was not surprising that Confederates, "whose whole lives have been spent in inventing atrocious and exquisite tortures for the punishment of their slaves," would stoop to cold-blooded murder. After all, they already had on their hands "the blood of hundreds of thousands sent to their graves without provocation, for their sport." Tragic as Fort Pillow was, it was "but the unmasking of the principles of slavery." For Fort Pillow from the Confederate perspective, see below.

64. Theodore Hodgkins to Hon. E. M. Stanton, April 18, 1864, in Berlin, Reidy, and Rowland, *Black Military Experience,* 587.

65. For growing dissent among blacks about enlistment, see McPherson, *The Negro's Civil War,* 173–79.

66. David Frances, Seventh Corps D'Afrique, to Editor, March 11, 1864, Port Hudson, La., *A-A,* April 9, 1864, p. 1.

67. G.E.S., Fifty-fourth Mass., to Editor, March 4, 1864, Jacksonville, Fla., *A-A,* April 2, 1864, p. 4.

68. G.E.S., Fifty-fourth Mass., to Editor, May 26, 1864, Folly Island, S.C., *A-A,* June 18, 1864, p. 1.

69. Tunnell, *Crucible of Reconstruction,* 80–81.

70. Sgt. Joseph Walker, Fifty-fifth Mass., to Editor, March 26, 1864, Yellow Bluff, Fla., *A-A,* April 16, 1864, p. 1.

71. Anon. Soldier, Twentieth U.S. Colored Troops, to "My Dear Friend" President Lincoln, August 1864, Camp Parapet, La., in Berlin, Reidy, and Rowland, *Black Military Experience,* 501–02.

72. See, for example, the letter of R. H. Isabelle, formerly of the La. Native Guards, to Editor, June 22, 1863, New Orleans, *A-A,* August 18, 1863, p. 4. Isabelle later reentered the Army, joining the Seventh La. For accounts of the La. Native Guards and their officers, see Mary F. Berry, "Negro Troops in Blue and Gray: The Louisiana Native Guards, 1861–1863," *Louisiana History* 8:2 (1967), 165–90; and James G. Hollandsworth, Jr., *The Louisiana Native Guards: The Black Military Experience During the Civil War* (Baton Rouge: Louisiana University Press, 1995).

73. Sgt. James Trotter, Fifty-fifth Mass., to friend Franky Garrison, August 21, 1864, Folly Island, S.C., in Trudeau, *Voices of the 55th,* 141–42.

74. "The Colored Mass Meeting," *New Orleans Tribune,* August 25, 1864, p. 2. For discussion of the black officers issue, see Glatthaar, *Forged in Battle,* ch. 9; Wilson, *The Black Phalanx,* ch. 4; and John W. Blassingame, "The Selection of Officers and Non-Commissioned Officers of Negro Troops in the Union Army, 1863–1865," *Negro History Bulletin* 30:1 (January 1967), 8–11.

75. Strong relationships between black enlisted men and white officers, and the ways in which shared goals and common experiences knit black and white together, form a major theme of Glatthaar's *Forged in Battle.*

76. D.I.I., Thirty-second U.S. Colored Troops, to Editor, July 18, 1864, Morris Island, S.C., *CR,* August 6, 1864, p. 1. In *Forged in Battle,* Joseph Glatthaar shows a wide spectrum of attitudes among white officers of black troops, ranging from hostility to respect and comradeship; see esp. ch. 5 and also chs. 3 and 9.

77. Sgt. John Cajay, Eighth U.S. Heavy Artillery, to Editor, June 25, 1864, New Orleans, *A-A,* July 16, 1864, pp. 1–2.

78. "Important to Colored Men," *A-A,* December 12, 1863, p. 4. The poster takes up the whole back page. For a thorough discussion of the evolution of black pay policy, see Herman Belz, "Law, Politics, and Race in the Struggle for Equal Pay During the Civil War," *Civil War History* 22:3 (1976), 197–213.

79. *Official Records,* ser. 3, vol. 5, pp. 632–33.

80. For an overview of the reaction of Mass. and S.C. regiments, see Belz, "Law, Politics, and Race in the Struggle for Equal Pay," 199–200.

81. Court-martial statement by Sgt. William Walker, Third S.C. Volunteers, on trial for mutiny for protesting unequal pay, January 12, 1864, Hilton Head, S.C., in Berlin, Reidy, and Rowland, *Black Military Experience,* 393. Walker was executed for mutiny.

82. Pvt. Loudon S. Langley, Fifty-fourth Mass., to Editor, January 23, 1864, *A-A,* January 30, 1864, p. 2.

83. Berlin, Reidy, and Rowland, *Black Military Experience,* reminds readers that a few dollars was not an inconsequential concern to black soldiers' families struggling to get by

(656–57 and 680–84). Still, many soldiers insisted that the main point transcended economics.

84. "Wolverine," Fifty-fifth Mass., to Editor, December 1863, *CR,* January 2, 1864, p. 2. Samuel Robinson similarly stressed that the motive for declining the state's offer to make up the difference in pay was "that we desire at this crisis, the recognition of our rights as men and as soldiers." See Sgt. Samuel Robinson, Fifty-fifth Mass., to *Liberator,* January 18, 1864, Folly Island, S.C., in Trudeau, *Voices of the 55th,* 61–62.

85. "A Soldier of the Fifty-fifth Mass. Volunteers" to Editor, January 12, 1864, Folly Island, S.C., *A-A,* January 30, 1864, p. 1. In June 1864, Congress finally passed an appropriations act equalizing the pay of all black troops to that of white soldiers, retroactive to January 1, 1864, and equalizing the pay of black troops who had been free before the war to the time of enlistment. See Berlin, Reidy, and Rowland, *Black Military Experience,* 367–68. Soldiers would actually begin to receive equal pay in the fall and winter of 1864–65.

86. Joseph Williams, formerly First N.C. Colored Volunteers, now recruiter, to Editor, September 7, 1863, Nashville, Tenn., *CR,* September 19, 1863, p. 1.

87. "Barquet," Fifty-fourth Mass., to Editor, November 18, 1863, Morris Island, S.C., *A-A,* January 2, 1864, p. 1. Similarly, Pvt. Daniel Walker, Fifty-fourth Mass., optimistically believed that once the threat of Civil War had passed, the U.S. government could not help but reward the contributions of black Americans, especially if they suppressed agitation until the crisis of the Union had passed. See Walker to Editor, January 15, 1864, Morris Island, S.C., *CR,* January 30, 1864, p. 1.

88. Sgt., Fifty-fifth Mass., to Editor, May 29, 1864, Folly Island, S.C., *CR,* July 9, 1864, p. 1. A letter from a member of the Fifty-fourth Mass. similarly assured readers that "the respectable part of the colored race consider that their own kind would make the most affectionate companions," and harbored no desire to intermarry with "Anglo Saxon" women. J. H. Hall to Editor, August 3, 1864, Morris Island, S.C., *CR,* August 27, 1864, p. 1.

89. G.W.H., First U.S. Colored Troops, to Editor, May 10, 1864, Wilson's Landing, Va., *CR,* May 28, 1864, p. 1.

90. "Africano," Fifth Mass. Cavalry, to Editor, June 11, 1864, City Point, Va., *A-A,* June 25, 1864, p. 1. In fact, added another soldier, Americans could only expect things to get worse "unless some plan is specially adopted to check [the] onward course" of prejudice, a "moral degradation and . . . one of the most fruitful sources of evil in our land." See Cpl. John Payne, Fifty-fifth Mass., to Editor, May 24, 1864, Morris Island, S.C., in *CR,* June 11, 1864, reprinted in Trudeau, *Voices of the 55th,* 148.

91. E.W.D., Fifty-fourth Mass., to Editor, June 9, 1864, Morris Island, S.C., *CR,* June 25, 1864, p. 1. The same letter continued its jeremiad tone: "Under such wrongs [as unequal treatment] no nation can prosper. If a strong power crush the weak and deprive them of the blessings which God has ordained for them, it must fall. God's supreme power will break them into pieces that will not obey His righteous laws."

92. Sgt. Richard White, Fifty-fifth Mass., to Editor, May 1, 1864, Folly Island, S.C., *A-A,* June 4, 1864, p. 1.

93. Q.M. Sgt. George Binford, Eighteenth Tenn. (CSA), to cousin, March 2, 1864, near Atlanta, Binford Papers, VHS.

94. Pvt. Henry Patrick, Forty-first N.C., to wife, August 13, 1864, near Petersburg, Va., Henry Machen Patrick Letters, NCDAH. Patrick exaggerated the figures: from the battle of the Wilderness through the "Crater" (the failed attack following the mine explosion at Petersburg), Army of the Potomac casualties totaled approximately 65,000. See E. B.

Long, *The Civil War Day by Day: An Almanac 1861–1865* (New York: DaCapo, 1971), 494, 500, 548; McPherson, *Battle Cry of Freedom,* 742. Yet Patrick rightly noted the impact of the high casualty count on both Union and Confederate morale.

95. Pvt. Thomas Kelley, unspecified Va. regiment in the ANV, but almost certainly the Thirty-second Va., to cousin, August 30, 1864, Henrico Co., Va., Thomas F. Kelley Papers, DU.

96. Drum Major Douglas Cater, Nineteenth La., to cousin, August 18, 1864, near Atlanta, Douglas J. and Rufus Cater Letters, *PAW,* Reel 11, Coll. 32.

97. Pvt. Peter Cross, Seventh N.C., to parents, March 30, 1864, Orange, Va., John Wright Family Papers, NCDAH.

98. Sgt. William Pitt Chambers, Forty-sixth Miss., journal, February 1864, Meridian, Miss., to Mobile, Ala., in Richard A. Baumgartner, ed., *Blood and Sacrifice: The Civil War Journal of a Confederate Soldier* (Huntington, W.Va.: Blue Acorn, 1994), 116–17. By 1864, Chambers also had reason to worry for the safety of Mississippi families at the hands of Confederate deserters and the irregular Confederate forces assigned to round up deserters, both of which preyed on civilians. See Weitz, *More Damning Than Slaughter,* 203–11.

99. Pvt. Louis Branscomb, Third Ala., to father, February 3, 1864, Camp Terrill, Va., Branscomb Family letters, ADAH. See also Pvt. John Everett, Eleventh Ga., who went "in for the hole Hog" for the sole reason that "I never intend to bee Cald a Conscript." Everett to mother, March 7, 1864, Blue Springs, Tenn., John A. Everett Papers, EU.

100. Pvt. Daniel Abernethy, Eleventh N.C., to wife, February 4, 1864, near Orange Court House, Va., Daniel Abernethy Papers, DU.

101. Pvt. John Killian, Twenty-third N.C., to sister, March 5, 1864, Talersville Station, Va., Eliza C. Killian Papers, SHC.

102. Pvt. Andrew Edge, Fifty-second Ga., to wife, April 14, 1864, near Dalton, Ga., Andrew Edge Correspondence, EU. The following month, Edge was wounded at New Hope Church, and was furloughed to recover at home. Once at home, he simply ignored the furlough's expiration date. Within the context of his regiment, Edge's experience was not extraordinary; the Fifty-second Ga. is identified by Mark Weitz as one of Georgia's "high desertion units." See Weitz, *A Higher Duty,* Table 3, p. 71.

103. Pvt. Louis Branscomb, Third Ala., to sister, April 15, 1864, Camp Terrill, Va., Branscomb Family Letters, ADAH.

104. Commissary Sgt. [name omitted to protect family], First Miss. Mounted Rifles, to Aunt, April 8, 1864, Memphis, Tenn., Anonymous Letters, 1864, Civil War Collection, Federal Collection, TSLA. This letter was written by a Mississippian who actually deserted the Confederacy to fight for the Union, in part because he believed the Confederacy was defeating its purpose by violating its own racial order.

105. Sgt. Marion Hill Fitzpatrick, Forty-fifth Ga., to wife, March 6, 1864, near Orange Court House, Va., in Jeffrey C. Lowe and Sam Hodges, eds., *Letters to Amanda: The Civil War Letters of Marion Hill Fitzpatrick, Army of Northern Virginia* (Macon, Ga.: Mercer University Press, 1998), 125.

106. Lt. E. L. Cox, Sixty-eighth N.C., diary, July 3, 1864, Norfolk, Va., CMM Ser. A, Reel 13. For another example of alarm about racial inversion, see Lt. James Ligon, Hampton's Legion, S.C., to mother, August 25, 1864, Henrico Co., Va., James Blackman Ligon Papers, SCL.

107. Pvt. John Washington Calton, Fifty-sixth N.C., to brother and sister-in-law, March 27, 1864, Weldon, N.C., John Washington Calton Letters, NCDAH. That the stories Calton relayed were untrue did not lessen the belief of many Southerners in their veracity, or their impact on soldiers' will to fight. For another soldier's remarks on the dangers of

black men seducing white women if the Yankees won, see Pvt. Thomas Kelley of Va. to his cousin, June 6, 1864, Henrico Co., Va., Thomas F. Kelley papers, DU.

108. Testimony of Pvt. George Shaw, Sixth U.S. Colored Heavy Artillery, Mound City Hospital, April 22, 1864, in "Fort Pillow Massacre," Senate Report 63, Thirty-eighth Congress, First Session (Washington, D.C.: Government Printing Office, 1864), 25.

109. Chaplain Richard Webb, Forty-fourth N.C., to fiancée, August 13, 1864, Petersburg, Va., Webb Family Papers, SHC.

110. Surgeon Charles Trueheart, Eighth Ala., to brother, August 28, 1864, defenses around Petersburg, Va., in Williams, *Rebel Brothers,* 115.

111. Capt. Reuben Allen Pierson, Ninth Ala., to father, April 19, 1864, Camp Hays, Va., in Cutrer and Parrish, *Brothers in Gray,* 234. Weitz details the depredations visited on Confederate civilians by both Confederate deserters and the regular and irregular Confederate Army forces detailed to round up deserters in *More Damning Than Slaughter,* esp. chs. 8 and 9.

112. Pvt. William Honnoll, Twenty-fourth Miss., to sister, April 13, 1864, Dalton, Ga., Honnoll Family Letters, EU.

113. Pvt. A. T. Holliday, First Ga. Militia, to Governor Joseph Brown, July 22, 1864, Washington, Ga., A. T. Holliday Letters, AHC. For many soldiers, the needs of their families were even more desperate, since few families were as well-to-do as Holliday's was. The clash between duty to the Confederacy and duty to provide for one's family is a major theme of Mark Weitz's *A Higher Duty,* esp. chs. 4 and 5.

114. For Davis's strategy, see Nelson, *Bullets, Ballots, and Rhetoric.* Desertion had been a significant fact of Confederate life since 1862, and it continued in the spring and summer of 1864 as Davis muted discussion of independence in hopes that Northerners would focus on the slavery issue, but it did not skyrocket. As had always been the case, exact desertion rates continued to vary by region. In *More Damning Than Slaughter,* Weitz shows that desertion rose for some states in 1864, but for others stayed steady or declined (see Tables 3 and 4, p. 246). Overall, he argues that desertion resulted from soldiers' concerns for the safety and well-being of their own loved ones and their home communities: when the best way to protect one's home and family seemed to be to fight against Yankees, men stayed in the ranks, but when the best way seemed to be to go home, they deserted. Weitz attributes fluctuations in different states not to Confederate political strategy or Davis's attempts to influence the Union's 1864 elections (which, logically, should have affected all states equally), but rather to the proximity of the Union Army, which made it easy for soldiers to cross over to Union lines and take an oath.

Other studies also show that factors other than Davis's campaign rhetoric influenced desertion. According to Mark Weitz in *A Higher Duty,* his study of Georgia soldiers, February 1864 marked the high point of desertion among Georgia troops, which was before Davis's strategy really came into play (see Table 2, p. 67). Ella Lonn and Bessie Martin identify the last quarter of 1864 as a period of high desertion, by which time Davis's strategy no longer applied, but fresh disasters, especially the fall of Atlanta and Lincoln's reelection, were raising new concerns for families' safety while also making Confederate victory look increasingly unlikely. Lonn, *Desertions During the Civil War,* 27; Martin, *Desertion of Alabama Troops from the Confederate Army,* 26–27. Weitz also credits Lincoln's reelection and the fall of Atlanta with boosting Confederate desertions in late 1864 (*More Damning Than Slaughter,* 270–71). The difference in timing noted by Weitz, Lonn, and Martin probably arises from the different sources used by the historians, and from different local triggers that made circumstances for Georgians different from circumstances for Alabamians (studied by Martin) or other Confederates. Weitz used the *Register of Con-*

federate Deserters, which counted only Confederates who deserted to the enemy and took the oath of allegiance, and did not come into existence until August 1863, while Lonn and Martin used the *Official Records* and newspaper advertisements for the capture of deserters. Also, the Union Army in Georgia in early 1864 both made it easier for Georgians to desert to the enemy and gave them more reason to worry about the safety of their families.

115. Pvt. Noble John Brooks, Cobb's Ga. Cavalry, diary, May 24, 1864, near North Anna River, Va., Noble John Brooks Civil War Diary and Letter, GDAH.

116. Pvt. John Killian, Twenty-third N.C., to sister, March 5, 1864, Talersville Station, Va., Eliza C. Killian Papers, SHC.

117. Ibid.

118. Pvt. Noble John Brooks, Cobb's Ga. Cavalry, diary, May 24, 1864, near North Anna River, Va., Noble John Brooks Civil War Diary and Letter, GDAH.

119. Sgt. Edward Brown, Forty-fifth Ala., February 5, 1864, Tunnel Hill, Ga., Edward Norphlet Brown Letters, ADAH.

120. Pvt. Joseph Stapp, Forty-first Ala., to mother, March 6, 1864, Petersburg, Va., Joseph Stapp Letters, VHS.

121. Lt. W. P. ("Joe") Renwick, Third La., to wife, April 14, 1864, Shreveport, La., CMM Ser. B, Reel 20.

122. Capt. Reuben Allen Pierson, Ninth La., to father, March 22, 1864, Orange Co., Va., in Cutrer and Parrish, *Brothers in Gray,* 228.

123. For discussion of Holden and the peace movement, and of the Vance-Holden election, see Harris, *William Woods Holden,* 127–52; Kruman, *Parties and Politics in North Carolina 1836–1865,* 249–65; and Gordon B. McKinney, *Zeb Vance: North Carolina's Civil War Governor and Gilded Age Political Leader* (Chapel Hill: University of North Carolina Press, 2004), 197–230.

124. Governor Zebulon Vance, "Address of Gov. Vance on the Condition of the Country," delivered in Wilkesboro, N.C., February 22, 1864, reprinted in *The Daily Conservative,* Raleigh, N.C., April 16, 1864, p. 1, from the shorthand report of G. Clinton Stedman, NCDAH.

125. Pvt. George Williams, Seventh N.C., to parents, April 5, 1864, near Gordonsville, Va., Williams-Womble Papers, NCDAH; Sgt. Martin Malone Gash, Sixty-fifth N.C., to sister, June 18, 1864, Kinston, Ga., Gash Family Papers, NCDAH.

126. Pvt. James M. Morris, Fifty-seventh N.C., to Governor Vance, April 27, 1864, near Kinston, N.C., Zebulon B. Vance Governor's Papers, NCDAH. Weitz notes the particularly violent North Carolinian home front in *More Damning Than Slaughter,* 188–95.

127. Pvt. Daniel Abernethy, Eleventh N.C., to wife, February 25, 1864, and to father, February 25, 1864, near Orange Court House, Va., Daniel Abernethy Papers, DU.

128. Pvt. Adelphos Burns, Forty-eighth N.C., to father, July 17, 1864, Petersburg, Va., Adelphos J. Burns Letters, NCDAH.

129. Governor Zebulon Vance, "Address of Gov. Vance on the Condition of the Country," reprinted in *The Daily Conservative,* Raleigh, N.C., April 16, 1864, p. 1, NCDAH.

130. Pvt. David Thompson, Twenty-seventh N.C., to mother, March 27, 1864, near Orange Court House, Va., Samuel Thompson Papers, SHC.

131. Pvt. Adelphos Burns, Forty-eighth N.C., to father, July 17, 1864, Petersburg, Va., Adelphos J. Burns letters, NCDAH. While neither Burns nor any other soldier who opposed Vance brought up the speech's sections on slavery or racial disorder, troops who supported Vance cited those very passages to explain their support for the governor.

132. Petition signed by "North Carolinians in prison at Johnson's Island, 231 in all," March 30, 1864, Johnson's Island, Ohio, Thomas Jefferson Green Papers, SHC.

133. Sgt. Isaac LeFevers, Forty-sixth N.C., to relatives at home, April 29, 1864, near Orange Court House, Va., Isaac Lefevers Papers, NCDAH.

134. On Union occupation of and black settlement in Plymouth, see Wayne K. Durrill, *War of Another Kind: A Southern Community in the Great Rebellion* (New York: Oxford University Press, 1990), 181–83.

135. Affidavit of Sgt. Samuel Johnson, Second U.S. Colored Cavalry, in the field, Va., July 11, 1864, in Berlin, Reidy, and Rowland, *Black Military Experience,* 588–89. For more on Confederate killing of black Union prisoners and violence against the town of Plymouth, see Durrill, *War of Another Kind,* 204–08.

136. *Richmond Examiner,* April 28, 1864, repeated in the New Bern *North Carolina Times,* May 21, 1864, as quoted in Durrill, *War of Another Kind,* 208.

137. For election results, see Kruman, *Parties and Politics in North Carolina, 1836–1865,* 265. The lopsided totals resulted in part from coercion. Sometimes officers prevented North Carolina troops from casting Holden ballots, either with threats or by tearing up Holden votes before they could be counted. William Holden complained that fully two-thirds of soldiers in the field had their right to vote as they wished suppressed. See "The Vote of the Army," North Carolina *Weekly Standard,* August 5, 1864, p. 3. Others without an obvious stake in the election's outcome verified incidents of coercion, if not at the rate that Holden claimed: Union general Winfield Hancock noted that two North Carolina men deserted to his lines "because they were not allowed to vote yesterday." See *Official Records,* series 1, vol. 40, part 3, p. 598; also available online through Cornell University's *Making of America* Web site. McKinney discusses election coercion in the Army in *Zeb Vance,* 228–29. Yet reports from soldiers in the field indicate that while fraud and intimidation happened, they were not universal. Pvt. Henry Patrick, Forty-first N.C., concluded "from *personal observation*" of the voting in his own company that "there never was a fairer election held that I ever witnessed." See Patrick to wife, August 13, 1864, near Petersburg, Va., Henry Machen Patrick Letters, NCDAH. Most men simply chose Vance of their own free will, and it is their behavior that needs explaining.

138. Sgt. Garland Ferguson, Twenty-fifth N.C., to brother, July 13, 1864, between Chattahoochee River and Atlanta, Evelyn McIntosh Hyatt Collection, NCDAH.

139. Sgt. Garland Ferguson, Twenty-fifth N.C., to brother, July 28, 1864, between Chattahoochee River and Atlanta, Evelyn McIntosh Hyatt Collection, NCDAH.

140. See Pvt. R. P. Allen, Fourth N.C. Cavalry, to wife, July 28, 1864, near Petersburg, Va., R. P. Allen Letters, MOC; Capt. Henry Chambers, Forty-ninth N.C., diary, July 1864, Suffolk, Va., Henry Chambers Papers, NCDAH; Richmond Mumford Pearson Papers, DU. The Richmond Mumford Pearson Papers contain not only election returns from numerous hospitals (General Hospital No. 5, Wilmington, N.C., and Tarboro Wayside Hospital, for instance), but also the returns for the First N.C. Battalion of Sharpshooters and for Yadkin County soldiers stationed at Salisbury, N.C., on July 28, the day of the vote. In each of these categories, Vance defeated Holden. All told, Vance won with 77 percent of the civilian vote and 87.9 percent of the soldier vote. See McPherson, *Battle Cry of Freedom,* 698. For more on the election, see Kruman, *Parties and Politics in North Carolina, 1836–1865,* 260–70; result statistics, 265.

141. Pvt. Henry Patrick, Forty-first N.C., to wife, August 13, 1864, near Petersburg, Va., Henry Machen Patrick Letters, NCDAH.

142. Pvt. William Templeton, Twelfth S.C., to sister, April 4, 1864, near Orange Court House, Va., Joseph and William Templeton Papers, SCL.

143. Pvt. John Everett, Eleventh Ga., to mother, March 7, 1864, Blue Springs, Tenn., John A. Everett Papers, EU.

144. Pvt. John Everett, Eleventh Ga., to mother, May 14, 1864, near Richmond, John A. Everett Papers, EU.

145. Drum Major Douglas Cater, Nineteenth La., to cousin, May 7, 1864, near Dalton, Ga., Douglas J. and Rufus Cater Letters, *PAW,* Coll. 32, Reel 11.

146. Exact numbers of Union dead are unobtainable because the regiments most heavily involved, the Sixth U.S. Colored Heavy Artillery, the Second U.S. Colored Light Artillery, and the Thirteenth Tenn. Cavalry (white unionists and some Confederate deserters), were all recruiting at the time, making the number of men on duty on April 12 obscure. Somewhere between 277 and 297 Union soldiers were killed, compared to 14 Confederate dead, according to Trudeau, *Like Men of War,* 168. Regimental records reveal mortality rates at 36 percent for white unionist troops and 66 percent for black soldiers. See John Cimprich and Robert C. Mainfort, Jr., "Fort Pillow Revisited: New Evidence About an Old Controversy," *Civil War History* 28:4 (December 1982), 295. Confederate sources first proclaimed a great victory at Fort Pillow and held the treatment of black troops up as a lesson intended for black soldiers and their supporters, but then downplayed the incident in response to harsh criticism and threats of retaliation from the Union. Northern sources immediately portrayed the event as a massacre, and a Congressional investigation revealed slaughter and atrocities such as the burning and burying alive of African Americans. The subsequently published Senate report, known as the "Fort Pillow Massacre Senate Report," or simply the "Fort Pillow Report" (1864), was certainly intended to sway northern public opinion toward a hard-line approach to the rebels. Although the more lurid claims of northern propaganda have been toned down by historians, objective accounts based on research agree that a massacre of mainly black and some white unionist soldiers took place after they had surrendered, and that the slaughter was extraordinarily brutal. Even historians initially sympathetic to southern denials of a massacre concur: see Albert Castel, "The Fort Pillow Massacre: Fresh Examination of the Evidence," *Civil War History* 4:1 (March 1958), 37–50. Castel admits that he began his study as "a wholehearted believer" in the southern version of Fort Pillow, but changed his mind in light of the evidence, 38. For additional accounts of Fort Pillow, see Bruce Tap, "'These Devils Are Not Fit to Live on God's Earth': War Crimes and the Committee on the Conduct of the War, 1864–1865," *Civil War History* 42:2 (June 1996), 116–32; Trudeau, *Like Men of War,* 156–69; and Richard L. Fuchs, *An Unerring Fire: The Massacre at Fort Pillow* (Cranbury, N.J.: Associated University Presses, 1994).

147. Sgt. Achilles Clark, Twentieth Tenn. Cavalry, to sister, April 14, 1864, near Brownsville, Tenn., quoted in Cimprich and Mainfort, "Fort Pillow Revisited," 297–99. Though more reticent than Clark, Samuel Caldwell also emphasized "how terrible was the slaughter" at Fort Pillow, and attributed the bloodletting to the fact that black Union soldiers "incensed our men." See Surgeon Samuel Caldwell, Sixteenth Tenn. Cavalry, to wife, April 15, 1864, near Brownsville, Tenn., quoted in Cimprich and Mainfort, "Fort Pillow Revisited," 300–01. Troops who heard about Fort Pillow, but did not participate in it, wrote favorably of the incident. Macon Bonner approved of the Fort Pillow affair, expressly because the victims were mainly black, while Thomas Warrick greeted word of the killing of blacks captured at Fort Pillow as "all good news." See Lt. Macon Bonner, Fortieth N.C. Artillery, to wife, April 21, 1864, Ft. Holmes, N.C., Macon Bonner Papers, SHC; Pvt. Thomas Warrick, Thirty-fourth Ala., to wife, April 18, 1864, in Ga., Thomas Warrick Letters, ADAH.

148. Pvt. Henry Bird, Twelfth Va., to fiancée, August 4, 1864, Petersburg, Va., Bird Family Papers, VHS. For more accounts of the killing of black prisoners at the Crater, see Pvt. Robert Mabry, Sixth Va., to wife, August 1, 1864, trenches around Petersburg, Robert

C. Mabry Papers, NCDAH; Pvt. Peter Cross, Seventh N.C., to brother, August 2, 1864, Petersburg, Va., John Wright Family Papers, NCDAH; Pvt. Daniel Abernethy, Eleventh N.C., to wife and father, August 7, 1864, Petersburg, Va., Daniel Abernethy Papers, DU; Pvt. R. P. Allen, Fourth N.C. Cavalry, to wife, August 1, 1864, near Petersburg, Va., R. P. Allen Letters, MOC.

149. Capt. Henry Chambers, Forty-ninth N.C., diary, March 9, 1864, Suffolk, Va., Henry Chambers Papers, NCDAH.

6: "Slavery's Chain Done Broke at Last": The Coming of the End

1. Sgt. John N. Keirns, Fifty-first Ohio, to wife and six children, February 1, 1865, near Huntsville, Ala., Tina May Doud Papers, JCHS. The song "Take Your Gun and Go, John," was written by an anonymous Union soldier in a Maine regiment; John Keirns probably received just the words and not the tune, because he referred to the piece as a "poem" rather than a song.

2. For accounts of the fall of Atlanta, see Albert Castel, *Decision in the West: The Atlanta Campaign, 1864* (Lawrence: University of Kansas Press, 1992); McPherson, *Battle Cry of Freedom,* 774–76; Robert A. Doughty and Ira D. Gruber, *The American Civil War: The Emergence of Total Warfare* (Lexington, Mass.: D.C. Heath, 1996), ch. 5; and Glatthaar, *The March to the Sea and Beyond,* 1–10.

3. Capt. Thomas Honnoll, Ninety-ninth Ohio, to friend, September 25, 1864, Decatur, Ga., T. C. Honnoll Papers, KSHS.

4. Chaplain Henry McNeal Turner, First U.S. Colored Troops, to Editor, September 10, 1864, Harrison's Landing, Va., *CR,* September 17, 1864, p. 1.

5. Sgt. Horatio Barrington, Fourteenth Ill., to Editor, December 18, 1864, Savannah, Ga., *Bloomington Pantagraph,* January 7, 1865, p. 1. Barrington wrote the letter weeks later in Savannah, based on his experiences in Atlanta.

6. For the centrality of Lincoln's election to Union victory, see David Long, *The Jewel of Liberty: Abraham Lincoln's Re-Election and the End of Slavery* (Mechanicsburg, Pa.: Stackpole Books, 1994); and Zornow, *Lincoln and the Party Divided,* chs. 14–16.

7. Capt. Thomas Honnoll, Ninety-ninth Ohio, to friend, September 25, 1864, Decatur, Ga., T. C. Honnoll Papers, KSHS.

8. Maj. W. W. Boatright, Seventy-first U.S. Colored Troops, to friend Harper, September 8, 1864, Natchez, Miss., in *Crawford Co.* (Ill.) *Argus,* September 22, 1864. Cpl. Charles Harris, 157th New York, also explained that McClellan catered more to soldiers' "self-interest" than Lincoln did, but that there was no way "any body which has suffered the hardships of a soldier two years could be willing to let every thing that has been accomplished be of no account," which is what would happen if McClellan won and instituted an "armistis." See Harris to parents, October 10, 1864, Morris Island, S.C., Charles J. Harris Letters, DU.

9. Lt. Nelson Newton Glazier, Eleventh Vt., to parents, August 31, 1864, hospital, Annapolis, Md., recovering from arm amputation, Nelson Newton Glazier Letters, VTHS. See also Lt. Sam Evans, Fifty-ninth U.S. Colored Troops, to father, October 16, 1864, Memphis, Tenn., Evans Family Papers, OHS; Pvt. George Hudson, One Hundredth Ill., to parents, September 11, 1864, Atlanta, George A. Hudson Collection, *PAW,* Coll. 138, Reel 54; Pvt. William Kesterson, Invalid Corps (USA), to brother, October 28, 1864, hospital, Springfield, Mo., William H. H. Kesterson Letters, MOHS.

10. Pvt. Oscar Cram, Eleventh Mass., to wife, September 11, 1864, near Petersburg,

Va., Oscar Cram Letters, CWMC. See also Capt. Peter Eltinge, 156th N.Y., to brother, September 2, 1864, near Charlestown, Va., Eltinge-Lord Family Papers, DU; Sgt. Edward Griswold, First Conn. Light Artillery, to sister, September 10, 1864, near Petersburg, Va., Edward, Charles, and Joel Griswold Papers, DU.

11. Pvt. George Hannaford, Seventeenth Conn., to wife, October 1864, St. Augustine, Fla., George W. Hannaford Letters, SHSW (typescript of letter also available at CAH). Naval engineer Augustine Sackett echoed Hannaford's sentiments when he described Republican victories in the October voting states of Pennsylvania, Ohio, and Indiana as equally "important to the preservation of the union as a great victory in the battlefield." See 2d. Asst. Engineer Augustine Sackett, U.S. Navy, October 14, 1864, aboard USS *Matabesett,* Fortress Monroe, Va., Augustine Sackett Letters, CTHS. For analysis of the "October states," see Long, *The Jewel of Liberty,* 244–48; and Zornow, *Lincoln and the Party Divided,* ch. 15.

12. Pvt. John Brobst, Twenty-fifth Wis., to Mary, September 27, 1864, hospital near Atlanta, in Margaret Brobst Roth, ed., *Well Mary: Civil War Letters of a Wisconsin Volunteer* (Madison: University of Wisconsin Press, 1960), 92–93. Pvt. John Foote agreed that "in [Lincoln's] hands [the war] will be closed *right* or not at all." See Foote to sister, November 10, 1864, near Richmond, John B. Foote Papers, DU.

13. Pvt. Oscar Cram, Eleventh Mass., to wife, September 11, 1864, near Petersburg, Va., Oscar Cram Letters, CWMC.

14. Sgt. Hermon Clarke, 117th N.Y., to father, October 3, 1864, Temple Hall Court House, Va., in Jackson and O'Donnell, *Back Home in Oneida,* 166. Lifelong Democrat Pvt. William Bean of the 182d Ohio also promised to vote the straight Democratic ticket as his family had always done. See Bean to brother, October 26, 1864, Camp Chase, Ohio, William E. Bean Papers, UMOC.

15. Pvt. Edwin Horton, Fourth Vt., to wife, November 6, 1864, Strasburg, Va., Edwin Horton Letters, VTHS.

16. Sgt. Charles Bates, Fourth U.S. Cavalry, to parents, November 15, 1864, near Nashville, Tenn., Charles Edward Bates Papers, VHS.

17. Sgt. James Taylor, Ninety-third U.S. Colored Troops, to Editor, April 14, 1865, Brashear City, La., *CR,* May 6, 1865, p. 4.

18. David R. Brown, Thirty-first U.S. Colored Troops, to Editor, November 15, 1864, City Point, Va., *A-A,* December 16, 1864, p. 2. Many black troops wrote to Lincoln requesting aid for their families, better conditions for soldiers, or clemency. Pvt. Samuel Roosa of the Twentieth U.S. Colored Troops wrote to the president to plead the case of some illiterate black troops accused of violating regulations. They had not been taught the rules and therefore, Roosa hoped to persuade the president, should not be harshly punished for disobeying. See Roosa to President Lincoln, January 24, 1865, Ft. Jefferson, Fla., in Berlin, Reidy, and Rowland, *Black Military Experience,* 477–78.

19. Chaplain Henry Turner, First U.S. Colored Troops, to Editor, September 10, 1864, Harrison Landing, Va., *CR,* September 17, 1864, p. 1. See also another soldier who withheld praise from Lincoln because the president decided only "tardily to do justice" to slaves when emancipation was "forced upon him by the irrepressible conflict of the times." R.H.B., Third U.S. Colored Troops, to Editor, September 7, 1864, Jacksonville, Fla., *CR,* September 17, 1864, p. 1.

20. Some states, such as Pennsylvania, had allowed absentee voting by soldiers in the election of 1812, but in 1862 the Pennsylvania Supreme Court prohibited the practice. See Margaret McKelvy Bird and Daniel Crofts, "Soldier Voting in 1864: The David McKelvy Diary," *Pennsylvania Magazine of History and Biography* 115:3 (July 1991), 373. Many

state constitutions specifically barred absentee voting. Josiah Henry Benton, *Voting in the Field: A Forgotten Chapter of the Civil War* (Boston: privately printed, 1915), surveys each Union state's constitution and applicable statutes.

21. Cpl. Charles Harris, 157th N.Y., to parents, October 15, 1864, Morris Island, S.C., Charles J. Harris Letters, DU.

22. Sgt. Nathan Parmater, Twenty-ninth Ohio, diary, October 11–12, 1864, near Atlanta, Nathan Parmater Papers, OHS. Parmater described the process by which his regiment conducted its state elections. Most regiments who voted in the field rather than sending ballots home, including Parmater's, followed similar procedures for the presidential election, though he did not describe the process so fully the second time around. J. Q. A. Campbell's Iowa regiment voted by a similar process, and Campbell himself served as judge. See Campbell, Fifth Iowa Cavalry, diary, November 8, 1864, near Mammoth Cave, Ky., in Grimsley and Miller, *The Union Must Stand*, 191.

23. Sgt. Henry Hart, Second Conn. Light Artillery, to wife, November 4, 1864, New Orleans, Henry Hart Letters, EU.

24. Sgt. Henry Hart, Second Conn. Light Artillery, to wife, October 21, 1864, New Orleans, Henry Hart Letters, EU.

25. Sgt. Charles Musser, Twenty-ninth Iowa, to father, November 9, 1864, Little Rock, Ark., in Popchock, *Soldier Boy*, 160–61. Musser reported the results from several other regiments, as follows. Thirty-third Iowa: Lincoln 431, McClellan 42. Third Iowa Battery: Lincoln 90, McClellan 14. Thirty-sixth Iowa: Lincoln 134, McClellan 6 (its numbers were depleted since many of its men had been taken prisoners of war months earlier); First Iowa Cavalry: Lincoln 480, McClellan 1. Several other regiments voted for Lincoln by wide margins, according to Musser, though he did not always give totals. In the Fortieth Iowa, an overwhelmingly Democratic regiment, Lincoln still beat McClellan by 25 votes.

26. For election results see Long, *The Jewel of Liberty*, 257–58 and Appendix D, 284–85; McPherson, *Battle Cry of Freedom*, 804–05; Zornow, *Lincoln and the Party Divided*, 200–202; and Nevins, *The War for the Union*, vol. 3, *The Organized War*, 138–40. In response to the lopsided vote, Democrats cried foul, alleging fraud and bullying of potential Democratic voters, but soldiers (including McClellan supporters) denied that unfair practices or tampering with the results had occurred, and historians have since validated soldiers' claims. Zornow examines various states where Democrats complained of fraud, and concludes that in some, such as Indiana, vote tampering probably occurred, but not enough to change the outcome dramatically (*Lincoln and the Party Divided*, 203–204). In *The Jewel of Liberty*, Long denies that tampering occurred in any meaningful way. McPherson points out that both parties habitually engaged in irregularities, and that "their partisan benefits tended to cancel each other out." New York Democratic commissioners, for instance, admitted to forging McClellan votes. In all, as McPherson concludes, "the voting of the soldiers in 1864 was about as fair and honest as 19th-century elections generally were, and Lincoln's majority was probably an accurate reflection of soldier sentiment" (*Battle Cry of Freedom*, 804–805 and n. 69). Some soldiers heard the charges and responded to them. Charles Tubbs, for instance, assured his wife that rumors of vote selling and other malfeasance were false, since he had seen no evidence of any such thing, even in Washington, D.C. "If there was aney such a thing in the Armey it would be practiced here as every thing that is rackaty is practiced here," he pointed out. See Tubbs to wife, September 17, 1864, Washington, D.C., C. H. Tubbs Letters, NCDAH.

27. Sgt. Henry Hart, Second Conn. Light Artillery, to wife, November 4, 1864, New Orleans, Henry Hart Letters, EU. Benton contends that only in Maryland did soldiers'

votes make the difference between loss or victory for McClellan (*Voting in the Field,* 223, 313), while Zornow and Long argue that only in Connecticut and New York did soldiers' votes provide the difference (*Lincoln and the Party Divided,* 202; *The Jewel of Liberty,* 256).

28. Pvt. Chauncey Welton, 103d Ohio, to father, September 19, 1864, Decatur, Ga., Chauncey B. Welton Letters, SHC. See also Cpl. James Beard, 142d N.Y., to brother and sister-in-law, October 23, 1864, before Richmond, James Beard Letters, CWMC, Ser. 2. Henry Riggs of the Ninety-second U.S. Colored Troops urged Democrats to do "as I have done" and "turn with disgust from their own political party" rather than elect a "*double-dyed Jeff Davis*" like McClellan. See Riggs to Editor, October 3, 1864, Morganza, La., *Bloomington Pantagraph,* October 19, 1864.

29. Lt. J. Q. A. Campbell, Fifth Iowa Cavalry, diary, November 16, 1864, Nashville, Tenn., in Grimsley and Miller, *The Union Must Stand,* 193.

30. Pvt. Justus Silliman, Seventeenth Conn., to mother, November 9, 1864, Jacksonville, Fla., in Marcus, *A New Canaan Private in the Civil War,* 83.

31. Pvt. John Brobst, Twenty-fifth Wis., to Mary, September 27, 1864, near Atlanta, in Roth, *Well Mary,* 92; Pvt. Wilbur Fisk, Second Vt., to *Green Mountain Freeman,* April 9, 1865, City Point, Va., in Rosenblatt and Rosenblatt, *Hard Marching Every Day,* 322–33. For just a few of the many additional examples of soldiers referring to the president as "Uncle" or "Father," see Pvt. Constant Hanks, Twentieth N.Y. Militia, to mother, September 13, 1863, Va., Constant Hanks Papers, DU; Pvt. Charles Tubbs, Tenth Veteran Reserve Corps, to wife, September 17, 1864, Washington, D.C., C. H. Tubbs Letters, NCDAH; Pvt. Amos Breneman, 203d Pa., to friend, October 25, 1864, near Richmond, Amos Breneman Letters, CWMC, Ser. 2; Pvt. Justus Silliman, Seventeenth Conn., to brother, April 24, 1864, Jacksonville, Fla., in Marcus, *A New Canaan Private in the Civil War,* 100.

32. Pvt. R. Matthew Perry, Fourteenth Wis., to brother, September 20, 1864, near Atlanta, R. Matthew Perry Letters, SHSW.

33. Many historians have characterized Sherman's March as an example of total warfare, by which they (and I) do not mean complete, indiscriminate destruction, but rather warfare waged between societies, not merely armies, with the home front as well as the front lines as its battlefield, and with social and political considerations as well as strictly military ones influencing strategic and tactical decisions. The Union Army's relative restraint in areas less associated with secession, but more ruthless destruction in South Carolina, which was most closely associated with secession, clearly meets this definition. See, for instance, Doughty and Gruber, *The American Civil War*; *The Emergence of Total Warfare,* ch. 5; Mark Grimsley, *The Hard Hand of War*; and Allan Nevins, *The War for the Union,* vol. 4, *The Organized War to Victory* (New York: Scribner, 1971), 144–69, 193–94.

34. For analysis of the march from the perspective of soldiers who took part, see Glatthaar, *The March to the Sea and Beyond,* which emphasizes the veteran character of Sherman's army, the commitment of the men to the campaign and to the cause of Union and emancipation that they believed it served, and soldiers' impressions of and interactions with black slaves and southern whites.

35. "Marching Through Georgia," by Henry Clay Work, 1865.

36. Pvt. Theodore Upson, One Hundredth Ind., diary, February 15, 1865, near Columbia, S.C., in Oscar Osburn Winther, ed., *With Sherman to the Sea: The Civil War Letters, Diaries & Reminiscences of Theodore F. Upson* (Baton Rouge: Louisiana State University Press, 1943), 136.

37. Cpl. Abial Edwards, Twenty-ninth Maine, to Anna, February 26, 1865, Camp

Sheridan, Va., in Kallgren and Crouthamel, *Dear Friend Anna,* 117. See also Jacob Seibert, Ninety-third Pa., to father, February 24, 1865, in front of Petersburg, Va., Seibert Family Papers, HCWRTC.

38. Sgt. David Blair, Forty-fifth Ohio, to sister, September 29, 1864, Atlanta, David Humphrey Blair Civil War Diary and Letters, CWMC. On October 13, Pvt. Charles Tubbs of the Tenth Veterans Reserve Corps, also wrote that "the constatution as it was looks to me as an utter imposability." See Tubbs to wife, Washington, D.C., C. H. Tubbs Letters, NCDAH.

39. Capt. Henry Riggs, Ninety-second U.S. Colored Troops, to Editor, October 3, 1864, Morganza, La., *Bloomington Pantagraph,* October 19, 1864.

40. Pvt. John Foote, 117th N.Y., to sister, September 28, 1864, near Petersburg, Va., and November 10, 1864, near Richmond, John B. Foote Papers, DU. For a description of the trials and sacrifices of war as "seeds sown" in the cause of national redemption, see *The Guidon,* 1:5, December 29, 1864, p. 3, MOHS. *The Guidon* was the camp paper of the Twelfth Pa. Cavalry.

41. Sgt. Henry Hart, Second Conn. Light Artillery, to wife, October 3, 1864, New Orleans, Henry Hart Letters, EU.

42. Asst. Surgeon John Moore, Twenty-second U.S. Colored Troops, to wife, September 25, 1864, Hanscom's Landing, Va., James Moore Papers, DU.

43. *Grant's Petersburg Progress,* 1:2, April 5, 1865, Petersburg, Va., p. 1, UVA. *Grant's Petersburg Progress* was written by a captain and a major in the Army of the Potomac, rather than by enlisted men in a particular regiment, as most camp newspapers were.

44. Chaplain Henry McNeal Turner, First U.S. Colored Troops, to Editor, September 10, 1864, Harrison's Landing, Va., *CR,* September 17, 1864, p. 1.

45. Asst. Surgeon John Moore, Twenty-second U.S. Colored Troops, to wife, February 7, 1865, Federal Point, N.C., James Moore Papers, DU. See also Sgt. J. Q. A. Campbell, Fifth Iowa, who committed to his diary the hope that "the doom of slavery may be irrevocably fixed" while "the nation is suffering from its chastisements." Campbell, diary, November 16, 1864, Nashville, Tenn., in Grimsley and Miller, *The Union Must Stand,* 193.

46. Lt. Henry Grimes Marshall, Twenty-ninth Conn., to folks at home, November 6, 1864, in the field, Va., Henry Grimes Marshall Papers, Schoff. For emancipation in Maryland, see Barbara Jeanne Fields, *Slavery and Freedom on the Middle Ground: Maryland During the Nineteenth Century* (New Haven: Yale University Press, 1985), 131–35, 142.

47. For more on the Maryland and Missouri state legislatures' overtures against slavery in 1864–65, as well as soldiers' votes in favor of emancipation in both states, see Michael Vorenberg, *Final Freedom: The Civil War, the Abolition of Slavery, and the Thirteenth Amendment* (New York: Cambridge University Press, 2001), 186–87; Benton, *Voting in the Field,* 46.

48. Lt. Francis Audsley, Forty-fourth Mo., to wife, January 30, 1865, Eastport, Miss., Audsley Papers, UMOC.

49. "Missouri is Free!!! Slavery is Buried!!," *Soldier's Letter,* January 28, 1865, Fort Riley, Kans., p. 3, KSHS. The same page also celebrated the news that Tennessee had abolished slavery, and reported that only four convention delegates had voted against emancipation in Missouri. *Soldier's Letter* was the regimental newspaper of the Second Colo. Cavalry.

50. Sgt. James Taylor, Second U.S. Colored Infantry, to Editor, January 29, 1865, Key West, Fla., *A-A,* February 25, 1865, p. 2. For a celebration in New Orleans, see Chaplain

George LeVere, Twentieth U.S. Colored Infantry, to Editor, February 2, 1865, Camp Parapet, La., *A-A,* February 25, 1865, p. 2.

51. For an account of the Thirteenth Amendment, see Vorenberg, *Final Freedom.* Voting tallies for the House and Senate appear in Tables 1 and 2 in the Appendix, 249–50.
Vorenberg demonstrates broad support for emancipation (or at least the unwillingness of
most Northerners to oppose emancipation) in ch. 4, and portrays the passage of the amendment and the North's positive response on 185–208.

52. Pvt. Joel Molyneux, 141st Pa., diary, February 3, 1865, near Petersburg, Va., in
Kermit Molyneux Bird, ed., *Quill of the Wild Goose: Civil War Letters and Diaries of Pri-
vate Joel Molyneux, 141st P.V.* (Shippensburg, Pa.: Burd Street Press, 1996), 264. See also
Soldier's Letter, February 4, 1864, Fort Riley, Kans., p. 2, KSHS.

53. Pvt. John Foote, 117th N.Y., to sister, February 8, 1865, Federal Point, N.C., John
B. Foote Papers, DU. Foote reiterated this point at the close of the war, when he wrote of
his jubilation at the "joyful tidings" that peace once again reigned, "and not a disgraceful
compromising peace, but one which will make this a land of liberty and a home for the
oppressed of every race. Let us give thanks unto the Lord & sing praises unto his holy
name." See Foote to mother, April 14, 1865, Wilmington, N.C., John B. Foote Papers, DU.

54. Rufus, Twenty-fifth U.S. Colored Troops, to Editor, February 7, 1865, Chapin's
Farm, Va., *A-A,* March 11, 1865, p. 1.

55. Cpl. Chauncey Welton, 103d Ohio, to parents, February 18, 1865, Washington,
D.C., Chauncey B. Welton Letters, SHC.

56. Lt. Edward Bartlett, Fifth Mass. Cavalry, to sister, February 5, 1865, Pt. Lookout,
Md., Edward J. Bartlett Correspondence, MHS.

57. Pvt. Theodore Upson, One Hundredth Ind., diary, November 18, 1864, Indian
Springs, Ga., in Winther, *With Sherman to the Sea,* 136.

58. Lt. Charles Brewster, Tenth Mass., to mother, October 12, 1864, Norfolk, Va., in
Blight, *When This Cruel War Is Over,* 332–33.

59. Capt. Van Bennett, Twelfth Wis., diary, October 16, 1864, near Resaca, Ga., Van S.
Bennett Diary, SHSW.

60. *The 83rd Illinoisan,* April 14, 1865, Clarksville, Tenn., p. 2, TSLA. For analysis of
the tension between racial justice and northern whites' desires for quick reunion, see David
W. Blight, *Race and Reunion: The Civil War in American Memory* (Cambridge, Mass.:
Harvard University Press, 2001). Chs. 5 and 6 specifically address soldiers.

61. Pvt. John English, Ninety-second Veteran Reserve Corps, October 5, 1864, hospital, Evansville, Ind., John English Letters, EU.

62. Pvt. George Hudson, One Hundredth Ill., to folks at home, April 10, 1865, Blue
Springs, Tenn., George A. Hudson Collection, *PAW,* Coll. 138, Reel 54.

63. Pvt. (acts as Ass't Sgn.) Robert Winn, Third Ky. Cavalry, to sister, January 22,
1865, near Savannah, Ga., Winn-Cook Papers, FC. Emphasis in original.

64. Pvt. Wilbur Fisk, Second Vt., to *Green Mountain Freeman,* February 8, 1865, City
Point, Va., Rosenblatt and Rosenblatt, *Hard Marching Every Day,* 308–09.

65. Sgt. Horatio Barrington, Fourteenth Ill., to Editor, December 18, 1864, Savannah,
Ga., *Bloomington Pantagraph,* January 7, 1865, p. 1.

66. A. Sanford, white officer of the Fiftieth U.S. Colored Infantry, to Editor, April 6,
1865, before Fort Blakely, Ala., *Canton* (Ill.) *Register,* October 3, 1864, p. 1.

67. *Soldier's Letter,* June 17, 1865 and February 13, 1865, Fort Riley, Kans., KSHS.

68. Lt. Rufus Kinsley, Seventy-fourth U.S. Colored Troops, diary, March 6, 1865, and
May 10, 1865, Ship Island, Miss., Rufus Kinsely Diary, VTHS.

69. Sgt. William Bradbury, 129th Ill., to wife, January 2, 1865, Chattanooga, Tenn., William H. Bradbury Papers, *PAW,* Coll. 26, Reel 6.

70. Affidavit of Pvt. William Jones, 124th U.S. Colored Infantry, March 29, 1865, Camp Nelson, Ky., in Berlin, Reidy, and Rowland, *Black Military Experience,* 276.

71. Chaplain A. B. Randall, Fifty-fourth U.S. Colored Troops, to Brig. Gen. Lorenzo Thomas, February 28, 1865, Little Rock, Ark., in Berlin, Reidy, and Rowland, *Black Military Experience,* 712.

72. R.H.B., Third U.S. Colored Troops, to Editor, September 7, 1864, Jacksonville, Fla., *CR,* September 17, 1864, p. 1.

73. Pvt. Henry Hoyle, Forty-third U.S. Colored Troops, to Editor, February 18, 1865, near Richmond, *CR,* March 18, 1865, p. 1.

74. Sgt. George Massey, Forty-third U.S. Colored Troops, to Editor, March 14, 1865, near Richmond, *CR,* April 8, 1865, p. 1.

75. Resolutions of the Fifty-fifth Mass., October 10, 1864, Folly Island, S.C., in both the *A-A,* November 12, 1864, p. 1, and the *CR,* November 12, 1864, p. 1. The resolutions were probably sent to the newspapers by Sgt. John Shorter, who acted as one of the secretaries of the committee on resolutions.

76. Pvt. Zack Burden, Eighth U.S. Colored Troops, to "Mr. Abebrem Lenken the President of the U.S. stats," February 2, 1865, City Point, Va., in Berlin, Reidy, and Rowland, *Black Military Experience,* 647–48.

77. John Cajay, Eleventh U.S. Colored Artillery, to Editor, March 24, 1865, Ft. Jackson, La., *A-A,* April 22, 1865, p. 4.

78. Sgt. Maj., One Hundredth U.S. Colored Infantry, to Editor, March 22, 1865, along the railroad line in Tenn., *A-A,* April 22, 1865, p. 4. See also Moses Foskey, Eleventh U.S. Colored Artillery, to Editor, December 20, 1864, Fort Banks, La., *A-A,* January 14, 1865, p. 4.

79. Sgt. Maj. Twenty-ninth Conn., to Editor, February 5, 1865, before Richmond, *A-A,* February 18, 1865, p. 1. The society was named for Frederick Douglass, famed abolitionist, orator, and political advocate, and Henry Highland Garnet, a black abolitionist minister.

80. Members of the society often wrote to the *Anglo-African* about their meetings. See, for instance, Sgt. A. H. Newton and Sgt. J. D. Kellies, Twenty-ninth Conn., to Editor, December 21, 1864, Chapin's Farm, Va., *A-A,* January 7, 1865, pp. 1–2; Newton and Kellies to Editor, January 19, 1865, in field before Richmond, *A-A,* February 4, 1865, pp. 1–2; Sgt. Maj. Twenty-ninth Conn., to Editor, February 5, 1865, before Richmond, *A-A,* February 18, 1865, p. 1.

81. Sgt. Maj. Dudley Asbury, 101st U.S. Colored Infantry, February 10, 1865, Nashville, Tenn., *A-A,* March 4, 1865, p. 1.

82. "Proceedings of the National Convention of Colored Men, Held in the City of Syracuse, N.Y., Oct. 4–7, 1864," in Howard Holman Bell, *Minutes of the Proceedings of the National Negro Conventions 1830–1864* (New York: Arno, 1969), 41–43.

83. R.H.B., Third U.S. Colored Troops, to Editor, September 7, 1864, Jacksonville, Fla., *CR,* September 17, 1864, p. 1.

84. Moses Foskey, Eleventh U.S. Heavy Artillery, December 20, 1864, Fort Banks, La., *A-A,* January 14, 1865, p. 1.

85. Pvt. T. H. Sands Pennington, Twentieth U.S. Colored Infantry, to father, September 22, 1864, Camp Parapet, La., reprinted in *A-A,* October 22, 1864, p. 1.

86. Rufus, Twenty-fifth U.S. Colored Troops, to Editor, February 7, 1865, Chapin's Farm, Va., *A-A,* March 11, 1865, p. 1. Despite his disillusionment, Rufus was confident

that there was "a power at work which will brook no delay nor submit to no deviation from that path" that led to justice for African Americans; he simply believed that God would have to take a more forceful role in nudging the nation down that path than he had once hoped would be the case.

87. Sgt. James Trotter, Fifty-fifth Mass., to Edward Kinsley, November 21, 1864, Folly Island, S.C., Edward Kinsley Papers, DU.

88. James Lewis, former captain, First La. Native Guards, to James Ingraham, November 1, 1864, New York City, reprinted in *A-A*, November 12, 1864, p. 1.

89. Chaplain J. R. Bowles, Fifty-fifth Mass., January 4, 1865, Beaufort, S.C., *A-A*, January 21, 1865, pp. 1–2.

90. Sgt. John Brock, Forty-third U.S. Colored Troops, to Editor, March 9, 1865, near Richmond, *CR*, March 18, 1865, p. 1.

91. Pvt. Henry Hoyle, Forty-third U.S. Colored Troops, to Editor, February 18, 1865, Richmond, *CR*, March 18, 1865, p. 1.

92. John Scott, Kans. Battery (Col'd), to Editor, January 27, 1865, Fort Leavenworth, Kans., *A-A*, February 11, 1865, p. 2.

93. Charles Gilbert, Twenty-sixth U.S. Colored Troops, to Editor, April 13, 1865, Beaufort, S.C., *A-A*, May 6, 1865, p. 1. A member of the Twenty-seventh U.S. Colored Troops who signed his name as "Spartan" also noted the promotion of Delany; he remarked that white reaction to the promotion was mixed. See Spartan to Editor, April 2, 1865, Faison's Station, N.C., *A-A*, May 6, 1865, p. 1.

94. John Cajay, Eleventh U.S. Colored Artillery, to Editor, March 24, 1865, Fort Jackson, La., *A-A*, April 22, 1865, p. 4.

95. Moses Foskey, Eleventh U.S. Colored Artillery, to Editor, February 15, 1865, Fort Banks, La., *A-A*, March 11, 1865, p. 1.

96. John Cajay, Eleventh U.S. Colored Artillery, to Editor, March 24, 1865, *A-A*, April 22, 1865, p. 4.

97. Sgt. James Payne, Twenty-seventh U.S. Colored Troops, to Editor, n.d., no place, *CR*, September 17, 1864, p. 1.

98. Drummer R. M. Smith, Third U.S. Colored Troops, to Editor, September 18, 1864, Jacksonville, Fla., *CR*, October 8, 1864, p. 1.

99. John Cajay, Eleventh U.S. Colored Artillery, to Editor, March 24, 1865, Fort Jackson, La., *A-A*, April 22, 1865, p. 4.

100. Lt. Charles Kerrison, Second S.C., to uncle, September 19, 1864, near Culpeper, Va., Kerrison Family Papers, SCL.

101. Capt. S. Hubert Dent, Ala. Light Artillery, to wife, September 10, 1864, near Lovejoy's Station, Ga., in Ray Mathis, ed., *In the Land of the Living: Wartime Letters by Confederates From the Chattahoochee Valley of Alabama and Georgia* (Troy, Ala.: State University Press, 1981), 110.

102. Commissary Sgt. William Chunn, Fortieth Ga., to mother, September 11, 1864, near Jonesboro, Ga., William A. Chunn Letters, EU. Capt. S. Hubert Dent Ala. Light Artillery, also emphasized the impact of Atlanta on the 1864 election. See Dent to wife, September 10, 1864, near Lovejoy's Station, Ga., in Mathis, *In the Land of the Living,* 110.

103. For Confederate hopes that McClellan would win the Union presidential election, see Nelson, *Ballots, Bullets, and Rhetoric.*

104. Pvt. Grant Taylor, Fortieth Ala., to wife, November 18, 1864, Holly Wood, Ga., in Blomquist and Taylor, *This Cruel War,* 304.

105. Pvt. Abel Crawford, Sixty-first Ala., to wife, Dora, November 16, 1864, near New Market, Va., Abel Crawford Letters, TSLA.

106. Lt. E. L. Cox, Sixty-eighth N.C., diary, November 9, 1864, Fort Delaware Prison, E. L. Cox Diary, CMM Ser. A., Reel 13.

107. Capt. George Dewey, First N.C. Cavalry, to sister, March 15, 1865, Stony Creek, Va., George Stanley Dewey Correspondence, SHC.

108. Pvt. Cornelius Oliver, Twenty-fourth N.C., to wife, December 14, 1864, Petersburg, Va., Mrs. O. H. Winstead Collection, NCDAH.

109. Pvt. Spencer Barnes, Thirtieth N.C., to sister, January 1, 1865, near Petersburg, Va., Spencer Barnes Letters, MOC.

110. Pvt. Jim Griggs, Forty-second Va., to cousin, late 1864, Petersburg, Va., Griggs Family Papers, VHS. Griggs further pointed out that if the men in the elite army of the Confederacy, Lee's army, felt that way, things could only be worse everywhere else. "If the troops of the victorious 1st Corp are this demoralized what do you expect of the men who have known nothing but defeat for the last seven months?" he asked.

111. Pvt. Felix Prior, Fifth Ga. Militia, to wife, near Savannah, December 7, 1864, Felix Prior Letters, GDAH.

112. Pvt. Robert A. Jackson, Thirty-fifth Ga., to parents, December 21, 1864, near Petersburg, Va., Daniel Andrew Jackson Sr. Collection, GDAH.

113. Pvt. William Barry, Fourteenth Miss., to sister, September 29, 1864, near Palmetto Station, Ga., Barry Letters, MDAH.

114. The strongest case for continued high Confederate morale even in the waning days of the war is made by Gary Gallagher in *The Confederate War*. Gallagher includes a barrage of blustery, fight-to-the-last-ditch quotations, but overlooks the fact that most of them come from the earlier days of the war rather than the winter of 1864–65, as well as the possibility that the tone bespeaks more desperate bravado than real assurance. Mark Grimsley and Brooks Simpson adopt a less impassioned tone in *The Collapse of the Confederacy* (Lincoln: University of Nebraska Press, 2001), but even their moderate contention that Southerners regarded the situation of 1864–65 as no worse than that of 1862 (1–2) underestimates the gloom expressed by most soldiers. George Rable, "Despair, Hope, and Delusion: The Collapse of Confederate Morale Reexamined," in Grimsley and Simpson, *The Collapse of the Confederacy*, 120–67, rightly attributes lingering optimism to "wishful thinking" (138–39), but he credits that wishful thinking with elevating morale more than it did, and conflates soldier and civilian morale in the process. Of his eighty-two footnotes, all but eleven cite exclusively civilian sources (especially politicians and newspapers), and of the eleven that quote at least one (usually only one) soldier, only five express optimistic sentiments, and only one expresses a gritty determination to fight to the end no matter how dark the situation appears. In other words, historians have habitually exaggerated high morale among Confederate soldiers in the winter of 1864–65. Even allowing for the exaggeration, some troops, especially in the Army of Northern Virginia, remained determined.

115. Surgeon John Kinyoun, Sixty-sixth N.C., to wife, October 9, 1864, southeast of Richmond, John Kinyoun Papers, DU.

116. Cpl. Ethelbert Fairfax, ANV Signal Corps, to mother, September 3, 1864, near Petersburg, Va., Randolph and Ethelbert Fairfax Letters, MOC.

117. Pvt. David Ballenger, Hampton's Legion, to mother, December 12, 1864, Shenandoah Valley, Va., David Ballenger Papers, SCL.

118. Sgt. Archie Livingston, Third Fla., to sister, November 20, 1864, near Florence, Ala., Livingston Family Letters, MOC. Pvt. Jesse Hill also expressed angry impatience with the "big secessionists" who so prolonged the war. See Hill to wife, January 27, 1865, Petersburg, Va., Jesse Hill Letters, NCDAH. Pvt. David Ballenger, Hampton's Legion,

who complained about the moral failings of Confederate citizens, found their leaders just as reprehensible. "I have at last come to the conclusion that I have been fighting to place despots and tyrants over me and my posterity," he announced. See Ballenger, to mother, December 12, 1864, Shenandoah Valley, Va., David Ballenger Papers, SCL.

119. "K." to *Richmond Enquirer,* December 20, 1864, trenches before Richmond, Va., reprinted in *Atlanta Daily Constitutionalist,* January 14, 1865, p. 1.

120. Pvt. Cornelius Oliver, Twenty-fourth N.C., to wife, February 5, 1865, Petersburg, Va., Mrs. O. H. Winstead Collection, NCDAH. Oliver's outburst against "drunken politicians" came in the context of a letter in which he explained to his wife why deserting was an honorable rather than dishonorable course of action, and one that he himself considered taking. In a later letter, Oliver said he would never desert, and in the end he lost his opportunity to do so. He was wounded and captured the following month, and died in prison.

121. Pvt. Cornelius Oliver, Twenty-fourth N.C., to wife, February 17, 1865, near Southerland Depot, Va., Mrs. O. H. Winstead Collection, NCDAH.

122. Pvt. Henry Morgan, Thirty-first La., to wife, January 24, 1865, Alexandria, La., Henry Morgan Letters, CWMC; Pvt. Spencer Barnes, Thirtieth N.C., to sister, January 1, 1865, near Petersburg, Va., Spencer Barnes Letters, MOC.

123. Pvt. Robert Jackson, Thirty-fifth Ga., to parents, December 21, 1864, near Petersburg, Va., Daniel Andrew Jackson Sr. Collection, GDAH; Pvt. Grant Taylor, Fortieth Ala., to wife, November 18, 1864, Baldwin Co., Ga., in Blomquist and Taylor, *This Cruel War,* 304.

124. Pvt. Jesse Hill, Twenty-first N.C., to wife, January 6, 1865. See also Hill's letters of November 26, 1864, and December 4, 1864, near Petersburg, Va., Jesse Hill Letters, MOC. See also Pvt. James Bracy, Fortieth N.C., to mother, October 14, 1864, near Plymouth, N.C., Lyman Wilson Sheppard Collection, NCDAH.

125. Quoted in Beringer et al., *Elements of Confederate Defeat,* 153.

126. For more on Orr's resolutions (for peace) in the Confederate Congress and Union cabinet member Francis Blair's overtures leading to the meeting, see Wilfred B. Yearns, "The Peace Movement in the Confederate Congress," *Georgia Historical Quarterly* 41:1 (March 1957), 12–15; Charles W. Sanders, Jr., "Jefferson Davis and the Hampton Roads Peace Conference: 'To Secure Peace to the Two Countries,' " *Journal of Southern History* 63:4 (November 1997), 808–15; Edward Chase Kirkland, *The Peacemakers of 1864* (New York: Macmillan, 1927), 141–42, 196–205, 222–26; and Steven E. Woodworth, "The Last Function of Government: Confederate Collapse and Negotiated Peace," in Grimsley and Simpson, *The Collapse of the Confederacy,* 28–29. For discussion of the February 3 meeting, see Sanders, "Jefferson Davis and the Hampton Roads Peace Conference," 816–24; Woodworth, "The Last Function of Government," 32; and Kirkland, *The Peacemakers of 1864,* ch. 5.

127. Cpl. William Andrews, Tenth Va. Battalion, first heard rumors of the mission of Stephens, Hunter, and Campbell on January 29. He hesitated to get his hopes up too high lest this rumor prove as false as so many earlier ones, but still, he "hope[d] it may be so." See Andrews to father, January 29, 1865, Darbytown Road, Va., William B. G. Andrews Papers, DU.

128. Woodworth, "The Last Function of Government," 31–35; Kirkland, *The Peacemakers of 1864,* 242–53.

129. Pvt. Cornelius Oliver, Twenty-fourth N.C., to wife, February 10, 1865, Petersburg, Va., Mrs. O. H. Winstead Collection, NCDAH.

130. Pvt. Hiram Harding, Ninth Va. Cavalry, diary, February 11, 1865, Richmond, Va., Hiram Harding Diary, MOC.

131. Lt. Charles James, Eighth Va., to sister, February 7, 1865, near Richmond, Va., Charles Fenton James Letters, VHS.

132. Chaplain Robert Bunting, Eighth Tex. Cavalry, to *Houston Telegraph,* February 17, 1865, Auburn, Ala., Robert Franklin Bunting Papers, TSLA.

133. For the effect of Union occupation on slavery, see Berlin, Fields, Glymph, Reidy, and Rowland, *Destruction of Slavery,* which argues that the war and the actions of slaves in the Confederacy had irreparably damaged slavery even before the end of the fighting, and that slavery could not have survived no matter who won the war. While the war, slaves' actions, and Union occupation certainly weakened slavery, to argue that it was dead regardless of the conflict's outcome misses the resilience of the institution. In areas that went back and forth between Union and Confederate occupation, slavery returned whenever Confederates got back in control, and in areas that never experienced Union occupation, it got stronger. For the strengthening of slavery in the North Carolina mountains during the war, see John Inscoe, "Mountain Masters: Slaveholding in Western North Carolina," *North Carolina Historical Review* 61 (April 1984), 143–73; and John C. Inscoe and Gordon B. McKinney, *The Heart of Confederate Appalachia: Western North Carolina in the Civil War* (Chapel Hill: University of North Carolina Press, 2000), ch. 9.

The necessary element in slavery's demise, even as late as 1865, remained Union victory, as Confederate soldiers and civilians knew. When the war ended, Confederates everywhere expressed shock that slavery was dead, which they would not have done if the institution had already been moribund anyway. For example, five days after the Union occupation of Richmond, slaveholder Fannie Taylor Dickinson reported in astonishment that her slave, Millie, no longer behaved as a slave. "Last night on ringing the bell for Millie, she was nowhere to be found," Dickinson confided to her diary. One week later, Dickinson was even more surprised when all the family's slaves left. In disbelief, she wrote, "our servants have all left. . . . This is indeed the unkindest cut of all. I cannot write about it." To the very end, she could not imagine that slavery would cease to exist. See Fannie E. Taylor Dickinson Diary, April 8 and April 17, 1865, Virginia Historical Society, quoted in Nelson Lankford, *Richmond Burning: The Last Days of the Confederate Capital* (New York: Viking, 2002), 235–36.

134. Pvt. David Thompson, Twenty-seventh N.C., to mother, January 9, 1865, near Petersburg, Va., Samuel Thompson Papers, SHC.

135. Robert Durden, *The Gray and the Black: The Confederate Debate on Emancipation* (Baton Rouge: Louisiana State University Press, 1972), 202–203, 268–69; Bruce Levine, *Confederate Emancipation: Southern Plans to Free and Arm Slaves During the Civil War* (New York: Oxford University Press, 2006), 119–20; Nelson, *Bullets, Ballot, and Rhetoric,* 167–78.

136. For three decades, Durden's *The Gray and the Black* remained the leading and generally unquestioned account of the Confederacy's black enlistment debate. Durden focuses mainly on the issue at official levels rather than on what soldiers thought about it, and contends that the question of black enlistment really amounted to a southern debate about emancipation, in which the Confederacy, led by Jefferson Davis, approached voluntary emancipation. When Durden does address soldiers' attitudes toward black enlistment, he draws almost exclusively on the resolutions in the *Official Records* to argue that enlisted men approved of the measure, especially nonslaveholding enlisted men who saw the move as a way to force the wealthy to make sacrifices, which many ordinary white Southerners felt they did too much of while the wealthy did too little. In *April 1865: The Month that Saved America* (New York: HarperCollins, 2001), Jay Winik uncritically repeats Durden's interpretation without particular attention to evidence.

A recent reexamination of the subject, Philip D. Dillard's dissertation, "Independence or Slavery: Confederate Debate over Arming the Slaves" (Ph.D. diss., Rice University, 1999), looks at newspapers in Virginia, Georgia, and Texas to conclude that "the vast majority of Virginians, Georgians, and even some Texans discovered that slavery could be sacrificed much more easily than southern independence," and therefore reluctantly came to support black enlistment in 1865 (11). While Dillard usefully notes three distinct stages in the debate over black enlistment, the conclusive one being the aftermath of the failed Hampton Roads conference, he misses some of the question's subtleties, for example, the distinction between actually freeing slaves and the loophole in General Orders No. 14, and the belief of many of the bill's supporters that, far from sacrificing slavery, black enlistment, if done correctly, could either help retain slavery, or at the very least, save white control-by-force over black labor as well as white supremacy, even if the legal institution was discarded. Further, Dillard's source base is very narrow. His conclusions come so exclusively from newspapers (he cites only two published soldiers' diaries and two memoirs of soldiers, and no manuscript sources) that they cannot be taken as indications of soldier opinion, especially in a war where soldiers' experiences and views diverged so widely from those of civilians, and in which soldiers complained about newspapers' misrepresentations. The narrowness of his source base might explain how he could miss, or at least underestimate, hostility and opposition to the measure.

J. Tracy Power touches briefly on the black enlistment debate in the Army of Northern Virginia in *Lee's Miserables,* noting that soldiers were "divided" on the issue. While he accurately attributes the support of those willing to tolerate the measure to their desire to exploit all available manpower rather than any "positive sentiments toward the prospect of black Confederates," he underestimates the heat and significance of the opposition to the measure in the ranks (250–55; quotation from 253).

The fullest and most recent treatment of this topic is Bruce Levine's *Confederate Emancipation.* Drawing on more thorough evidence than previous accounts, Levine conclusively shows that arming some black slaves to stave off imminent defeat, which the Confederacy ultimately accepted, and emancipation, which it avoided, were two very separate things. With a focus encompassing Congress, Davis, political leaders, military leaders, and civilians from all social classes, Levine shows that black enlistment did *not* mark willingness to give up slavery for independence, nor did it signal a softening of white racism. Instead, it was a desperate last measure brought about by military disasters and the actions of slaves who forced Confederates to consider the previously unthinkable, but who also rejected enlistment because their own interests were served by Union victory. Through black enlistment, Levine argues, white supporters hoped to retain as many aspects of slavery as possible, including control over black labor and white supremacy. Levine does not aim to examine exhaustively enlisted soldiers' views on the subject of black enlistment. Left with a short space to consider the topic (113–17), he concludes that until the spring of 1865, soldiers opposed black enlistment, and many continued to oppose the proposition to the bitter end, but that in the final months of the war the Army experienced a "shift in its center of gravity" in which small majorities, but majorities nonetheless, were willing to countenance black enlistment, though he is less clear about emancipation (115). The analysis offered here will differ, largely due to the use of different sources: Levine quotes overwhelmingly from officers and slaveholding soldiers rather than enlisted troops (mainly nonslaveholders), who are the main focus here. He also accepts uncritically the results of regimental votes that enlisted men's private writings suggest need to be considered with more circumspection.

137. For General Cleburne's proposal and official response (including Davis's order

that discussion of it cease, and denial of promotion to Cleburne), see Beringer et al., *The Elements of Confederate Defeat,* 168–69; Dillard, "Independence or Slavery," 17–20; Durden, *The Gray and the Black,* 53–67; Escott, *After Secession,* 242; Levine, *Confederate Emancipation,* 27–29; McPherson, *Battle Cry of Freedom,* 832–33; Thomas, *Confederate Nation,* 261–64.

138. Sgt. Edward Brown, Forty-fifth Ala., to wife, January 3, 1864, Tunnel Hill, Ga., Edward Norphlet Brown Letters, ADAH.

139. Sgt. Edward Brown, Forty-fifth Ala., to wife, January 12, 1864, Tunnel Hill, Ga., Edward Norphlet Brown Letters, ADAH.

140. Governor Henry Allen to Secretary of War James Seddon, September 26, 1864, quoted in Durden, *The Gray and the Black,* 74. See also Dillard, "Independence or Slavery," 22–23; Levine, *Confederate Emancipation,* 31–32.

141. On the contributions of slaves and freed blacks to the Army of Northern Virginia, see James H. Brewer, *The Confederate Negro: Virginia's Craftsmen and Military Laborers, 1861–1865* (Durham: Duke University Press, 1969).

142. For discussion of public opinion on black enlistment in the fall of 1864, see Dillard, "Independence or Slavery," 12–43, 89–113, 117–202; Levine, *Confederate Emancipation,* 110–11.

143. Sgt. Marion Hill Fitzpatrick, Forty-fifth Ga., to wife, November 3, 1864, near Petersburg, Va., in Lowe and Hodges, *Letters to Amanda,* 182.

144. Cpl. Charles Baughman, Thirteenth Battalion Va. Light Artillery, to father, October 23, 1864, near Petersburg, Va., Charles Baughman Letters, MOC.

145. Pvt. Peter Cross, Seventh N.C., to wife, November 4, 1864, somewhere in Va., John Wright Family Papers, NCDAH.

146. For further discussion of the impact of the Hampton Roads conference, see Dillard, "Independence or Slavery," 71–88, 147–75, 236–68; Levine, *Confederate Emancipation,* 111–12. Dillard and Robert Durden hold that Lee's endorsement of black enlistment led to a shift in opinion among leaders, civilians, and soldiers. Michael Fellman, in *The Making of Robert E. Lee,* counters that even despite Lee's support, most soldiers remained hostile to the measure (213–15).

147. Gen. Robert E. Lee to Ethelbert Barksdale, February 18, 1854, in Durden, *The Gray and the Black,* 206. The *Examiner*'s doubts appeared on February 16. See Durden, *The Gray and the Black,* 199.

148. Lt. William Andrews, Tenth Va. Battalion, to father, February 21, 1865, Chaffin's Farm, Va., William B.G. Andrews Papers, DU. Levine notes Lee's influence in changing some soldiers' minds; see *Confederate Emancipation,* 115.

149. Camp Davis's Brigade, February 14, 1865, near Petersburg, VA, *Richmond Sentinel,* February 21, 1865, reprinted in Durden, *The Gray and the Black,* 219.

150. "Resolutions of Thomas's Brigade," *Richmond Examiner,* February 18, 1865, in Durden, *The Gray and the Black,* 218.

151. See esp. Durden, *The Gray and the Black;* Winik, *April 1865.*

152. See, for example, "Resolutions of the Fredericksburg Artillery," January 18, 1865, *Richmond Examiner,* January 22, 1865; "Resolutions of the 57th Virginia Infantry," January 26, 1865, *Richmond Examiner,* January 30, 1865; "Resolutions of the 36th and 60th Va., 45th Va. Battalion," "Resolutions of the 54th North Carolina," "Resolutions of the 17th South Carolina," *Richmond Examiner,* February 18, 1865. Resolutions like these dwelled on the danger of "our ruin as a people" if Southerners were to surrender to the Yankees, who intended to "consign us and our children to bondage and slavery which would be insupportably base and degrading"; they mention nothing about black soldiers.

153. See numerous soldiers' letters to newspapers in January and February 1865, such as one of mid-January 1865 from "Soldier," *Richmond Examiner,* January 18, 1865. J. Tracy Power notes the significance that Army of Northern Virginia soldiers attached to regimental consolidation in *Lee's Miserables,* ch. 8, esp. 239–40.

154. "Resolutions from the Army," January 1, 1865, Jordan's Battery (ANV), *Richmond Examiner,* January 1, 1865; "B." in "camp" to Editor, February 14, 1865, *Richmond Examiner,* February 24, 1865.

155. South Carolina Soldiers to Editor, *Charleston Mercury,* January 13, 1865.

156. Pvt. J. C. Wright, Fortieth N.C., to sister, February 19, 1865, Petersburg, Va., Corpening Family Papers, DU.

157. "Your's &c," Wise's Brigade, to Editor, February 8, 1865, Petersburg, Va., *Richmond Examiner,* February 11, 1865.

158. Pvt. Daniel Abernethy, Eleventh N.C., to parents, February 16, 1865, Petersburg, Va., Daniel Abernethy Papers, DU.

159. Pvt. Joseph Maides, Twenty-seventh N.C., to mother, February 18, 1865, Petersburg, Va., Joseph Maides Papers, DU.

160. La. soldier to friend, February 4, 1865, Keachie, La., "The Color of Gray: African Americans in Confederate Service," MOC.

161. Pvt. J. C. Wright, Forty-sixth N.C., to mother, February 15, 1865, Petersburg, Va., John Henry Murphy Papers, SHC.

162. Sgt. Edward Brown, Forty-fifth Ala., to wife, March 16, 1865, Hamburg, S.C., Edward Norphlet Brown Letters, ADAH.

163. "A Private Soldier" from Ga., to Editor, January 16, 1865, Warrenton, Ga., *Augusta Daily Constitutionalist,* January 26, 1865, p. 2.

164. Chaplain Robert Bunting, Eighth Tex. Cavalry, to *Houston Telegraph,* February 17, 1865, Auburn, Ala., Robert Franklin Bunting Papers, TSLA.

165. Pvt. Grant Taylor, Fortieth Ala., to wife, January 11, 1865, Spanish Fort, Ala., in Blomquist and Taylor, *This Cruel War,* 322–23.

166. Levine makes a similar point, arguing that the late and desperate date of the Confederacy's adoption of black enlistment, despite much earlier indications that such a measure offered the only hope of avoiding defeat, shows exactly how central slavery and white supremacy were to the Confederate cause. See *Confederate Emancipation,* 15, 148, 156–59.

167. Lt. J. G. Sills, Sixty-sixth N.C., to brother, April 3, 1865, near Smithfield, N.C., Roy Vernon Howell Papers, NCDAH.

168. For Confederate desertion in the final weeks of the war, see William Marvel, *Lee's Last Retreat: The Flight to Appomattox* (Chapel Hill: University of North Carolina Press, 2002), 5–6; Weitz, *More Damning Than Slaughter,* 281.

Conclusion: What This Cruel War Was Over

1. Pvt. Charles Beman, Fifth Mass. Cavalry, to father, April 5, 1865, Richmond, reprinted in *A-A,* April 22, 1865, p. 1. Lt. Edward Bartlett, Fifth Mass. Cavalry, also told of the regiment's arrival as one of the first Union regiments to enter the Confederate capital. See Bartlett to sister, April 3, 1865, Richmond, Edward J. Bartlett Correspondence, MHS.

2. Sgt. Major Griffin, Twenty-ninth Conn., to Editor, April 12, 1865, Richmond, *A-A,* April 29, 1865, p. 1.

3. Pvt. Charles Beman, Fifth Mass. Cavalry, to father, April 5, 1865, Richmond, in *A-A,* April 22, 1865, p. 1.

4. On April 18, Gen. Joseph Johnston and Gen. William T. Sherman reached terms; Jefferson Davis was captured on May 10; and the last on-land fight sputtered out at Palmito Ranch, Texas, on May 12. Because the terms offered by Sherman to Johnston were deemed too lenient, President Andrew Johnson and the cabinet revoked them and sent Grant to negotiate new terms. Johnston's official surrender according to these terms took place April 26. After Palmito Ranch, a few Confederate raiders were still afloat on the high seas, but they did not engage Union ships in any major sea battles. A small amount of guerrilla activity broke out in Missouri, whose residents had gotten into the habit in the 1850s, but it never amounted to enough to constitute a serious threat to the peace between the United States and the erstwhile Confederate States of America.

5. Pvt. John Franklin Smith, a Tex. regiment (probably Twelfth Tex. or Nineteenth Tex.), to cousin, May 19, 1865, Galveston, Tex., John Franklin Smith Letters, CAH.

6. Cpl. Lewis Bissell, Second Conn. Heavy Artillery, to family, April 9, 1865, Appomattox Court House, Va., in Olcott and Lear, *The Civil War Letters of Lewis Bissell,* 374. See also Thomas Low's report of "the wild joy of the hour." Capt. Thomas Low, Eighth N.Y. Heavy Artillery, to brother, April 12, 1865, City Point, Va., Thomas Low Papers, DU.

7. See, for instance, Capt. Peter Eltinge, 156th N.Y., to father, April 20, 1865, Goldsboro, N.C., Eltinge-Lord Family Papers, DU; Pvt. Justus Silliman, Seventeenth Conn., to brother, April 24, 1864, Jacksonville, Fla., in Marcus, *A New Canaan Private in the Civil War,* 100.

8. Sgt. Nathan Parmater, Twenty-ninth Ohio, April 17, 1865, Raleigh, N.C., Nathan Parmater Papers, OHS.

9. Richard H. Black, Third U.S. Colored Troops, to Editor, May 1865, Fernandina, Fla., *A-A,* May 27, 1865, p. 2.

10. Sgt. Charles Harris, 157th N.Y., to parents, April 1865, near Statesburg, S.C., Charles J. Harris Letters, DU.

11. *The 83rd Illinoisan,* 1:6 (April 21, 1865), Clarksville, Tenn., p. 2, TSLA.

12. Jack Halliards, U.S. Gunboat *Kennebec,* to Editor, off Galveston, Tex., May 1, 1865, *A-A,* May 27, 1865, p. 1.

13. Sgt. William Ellis, Washington Artillery, diary, April 18, 1865, near Abbeville, S.C., William H. Ellis Family Papers, CMM Ser. B, Reel 5; Lt. E. L. Cox, Sixty-eighth N.C., diary, April 16, 1865, Fort Delaware Prison, E. L. Cox Diary, CMM Ser. A, Reel 13.

14. For more on southern reaction to the assassination, see Thomas Reed Turner, *Beware the People Weeping: Public Opinion and the Assassination of Abraham Lincoln* (Baton Rouge: Louisiana State University Press, 1982), ch. 7.

15. Pvt. Rudolf Coreth, Thirty-sixth Tex. Cavalry, to family, April 28, 1865, near Richmond, in Goyne, *Lone Star and Double Eagle,* 169.

16. Pvt. William Pitt Chambers, Forty-sixth Miss., diary, May 16, 1865, Fertile Glade, Miss., in Baumgartner, *Blood and Sacrifice,* 225.

17. Capt. Henry Richardson, Confederate Corps of Engineers, to parents, June 21, 1865, Tensas Parish, La., Henry Brown Richardson Papers, CMM Ser. B, Reel 17. See also Ga. soldier John Speer to mother, April 2, 1865, Natchitoches, La., Soldiers' Letter Collection, Louisiana File, MOC; Lt. James Green, Fifty-third N.C., diary, May 4, 1865, home in N.C., James E. Green Diary, SHC; Lt. Hannibal Paine, Twenty-sixth Tenn., to sister, May 21, 1865, Fort Delaware Prison, Hannibal Paine Letters, TSLA.

18. See Cpl. Theodore Livingston, Third Fla., to brother, May 22, 1865, home in

Madison Court House, Fla., Livingston Family Letters, MOC; Lt. George Dillon, Eighteenth Tenn., May 26, 1865, Talladega, Ala., George Dillon Letters, TSLA.

19. Captain Samuel Foster, Granbury's Texas Brigade, diary, 1865, quoted in Mitchell, *Civil War Soldiers,* 205.

20. See, among others, Pvt. David Thompson, Twenty-seventh N.C., to mother, January 9, 1865, near Petersburg, Va., Samuel Thompson Papers, SHC; "Poor [Georgia] soldier" to Editor, January 21, 1865, near Augusta, Ga., *Augusta Daily Constitutionalist,* January 26, 1865, p. 2; Lt. Charles James, Eighth Va., February 7, 1865, Richmond, Charles Fenton James Letters, VHS. Chaplain Robert Bunting, Eighth Tex. Cavalry, wrote repeatedly about the federal government's alleged intentions of redistributing land, disenfranchising whites and enfranchising blacks, and otherwise elevating blacks at the expense of southern whites. See also Blight, *Race and Reunion;* Faust, *Mothers of Invention;* Mitchell, *Civil War Soldiers,* 204–06; Wells, *The Origins of the Southern Middle Class,* 231–33.

21. *The Third Brigade,* 1:1, May 19, 1865, Danville, Va., p. 2, LOV. *The Third Brigade* was the paper of the 122d N.Y. See also *Soldier's Letter,* February 13, 1865, Fort Riley, Kans., p. 3, KSHS.

22. Pvt. G. Haven Putnam, 176th N.Y., to Mary Loines, May 29, 1865, Savannah, Ga., Papers of the Low-Mills Family, LC. For just a few of many enthusiastic letters about black education, see Sgt. William Bradbury, 129th Ill., to wife, January 2, 1865, Chattanooga, Tenn., William H. Bradbury Papers, *PAW,* Coll. 26, Reel 6; Pvt. Justus Silliman, Seventeenth Conn., to mother, October 18, 1864, Jacksonville, Fla., and to cousin, January 13, 1865, Jacksonville, Fla., in Marcus, *A New Canaan Private in the Civil War,* 80 and 91.

23. David Williamson, Eleventh U.S. Heavy Artillery, to Editor, March 1865, Fort Banks, La., *A-A,* April 8, 1865, p. 2.

24. The postwar backsliding did not happen right away. In the 1860s and 1870s, black Americans voted, enjoyed economic advances, and held political office. By 1870, both the Fourteenth Amendment (guaranteeing citizenship rights to African Americans) and the Fifteenth Amendment (guaranteeing the right to vote to black men) had passed. In 1875 Congress passed the Civil Rights Act. But the tide turned in the 1880s. In 1883 the Supreme Court struck down the Civil Rights Act, and a series of decisions progressively weakened the Fourteenth and Fifteenth Amendments. In the 1890s, segregation became the law in many southern states. As Frederick Douglass bleakly noted, white racism and its manifestations rose in direct relation to "increasing distance from the time of the war." In other words, the further away in time Americans moved from the war, the more willing whites proved to forget and abandon racial equality. See Frederick Douglass, *The Life and Times of Frederick Douglass, Written by Himself: His Early Life as a Slave, His Escape from Bondage, and His Complete History* (1892), quoted in Blight, "For Something Beyond the Battlefield," 1159. For the end of Reconstruction, the fading of its gains, and the onset of segregation, see William Gillette, *Retreat from Reconstruction, 1869–1879* (Baton Rouge: Louisiana State University Press, 1979); Heather Richardson, *The Death of Reconstruction: Race, Labor, and Politics in the post–Civil War North 1865–1901* (Cambridge, Mass.: Harvard University Press, 2001); C. Vann Woodward, *The Strange Career of Jim Crow,* commemorative edition (New York: Oxford University Press, 2002).

PRIMARY SOURCES

Secondary sources may be found in Notes.

Manuscripts, Soldiers' Letters, and Diaries

Alabama

Alabama Department of Archives and History
Alpheus Baker Diary
Branscomb Family Letters
Edward Norphlet Brown Letters
Newton N. Davis Letters
Henry J. Hunt Letter
William Lowery Diaries
Mark Lyons Letters
W. E. Riser Letter
C. A. Ryder Diary
James T. Searcy Letters
Reuben Martin Searcy Letters
Thomas S. Taylor Letters
E. W. Treadwell Letters
Turner Vaughan Diary
Thomas Warrick Letters
Robert A. Williams Civil War Letters
Henry Wilson Letters
H. B. Wood Letter

Hoole Library, University of Alabama, Tuscaloosa
Allen Family Papers
Cameron Collection
Ross-Searcy-Snow Papers

Arkansas

University of Arkansas Special Collections
Jonathan W. Callaway Civil War Letters and Papers
Milton Chambers Correspondence
James M. Harrison Letters
Thomas Jefferson Jobe Diary
Elihu G. Martin Letter
Robert and Sephronia Clark McCollom Papers

Minos Miller Papers
Thomas R. Stone Diary
SELECTED ARKANSAS MANUSCRIPTS FROM THE CHICAGO HISTORICAL SOCIETY COLLECTION (MICROFILMED AND HELD AT UNIVERSITY OF ARKANSAS SPECIAL COLLECTIONS)
 Mason Brayman Papers
 J. W. Gambill Letters
 E. C. Hubbard Papers
 J. B. Hubbard Letters
 James I. Lawrence Letters
 Robert Mitchell Diary

Connecticut

Connecticut Historical Society
Orra B. Bailey Letters
Milton Humphrey Bassett Papers
Caleb Blanchard Letters
Andrew Byrne Diary
Charles Henry Camp Letters
Leander Chapin Letters
George Clary Papers
Charles S. Crain Letters
Joseph Orin Cross Letters
John Best Cuzner Papers
Charles Greenleaf Letters
John Holwell Letters
Leroy D. House Letters
Robert McNaughton Diary
Augustine Sackett Letters
Homer S. Sackett Letters
Henry D. Sexton, Isaac H. Tuller, and Martin L. Wadhams Papers
Francis Simpson Papers
Henry Snow Letters
George Wetmore Letters

Georgia

Atlanta History Center
James P. Crane Letters
John Dunlap Letters
Colin Dunlop Letters
Hosea Garrett Letters
A. T. Holliday Letters
John Matthew McCrary Letters
Leander Parker Letters
Roderick Gaspero Shaw Letters
Samuel J. Spencer Letters
Jim L. Wilson Letters

Chickamauga National Military Park Vertical Files
Thaddeus Marion Brindley Letters, Twenty-second Alabama File
John Forbes Davenport Letters, First Alabama Battalion, Hilliards Legion File
Richard B. Ledbetter Letters, Fortieth Alabama Infantry File
Francis Livingston Wadsworth Letters, Hilliards Alabama Legion File

Emory University
John D. Babb Family Papers
William Baugh Letters
Thomas Stuart Birch Papers
Henry S. Campbell Family Letters
Thomas M. Carter Papers
William A. Chunn Letters
CONFEDERATE MISCELLANY
　James Atkins Papers
　Thomas Carson Letter
　Thomas R. R. Cobb: Petition
　J. C. Daniel Poem
　Isaac Domingos Letter
　J. R. Garber Letters
　Lewis Groce Papers
　Joseph Hilton Letters
　Dickerson Holliday Letters
　G. H. Keahey and Niel Godwine Letters
　John and W. F. Price Letters
Henry Crydenwise Letters
Andrew J. Edge Correspondence
John A. Everett Papers
James Garrison Letters

John A. Harris Letters
Honnoll Family Papers
William McFall Letters
Peter Oswald Letters
William Parkinson Papers
Reid-Jordan Family Papers
Oliver Strickland Letters
Charles Brown Thurston Papers
UNION MISCELLANY
　Daniel Ammell Letter
　John English Papers
　Henry W. Hart Letters
　Gideon Merritt Letter
　George W. Pennington Papers
　Elias Prichard Papers

Georgia Department of Archives and History
Noble John Brooks Letters and Diary
Addison M. Burnside Letters
Thomas and Warren Campbell Confederate Letters
William Smith Carson Collection
CIVIL WAR MISCELLANY, PERSONAL PAPERS
　Stand Watie Papers
　Wilkinson Family Papers
Jeremiah Jefferson Davis Letters
William P. Davis Diary
Ivy Duggan Letters
Berrien W. Durden Family Papers
Thomas Forrester Letters
Malachi Henry Foy Collection
Jasper A. Gillespie Family Papers
Hagan/Roberts Family Papers
Roderick Henry Harper Civil War Letters
Daniel Andrew Jackson Sr. Collection
William H. Johnson Letters
Megarity Family Papers
Jasper Norris Letters
Thomas Omary Letters
Josiah Blair Patterson Letters
Andrew Perkins Letter
Photostat File: Civil War Collection A–M and N–Z
Prescott/Jones Family Papers
Felix W. Prior Letters
James Snell Diary
United Daughters of the Confederacy: LaGrange Chapter: Miscellaneous Letters and Diaries

Wright Vinson Letters
John Wilson Civil War Letter

Illinois

Chicago Historical Society
Sullivan Ballou Letter
M. A. Barber Letters
Henry Brimhall Letter
Raleigh Edward Colston Folder
Judson Crary Letter
J. H. Dennard Letters
Jacob T. Esher Letters
Michael Gapen Letters
Gustav Haller Papers
Frederick H. Harris Letters
Charles Jarvis Letter
Delazon Ketchum Letters
George W. Little Diary
John J. Lynch Letters
Hugh McGrath Letters
William McMullen Letters
James A. Mulligan Papers
D. Myers Letters
John A. Nurse Papers
Cyrus Randall Letters
William H. Ross Letters
Frederick W. Russell Papers
Joseph F. Ward Papers
James Westervelt Papers
John Winterbotham Papers

Illinois State Historical Library
Andrews Family Papers
John Andrews Letters
Adin Ballou Letters
Henry Bandy Letters
Alphonso Barto Letters
Newton Bateman Papers
Sylvester Beckwith Letters
Ransom Bedell Papers
Thomas B. Bourne Letters
Carpenter Bull Papers
Samuel L. and George D. Carpenter
    Papers
Civil War Letters 1863–64 Written by
    Indiana Soldiers
Landsden Cox Letters
John Gayle Davis Letters
Charles Deamude Letters

John C. Dinsmore Letters
James F. Drish Papers
Engleman-Kircher Papers
Everson Letters
John A. Griffin Papers
John L. Harris Papers
William Hinshaw Letter
Amos Hostetter Letters
Edward Howe Letter
August Kautz Papers
King Family Papers
Tilmon D. Kyger Letters
Christian E. Lanstrum Papers
Henry Newhall Letters
Anson Patterson Papers
W. H. Price Letters
I. V. Reynolds Letter
Edwin Sackett Diary and Letters
M. W. Shanahan Letter
James B. Turner Papers
Augustine Vieira Letters
Robert M. Woods Letter

Kansas

Kansas State Historical Society
Aaron Beck Diary
C. S. Bolton Diary
David R. Braden Diaries
Charles Dennison Brandon Diary
George Brinsmaid Papers
John S. Brown Family Papers, Reels 2
    and 3.
John M. Brunt Papers
T. H. Connell Letters
Warren and Mary A. Day Letters
George E. Flanders Letters
George Fleischer (Collector) Civil War
    Letters
James H. Guthrie Diary
Daniel B. Holmes Papers
Webster Moses Letters and Diaries
Margaret Price Papers
William B. and Lewis Sherman
    Collection
William Smith Diary
Joseph Trego Collection
Samuel Worthington Papers

Kansas Collection, Spencer Research Library, University of Kansas

John C. Belleville Papers
James Denver Papers
Henry C. Fike Correspondence
Isaiah Morris Harris Journal and
 Correspondence
William P. Harrison Letters
Isely Family Correspondence and
 Documents
James W. Jessee Diaries
Charles Oren Letters

Louisiana

Confederate Military Manuscripts, Series B: Holdings of Louisiana State University, Baton Rouge

Israel Adams and Family Papers
William M. Allen Correspondence
Michel Thomassin Andry and Family
 Papers
Henry Baines Papers
Albert A. Batchelor Papers
John W. Bell Papers
George M. Dixon Papers
William Y. Dixon Papers
James and John Durnin Papers
E. P. Ellis and Family Papers
William H. Ellis Family Papers
James Foster and Family Correspondence
G. W. Giles Letters
Arthur W. Hyatt Papers
William H. Ker Letters
Josiah Knighton Family Papers
Lemanda E. Lea Papers
Edwin Leets Letters
Thomas Railey Markham Papers
Robert H. Miller Letters
John A. Morgan Papers
Robert A. Newell Papers
William Nicholson Letters
Frank P. Peak Narrative
Prudhomme Family Papers
W. G. Raoul Letters
Major John Reid Papers
W. P. and Joseph Renwick Papers
Henry Brown Richardson Family
 Papers

John N. Shealy Letters
John F. Stephens Correspondence
Frederick R. Taber Papers
William Tamplin Letters
William Terry and Family Papers
George Tichenor Diary

Williams Research Center

Black Soldiers Collection

Massachusetts

Boston Atheneum

Cutter, Orlando Phelps. *Our Battery; or, The journal of Company B, 1st O.V.A.* Cleveland: Nevins Book and Job Printing, 1864.
Foxcroft, G. A. *A Trackt for the Soldiers.* Walpole, Mass.: May 1, 1863.
Cornelius Johnson Letter
Kirwan, Thomas. *Soldiering in North Carolina; being the experiences of a 'typo' in the pines, swamps, fields, sandy roads, towns, cities, and among the fleas, wood-ticks, 'gray-backs,' mosquitoes, blue-tail flies, moccasin snakes, lizards, scorpions, rebels, and other reptiles, pests, and vermin of the 'Old North State.' Embracing an account of the three-years and nine-months Massachusetts regiments in the department, the freedmen, etc, etc., etc., By "one of the Seventeenth."* Boston: Thomas Kirwan, 1864.
L. N. Peters Letter
"Petition to Abraham Lincoln for exchange of officers held as prisoners of war in Texas, 1864"

Massachusetts Historical Society

Edward J. Bartlett Correspondence
George H. Baxter Letters
Caleb Hadley Beal Papers
Edwin Bearse Correspondence
Lorin Low Dame Papers
Edward L. Edes Correspondence
Stephen G. Emerson Correspondence
Thomas S. Howland Papers
Oliver Ricker Diary
Samuel Storrow Papers

J. Chapin Warner Papers
Henry F. Wellington Papers

Michigan

*Schoff Collection, Clements Library,
University of Michigan*
Numa Barned Papers
Hacker Brothers Papers
Charles Henthorn Letters
Levi Hines Papers
Cornelius Hulsapple Papers
Henry Johnson Letters
Christopher Keller Papers
Henry Grimes Marshall Papers
Charles M. Maxim Letters
Miller Brothers Letters
Hugh P. and George Roden Papers
Henry H. Seys Letters
William Henry Shaw Letters
C. Frank Shepard Papers
Ezra Stearns Papers

Minnesota

Minnesota Historical Society
George R. Adams Papers
Joseph Allen Letters
Peter Daniel Anderson Letters
Lyman Warren Ayer Papers
John Reed Beatty Papers
Brookins Family Letters
Pehr Carlson Papers
William Z. Clayton Papers
Loren Collins Papers
Elijah Evans Edwards Civil War Journals
FIRST MINNESOTA INFANTRY LETTERS
  Capt. Napoleon Jackson Tecumseh Dana
    Letters
  Edward L. Davis Letters
  Edward A. Walker Letters
Lucius F. Hubbard and Family Papers
John B. Leo Letters
Adam Marty Correspondence
Hans Mattson and Family Papers
William McGrorty and Family Papers
John Nelson Papers
Axel Hayford Reed Diaries
Jesse A. and Luman P. Washburn Papers

Mississippi

*Mississippi Department of Archives and
History*
Barry Letters
J. A. Bigger Manuscript
CIVIL WAR PAPERS (MISCELLANEOUS)
1861–65
  R. W. Banks Letters
  G. W. Bynum Letters
  W. D. Cobb Letters
  Sgt. A. Fishe Cove Letters
  B. H. Develin Letters
  Thomas Hemphill Letters
  Conrad Anderson Lusk Letters
  Arch McLaurin Letters
  Samuel E. Rankin Letters
  W. H. Simrall Letters
  Thomas Trotter Weathersby Letters
William L. Davis Letters
A. G. Fraser Papers
George L. Hiatt Diary
T. J. Koger Collection
T. McNamara Diary
McWillie-Compton Papers
John C. Rietti Papers
W. A. Rorer Letter
J. B. Sanders Papers
J. F. Sessions Papers
John A. Wilson Letters

Missouri

*Jackson County Historical Society,
Independence, Mo.*
Isaac Adair Papers
James H. Booth Letter
Tina May Doud Collection
Holloway Letters
James H. Hougland Civil War Diary
Iserman Letters
C. C. Robottom Papers
Sandford Family Papers
Mary Overton Gentry Shaw Family Papers
H. C. Van Smith Collection
Margaret Woodson Collection

*Special Collections, Kansas City Public
Library*
Cyrus F. Boyd Collection

Dixon and Jordan Family Papers and
Letters
Guitar-Leonard Family Papers
Myers Family Collection

*Missouri Historical Society, St. Louis,
Mo.*
John Conway Family Papers
CIVIL WAR COLLECTION
John T. Appler Diary
Bell Family Diaries
Joseph A. Fardell Papers
Edward Hartley Papers
Samuel M. Kennard Letters
William H. H. Kesterson Letters
David T. Massey Letters
David Monlux Letters
William Renken Letters
Henry Voelkner Letters
Thomas Copernicus Wright Papers
William R. Donaldson Civil War
Correspondence
Thomas S. Hawley Papers
Herman B. Miller Papers

*Western Historical Manuscripts
Collection, University of Missouri,
Columbia*
John H., James, and William Alker Papers
Alley-Brewer Family Letters
Audsley Papers
William E. Bean Papers
Columbus and Bennet Bryan Letters
John T. Buegel Diary
CIVIL WAR LETTERS
Albert Allen Letters
Robert LaValley Letters
H. C. and W. H. Crawford Letters
John W. Garriott Letters
William Emmerson Lewis Letters
David Wilson Pollock Letters
Virginia Southwood Collection
Stephan Werly Diary

*Western Historical Manuscripts
Collection, University of Missouri,
Kansas City*
Maschel Manring Papers

*Western Historical Manuscripts
Collection, University of Missouri,
Rolla*
Moses Jasper Bradford Letters
Phillip A. Reilly Letters

New York

New-York Historical Society
William Butler Letters
Henry Hubble Papers
James Monroe Lyon Papers
Peter Welsh Letters

*New York Public Library, Manuscripts
and Special Collections*
Brown Family Papers
THOMAS MADIGAN COLLECTION
James Butler Diary
Cabot Jackson Russell Papers
DORE SCHARY COLLECTION OF LETTERS BY
CONFEDERATE SOLDIERS
Henry Higginbotham Letters
A. W. Tower Diary
UNION ARMY BOXES
John England Letters
Robert Pitts Diary
Austin D. Thompson Letters
Charles Upson Letters
U.S. Army 1861
U.S. Army 1862

*New York State Library Special
Collections, Albany, N.Y.*
Albert N. Ames Papers
F. W. Baker Letters
A. Clark Baum Letters
Lewis Benedict Letters
Abram Bogart Letters
Andrew Brockway Letters
U. A. Burnham Papers
Cornelius Carmody Papers
George H. L. Coggeshall Letters
John C. Cooper Family Papers
"Dear Hen" Letter, August 5, 1861
Eaton Family Papers
E. W. Everson Letters
William Arnold Fuller Letters
Calvin A. Haynes Letters
John H. Horton Letters

F. A. Ludlam Letters
John Muldoon Papers
Penny Family Papers
John Pettengill Papers
James Randall Papers
Charles Reynolds Papers
Byron Strong Papers
James B. Turner Papers

Schomburg Center for Research in Black Culture, New York

Baird, Henry Carey. *Washington and Jackson on Negro Soldiers. Gen. Banks on the Bravery of Negro Troops.* Philadelphia: Printed for Gratuitous Distribution, 1863.

Henry Colman Papers
Isaac Gardner Diaries

Green, Alfred M. *Letters and Discussions on the Formation of Colored Regiments: and the duty of Colored People in Regard to the Great Slaveholder's Rebellion in the United States of America.* Philadelphia: Ringwalt and Brown, 1862.

SPIKE HARRIS COLLECTION

Confederate Impressment, Union Employment Papers
Joseph Brown Papers
Martin Delany Papers
James H. and Samuel Harris Papers

MISCELLANEOUS LETTERS AND PAPERS

"The Second Louisiana" by George Boker
General Orders No. 15
Quincy A. Gillmore Letter
E. P. McCrea Memo
Recruitment bulletin from Supervisory Committee on Colored Enlistments
Resolutions of the Colored People of Charleston, S.C.

John Payne Civil War Collection

Syracuse University Special Collections, Bird Library

James Barnes Correspondence
John A. Bogert Papers
Albert M. Cook Papers
John E. Foster Papers
William W. Hawkins Letters

Hervey Lane Howe Letters
Reuben Kirk Papers
Alexander D. Masekes Papers
C. D. Pattie Collection
Henry B. Walker Letters

North Carolina

Duke University Special Collections

Daniel Abernethy Papers
William B. G. Andrews Papers
Samuel Simpson Biddle Letters and Papers
Asa Biggs Papers
Eliza H. (Ball) Gordon Boyles Papers
Samuel Bradbury Papers
Kate Camenga Papers
John Cantey Papers
Lunsford R. Cherry Papers
Corpening Family Papers
Confederate Miscellany: Officers' and Soldiers' Letters
Confederate States of America, Archives: State Government Papers 1861–65
Columbus H. Dixon Papers
Eltinge-Lord Family Papers
Alexander T., Joseph R., and William M. Findley Papers
John B. Foote Papers
Noah L. Gebbart, Sr., and Emmanuel Martin Gebbart Papers
Adolphus Washington Greely Papers
Edward, Charles, and Joel Griswold Papers
Constant C. Hanks Papers
Charles J. Harris Letters
Il Recrutio: An Original Opera performed by a troupe of the Massachusetts Forty-fourth Regiment, in barracks, at Newbern, N.C., on Wednesday Evening, March 11, 1863, under the auspices of the Regimental Dramatic Club
John O. Johnson Papers
Thomas F. Kelley Papers
Edward W. Kinsley Papers
John Hendricks Kinyoun Papers
Thomas Low Papers and Diary
James Otis Moore Papers
Richmond Mumford Pearson Papers
Benjamin Pedrick Papers
Person Family Papers

David Reynolds Diary and Papers
Isaac Reynolds Letters
Irby H. Scott Papers
Lewis O. Sugg Papers
James A. Whitehead Papers
James Zimmerman Papers

North Carolina Division of Archives and History

John H. Armfield Letters
R. H. Bacot Letters
R. T. Barnes Diary
Branson Family Papers
Henry C. Brown Papers
Isaac Brown Collection
Adelphos J. Burns Papers
John Washington Calton Letters
Henry A. Chambers Papers
John Willis Council Diary
Alexander England Family Papers
Gales Papers
Gash Family Papers
Bryan Grimes Papers
Oliver C. and Calier G. Hamilton Letters
Hampton Family Papers
Marcus Hefner Papers
Jesse Hill Letters
Roy Vernon Howell Papers
Robert H. Hutspeth Letters
Evelyn McIntosh Hyatt Collection
Henry Champlin Lay Diary
Isaac LeFevers Papers
Albert Moses Luria Journal
Robert C. Mabry Papers
William G. Parker Papers
Henry Machen Patrick Letters
Poteet-Dickson Letters
Shaffner Diary and Papers
Williams-Womble Papers
Lyman Wilson Sheppard Collection
C. H. Tubbs Letters
Zebulon Baird Vance Papers, Governor's Papers
Zebulon Baird Vance Papers, Private Collections
Mrs. O. H. Winstead Collection
John Wright Family Papers
John G. Young Papers

Southern Historical Collection, University of North Carolina, Chapel Hill

Isaac Alexander Papers
S. G. Barnard Papers
William James H. Bellamy Papers
Macon Bonner Papers
John H. Brown Diary
Buchanan-McClellan Family Papers
Calder Family Papers
Confederate Papers, Series 1 and 2
Thomas Benjamin Davidson Papers
George Stanley Dewey Correspondence
Fitzgerald Family Papers
Frank Family Letters
Graves Family Correspondence
James E. Green Diary
Thomas Jefferson Green Papers
John Wesley Halliburton Papers
Catherine Hanes Papers
Eliza C. Killian Papers
McBride Family Papers
Neill McLeod Papers
John Hunt Morgan Papers
William Groves Morris Papers
John Henry Murphy Papers
Patton Family Letters
Phifer Family Papers
Julius Ramsdell Papers
Frank Liddell Richardson Papers
Joseph Sams Papers
Skinner Family Papers
Andrew J. Sproul Letters
James H. Stanley Correspondence
Steed and Phipps Family Papers
John K. and Melinda East (Pace) Street Papers
Charles A. Tanner Papers
Samuel Thompson Papers
George Warfield Letters
Webb Family Papers
Chauncey Brunson Welton Letters
Edward Augustus Wild Papers
George Whitaker Wills Papers

Ohio

Ohio Historical Society
John W. Baldwin Papers

Evans Family Papers
Samuel J. Harrison Papers
Ephraim Holloway Papers
John Inskeep Diary
John Wesley Marshall Papers
Abram McClellan Papers
Nathan Parmater Papers
William H. Philips Papers
Albert Rogall Diary
Shotwell Family Papers
George B. Turner Papers
John D. Vail Diary

Western Reserve Historical Society
Alexander Bunts Family Papers
Civil War Miscellany
Civil War Regimental Papers: Negro
    Regiments
Thomas Covert Papers
Henry G. Crickmore Papers
Wilbur F. Hinman Letters
George W. Hodges Letters
Morris I. Holly Letters
George W. Landrum Papers
Carlos Parsons Lyman Papers
McMeekin Family Papers
James Nesbitt–Isaac Raub Papers
William Rapson Papers
Isaac G. Thorne Papers
Charles Albert Turner Letters
Marion D. Ward Letters
E. G. Wood Family Papers

Pennsylvania

U.S. Army Military History Institute,
Carlisle Barracks
CIVIL WAR MISCELLANEOUS COLLECTION
    Alvin Alexander Letters
    Samuel Alexander Correspondence
    George Aux Letters
    David Humphrey Blair Civil War Diary
        and Letters
    John Boyer Letters
    Ephraim Franklin Brower Diary
    Charles Coward Letters
    Oscar Cram Letters
    John Marshall Eaton Letters
    Evans Family Papers
    William Fairbanks Letters

James A. P. Fancher Diary
Foster Family Papers
Jacob Freyburger Letters
William B. Gates Letters
Liston Gray Letters
Joshua Hamlin Letters
Henry Hoyt Letters
George W. Johnson Papers
Lewis Jones Letters
Edwin Keen Papers
Jacob Klein Letters
James Magill Papers
Charles Maxim Letters
Henry Morgan Letters
Theodore Skinner Letters
Stephen Smith Diary
John Wall Letters
Francis Wheaton Letters
Isaac Williams Letters
CIVIL WAR MISCELLANEOUS COLLECTION,
SERIES 2
    James Beard Letters
    J. Henry Beatty Letters
    Boucher Family Papers
    Amos Breneman Letters
    Morris Chalmers Letters
    Charles Chapin Letters, Diary and
        Papers
    Samuel Condé Letters and Papers
    Dayton Flint Letters
    Thomas Grant Letters
    Alonzo G. Rich Papers
    Louis Rowe Letters
Civil War Times Illustrated COLLECTION
    Jacob Behm Correspondence
    Caldwell Family Correspondence
    Henry Henney Diary and Letters
    Thomas Hodgkins Letters
    Samuel Richards Letters
    Joseph Scroggs Diary
HARRISBURG CIVIL WAR ROUND TABLE
COLLECTION
    Benjamin Ashenfelter Letters
    Ellis-Marshall Family Papers
    Luther Furst Diary
    William J. Gibson Letters
    John and Samuel Hamer Papers
    David Nichol Papers
    Seibert Family Papers

South Carolina

South Carolina Archives and History Center
Campbell Family Papers
Recordsbooks of Palmetto Riflemen, 1861

South Caroliniana Library, University of South Carolina, Columbia
David Ballenger Papers
John B. Bannon Papers
Frederick Bischoff Journal
Barham Bobo Foster Papers
Ralph S. Goodwin Letters
John Head Diary
Francis Henry Correspondence
Chesley Worthington Herbert Papers
Theodore Augustus Honour Papers
Kerrison Family Papers
Calvin King Papers
C. R. Knapp Letters
William Henry Harrison Lee Papers
James Blackman Ligon Papers
Samuel Catawba Lowry Journal
McGaw Family Papers
McGee and Charles Family Papers
Andrew McIlwaine Papers
Roderick Salley McLucas Papers
George W. Northam Papers
John Putnam Papers
James Tinkler Papers
Willis Family Papers
Moultrie Reid Wilson Papers

Tennessee

Tennessee State Library and Archives
George Thompson Blakemore Diaries
R. P. Boswell Letters
Robert Franklin Bunting Papers
CIVIL WAR COLLECTION, CONFEDERATE
COLLECTION
 John J. Blair Letters
 John W. Buford Letters
 Ben W. Coleman Letters
 William E. Coleman Letters
 Abel H. Crawford Letters
 George Davis Letters
 Charles B. Douglass Letters
 John D. Floyd Letters
 J. M. Gentry Letters

Joel T. Haley Letters
William J. Hine Diary
Stephen A. Jordan Diary
Hugh G. Moore Letters
Joseph Mothershead Diary
Hannibal Paine Letters
James Parrott Letters
William Mebane Pollard Diary
D. L. Smythe Letters
Walter Kibbell Wendel Diary
W. H. Williams Letters
CIVIL WAR COLLECTION, FEDERAL
COLLECTION
 Anonymous Letters — 1864
 Lyman Ayer Letters
 George Hovey Cadman Letters
 Thomas Hopkins Deavenport Diaries
 George Washington Dillon Papers
 Azariah Dorton Letters
 James W. King Letters
 Nat. G. Pierce Letters
 Mitchell Andrew Thompson Letters
 Benjamin Franklin Wade Letters
 Harrison White Letters
 Henry F. Wright Letters
John D. Floyd Letters
Polk Hollaway Letter
Ragland Family Papers
Captain Samuel Rankin Latta Papers
R. M. Rucker Letters
Shahan Family Papers

Texas

Center for American History, University of Texas, Austin
Edwin Pinckney Becton Papers
Jacob DeWit Brewster Papers
George Claver Brightman Papers
John Claver Brightman Papers
Joseph Bruckmuller Notebook
Edward Burleson, Jr., Papers
Bluford Alexander Cameron Papers
Josephus B. Cavitt Papers
CIVIL WAR BIOGRAPHICAL FILE
 B. Bradbury Letter
 W. S. Douglas Letter
 B. P. Gandy Letters
 Alexander Cameron Hill Letters

William A. Leach Letters
D. W. Marsh Letters
J. S. Moffatt Letters
B. A. Simms Letters
"Tip" Letter
J. W. Yale Letter
Civil War Miscellany Collection
J. D. Davidson Papers
S. G. Davidson Papers
Green C. Duncan Papers
George Achile Feris Papers
Robert T. Frazier Family Papers
James Madison Hall Family Papers
Thomas B. Hampton Letters
Christian Wilhelm Hander Family
   Collection
William P. Head Papers
Richard Jacques Letters
John W. Keith Family Papers
James H. Manahan Letters
Friedrich Heinrich Niehbuhr Papers
Benjamin F. Piper Family Papers
George W. Root Letters
John Franklin Smith Letters
Robert Anderson Sullivan Papers
Lee Ray Wylie Letters

Vermont

Vermont Historical Society, Montpelier
Valentine G. Barney Letters
Barton Family Papers
Bixby Family Papers
Zenas H. Bliss Correspondence
Thomas H. Brown Letters
Henry P. Burnham Papers
Abel Conant Diary
Jerome Cutler Letters
Henry F. Dix Letters
Albert A. Dodge Letters
Nelson Newton Glazier Letters
E. C. Hall Papers
George B. Harrison Letters
Roswell Holbrook Letters
Edwin Horton Letters
William Elmore Howard Letters
Rufus Kinsley Diary
Rufus Kinsley Papers
Timothy Messer Civil War Letters

Cassius Newell Civil War Letters
John Brown Pollard Diaries
George Sawtell Letters
Stephen F. Spaulding Letters
Irvin Spooner Letters
William White Civil War Letters
John Williams Diary

Virginia

Eleanor S. Brockenbaugh Library,
   Museum of the Confederacy
AFRICAN AMERICAN COLLECTION
   Invitation by Freedmen of St. Augustine,
      Fla. to Attend Celebration of
      Anniversary of Emancipation
      Proclamation, Jan. 1, 1864, issued to
      Capt. Durgan, Seventh N.H. Vols.
   Petition from Officers of Nelsen's
      Battalion, S.C. Volunteers, May 1862,
      Asking for Transfer of (Named)
      Mulattoes from Unit
   Slave-Hiring Notes from Tenn. RR and
      Confed. Quartermaster Dep't.
   Slave Impressment Receipts, 1863
      (requiring owner to provide able-
      bodied male slaves to work on
      fortifications, Talladega, June 1864)
Harrison Alexander Letter
Richard P. Allen Letters
Addison Ashburn Letter
Isaiah Baker Letters
Spencer Barnes Letter
Charles Baughman Letters
Samuel Y. Brown Letter
Edward Clifford Brush Diary
Clayton Coleman Letters
Department of S.C. and Ga. Collection:
   Inspection Reports
William K. Estes Diary
Arthur Evans Letters
Randolph and Ethelbert Fairfax Letters
John Harvey Fryar Diary and Letters
Milo Grow Letters
Jessee Hill Letters
John R. Hill Letters
R. G. Holloway Diary
James Montgomery Lanning Diary
Livingston Family Letters

Eugene Frederick Lykes Letters
Albert McCollom Letters
Angus McDonald Letter
John J. Mendenhall Letter
James Montgomery Letter
Joseph Mullen Diary
John Piney Oden Diary
Thomas D. Osborne Letters. Transcripts of
   Eastern Kentucky University originals
   transcribed by EKU students.
J. Thomas Petty Diary
H. O. Pitts, ed. *Letters of a Gaston Ranger:
   2nd Lt. James Wellington Lineberger.* H.
   O. Pitts, 1991.
J. Tucker Randolph Letters and Diaries
Royall Family Letters
W. H. and J. S. Shibley Letters
William B. Short Letters
John A. Speer Letter in "Louisiana Men
   File" of "Soldier's Letters" Collection
Gordon Thompson and George Bailey
   Letters
Valor, a publication of Hood's Texas
   Brigade Association (1973), including
   letters of Joseph B. Polley, William H.
   Foster, and Jack Burke
John P. Wilson Letters
John Christopher Winsmith Papers
William S. Woods Letters

University of Virginia, Alderman Library
Franklin A. Setzer Papers
Williams Papers

Valley of the Shadow Civil War Project
William Tell Barnitz Letters
John H. Cochran Letters
John Hamer Letters
McCutchan Family Letters
Samuel M. Potter Letters

Virginia Historical Society
Charles Edward Bates Papers
George C. Binford Papers
Bird Family Papers
Bowler Family Papers
Carrington Family Papers
William Thomas Casey Papers
Griggs Family Papers, 1861–1865
Griggs Family Papers, 1862–1879
William Southall Harrison Letter

Charles August Henninghausen Papers
Charles Fenton James Letters
Keiley Family Papers
Henry Klag Diary
Langhorne Family of Montgomery Co., Va.
   Papers
Liebermann Family Papers
John Marshall Martin Papers
Richard Launcelot Maury Diary
Daniel Thurber Nelson Papers
Henry Thweatt Owen Papers
Pegram-Johnson-McIntosh Family Papers
James L. Power Letter
Prisoners' Club, Libby Prison: Constitution
Ringler Letters
Llewellyn Traherne Bassett Saunderson
   Diary
J. E. Shuman Letter
John A. Williams Letters

**Confederate Military Manuscripts,
   *Series A: Holdings of the Virginia
   Historical Society***
Henry Robinson Berkeley Papers
Camp Chase, Columbus, Ohio Papers
   1862–1863
John Herbert Claiborne Papers
E. L. Cox Diary
Creed Thomas Davis Diary
John Walter Fairfax Papers
Harlow Family Papers
Richardson Wallace Haw Diary
John Lyon Hill Diary
Jordan-Bell Family Letters
Keith Family Papers
James Henry Langhorne Diary
David Gregg McIntosh Papers
Meade Family Papers
George Washington Peebles Diary
William W. Sherwood Diary
Robert Winn Snead Papers
Murray Forbes Taylor Papers
Watson Family Papers
John French White Papers

Washington, D.C.

Catholic University of America
Charles Quinn Letters in O'Donovan
   Rossa Papers, Reel 1

Library of Congress, Manuscripts
J. J. Asbill Letters
Daniel C. Beard Family Papers
Low-Mills Family Papers
Montgomery Family Papers
E. J. More Collection
Jonathan Roberts and Family Papers
William Rufus Shafter Collection
Spaulding Family Papers
Lyman Potter Spencer Papers
Hazard Stevens Collection
Arthur Van Horn Papers
Andrew J. Walker Papers
James Walker Letters
Edwin Oberlin Wentworth Papers

Library of Congress, **People at War**
Microfilm Collection
John S. Anglin Letters
Orra B. Bailey Letters
William H. Bradbury Papers
Felix Brannigan Papers
Caleb Henry Carlton Papers
Douglas J. and Rufus W. Cater Papers
Sylvester Crossley Diary
George Washington Hall Collection
William Hamilton Papers
Esther Hill Hawks Collection
A. C. Hills Letter
William G. Hills Diary
George A. Hudson Collection
George O. Jewett Collection
John Griffith Jones Collection
Joseph Lester Collection

Wisconsin

State Historical Society of Wisconsin
John J. Barney Papers
Charles E. Beecham Letters
Van S. Bennett Diary
Adelbert M. Bly Correspondence
Hiram H. G. Bradt Letters
John Brandon Letters
Edward P. Bridgman Papers
William Brown Letters
Amasa Cobb Papers
Richard Robert Crowe Letters
Michael Hayes Branniger Cunningham
 Letters

Edward C. Dwight Papers
James Ghormley Diary
George W. Hannaford Letters
William Hanson Letters
Harrison Family Papers
Theron P. Holt Papers
David Goodrich James Correspondence
Karl Karsten Letters
John W. Kennedy Letters
Kimberley Family Papers
Samuel Cotter Kirkpatrick Letters
John Knaus Letters
Ferdinand Kurz Diary
Stanely E. Lathrop Letters
[Leigram], Ole Kittelson Diary
"Letter from Second Floor Prison,
 Danville, Va."
John MacLachlan Letters
William H. Mason Letters
John W. McCann Letters
Hugh A. McLaurin Correspondence
William C. Meffert Diaries
Adam Muezenberger Letters
Rollin Olson Civil War Letters, translated
 by Morgan Olson
Orson Parker Letters
R. Matthew Perry Letters
E. B. Quiner Correspondence of Wisconsin
 Volunteers. Ten volumes of letters from
 Wisconsin Civil War soldiers published
 in Wisconsin newspapers, 1861–65,
 arranged by regiment.
Walter V. Reeder Papers
Israel, William, and Jesse M. Roberts
 Letters
John H. Roberts Letters
George W. Root Papers
Horace Smith Civil War Diary
Charles Spencer Letters
Jonathan Dwight Stevens Letters
Benjamin F. Strong Letters
Henry J. Traber Letters
Peter Stillman Cottrell Tubbs Letters
Henry Harrison Twining Letters
Charles D. Waldo Diaries
Albert F. Waugh Letters
Frank Wittenberger Diary

Miscellaneous Manuscript Sources

Republic of Ireland

National Archives
Michael Brennan to Edward Murray, May
   30, 1863. U.S. Consular Despatches,
   Dublin, vol. 4

National Library of Ireland
Charles Locke Letters
Robert D. Webb Letters

Northern Ireland

Public Record Office, Northern Ireland
James Carlisle Letters
Abraham Irvine Letters
Robert McElderry Letters
William McSparron Letters
John Thompson Letters

Private Collections
Aaron T. Hess Diary, Private Collection of
   William E. Gienapp
David McGiffert Letters, Private
   Collection of Kerby Miller

Regimental Newspapers, by Current Location

Alabama

***Alabama Department of Archives and
   History***
The Pioneer Banner

Arkansas

University of Arkansas
Campaign Hornet
The Reveille
Stars and Stripes

Connecticut

Connecticut Historical Society
Connecticut Fifth
Twenty-Sixth

Georgia

Emory University
The Spirit of '61

Illinois

Chicago Historical Society
Lauman's Own
The Sixth Corps
The Union Volunteer
The War Eagle
*The War Eagle & Camp Journal of the
   Army of the West*

Illinois State Historical Library
Camp Illuminator
Camp Kettle
Camp Register
The Federal Scout
First Division Proclamation
Grant's Petersburg Progress
The Illinois Fifty-Second
New South
Normal Picket
Our Camp Journal
Our Flag
Our Regiment
Pennsylvania Thirteenth
Sixth Corps
Soldier's Friend
*Soldiers' Letter of the 96th Illinois
   Volunteer Infantry*
The Tenth Legion
Traveler
The Union Volunteer
Van-Guard
War Eagle

Kansas

Kansas State Historical Society
Buck and Ball
The Clinton Journal
The First Kansas
Fort Smith Union
Soldier's Letter
The Wisconsin Volunteer

Massachusetts

American Antiquarian Society, Worcester
The Advance Guard
The American Union
The Corinth War Eagle
The Pennsylvania Fifth

Massachusetts Historical Society
The Camp Kettle
The Crutch
The Daily Rebel Banner
The Free South
The Haversack
The Nashville Daily Times and True
    Union
The Opelousas Courier
The Peninsula
The Swamp Angel
Unconditional S. Grant
The Vicksburg Daily Citizen

Widener Library
Bates, William C. *The Stars and Stripes in
    Rebeldom: A Series of Papers Written by
    Federal Prisoners (Privates) in
    Richmond, Tuscaloosa, New Orleans,
    and Salisbury, N.C.* Boston: T.O.H.P.
    Burnham, 1862.
"Fort-La-Fayette Life." *1863–1865 in
    Extracts from The "Right Flanker," A
    Manuscript Sheet Circulating Among
    the Southern Prisoners in Fort-La-
    Fayette, in 1863–64.* London: Simpkin,
    Marshall, 1865.

Minnesota

Minnesota Historical Society
The Berryville Conservator
The Corinth Chanticleer
The First Minnesota

Mississippi

Mississippi Department of Archives and History
The Corinth Chanticleer
The Corinth War Eagle

Missouri

Kansas City Public Library Special Collections
The Arkansas Traveller

Missouri Historical Society
The American Patriot
The Batesville Bazzoo
Camp Sweeny Spy
The Guidon
Military News of the Missouri Volunteers
The Missouri Army Argus
The Missouri Army Argus—Extra
Our Whole Union
The Red River Rover
The U.S. American Volunteer
The Vidette Extra
The Volunteer

Western Historical Manuscripts Collection, University of Missouri, Columbia
The Zouave Register

North Carolina

Duke University
The American and Union
The Army and Navy Herald
The Clarendon Banner of Freedom
The Knapsack
The New Era
The Old Flag
The Port Hudson Freeman
The Regimental Flag
The Sixth Corps
The Soldier's Paper

North Carolina Division of Archives and History
New Era
Union Advance Picket

Southern Historical Collection, University of North Carolina, Chapel Hill
The Fort Delaware Prison Times
The Vidette

Ohio

Western Reserve Historical Society
The Banner of the Ironsides
Camp Illuminator
The Chattanooga Army Bulletin
The Ohio Seventh
The Winchester Army Bulletin

Tennessee

Tennessee State Library and Archives
Athens Union Post
The Battery Reveille
The Battle Flag
The Chattanooga Army Bulletin
Daily Rebel Banner
The 83rd Illinoisan
The Federal Knapsack
Our Old Flag
Pulaski Chanticleer
The Reveille
Seventh Brigade Journal
The Soldier's Budget
Union Banner
The Union Herald
The Vidette

Virginia

Library of Virginia
The American Union
The Sixth Corps
The Third Brigade

**Eleanor S. Brockenbaugh Library,
    Museum of the Confederacy**
The American and Union
The First Minnesota
The Grapeshot
The Haversack
The Port Hudson Freemen

Alderman Library, University of Virginia
The Camp Kettle
Grant's Petersburg Progress
The New York Ninth
The Palmetto Herald
The Regimental Flag

Virginia Historical Society
The Blower
The Cavalier
The Missouri Army Argus
The Pennsylvania Fifth
The Soldier's Visitor

Washington, D.C.

Library of Congress
Cartridge Box
The Reveille
Soldier's Casket

Wisconsin

State Historical Society of Wisconsin
The Black Warrior
The Camp Kettle
The Hospital Transcript
The National Guard
The Opelika Union

Civil War Broadsides and Other Ephemera

Alabama

**Alabama Department of Archives and
    History**
Confederate Patriotic Songs of I. A.
    Dodge, Texas Cavalry

Georgia

**Georgia Department of Archives and
    History**
Notice to Conscripts
Partizan Rangers Recruiting Broadside

Illinois

Chicago Historical Society
"Chronological Record of the War for
    the Union. With Patriotic Songs
    Distributed in Heck's Champion
    Prize Package."

South Carolina
Charleston Mercury
Edgefield Advertiser

Tennessee
Nashville Times and Daily Union

Texas
Houston Telegraph
San Antonio Herald

Virginia
Richmond Enquirer
Richmond Examiner
Richmond Sentinel

Other Primary Sources: Military, Official, and Miscellaneous

Congressional Globe. Washington, D.C., 1861–65.

"Fort Pillow Massacre." Senate Report 63, Thirty-eighth Congress, First Session. Washington, D.C.: Government Printing Office, 1864.

Official Army Register of the Volunteer Force of the United States Army for the Year 1861, '62, '63, '64, '65. Part 4. Washington, D.C.: Government Printing Office, 1865.

Porter, Kirk H., compiler. *National Party Platforms.* New York: Macmillan, 1924.

Report of the Adjutant General of the State of Illinois Containing Reports for the Years 1861–1865. Revised by Brig. Gen. J. W. Vance. Springfield, Ill., 1886.

Union Soldiers and Sailors Monument Association. *The Union Regiments of Kentucky.* Louisville, Ky.: Courier-Journal Job Printing, 1897.

War of the Rebellion: A Compilation of the Official Records of the Union and Confederate Armies. 128 vols. Washington, D.C., 1880–1901.

Other Primary Sources: Published Letters, Diaries, and Papers

Angle, Paul M., ed. *Three Years in the Army of the Cumberland: The Letters and Diary of Major James A. Connolly.* Bloomington: Indiana University Press, 1959.

Athearn, Robert G., ed. *Soldier in the West: The Civil War Letters of Alfred Lacey Hough.* Philadelphia: University of Pennsylvania Press, 1957.

Barrett, John G., ed. *Yankee Rebel: The Civil War Journal of Edmund DeWitt Patterson.* Chapel Hill: University of North Carolina Press, 1966.

Basler, Roy P., ed. *The Collected Works of Abraham Lincoln.* Nine vols. New Brunswick, N.J.: Rutgers University Press, 1953–57.

Baumgartner, Richard A., ed. *Blood and Sacrifice: The Civil War Journal of a Confederate Soldier.* Huntington, W. Va.: Blue Acorn, 1994.

Bee, Robert L., ed. *The Boys from Rockville: Civil War Narratives of Sgt. Benjamin Hirst, Company D, 14th Connecticut Volunteers.* Knoxville: University of Tennessee Press, 1998.

Bell, Howard Holman, ed. *Minutes of the Proceedings of the National Negro Conventions 1830–1864.* New York: Arno, 1969.

Bergen, Theodore C., ed. *The Civil War Letters of Colonel Hans Christian Heg.* Northfield, Minn.: Norwegian-American Historical Association, 1936.

Berlin, Ira, Barbara J. Fields, Thavolia Glymph, Joseph P. Reidy, and Leslie S. Rowland, eds. *Freedom: A Documentary History of Emancipation 1861–1867: The Destruction of Slavery* Series I, Volume I. New York: Cambridge University Press, 1985.

Berlin, Ira, Steven F. Miller, Joseph P. Reidy, and Leslie S. Rowland, eds. *Freedom: A Documentary History of Emancipation 1861–1867: The Wartime Genesis of Free Labor: The Upper*

South, Series I, Volume II. New York: Cambridge University Press, 1993.

Berlin, Ira, Thavolia Glymph, Steven F. Miller, Joseph P. Reidy, Leslie S. Rowland, and Julie Saville, eds. *Freedom: A Documentary History of Emancipation 1861–1867: The Wartime Genesis of Free Labor: The Lower South,* Series I, Volume III. New York: Cambridge University Press, 1990.

Berlin, Ira, Joseph P. Reidy, and Leslie S. Rowland, eds. *Freedom: A Documentary History of Emancipation, 1861–1867, Selected from the Holdings of the National Archives of the United States.* Series 2: *The Black Military Experience.* New York: Cambridge University Press, 1982.

Bird, Kermit Molyneux, ed. *Quill of the Wild Goose: Civil War Letters and Diaries of Private Joel Molyneux, 141st P.V.* Shippensburg, Pa.: Burd Street Press, 1996.

Blight, David W., ed. *When This Cruel War Is Over: The Civil War Letters of Charles Harvey Brewster.* Amherst: University of Massachusetts Press, 1992.

Blomquist, Ann K., and Robert A. Taylor, eds. *This Cruel War: The Civil War Letters of Grant and Malinda Taylor, 1862–1865.* Macon, Ga.: Mercer University Press, 2000.

Bryant, William Cullen, II. "A Yankee Soldier Looks at the Negro." *Civil War History* 7 (1961), 133–48.

Buckley, Cornelius M., ed. and trans. *A Frenchman, A Chaplain, A Rebel: The War Letters of Pere Louis-Hippolyte Gache, S.J.* Chicago: Loyola University Press, 1981.

Burgess, Lauren Cook, ed. *An Uncommon Soldier.* New York: Oxford University Press, 1994.

Byrne, Frank L., and Jean Powers Soman, eds. *Your True Marcus: The Civil War Letters of a Jewish Colonel.* Kent, Ohio: Kent State University Press, 1985.

Cate, Jean M., ed. *If I Live to Come Home:*

The Civil War Letters of Sergeant John March Cate. Pittsburgh: Dorrance, 1995.

Chesebrough, David B., ed. *"God Ordained This War": Sermons on the Sectional Crisis, 1830–1865.* Columbia: University of South Carolina Press, 1991.

Coco, Gregory A., ed. *From Ball's Bluff to Gettysburg . . . and Beyond: The Civil War Letters of Private Roland E. Bowen, 15th Massachusetts Infantry, 1861–1864.* Gettysburg, Pa.: Thomas, 1994.

Cooke, Chauncey H. "A Badger Boy in Blue: The Letters of Chauncey H. Cooke." *Wisconsin Magazine of History* 4: 1 (September 1920), 75–100; 4:2 (December 1920), 208–17; 4:3 (March 1921) 322–44; 4:4 (June 1921) 431–56; 5:1 (September 1921), 63–90.

Cutrer, Thomas, and T. Michael Parrish, eds. *Brothers in Gray: The Civil War Letters of the Pierson Family.* Baton Rouge: Louisiana State University Press, 1997.

Dennis, Frank Allen, ed. *Kemper County Rebel: The Civil War Diary of Robert Masten Holmes, C.S.A.* Jackson: University and College Press of Mississippi, 1973.

Duganne, A. J. H. *The Fighting Quakers, A True Story of the War for Our Union.* New York: J. P. Robens, 1866.

Elkins, Vera Dockery, ed. *Letters from a Civil War Soldier.* New York: Vantage, 1969.

Everson, Guy R., and Edward H. Simpson, Jr., eds. *Far, Far from Home: The Wartime Letters of Dick and Tally Simpson, Third South Carolina Volunteers.* New York: Oxford University Press, 1994.

Fitzhugh, George. *Cannibals All! or Slaves Without Masters.* Cambridge, Mass.: Belknap, 1960. Originally published 1857.

Fleet, Betsy, and John D. P. Fuller, eds. *Green Mount: A Virginia Plantation*

Family during the Civil War. Lexington: University of Kentucky Press, 1962.

Flower, Milton E., ed. *Dear Folks at Home: The Civil War Letters of Leo W. and John I. Faller with an Account of Andersonville*. Carlisle, Pa.: Cumberland County Historical Society, 1963.

Folmar, John Kent, ed. *From That Terrible Field: Civil War Letters of James M. Williams, Twenty-First Alabama Infantry Volunteers*. Tuscaloosa: University of Alabama Press, 1981.

Freehling, William W., and Craig M. Simpson, eds. *Secession Debated: Georgia's Showdown in 1860*. New York: Oxford University Press, 1992.

Gavin, William Gilfillan, ed. *Infantryman Pettit: The Civil War Letters of Corporal Frederick Pettit, Late of Company C 100th Pennsylvania Veteran Volunteer Infantry Regiment, "The Roundheads."* Shippensburg, Pa.: White Mane, 1990.

Gemant, Sophie S., trans., and Fanny J. Anderson, ed. "The Shelly Papers." *Indiana Magazine of History* 44:2 (June 1948), 181–90.

Goodell, Robert C., ed. and trans., and P. A. M. Taylor. "A German Immigrant in the Union Army: Selected Letters of Valentin Bechler." *Journal of American Studies* 4:2, 145–62.

Goyne, Minetta Altgelt, ed. and trans. *Lone Star and Double Eagle: Civil War Letters of a German-Texas Family*. Texas Christian University Press, 1982.

Greenleaf, Margery, ed. *Letters to Eliza from a Union Soldier, 1862–1865*. New York: Follett, 1970.

Grimsley, Mark, and Todd D. Miller, eds. *The Union Must Stand: The Civil War Diary of John Quincy Adams Campbell, Fifth Iowa Volunteer Infantry*. Knoxville: University of Tennessee Press, 2000.

Hallock, Judith Lee, ed. *The Civil War Letters of Joshua K. Callaway*. Athens: University of Georgia Press, 1997.

Harris, Robert F., and John Niflot, eds. *Dear Sister: The Civil War Letters of the*

Brothers Gould. Westport, Conn.: Praeger, 1998.

Harwell, R. B., ed. "Edgar Dinsmore Letters." *Journal of Negro History* 35:3 (July 1940), 363–71.

Hatley, William F., and Linda B. Huffman, eds. *Letters of William F. Wagner, Confederate Soldier*. Wendell, N.C.: Broadfoot's Bookmark, 1983.

Heller, J. Roderick, III, and Carolyn Ayres Heller, eds. *The Confederacy Is on Her Way Up the Spout: Letters to South Carolina, 1861–1864*. Athens: University of Georgia Press, 1992.

Jackson, Henry F., and Thomas F. O'Donnell, eds. *Back Home in Oneida: Hermon Clarke and His Letters*. Syracuse, N.Y.: Syracuse University Press, 1965.

Janvier, Francis De Haes. "The Sleeping Sentinel." In James E. Murdoch, compiler, *Patriotism in Poetry and Prose*. Philadelphia: Lippincott, 1866.

Jaquette, Henrietta Stratton, ed. *South After Gettysburg: Letters of Cornelia Hancock, 1863–1868*. New York: Crowell, 1956.

Joslyn, Mauriel Phillips, ed. *Charlotte's Boys: Civil War Letters of the Branch Family of Savannah*. Berryville, Va.: Rockbridge, 1996.

Kallgren, Beverly Hayes, and James L. Crouthamel, eds. *"Dear Friend Anna": The Civil War Letters of a Common Soldier from Maine*. Orono: University of Maine Press, 1992.

Kohl, Lawrence Frederick, and Margaret Cosse Richard, eds. *Irish Green and Union Blue: The Civil War Letters of Peter Welsh, Color Sergeant 28th Regiment Massachusetts Volunteers*. New York: Fordham University Press, 1986.

Lane, Bessie Mell, ed. *Dear Bet: The Carter Letters: 1861–1863*. Clemson, S.C.: Bessie Mell Lane, 1978.

Lane, Mills, ed. *"Dear Mother: Don't Grieve About Me. If I get Killed, I'll only be Dead." Letters from Georgia Soldiers in the Civil War.* Savannah: Beehive Press, 1977.

Lewis, A. S., ed. *My Dear Parents: An Englishman's Letters Home from the American Civil War.* London: Victor Gollancz, 1982.

Lowe, Jeffrey C., and Sam Hodges, eds. *Letters to Amanda: The Civil War Letters of Marion Hill Fitzpatrick, Army of Northern Virginia.* Macon, Ga.: Mercer University Press, 1998.

Marchand, Edward, ed. *News from Fort Craig, New Mexico, 1863: Civil War Letters of Andrew Ryan with the First California Volunteers.* Santa Fe: Stagecoach Press, 1966.

Marcus, Edward, ed. *A New Canaan Private in the Civil War. Letters of Justus M. Silliman, 17th Connecticut Volunteers.* New Canaan, Conn.: New Canaan Historical Society, 1984.

Marshall, Jeffrey D., ed. *A War of the People: Vermont Civil War Letters.* Hanover, N.H.: University Press of New England, 1999.

Martin, Kenneth R., and Ralph Linwood Snow, eds. *"I Am Now A Soldier!": The Civil War Diaries of Lorenzo Vanderhoef.* Bath, Maine: Patten Free Library, 1990.

Mathis, Ray, ed. *In the Land of the Living: Wartime Letters by Confederates from the Chattahoochee Valley of Alabama and Georgia.* Troy, Ala.: Troy State University Press, 1981.

Montgomery, George, ed. *Georgia Sharpshooter: The Civil War Diary and Letters of William Rhadamanthus Montgomery.* Macon, Ga.: Mercer University Press, 1997.

Mumey, Nolis, ed. *Bloody Trails Along the Rio Grande: A Day-by-Day Diary of Alonzo Ferdinand Ickis.* Denver: Old West, 1958.

Olcott, Mark, and David Lear, eds. *The Civil War Letters of Lewis Bissell.* Washington D.C.: Field School Educational Foundation, 1981.

Olmsted, Frederick Law. *The Cotton Kingdom: A Traveller's Observations on Cotton and Slavery in the American Slave States.* New York: Knopf, 1962.

Patrick, Jeffrey L., ed. " 'This Regiment Will Make a Mark': Letters of a Member of Jennisons's Jayhawkers, 1861–1862." *Kansas History* 20:1 (spring 1997), 50–58.

Popchock, Barry, ed. *Soldier Boy: The Civil War Letters of Charles O. Musser, 29th Iowa.* Iowa City: University of Iowa Press, 1995.

Post, Lydia Minturn, ed. *Soldier's Letters from Camp, Battle-field and Prison, Published for the U.S. Sanitary Commission.* New York: Bunce & Huntington, 1865.

Redkey, Edwin S., ed. *A Grand Army of Black Men: Letters from African-American Soldiers in the Union Army, 1861–1865.* New York: Cambridge University Press, 1992.

Reid-Green, Marcia, ed. *Letters Home: Henry Matrau of the Iron Brigade.* Lincoln: University of Nebraska Press, 1993.

Reyburn, Philip J., and Terry L. Wilson, eds. *"Jottings from Dixie": The Civil War Dispatches of Sergeant Major Stephen F. Fleharty, U.S.A.* Baton Rouge: Louisiana State University Press, 1999.

Rhodes, Robert Hunt, ed. *All for the Union: The Civil War Diary and Letters of Elisha Hunt Rhodes.* New York: Orion, 1991.

Rosenblatt, Emil, and Ruth Rosenblatt, eds. *Hard Marching Every Day: The Civil War Letters of Private Wilbur Fisk, 1861–1865.* Lawrence: University Press of Kansas, 1992.

Roth, Margaret Brobst, ed. *Well Mary: Civil War Letters of a Wisconsin Volunteer.* Madison: University of Wisconsin Press, 1960.

Rozier, John, ed. *The Granite Farm Letters: The Civil War Correspondence of Edgeworth & Sallie Bird.* Athens: University of Georgia Press, 1988.

Runge, William H., ed. *Four Years in the Confederate Artilley: The Diary of Private Henry Robinson Berkeley.* Chapel Hill: University of North Carolina Press for the Virginia Historical Society, 1961.

Sears, Stephen W., ed. *The Civil War Papers of George B. McClellan: Selected Correspondence.* New York: Ticknor and Fields, 1989.

———, ed. *For Country, Cause and Leader: The Civil War Journal of Charles B. Haydon.* New York: Ticknor & Fields, 1993.

Shannon, Fred Albert, ed. "The Civil War Letters of Sergeant Ondley Andrus." *Illinois Studies in the Social Sciences* 28:4 (1947), 5–147.

Silber, Nina, and Mary Beth Steven, eds. *Yankee Correspondence: Civil War Letters between New England Soldiers and the Home Front.* Charlottesville: University of Virginia Press, 1996.

Silver, James W., ed. *A Life for the Confederacy: As Recorded in the Pocket Diaries of Pvt. Robert A. Moore.* Wilmington, N.C.: Broadfoot, 1991.

Simpson, Col. Harold B., ed. *The Bugle Softly Blows: The Confederate Diary of Benjamin M. Seaton.* Waco, Tex.: Texian, 1965.

———, ed. *A Soldier's Letters to Charming Nellie.* Gaithersburg, Md.: Butternut, 1984.

Stevenson, Benjamin Franklin. *Letters from the Army, 1862–1864.* Cincinnati: Robert Clark, 1886.

Stirling, James, ed. *Letters from the Slave States.* New York: Negro Universities Press, 1969.

Summers, Festus P., ed. *A Borderland Confederate.* Pittsburgh: University of Pittsburgh Press, 1962.

Swiger, Elizabeth Davis, ed. *Civil War Letters and Diary of Joshua Winters, a Private in the Union Army Company G, First Western Virginia Volunteer Infantry.* Parsons, W. Va.: McClain, 1991.

Throne, Mildred, ed. *The Civil War Diary of Cyrus F. Boyd, Fifteenth Iowa Infantry, 1861–1863.* Millwood, N.Y.: Kraus Reprint, 1977.

Trimble, Richard M., ed. *Brothers 'Til Death: The Civil War Letters of William, Thomas and Maggie Jones, 1861–1865.* Macon, Ga.: Mercer University Press, 2000.

Trudeau, Noah Andre, ed. *Voices of the 55th: Letters from the 55th Massachusetts Volunteers, 1861–1865.* Dayton, Ohio: Morningside, 1996.

Twichell, Joseph. "Army Memories of Lincoln." *Congregationalist and Christian World,* January 30, 1913, p. 154.

Vanderslice, Catherine H., ed. *The Civil War Letters of George Washington Beidelman.* New York: Vantage, 1980.

Welker, David A., ed. *A Keystone Rebel: The Civil War Diary of Joseph Garey, Hudson's Battery Mississippi Volunteers.* Gettysburg, Pa.: Thomas, 1996.

Williams, Edward B., ed. *Rebel Brothers: The Civil War Letters of the Truehearts.* College Station: Texas A&M University Press, 1995.

Winther, Oscar Osburn, ed. *With Sherman to the Sea: The Civil War Letters Diaries & Reminiscences of Theodore F. Upson.* Baton Rouge: Louisiana State University Press, 1943.

Wittenberg, Eric J., ed. *"We Have It Damn Hard Out Here": The Civil War Letters of Sergeant Thomas W. Smith, 6th Pennsylvania Cavalry.* Kent, Ohio: Kent State University Press, 1999.

Woodworth, Steven E., ed. *The Musick of the Mocking Birds, the Roar of the Cannon: The Civil War Diary and Letters of William Winters.* Lincoln: University of Nebraska Press, 1998.

Yearns, Buck, and John G. Barrett, eds. *North Carolina Civil War Documentary.* Chapel Hill: University of North Carolina Press, 1980.

ACKNOWLEDGMENTS

As I was completing the dissertation that gave this book its start, my friend David Konigsberg cheerfully (and superfluously) pointed out that I had spent longer working on the dissertation than it took soldiers to fight the Civil War. Recently, he "helpfully" reminded me that in the time it has taken me to revise the dissertation into a book, I could have fought the war all over again. Any project that takes that long benefits from a lot of help along the way, and it gives me enormous pleasure to say "thank you" to some of the people and institutions that have provided assistance.

Long campaigns require supply lines and other forms of logistical support. I appreciate the support provided by the Harvard University Department of History, the Harvard University Graduate Student Council, the Harvard University Graduate School of Arts and Sciences, the Packard Fellowship, the Oscar Handlin Fellowship, the Charles Warren Center, the King V. Hostick Award of the Illinois State Historical Library, the Alfred Landon Grant of the Kansas State Historical Society, the Jacob Price Visiting Research Fellowship of the Clements Library at the University of Michigan, the Archie K. Davis Fellowship of the North Caroliniana Society and the Mellon Research Fellowship Program of the Virginia Historical Society. The C. Vann Woodward Prize awarded by the Southern Historical Association allowed me to get started on revising; the existence of the prize testifies to the SHA's genuine commitment to fostering the development of junior scholars. I also appreciate the Regency Fellowship provided by Pacific Lutheran University, which enabled me to dedicate the summer of 2004 to writing, and the generosity of the Georgetown University Department of History in lightening my teaching load in the fall of 2005, which sped up the completion of the manuscript.

The men and women who work at libraries and archives possess the keys to the researcher's kingdom, and I am very grateful for the generosity with which so many shared those keys. The staff of the North Carolina Division of Archives and History, John White of the Southern Historical Collection at the University of North Carolina, Wayne Moore of the Tennessee State Library and Archives, David Keogh at Carlisle Barracks, and the staff at the Vermont Historical Society all deserve special thanks for unusual helpfulness and friendliness. Dr. Edwin Bridges not only put out the welcome mat at the Alabama Department of Archives and History, but he also provided a terrific tour of Montgomery. John Coski of the Museum of the Confederacy seemed to know the whereabouts and content of collections relating to every Confederate soldier, and he could also talk about baseball with a glee similar to my own. The one thing I do not like about archives is that they all maintain the temperature of a standard meat locker. For this reason, I especially thank Judy Johnson of the Connecticut Historical Society, who brought me a cup of hot tea one day that hit the spot.

As I embarked on my research travels, I always carried a tent in my backpack in case I got stuck for a place to stay. Thanks to the hospitality of an almost embarrassing number of good-hearted souls, I only had to use the tent twice. More important, that hospitality gave me the opportunity, after long days spent communing with dead soldiers who never laughed at my jokes, to talk to people who were still alive. Many thanks to Janet Baker-Carr, John Belcher, Celeste Dixon (for tours of Chickamauga and Lookout Mountain, as well as a place to sleep), Mary Fleischli and Allan da Costa Pinto, Dan Hubbard, Marvin and Carla Johnson, Barb Keys and Jeff Shimeta, Tim and Liza Kirchgraber, Michelle Manning and Eli Eastman, Richard and Rita Manning, Ethelmae and Harold Mason, Jennie and the late Robert McCormick, Jennifer Mattson, Ann O'Leary, Karla, David, Zachary, and Erin Principe, Asha and Stephen Shipman, Janet Stateman, Clemmie Stringfellow, Bill and Máire Tennant, and Erika Teschke and Tim Koeppe.

Friends and fellow travelers from graduate school contributed to this project in direct and indirect (but always invaluable) ways. I especially want to thank Andy Coopersmith, Brian Delay, Jennie Goloboy, Dan Hamilton, Isadora Helfgott, Libra Hilde, Barbara Keys, Rob MacDougall, Jon Schrag, Eva Shepard Wolf, and Julia Torrie. Christine Dee made two especially notable contributions: in the middle of the dissertation she pointed out that the manuscript flipped back and forth between two different organizational patterns and one worked better than the other (she was right), and she also provided an invaluable reading of the first draft of the Introduction. Silvana Siddali invariably reminds me of why I find working on the nineteenth century so exciting. Lisa Laskin, one of the most unfailingly sensible people I know, generously shared her inexhaustible font of advice and insight on Civil War soldiers, and on much else besides; she was also a great traveling companion and river rafting partner on a trip down the James River in Richmond. The all-time research travel companion award, though, must go to Susan Wyly, thanks to whom I have more good stories about a trip through Alabama, Tennessee, and Mississippi than any one person has a right to. How her car got home in one piece I will never fully understand (in fact, strictly speaking, I don't think it did get home in one piece, though it did get home). Even before graduate school, my undergraduate years at Mount Holyoke College molded me in more ways than I can recount, and I want to thank every inch of that place, which opened up for me the life of the mind.

Colleagues and members of the historical profession have proven unstinting with their help and advice. Kerby Miller shared valuable sources. Drew Gilpin Faust, Evelyn Brooks Higginbotham, and Reid Mitchell all read and commented on the dissertation, a herculean feat appreciable only to those who know how very long that dissertation was. Catherine Allgor and Susan O'Donovan have both served as savvy guides and firm friends who helped me make the transition from graduate student to a historian with a job; just as important, Susan continues to serve as a "virtual" marathon training partner. Colleagues in the Georgetown University Department of History, especially Alison Games, Maurice Jackson, Michael Kazin, Christine Kim, Amy Leonard, Joe McCartin, Adam Rothman, and John Tutino helped make the transition to Georgetown so smooth that I could begin a new job and finish a book in the same year, and enjoy both processes (usually). Heather Cox Richardson and Michael Vorenberg each commented on the first two chapters in ways that provided me with breakthroughs as I began to transform the dissertation into a book. William Cooper, Leonard Richards, and James McPherson read the manuscript draft with generosity and an exactitude that saved me from embarrassing errors. Fred Bailey read both the dissertation and the manuscript, and offered key advice for making explicit a theme that had first been implicit. Robert Bonner also read the manuscript draft and offered several perceptive comments that helped me clarify what I was really trying to say. Although Adam was chagrined to learn that he was "tied," the fact remains that Adam Rothman and Aaron Sheehan-Dean tied for the most incisive reading of the manuscript. Adam's thoughtful comments helped sharpen both argument and prose. Aaron possesses an uncanny knack for figuring out what I am trying to say and articulating it far more clearly than I have done, and he generously applied that knack to many places in the manuscript. Several of the above-mentioned labored valiantly but fruitlessly to dissuade me from certain points or to change my mind; all errors of fact or judgment that remain are mine alone.

The historian who contributed the most to this project was surely the late William Gienapp, who saw the dissertation but none of the revisions that followed. From loaning books to listening to ideas to critiquing prose with trademark care and precision, he consistently demonstrated the most sincere dedication to teaching that I have ever seen. In my first year of graduate school he said, "There are professors who want you to think like them, and there are professors who want you to think. I am the second kind." He proved that he meant it, even when he thought I was daft, and he served as the model for the sort of scholar and teacher I hope to be. His wife, Erica Gienapp, continues to inspire and foster the development of his students.

Transforming a manuscript into a book is a mysterious process for a first timer, and I would like to thank the people who helped demystify it. Michael Kazin very kindly put me in touch with his agent, Sandy Dijkstra, who shepherded the project through with helpfulness and efficiency. Jane Garrett, Leslie Levine, and Emily Molanphy at Knopf always answered questions immediately and helpfully. Jane Garrett also paid me the great compliment of simply letting me work on the manuscript in my own way and time. Jenna Bagnini's light and careful touch smoothed out rough spots while making the editing process painless.

Several friends who have nothing to do with the historical or editorial professions proved indispensable to this project. Nobody could ask for better cheerleaders than Eileen and Les Bernal, who have seen me through all manner of life transitions. Kate Baker-Carr exemplifies grace and friendship; there were patches along the way that I simply could not have navigated without her. Erika Teschke and I have been the closest of friends since college, and I can imagine neither this book nor my life without her friendship.

My family has been as central to this project as soldiers' families were to their worlds. My parents, Howard and Kathy Miller, helped me purchase the laptop computer that accompanied me on many of my research travels and on which I wrote the original dissertation, but even before that, my mother made sure that no matter how many times we moved, from the age of three on, I always had a library card. My mother- and father-in-law, Richard and Rita Manning, put me up during research trips, always knew when and when not to ask about the book project, and provided silent help that kept our household going. They also provided an afternoon of babysitting that allowed me to finish proofreading. Michelle Manning and Eli Eastman also put me up, as did Erica Eastman on a later trip (though

Erica had little say in the matter, since she could not yet talk). Michelle even went back to an archive for me to make another copy of a source after I lost my copy. My grandparents deserve special mention. My grandfather, Jack Pluta, believed resolutely in the value of education and of me even—especially—when I had a hard time sharing his confidence. My grandmother, who reduced all the syllables of Virginia Mary Grace Houghney Barker Pluta down to the essentials and went by "Jean," was fascinated by the Civil War and she taught me to read when I was two. Anything about my grandmother was bound to rub off on me, but that particular combination has turned out to shape my life.

My son, Aidan Douglass Manning, gracefully timed his arrival to permit the timely completion of this book. He makes it easy to understand how Confederates could justify nearly anything out of love and concern for their children; because I care about the kind of world he grows up in, he also serves as a reminder of the importance of resisting that urge.

Finally, there is Derek. When I began my research travels, he lived in a one-room apartment, but still he offered his address as a destination for the shipping of photocopies, and then built a bookcase to contain the overflow. He put up with side trips to archives on our camping trips, agreed to have some of our wedding photos taken at the Massachusetts Fifty-fourth Monument in Boston, and learned far more about the nineteenth century than he ever wanted to know. He has also, uncomplainingly, become a citizen-by-marriage of Red Sox Nation, even though he had no interest in baseball before we met (a fact he wisely hid from me until well into our courtship, which consisted of many Red Sox games). He was so sure I would finish the dissertation on time that he got tickets to Fenway Park for a Red Sox–Yankees game the night *before* the dissertation was due. (The Red Sox won 3–2, in a beautiful pitching duel.) Since then we have moved across the country twice, but never left the bounds of Red Sox Nation; he also got tickets to a Red Sox game in Baltimore for the week after I submitted this manuscript. He has shared his home with thousands of dead soldiers and his life with me, and even though I have had years to think up words adequate to convey my love and thanks, I still remain powerless to do so, leading me to the conclusion that words powerful enough simply do not exist.

INDEX

BLOOD AND THUNDER
*The Epic Story of Kit Carson and the Conquest of the
American West*
by Hampton Sides

In *Blood and Thunder*, Sides gives us a magnificent history of the American conquest of the West. At the center of this sweeping tale is Kit Carson, the trapper, scout, and soldier whose adventures made him a legend. Sides shows us how this illiterate mountain man understood and respected the Western tribes better than any other American, yet willingly followed orders that would ultimately destroy the Navajo nation. Rich in detail and spanning more than three decades, this is an essential addition to our understanding of how the West was really won.

History/Biography/978-1-4000-3110-8

FREEDOM RISING
Washington in the Civil War
by Ernest B. Furgurson

This luminous portrait of wartime Washington brings to vivid life the personalities and events that animated the capital during its most tumultuous time. Here among the sharpsters and prostitutes, slaves and statesmen are detective Allan Pinkerton, tracking down Southern sympathizers; poet Walt Whitman, nursing the wounded; and Abraham Lincoln, wrangling officers, pardoning deserters, and inspiring the nation. *Freedom Rising* is a gripping account of the era that transformed Washington into the world's most influential city.

History/Civil War/978-0-375-70409-3

FOREVER FREE
The Story of Emancipation and Reconstruction
by Eric Foner

Drawing on a wide range of long-neglected documents, Eric Foner places a new emphasis on black experiences and roles during the era. We see African Americans as active agents in overthrowing slavery, in shaping Reconstruction, and creating a legacy long obscured and misunderstood. He compellingly refutes long-standing misconceptions of Reconstruction, and shows how the failures of the time sowed the seeds of the civil rights struggles of the 1950s and 60s.

History/978-0-375-70274-7

TWILIGHT AT LITTLE ROUND TOP
July 2, 1863—The Tide Turns at Gettysburg
by Glenn W. LaFantasie

On July 2, 1863, forces from the Confederate Army of Northern Virginia and the Union Army of the Potomac clashed over the rocky hill known as Little Round Top. This battle was one of the most brutal engagements of the American Civil War, and the North's bloody victory there ensured their triumph at Gettysburg, setting the stage for the South's ultimate defeat. Using newly discovered documents and rare firsthand sources, LaFantasie sheds light on the dramatic story of this pivotal battle.

History/978-0-307-38663-2

THE NEGRO'S CIVIL WAR
How American Blacks Felt and Acted During the War for the Union
by James M. McPherson

In this classic study, Pulitzer Prize–winning author James M. McPherson narrates the experience of blacks—former slaves, soldiers, intellectuals, and common people—during the Civil War. Drawing on contemporary journalism, books, and letters, he presents a chronicle of their fears and hopes as well as their essential contributions to their own freedom. Above all, we are allowed to witness the dreams of a disenfranchised people eager to embrace the rights and the equality offered to them, finally, as citizens.

History/Civil War/978-1-4000-3390-4

THE CALIFORNIA GOLD RUSH AND THE COMING OF THE CIVIL WAR
by Leonard L. Richards

When gold was discovered at Sutter's Mill in 1848, Americans of all stripes saw the potential for both wealth and power. Among the more calculating were Southern slave owners. By making California a slave state, they could increase the value of their slaves, and expand Southern economic clout. Yet, despite their machinations, California entered the union as a free state. Disillusioned Southerners would agitate for even more slave territory, leading to the Kansas-Nebraska Act and, ultimately, to the Civil War itself.

History/978-0-307-27757-2

VINTAGE AND ANCHOR BOOKS
Available at your local bookstore, or visit www.randomhouse.com